Peace, Politics and Violence
in the New South Africa

African Discourse Series

General Editor: Abebe Zegeye

Peace, Politics and Violence
in the New South Africa

Edited by
Norman Etherington
Head, Department of History
The University of Western Australia

HANS ZELL PUBLISHERS
London • Melbourne • Munich • New York • 1992

© 1992 Hans Zell Publishers and individual contributors
Hans Zell Publishers
is an imprint of Bowker-Saur, a division of Reed Reference Publishing,
60 Grosvenor Street, London W1X 9DA, United Kingdom.

British Library Cataloguing in Publication Data

Peace, Politics and Violence in the New South Africa. - (African Discourse Series
    No. 5)
    I. Etherington, Norman II. Series
    320.968

    ISBN 1-873836-75-9

Library of Congress Cataloging in Publication Data

Peace, Politics and Violence in the New South Africa / edited by Norman Etherington.
    370p. 220cm. — (African discourse series : no. 5)
Papers from a conference held at the University of Western Australia in December 1991.
    ISBN 1-873836-75-9
    1. South Africa—Politics and government—1961-1978—Congresses.
    2. South Africa—Politics and government—1978- —Congresses.
    I. Etherington, Norman. II. Series.
    DT1945.P43 1992
    968.06—dc20   92-25670

                                                              CIP

Cover design by Robin Caira

Printed on acid-free paper.

Disk conversion and typesetting by
Judy Bolton, Department of History,
University of Western Australia

Printed and bound in Great Britain
by Antony Rowe Ltd,
Chippenham, Wiltshire.

Contents

v

Preface & Acknowledgements

Background to the Project

In December 1991, the Indian Ocean Centre for Peace Studies brought together an outstanding panel of scholars to assess the prospects for a peaceful transition to a new constitutional order in South Africa. The timing was deliberate. The Codesa talks had just begun and there was a general consciousness that the culmination of the process might be just around the corner. One of the most tantalizing prospects available to such a gathering was to see how historical perspectives could help illuminate events that are still unfolding. In addition to the historians present, the panel included individuals from other disciplines who have worked at one time or another at unravelling the meaning of past events. All were acutely aware of the pitfalls lying in wait for those who attempt to make historical judgments on the basis of fragmentary evidence. At the same time, there was general agreement that historians have important insights to offer *now*. The business of providing the best possible academic interpretations for current events must wait until archives now closed to public view disgorge their secrets.

The contributors hoped, for all sorts of reasons, that the framework for negotiating a new South African constitution would be worked out before this book appeared. Initial euphoria was tempered by the shock of Boipatong. While contributors' spirits have ebbed and flowed as events have unfolded, we have tried hard to produce something without a 'use by' date stamped on the cover. For that reason room was left for some of the papers to be modified as events unfolded. Although this is not a book of prophecy, it may lend some assistance to prophets. Those who want to predict where a projectile will land need to know its trajectory from the point of launch. In South Africa the air is thick with all sorts of lethal projectiles, some of which were launched a very long time ago.

Unexpected Events

When the ANC walked out of the Codesa talks, many of our contributors, including the editor, believed that external pressures would force the main parties back to the negotiating table within a few weeks. Our publisher, Hans Zell, agreed to let our deadline run beyond its original June target. Boipatong, while a tragedy and a shock, conformed to a pattern of violence which Joan Wardrop shows in Chapter 2 had developed well before the ANC joined the initial negotiations. It therefore seemed unlikely to be the sort of epoch-making event that could shut down Codesa for good. When the ANC called for two days of Mass Action in the first week of August, few of us were surprised. We were aware, as Frene Ginwala points out in Chapter 1, that large numbers of ANC supporters were worried that its leadership had lost touch with common people while hobnobbing with National Party luminaries at Codesa. Chapter 14 explains why the ANC had good reasons for believing that a mass 'stayaway' would succeed. Having shown solidarity with the township dwellers who have been in the frontline of political violence, and having shown the De Klerk government as well as the world that it could orchestrate peaceful, disciplined, mass action, the ANC could return to the negotiating table. De Klerk had already conceded much of the ground which was most heatedly contested at the point at which talks broke down.

Although the precise details may not be known for quite some time, it seems fairly clear that the ANC leadership was divided over the proper course to take during the last week of August. In the end, it appears to have concluded that the De Klerk government would not abandon the goal of a 'power-sharing' constitution. As Frene Ginwala notes in Chapter 1, De Klerk had signalled as much during the brief campaign preceding the all-white referendum of March, 1992. A continued insistence on parity of representation from many different groups, including 'homeland' leaders, and plans to provincialize key services also indicated that the infrastructure for a 'power-sharing' constitution was being progressively put into place. Hermann Gilliomee's chapters in this book show why such an undeviating purpose should come as no surprise — why, despite many stunning departures, FW De Klerk stands in a direct line of descent from his Afrikaner nationalist forbears. Of course, to the ANC 'power sharing' is a euphemism for power denying. That is to say, it is a device for preventing majority rule.

What *was* unexpected was the shift of mass action from the cities to the countryside. Why was ANC Secretary-General Cyril Ramaphosa leading thousands in a non-violent march on the Ciskei? Why was this to be followed up almost immediately by another monster march on Qwaqwa? Several possibilities sprang to mind, all of them suggesting that Codesa would not be revived by anything short of a virtual capitulation by De Klerk. The ANC, like many scholars, had steadfastly refused to take seriously claims that the homelands are independent in any meaningful sense. Puppets and stooges were the nicest epithets used to describe homeland leaders. On the other hand, it is upon those territories that any edifice of 'power sharing' must largely rest.

If, by focussing attention on the weaknesses of the homelands, the ANC discredited them as credible power sharers, the concept of power sharing itself might be fatally crippled. If attempts to topple their leaderships were thwarted by actions of the South African security forces, the pretence of independence would be exposed. If ANC action actually succeeded in displacing homeland leaderships, then a 'power sharing' constituent assembly might conceivably consist of several ACN cadres talking with one another around the table. In any of these eventualities the ANC could not lose.

However, in making this calculation, the ANC disclosed its confidence that De Klerk, unlike PW Botha, does not have the option of throwing the reform process into reverse. There must be a new constitution for South Africa one way or another. The events of 1992 increased the odds that the new order would not be reached through open collusion between the major parties.

The Shape of this Book

Whatever the turn of events, there is much between the covers of this book which may be of enduring importance. Four areas of concern are singled out for special attention. Part 1 focusses on current events. Frene Ginwala, a trained historian who now serves as Head of Research for the ANC, charts the changing fortunes of the Codesa talks from her perspective inside ANC headquarters in Johannesburg. Hermann Giliomee, whose dual background as a historian of political thought and a commentator on current politics gives him an unrivalled vantage point for understanding the National Party, asks whether this is 'the last trek' for Afrikaners. Joan Wardrop, by taking a close look at the unfolding of events in the crucial period 1989-91, is able to point up disturbing ambiguities in the behaviour of the ruling regime — ambiguities which prefigured the revelations and scandals which bedevilled and derailed negotiations in 1992. Deryck Schreuder, recently returned from observing a Commonwealth Heads' of Government Meeting (CHOGM), uses his knowledge of history to explore the prospects for international mediation by the Commonwealth, the United Nations or other outside forces. Norman Etherington looks at the merits of some explanations that have been advanced for 'the death of apartheid'.

Part 2 fills in the background to the ethnic self-consciousness which has moved many South Africans to seek violent solutions to their problems. Shula Marks puts together her work on different eras of Zulu history to show how the Inkatha movement has 'hijacked' the past to serve its present political objectives. James Shuttleworth provocatively argues that today's image of the Zulu is as much a construction of white minds as black ones, while Hermann Giliomee systematically demolishes myths of Afrikaner ethnic solidarity. On the other hand, Giliomee's analysis confirms the ANC perception that the surrender of Afrikaner power was never on FW De Klerk's agenda. Part 3 looks across the frontier to two of the so-called Front Line States, a phrase which threatens to be drained of meaning as South Africa changes. James Polhemus shows that behind the facade of implacable hostility, Zimbabwe and South Africa have been evolving a new relationship during the last decade and suggests that even after apartheid there will be difficulties. Christopher Saunders and Michael Evans look for lessons in the transitions to democracy made by Namibia and

Zimbabwe. In the case of Namibia, decades of foot-dragging and obfuscation were followed by a sudden and apparently successful rush to a new order. In Zimbabwe, three different armies harbouring deep mutual suspicions were welded into a single unit. Implicit in Major Evans' analysis is the long-shot possibility that a similar welding could occur in the South African security forces.

The last section of the book looks at ideology and political action in relation to the black workers of South Africa. Until very recently it has been common among elements of both right and left to treat the *Freedom Charter* as a socialist blueprint for revolution. Political commentators have earnestly debated whether the ANC can or will sacrifice its revolutionary heritage in the negotiating process. Paul Rich delves into the origins of the *Freedom Charter* and finds a more multifarious, flexible and populist lineage — one that has continued relevance to 'the new South Africa'. From a quite different perspective Peter Limb questions whether the gap between ANC nationalists and ordinary workers was ever so large as some scholars have claimed. In the final chapter Glenn Adler, Judy Maller and Eddie Webster find growing contemporary linkages between organized labour and political action. Against that background, the August 1992 mass action campaign can be seen to be not an isolated experiment, but the culmination of a long series of 'stayaways'.

One last feature of the book which deserves a mention is the Australasian perspective taken by the gathering which generated the project. Australia and New Zealand assume far more importance in South African imaginations than the economic or political significance of either country would warrant. When sanctions ruptured ancient sporting rivalries, the wounds festered more openly than any hurts inflicted by curbs on investment and trade. For many white South Africans, New Zealand and Australia are might-have-been versions of their own country. New Zealand holds out a vision of a multi-racial society in which relative social harmony and civilization survive, despite a one-man/one-vote constitution. Australia, on the other hand, seems to approach the abandoned fantasy of ideal apartheid: a mineral-rich, continent-sized, white homeland where smoke rises daily from a million backyard barbecues.

Comparing the way the three countries have coped with the economic shocks of the last two decades is instructive. Pick up a newspaper in New Zealand or Australia, and you will most likely read that the country's situation is uniquely awful. Inflation, recession, unemployment are all the fault of bungling local politicians or bureaucrats. Governments reply to these charges by insisting that they are blameless — no one could withstand the cyclonic outside forces that beset them . These debates among Australians and New Zealanders about whether internal or external forces are responsible for their predicaments resemble scholarly discussions on the reasons for the death of apartheid. Indeed, they may be more germane than the comparison frequently drawn between Gorbachev's Soviet Union and De Klerk's South Africa.

Debts

Many people beside the authors contributed to the making of this book. The Indian Ocean Centre for Peace Studies and its director, Ken McPherson, supplied a vital early injection of funds. The University of Western Australia's Octagon Lecture Series, Qantas Airlines and Scott Spencer from the Australian Department of Foreign Affairs made Frene Ginwala's participation possible. Alan Dodds and Judy Bolton turned raw computer text into finished pages. Pen Hetherington's proof reading uncovered and eliminated unsuspected blemishes.

Norman Etherington
September 1992

Contributors

Glenn Adler is an associate of the Sociology of Work Unit in the Department of Sociology at the University of the Witwatersrand, and is completing a doctoral dissertation at Columbia University entitled '"The Factory Belongs to all who Work in it": the Organization of Non-racial Trade Unions in the South African Motor Industry, 1968-1983'. He is also co-editor of a volume on American trade unionism, *Union Voices: Labor's Response to Crisis*.

Norman Etherington is Professor of History and Head of the Department of History at the University of Western Australia. He is the author of *Preachers, Peasants and Politics in Southeast Africa*, *Theories of Imperialism: War, Conquest and Capital*, and *Rider Haggard*. He writes regularly on contemporary issues for the *Southern African Review of Books*.

Michael Evans is in the History Department at the University of Western Australia. He has served as a Major in the Zimbabwe Defence Forces and during his service was responsible of the development of War Studies at the University of Zimbabwe. He holds an MA in War Studies from King's College, University of London, and in 1987-88 was Honorary Visiting Fellow at the Centre for Southern African Studies, University of York.

Hermann Giliomee is Professor of Political Studies at the University of Cape Town. He has been a prolific writer on South African political history and is well known as a media commentator on current politics. Among his most recent books are *Negotiating South Africa's future* and *From Apartheid to Nation-building: Contemporary South African Debates*.

xiii

Frene Ginwala is Head of Research for the African National Congress. She has had a distinguished career in African journalism, and holds both a law degree and a Ph.D. in history. The unbanning of the ANC paved the way for her return to South Africa from exile. While in London she served for several years as assistant to ANC President-in-Exile Oliver Tambo.

Peter Limb is a member of staff at the Library of the University of Western Australia where he is completing a study of the relationship between the ANC and black workers in the first half of the twentieth century.

Judy Maller is an associate of the Sociology of Work Unit in the Department of Sociology at the University of the Witwatersrand. She is the author of the recently published *Conflict and Cooperation: Case studies in Worker Participation*, and has worked for a number of trade union research organizations.

Shula Marks is Professor and Director of the Institute of Commonwealth Studies in the University of London. She is well known in the field of Southern African studies for her work on Natal/Zulu history and for helping to edit many collections of historical essays. Among her recent books are *The Ambiguities of Dependence in South Africa: Class, Nationalism, and the State in Twentieth-century Natal*, and *Not either an Experimental Doll: the Separate Worlds of Three South African Women*.

James Polhemus is Dean of Social Sciences at Deakin University in Australia and has written extensively on politics in Botswana and other parts of Southern Africa. His published works include *Development Experience in the Third World: a Political Science Perspective*.

Paul Rich is in the Department of Politics at the University of Melbourne where he is associated with the Drakensberg Trust. He is the author of *White Power and the Liberal Conscience: Racial Segregation and South African Liberalism, 1921-1960* and *Hope and Despair: English Speaking Intellectuals and South African Politics, 1896-1976*.

xiv

Christopher Saunders is Head of the Department of History at the University of Cape Town, where he has had a longstanding association with the editorial board of the cross-disciplinary journal *Social Dynamics*. His most recent book is *The Making of the South African Past: Major Historians on Race and Class*.

Deryck Schreuder is Challis Professor of History at the University of Sydney and Associate Director of the Humanities Research Centre in the Australian National University. His major works include *Gladstone and Kruger* and *The Scramble for Southern Africa, 1877-1895*.

James Shuttleworth is in the Department of History at the University of Western Australia, and has been engaged for some time in a study of the use and abuse of history by MG Buthulezi and the Inkatha Movement.

Joan Wardrop is in the School of Social Science, Curtin University of Technology, Western Australia, and has recently published *Rhetoric and Reality: the New South Africa*.

Eddie Webster is Professor and Head of the Department of Sociology at the University of the Witwatersrand, where he is also Director of the Sociology of Work Unit. He is the author of *Cast in a Racial Mould: Labour Process and Trade Unionism in the Foundries* and has published widely on South African labour studies. He is a member of the editorial board of the *South African Labour Bulletin*, and has a long-standing relationship with the labour movement through his research and teaching activities.

Acronyms

AAC	All African Convention
AG	Administrator General (Namibia)
AHI	Afrikaanse Handelsinstituut
AMWU	African Mine Workers' Union
ANC	African National Congress
AZAPO	Azanian African People's Organization
BBC	British Broadcasting Corporation
CAAA	Comprehensive Anti-Apartheid Act (USA)
CASE	Community Agency for Social Enquiry
CHOGM	Commonwealth Heads of Government Meeting
CNETU	Council of Non-European Trade Unions
CNS	Accord between COSATU, NACTU & SACCOLA
COD	Congress of Democrats
Codesa	Convention for a Democratic South Africa
COP	Congress of the People
COSATU	Congress of South African Trade Unions
COSATU	Congress of South African Trade Unions
CP	Conservative Party
CPSA	Communist Party of South Africa
CYL	Congress Youth League
DFHQ	Defence Force Headquarters
DP	Democratic Party
DTA	Democratic Turnhalle Alliance
EAC	Economic Advisory Council
FAK	Federasie van Afrikaanse Kultuurverings
FRELIMO	Front for the Liberation of Mozambique
G7	The Group of Seven nations
HNP	Herstigte Nasionale Party
IBIIR	Independent Board of Inquiry into Informal Repression
ICU	Industrial and Commercial Workers Union
IFP	Inkatha Freedom Party
IMF	International Monetary Fund
JHC	Joint High Command
JPS	Joint Planning Staff
LMG	Labour Monitoring Group
LRAA	Labour Relations Amendment Act

MK	Umkhonto we Sizwe, military arm of the African National Congress
MNR	Mozambique National Resistance Movement
NAC	National Action Council
NACTU	National Council of Trade Unions
NCA	Namibia Constituent Assembly
NENF	National Economic Negotiating Forum
NMC	National Manpower Commission
NP	National Party
NRC	Natives Representative Council
OAU	Organization of African Unity
PAC	Pan African Congress
RAR	Rhodesian African Rifles
SABC	South African Broadcasting Corporation
SACCOLA	South African Employers' Consultative Committee on Labour Affairs
SACP	South African Communist Party
SACPO	South African Coloured People's Organization?
SACTU	South African Congress of Trade Unions
SADCC	Southern African Development Coordination Conference
SADF	South African Defense Force
SAIC	South African Indian Congress
SAIRR	South African Institute of Race Relations
SANC	South African National Native Congress
SAP	South African Police
SR	Special Representative (Namibia)
SSRC	Soweto Students' Representative Council
STF	Special Task Force
SWAPO	South West African People's Organization
SWAPOL	South West African Police
TIC	Transvaal Indian Congress
TVBC states	Transkei, Venda, Bophutustwana, Ciskei
UDF	United Democratic Front
UDI	Unilateral Declaration of Independence, Southern Rhodesia, 1965
UF	Urban Foundation
UNHCR	United Nations High Commission for Refugees
UNSC	United Nations Security Council
UNTAG	United Nations Transitional Assistance Group
UWUSA	United Workers Union of South Africa
VAT	Value Added Tax
ZANLA	Zimbabwe African National Liberation Army
ZANU	Zimbabwe African National Union
ZAPU	Zimbabwe African People's Union
ZIPRA	Zimbabwe People's Revolutionary Army
ZNA	Zimbabwe National Army

1

Into and Out of Codesa Negotiations: the View from the ANC

Frene Ginwala

This chapter has two parts. The first part is a transcription of a public address given two days after the Codesa talks began. The second part takes the form of an epilogue reflecting on the first seven months of negotiations. While both parts are informed by Dr Ginwala's vantage point as Head of Research for the ANC, they should not be regarded as official views of the organization.

2 December 1991

Two days ago, a preparatory meeting of over 20 parties finally gave shape to South Africa's negotiating table, and set the broad agenda for the negotiations, which are scheduled to begin on December 20th. This agreement comes one year and ten months after the National Party leadership accepted the necessity of negotiating with representative black leaders, and unbanned the ANC, PAC and other organizations.

The question we have to ask is why has it taken so long even to start negotiations. The answers are important not just for the historical record, but because some of the issues are still unresolved, and will affect the speed with which the negotiations will be able to proceed. And I must at the outset distinguish negotiations from the talks that have happened up to now. Up to now we have been talking about how to get to the point of negotiations. Negotiations on substantive matters will begin on December 20th.

I want briefly to contextualize what comes now by summarizing what was actually agreed. Firstly we agreed on the name. This may seem strange but for more than a year we had been talking about an All Party Congress which was the ANC's preferred terminology, a Multi-Party Conference which was the National Party's, a Pre-Constituent Assembly Meeting which was the Pan-African Congress's. People were getting tired of putting slashes between all these initials. Now the name will be the Convention for a Democratic South Africa, or Codesa for short.

We agreed also on a number of agenda items. Among the main ones are
- the creation of a climate for free political
  participation
- general political and constitutional principles
- the constitution making body or the process
- transitional arrangements
- the future of what are known as the TVBC states
  (the four Bantustans that were given
  independence by Pretoria)
- the role of the international community
- the time frames for the exercise and, most
  importantly, the implementation of the
  decisions of Codesa.

So that will be what we have to discuss. We agreed that the venue should be inside South Africa. We have also said it should not be a State venue, so we will have to find one. And there has been a long debate, which is still unresolved, about who will attend this Conference.

At the meetings last week, all the major political parties in the country were invited as were governments of the independent Bantustans. The National Party and the South African government were separately represented. However, the Government delegation is supposed to be only there as an observer.

Those who did not accept the invitation included the three parties of the far right (the HNP, the AWB and the Conservative Party) and, on the left, AZAPO. What we have still to resolve is a request from the Inkatha Freedom Party, who have asked for separate representation of the government of Kwazulu, which is a non-independent homeland, and of 'the Zulu people' through the King. This will be discussed by the Steering Committee. Consideration was also given to the possibility of the Trade Unions participating and it was generally agreed that that would not happen at this meeting. Consideration was given to an economic forum which can discuss economic policy during the transition.

What was absent both in the preparatory meetings and in the formal discussion was the participation of women. There were virtually no women delegates there at all; there were a few women in the supporting staff. There is in the country some talk of forming a women's political party in order to make sure we gain entry.

There was also agreement on foreign participation. There has been resistance until very recently from Pretoria to any foreign participation. What has now been agreed is that ambassadors will be able to participate and that there will be representatives from a number of international organizations, the OAU, the United Nations, the European community and the Non-aligned Movement. What role the international community will play in the actual process will be an agenda item to be discussed.

There was a major problem as to who should convene the meetings. This was a problem because until recently Pretoria had assumed that it would act as convenor. This, of course, has been challenged. In the event — since everyone got there one way or the other — the feeling was that we did not need anyone else to convene the next conference. It has been agreed that two judges will chair the whole conference. Proposals that the Chief Justice or religious leaders chair failed to gain sufficient consensus. The Chief Justice was considered to be part of the state structures by the ANC and religious leaders as not sufficiently neutral by the Government and the IFP. As a compromise, the Chief Justice will open the meeting and call on the religious leaders to say prayers.

Now, you may well ask, what on earth are you going to sort out in two days? The idea is that in two days we will demarcate the agenda items, we will then set up working groups to look at each of these issues and also we will have to discuss how decisions are going to be made. The way we made decisions at this preparatory meeting was according to a new procedure, which I think we invented in South Africa, called 'sufficient consensus'. We turned to this doctrine because we faced a situation in which, if everybody was able to attend and there was no election, no way of gauging strength, you could have a very small political party holding up the whole process by exercising a solitary veto. The doctrine of sufficient consensus enables the chairperson of the conference to decide that despite some opposition, sufficient agreement exists to allow the process to move. In other words there is sufficient consensus. I suspect you will be hearing more of that as the discussions proceed.

Background to the talks

Why did it take us so long to get to this stage? As of February 2nd, 1990, I think whites generally and the Pretoria regime believed that by unbanning the ANC and the major political organizations, and repealing legislation that had become known as the 'pillars of apartheid', not by us I hasten to say, the situation in South Africa would be 'normalized'. Many whites, I believe, expected immediate benefits to be gained through solving some of the country's economic and social problems. Certainly, the authorities saw it as a way of opening the way for engaging Nelson Mandela and other leaders in resolving the country's problems, without first having to make fundamental changes.

The question of how much change they were prepared to countenance at that point, or even now, is still open to debate.

However the unbanning of the organizations and releasing leaders did not normalize the situation, it merely took us back to where we were in 1960. The repeal of legislation such as the Group Areas Act took us back to 1950 — and by no stretch of imagination can the system that obtained in that period be accepted as normal in 1991.

So perceptions of South Africa's political reality differed

from the outset of this process and that has had important consequences for the way events unfolded. Clearly there were, and there still are, very different perceptions of the nature of oppression in South Africa. Is what we are dealing with structured oppression or simply discrimination? There are also different perspectives on the legitimacy of the Pretoria regime and on the status of the liberation struggle.

The National Party view of apartheid is illustrated in a recent interview given by the Director General of Foreign Affairs, Neil van Heerden, which I saw reproduced in a copy of the *Financial Times* on the flight coming over. He casually makes a very telling point when he says, 'Now that apartheid is removed, our strategy should be ....'. So, clearly in his eyes non-racialism, democracy, and the need for changes that will allow political participation by all citizens in South Africa have nothing to do with apartheid. With 'apartheid removed', the ANC is expected to operate within the existing political system as a political party. Although not even the National Party suggests that we put up candidates (of the appropriate race) for elections, the demand is there and constantly repeated for the ANC to abandon mass action and other forms of extra-parliamentary activity. Instead we are supposed to join with government in resolving some of the present problems and in that way be co-opted to operate within the apartheid system and its institutions.

In this scenario, what is being ignored is that it is the present constitution that defines the character of the ANC, the PAC and other liberation organizations, in fact of almost any black political organization. The majority of membership is still outside the South African polity and has no constitutional way of expressing itself. Unlike a political party, which operates within constitutional parameters and institutions, the ANC must still endeavour to change that constitution and those institutions. Therefore, where necessary, it has to engage the parliament of the streets, through boycotts, through demonstrations, mass action, strikes and similar activity.

The necessity for this action is incomprehensible to the authorities and to many white South Africans. At the same time there is little comprehension of how the South African government and the ANC are perceived both internationally and internally — legally, and in the political culture. The internal perception is something that goes beyond the usual hostility and lack of allegiance and loyalty that oppressed people feel for any repressive government.

Anti-colonial struggles and international law have developed since 1948 when the National Party came into power. The status of the South African Government and that of the liberation movements have been affected by the International Convention that declared the practice of apartheid a crime in international law — the first occasion since the Nuremburg trials that this has been done. The right of the people to self-determination is now recognized as inalienable. Over the period of UDI in Southern Rhodesia, it came to be recognized that by definition minority governments are illegitimate. In the instance of what was formerly the Spanish Sahara, the right of one colonial power (Spain) to 'decolonize' by handing power over to another (Morocco) without the people in the territories being consulted has been decisively challenged. Those debates had relevance for South Africa, because Pretoria claimed it had decolonized the bantustans. They may yet be important should there be difficulties reincorporating the TVBC (ex-banstustans) into South Africa. I am sure that we are going to hear tired, out-dated arguments in the talks by those who want to resist the re-incorporation.

The United Nations General Assembly has refused to accept the credentials of the Pretoria regime for many years now, while it has recognized the National Liberation Movements, the ANC and PAC as entitled to speak on behalf of the people of South Africa on the international stage. The legitimacy of the liberation struggle was explicitly recognized and even the Security Council — which has in the past not hesitated to exercise vetos to protect Pretoria — even the Security Council has recognized the legitimacy and the right of the people of South Africa to use 'all means at their disposal' to assert their rights, which is understood to include the right 'to take up arms'. Further undercutting Mr De Klerk's claim to a legitimate status, a Security Council resolution has declared the Tri-cameral constitution, from which he now draws his powers, to be 'null and void'.

In contrast, the political stature of the ANC has grown as it has increasingly been accorded recognition and status, even by governments which had previously supported Pretoria without reservation. This status, in the eyes of the ANC, the PAC and the international community, was neither altered nor wished away on 2nd February when the ANC was unbanned.

Pretoria, however, simply closes its eyes to this reality, or possibly may not have appreciated its full significance. Self-deluding propaganda and censorship inevitably affect the perceptions and understanding of those who do the censoring. Time and again since I have returned to South Africa, I have realized just how much of an impact that self-deluding propaganda has on the actions of Pretoria.

For Pretoria, of course, the world is still normal from its own perspective. It assumes it has the legal and constitutional right to rule, which gives it the authority to remain in power and to exclusively manage the transition. Hence the statements, which we constantly had, about the National Party refusing to accept any changes it did not like, about National Party values prevailing, whatever anyone else decided, and of course the resistance to an interim government. To this point I will return later.

Now these differing perceptions of the South African political reality held by the major parties, underlay many of the problems that arose during this intervening period of nearly two years. The actors did not necessarily articulate issues in these terms, but they acted upon the basis of assumptions about their own status and that of their opponents.

For the liberation movements also, the situation was not simple or unambiguous — nor indeed was it anything like what we might have envisaged. Commentators have often compared our situation to that in Latin America, but we cannot draw on that experience. As I already explained, we are not faced simply with a situation in which an authoritarian government suddenly unbans or lifts restrictions on political parties that operate within that system. Nor is the situation precisely similar to that of Angola or Mozambique. Now of course all of us were convinced in the many years of liberation struggle that victory was certain. That was one of our favourite slogans. But, there was never a

clear cut and unequivocal scenario of how that victory was going
to come about and what would actually happen.

` A move to a people's war and the possibility of insurrection
were avidly debated and questioned in the columns of the ANC
organ *Sechaba*, in other ANC journals and in internal meetings.
And many a fantasy was woven of an embattled regime
regrouping around the Voertrekker Movement behind a laager
formed of ox-wagons and Caspirs, tanks, sneeze machines,
rocket launchers and so on, while in the cities and countryside
ordinary people took over public buildings, factories and the
institutions of power. We had visions of MK Commanders
striding at the head of their troups into Pretoria, Johannesburg
and all the cities of South Africa, while people formed
spontaneously into a national convention to write the new
constitution.

Of course, the reality we find today is very very different.
We find ourselves legalized in a situation where, de facto, the
levers of state powers still remain in the hands of the very
authorities against whom we fought for so long. This power
covers all the institutions of government, the military
establishment and the police — and not only the institutions of
the state, but of the economy and in fact wherever legal power is
vested. It was one thing to commit ourselves to a negotiated
solution as we have done — but another to work out how we
could retain any power in this situation, how we could avoid
being co-opted, and how we could engage in meaningful
negotiations. So we too have faced very serious problems.

Within weeks of the unbanning and the release of Nelson
Mandela, the ANC made major and significant concessions. In
accordance with the Harare Declaration and the UN Consensus
Declaration of December 1989, Pretoria was required to create a
climate conducive to negotiations by releasing political
prisoners, unbanning organizations, allowing exiles to return
and repealing repressive legislation. Instead of waiting for
Pretoria to act on its own timetable, the ANC decided to meet the
authorities in order to discuss the removal of the obstacles that
stood in the way of the start of negotiations. Pretoria in its turn
added the continuation of the armed struggle to the list of
obstacles. On the understanding that agreement had been

reached on the removal of the other obstacles, the ANC agreed to suspend armed action.

However, we found that agreements reached would not be implemented — either because of bad faith by the negotiators or because implementation was being frustrated by civil servants. We were constantly being told 'the door was open' for exiles to return. In fact, the first time I ever confronted an official of the South African government was on 2nd February on a BBC interview when he said to me 'the door is open, go back home'. But what we found were detailed indemnity forms to be filled in which had to be processed by security police and bureaucrats. Later we faced difficulties of funding and support, when Pretoria refused to allow the U.N. High Commission for Refugees (UNHCR) to operate on the same basis as it has operated in other countries.

Having begun with the perception that the National Party was led by a man of integrity and was genuinely seeking a negotiated solution, the feeling grew that in fact the levers of state power were being manipulated in order to weaken the ANC and hence to force it in whatever negotiations followed to make compromises over the types of changes that we believed were necessary in any political dispensation. There was considerable anger at the grass roots and within the ANC leadership.

This was further fuelled by the escalating violence and the failure of the security forces to control that violence. Instead of the normal process of the police investigating and finding the evidence, we were told that evidence had to be supplied by the victims. And, of course, there were mounting reports and evidence of police involvement in crimes and the failure of Pretoria to act on those reports. So by September 1990, the National Executive of the ANC was considering breaking off all talks with the government. The view was being expressed more and more that whether De Klerk could not control the police or would not control the police was a debate that might be of relevance in one context but in another was totally irrelevant because in neither case would he make a credible negotiating partner. Because he could not deliver.

Apart from the human aspect, the frightening violence made

it difficult for the ANC to organize. It worked, and still works to intimidate and frighten people from showing their political allegiance or expressing their views, and it undermined the climate of free political debate that was required for negotiations.

Earlier this year, the ANC finally refused to have any further dealings on the constitution with the government and issued an ultimatum requiring Pretoria to address the issue of violence and meet the previously agreed deadlines. With little publicity, the log jams began to shift — prisoners were released before the 30th of April, nearly 5,000 indemnity forms were suddenly processed, and the Cabinet was reshuffled.

But the most significant shifts came in the events leading up to the Peace Accord and in the agreements that were reached there. Initially, Pretoria unilaterally decided to call a Peace Conference — a meeting to deal with the question of violence. Mr De Klerk phoned President Mandela and informed the ANC what was happening and when. There had been no prior consultation or discussion. Once again there was the assumption that Pretoria had the right to take unilateral decisions about the process of change — an assumption that the ANC, on this occasion, explicitly rejected. We demanded from the government de facto recognition as an equal partner in determining the processes, and refused to participate unless this was accepted. Though there is no formal agreement to that effect, in practice that is what is now happening.

De Klerk's Conference went ahead, and was boycotted by all the democratic and anti-apartheid forces. The ANC, in the meantime, had proposed a Conference convened by neutral individuals or organizations, and we later supported a proposal initiated by the church and business. Through a face saving formula, Pretoria was able to support this initiative also, and so the Peace Accord was born.

In the leadup discussions and in the content of the Accord, both sides had made concessions. The government implicitly accepted that it could not act on its own, and accepted the need for neutral conveners and neutral chairing of any meeting where agreements had to be reached. Within the Accord itself, Pretoria accepted the need for joint management of certain sectors of the state pending a final settlement. (I am now talking of joint committees of the police and the ANC for security, monitoring and a whole range of other activities). On its side, the ANC effectively accepted that the existing constitutional institutions — including the Tri-cameral Parliament would have to be used to make necessary changes and provide legislative backup to agreements that were reached.

Now this is a very major concession, but strangely it has gone unnoticed, perhaps because it seems a return to what previously was seen as 'normality'. But what it does mean is that in the Peace Accord there is an acceptance that agreements that we reach will then have to be legislated for by the existing institutions. The reasons for this are obvious; there is no other way. De Klerk wants constitutional continuity so that some right-wing general does not go to the courts to say he won't accept orders from a new government. We equally do not want a police general going to the courts and refusing to obey the orders of the new government on the ground that there is no constitutional continuity. It is thus in the interests of both of us to make sure of a smooth transfer of power to whatever new structures are actually agreed.

Many substantive issues even in the Peace Accord remain unresolved, especially the question of banning cultural weapons. Revelations that the government was secretly funding Inkatha precipitated a strategic shift in the ANC approach. There was disquiet over the use of government machinery and taxpayers' money to try and weaken the ANC while strengthening the National Party or forces supporting it. This has been growing all the time. With evidence of direct funding for Inkatha, the ANC felt that it could no longer depend on Pretoria to create the necessary climate for negotiations. This was significant because, as I said earlier, under the Harare and UN Declarations, the right climate had to be created before negotiations could begin.

The continuation in office of the National Party government was now recognized as the main obstacle to progress. It was therefore decided to move speedily to convene an All Party Congress, which would decide on the removal of obstacles and pave the way for an Interim Government. It is this decision, and the rigour with which it has been pursued, that brought about the preparatory meeting of this last weekend. The process was facilitated by the intense lobbying and consultation in which both sides have engaged in the last two months.

Guidelines for the Codesa Talks

Since its unbanning, the ANC has had discussions with every black political party in the country, except the parties in the Indian House of Delegates (the Indian community refuses to countenance such discussions). As a result, there is an informal grouping around certain common understandings of the negotiating process among black political parties, among traditional rulers who have been organized under Contralesa, and among some of the Bantustan governments. The Patriotic Front which met six weeks ago brought these organizations, the political ones, together with trade unions, civic and other community organizations. The common understanding of the negotiating process encompasses —

Firstly, a participatory process, including an elected constituent assembly; because what we are opposed to is the tradition in South Africa of constitutions being decided at the top and then being imposed. Even whites at a popular level have not been involved in constitution making in the past and there is a very strong feeling that we need a participatory process as much to make the constitution democratic as to ensure support for the difficult decisions that a democratic government is going to have to take.

Second, a common understanding that the present government cannot unilaterally supervise the transition. Hence there is a need for some kind of transitional authority or Interim Government that commands broad support.

Parties to the Talks

Now the present broad grouping is, to me as an exile, a very strange one. I must say I find ANC headquarters these days very strange. We find homeland leaders, suspect for decades, trouping in and out of meetings, the Democratic Party from the white House of Assembly, the Labour Party from the Coloured House of Representatives, General Holomisa of the Transkei

Bantustan. We find the ex-Regent to the Zulu King and leader of the BOP coup attending meetings of the National Executive Committee and so on. So, in a sense, the world has changed from that very simple thing of us versus the police and the 'baddies', and what we are finding now is that a lot of the people we had characterized as 'baddies' are now seeing the process of change as inevitable and are coming across. I am not suggesting any particular motivation, but they are beginning to see that, since there is going to be a democratic process, they better decide whether they want to be with the National Party or with the forces for change.

Now among all these groups that I have mentioned, you will have noticed, I am sure, that I have not mentioned the Inkatha Freedom Party. Our relations with the IFP have been problematic for some considerable time. We have resisted the attempt lately in some quarters to project the IFP, the ANC and the government as a Troika that could decide what happens in South Africa. This almost halted the recent preparatory meeting which was to have consisted of five or six of the major political parties as a preparatory committee for these talks. After there had been preliminary agreement on these lines, the IFP said no, there would have to be only the ANC, the government and the IFP. At which point the other homeland leaders started going to Mr De Klerk and saying,'but why that homeland and not us?' So you then began to get challenges to the IFP, coming not from the ANC but from other homeland leaders. Even though relations are problematic, at the talks themselves last week, IFP supported ANC positions to a considerable extent. So perhaps there are changes coming there but I would not predict that any breakthrough will happen. What we do have is a broad front including many of the elements that De Klerk had assumed would support him.

On the other hand the National Party has also been busily canvassing and having its talks at a bi-lateral and multilateral level. It has made inroads, especially in the coloured and Indian community. The control of the media in South Africa makes it very difficult for any opposing views to be heard broadly. And, this is why one of the items on the agenda for the Codesa will be the control of theSouth African Broadcasting Commission and an attempt to make sure that it is open to all participating parties.

What was a surprise, however, was the isolation of the Pretoria regime, over this weekend, on the question of who should be in the chair. They had accepted for some considerable time now that neither the government nor the National Party could chair or convene any of these talks. Then they put forward the idea of the Chief Justice, who for us is, quite as much as the National Party, a symbol of a state and the constitution we are trying to change. So we were opposed to this. What has happened is that two other judges, the first black judge, Ismail Mahomed and another judge in the Transvaal, have been elected as Co-Chairmen. The Chief Justice will have a ceremonial role in opening the Conference and calling upon the religious leaders to lead the prayers.

Nobody, except one minor Bantustan party, supported the National Party on this decision. Even the IFP supported the idea that the Chief Justice should not chair. And this to us was quite a pleasant surprise, if I may put it that way, because it did show that there were significant shifts within the parties that had traditionally supported the National Party.

Questions still to be decided

There are crucial issues still outstanding. The first is the question of the transitional authority, Interim Government or transitional government (even on the agenda we have had to use all those words). Initially the proposal from the liberation movements was that there should be full transfer of sovereignty to an Interim Government. The reasons for this were obvious. There was a feeling that we could not trust the present government to maintain a neutral stance in the interim period. We certainly could not trust them to supervise the new elections. But, lately, some have wondered whether a transitional government with full sovereignty is such a good idea. Any Interim Authority or government, whatever its standing, will be a coalition government. By definition, coalition governments favour the status quo; you have to take a positive position to make a change.

So there is a danger involved in going into an Interim Government and finding ourselves unable to make changes. The result, of course, will be that we then have responsibility but no power. Under those circumstances we are likely to lose support and there will be serious problems with our own supporters. So a lot of rethinking is now going on about whether we want a full Interim Government.

Another problem is that we believe that any Interim Authority should have a limited time span. If you have a fully sovereign government, you can't just walk out. If we did that, the National Party would gain an important advantage. We would leave them in control and nothing would change. A possibility now is that we might assume authority over certain vital areas. The media, the SABC, security, defence — these are obvious areas which would have to be controlled by some joint authority.

Handling the economy with an Interim Government is also difficult. We would obviously want to allocate national resources in a very different way to the way the government is doing now. If we went into the Ministry of Housing, we would certainly want to deal with the funding of housing very differently. If we went into the Department of Education we could not accept schools paying different subsidies for white children and black children. These are not situations which we want even for a temporary period.

So, the debate on the Interim Government within the ANC, among the democratic forces, is still wide open in terms of what actually we will ask for when we come to the negotiating table. On its side, the present government, having refused to transfer any sovereignty at the beginning, has argued that all that is needed is some leaders from the liberation movements to join the present cabinet. The government is anxious to engage us in responsibility for areas like Education, Housing and the Budget so that the responsibility for problems land on our shoulders as much as theirs.

Another vital question is timing. When will an Interim Government take authority? The probability is that an Interim Government can only come into being when we have agreed on issues, such as the mechanisms for actually arriving at a Constituent Assembly .

The Constituent Assembly is itself a matter on which there are grave and major differences. At no point does it appear that the government is prepared to countenance the Constituent Assembly. It would like Codesa to become, in fact, the constitution-making body. However, as I have indicated, Codesa is not based upon popular participation and does not give any indication of the strength of the parties who are engaged in the negotiations.

But perhaps the greatest problem of all is agreeing on the principles that will underlie the new Constitution. The National Party appeared to have abandoned its previous dream of a new Constitution based on group rights with an electoral system based on racial and ethnic groups. Nonetheless, their latest proposals strangely seem to revert to group and ethnic concepts. While racial and ethnic definitions of groups are abandoned, the National Party defines participatory democracy as based on the effective participation of political parties, not of citizens individually and collectively. And it is the effective participation of individual citizens that is the true barometer of a genuine democracy.

Furthermore, the National Party still totally rejects the principle of majority rule regardless of any safeguards or checks and balances that might be devised. So, though we have general agreement among all the parties that there will be guarantees of rights, a multi-party system and so on, there is a chasm between us on the fundamental principles of democracy as well as the nature of the future of South Africa. To the National Party, it would appear that the political and social institutions of the new society should maintain in perpetuity the divisions created by apartheid.

The liberation movement recognizes there is a legacy of apartheid but we seek new institutions that will overcome this legacy and help to create a common society, however far away the fulfilment of that prospect may be. Thus the differences between us are not simply about mechanisms — whether you have an Interim Government or not, whether you have a Constituent Assembly or not — but they are about the very objectives of the liberation struggle and the character of the new South Africa. The message is that we are in transition from apartheid but at the moment there is no agreement about where we are going and, unless we agree on the ultimate destination, any agreement on mechanisms will have no meaning and the struggle in South Africa will have to continue until we are able to give meaning to the objectives for which so many people have fought.

3 September 1991

The final paragraph of the first section, written nine months ago, proved to be prophetic. At the Codesa talks, while agreement could be reached on a number of matters including some of the mechanisms for the transition, there was no agreement on the constitutional principles upon which the new order should be based nor on the nature of the constitution making body. As a result, just six months after the negotiations began, they broke down.

Major issues of both substance and procedure still divide the two sides, but beneath these remain the fundamentally different concepts of the nature of democracy and the character of the future South African. The negotiations began on December 20th, 1991 with a two day plenary session of the Convention which was broadcast live across the country. There were nineteen participants and much fanfare and official euphoria. (Neither the Conservative Party nor the PAC participated.) A Declaration of Intent with a commitment to establish a united non-racial non-sexist democratic South Africa was speedily agreed upon. Seventeen of the participants found the formulations acceptable, though there were different understandings of what the words meant. The government of Bophuthatswana refused to be bound by any declaration of Codesa, while the IFP considered that the Declaration did not allow for a federal option. (The IFP has subsequently signed the Declaration.)

However, hardly had the ink dried on the Declaration when the country was electrified as Nelson Mandela publicly dressed down FW De Klerk in the closing hour of the Convention. A request that De Klerk speak at the end of the proceedings had been conceded by the ANC as a courtesy. However, De Klerk abused the concession and used the opportunity to attack the ANC over issues such as the role of the armed wing Umkhonto we Sizwe which were still the subject of bilateral negotiations. Moreover, he assumed the style of a headmaster reprimanding a class of children.

Rarely, if ever, has any Head of State (albeit of a regime considered illegitimate) been publicly chastised as De Klerk was when the ANC leader stood to speak on a 'matter of national concern'. That a black man would do so in South Africa was unthinkable. That such an impossible event would be broadcast on the state-run television was beyond the realms of fantasy. Yet that is what happened.

Millions had ring-side seats, watching as Mandela's quiet but stinging words met first with disbelief and then a variety of reactions: amazement followed by anger among the National Party and government delegations, faces flushed and in some cases almost apoplectic; Democratic Party members stunned and finally lowering heads into hands in a mixture of consternation and despair; discomfitted Bantustan leaders, eyes downcast with uncertainty or bulging with astonishment; while, among the members of the anti-apartheid delegations, shock mixed with surprise and, slowly, barely concealed pleasure spread on black and white faces.

In the townships the atmosphere was electric. Drivers hooted and headlights blazed as cars were stopped and the word passed on. Phones rang, spreading the message to switch on television sets and watch the incredible. Disbelief turned to joyous dancing in the streets as blacks who had been alienated by the courtesies, formal handshakes and smiles of the two day proceedings, gave vent to their relief. To what extent later reports of these events helped white South Africans to begin to comprehend the depth of black suffering and anger over the years of apartheid is unclear.

The much publicised 'chemistry' between De Klerk and Mandela — on which so much hope had been pinned by optimists — evaporated as Mandela demonstrated that though he had risen above bitterness, his attempts to seek reconciliation should not be mistaken for naïvete or weakness, and that neither he nor the ANC would accept being treated with disrespect or as less than equal. Apartheid was not yet dead, but the days when blacks would put up with white notions of superiority were over.

For blacks it had been demonstrated that while negotiations may require consorting with the 'enemy' this does not have to be done on the enemy's terms.

In the following months, the negotiations were conducted in a Management Committee, in five working groups and in bilateral meetings between the ANC and government. The recommendations of the working groups were to be presented and approved at a second Codesa summit.

Codesa was intended to be all inclusive. There was an ongoing debate on whether there should be participation by non-party political organizations. This focused largely on whether COSATU, the country's major trade union federation, should have a seat. Unionists were themselves divided. Some women's organizations also sought to participate. Nonetheless, there was agreement that the Convention should be confined to political organizations.[1] Regardless of size, existing political groupings were all given the same status, powers and representation. Among the participants were the political parties in the various houses of the Tricameral Parliament, political parties formed in the homelands, the 'governments' of the four nominally independent bantustans (including the military rulers who took power in coups in three of them). Each of the 19 participants was entitled to field ten delegates and ten advisers for the working groups, representatives on the Management Committee and the Gender Advisory Committee plus a number of support staff. Some of the parties were so weak that they had considerable difficulty in mustering and sustaining such large delegations over the months of negotiations. Many featured civil servants seconded by Pretoria, non-South African academic advisers, lawyers and others retained for the purpose.

Members of the liberation movement delegations had been instructed to clear their desks on the assumption that negotiations were a priority. For others, negotiations appeared to be a part time activity, to be fitted in when they were not engaged in other more important tasks. During the initial discussions on procedure, delegation after delegation indicated that they could only spare one day a week, or, on occasion, two for negotiations, but that in no circumstances could meetings be held on Wednesdays. With a mixture of wonder and amusement the realization dawned on those who were not parties to the 'governing' of South Africa that the country's multitude of cabinets (one from each of the eight self-governing homelands, the four 'independent' Bantustans, and the three Tricameral Houses) had synchronised their weekly cabinet meetings.[2]

The process was slow and, in the Working Groups, highly ritualized. There was no sharp focus on fundamental issues, and little cut and thrust of debate on the position of a particular party. The procedure seemed to have been deliberately devised to avoid that possibility. Each of the participants presented its position on almost every agenda item, reading lengthy and repetitive documents into the record. Those parties with the least support in the country appeared to make the longest and most frequent interventions. After each individual presentation, clarification could be sought, but the issues raised could not be debated. Thereafter, the Steering Committee of the working group would produce a draft formulation, on which it believed consensus might be achieved. This potential compromise was then discussed.

Throughout the proceedings, bilateral meetings between the ANC and Government continued. There were also other meetings. Members of the Patriotic Front met regularly to formulate strategies and sort out common positions among the various working groups. The NP met with its allies.
Despite the cumbersome procedures, agreement was reached on a number of matters in some working groups. The fundamental differences were never really addressed, but underlay the difficulties in two working groups: Working Group 2, which dealt with constitutional principles and the constitution-making body, and Group 3, which dealt with the transitional arrangements.[3]

The ANC, which had started by calling for an immediate transfer of power to a full Interim Government, shifted its ground and put forward proposals for a two-stage transition. In the first an Interim Governing Council would assume full control over four areas of Government: security, local and regional government, foreign affairs and finance. The Council would also appoint an independent commission to supervise the state-owned media, and an election commission, which would be responsible for preparing and conducting elections for the constitution-making body. In the second stage, a multi-party interim government would be appointed, proportionately representing those parties who secured seats in the elections. The ANC also accepted the NP proposal that an elected Assembly should act as both the legislature and the constitution-making body. Initially, the NP insisted on retaining power during the first phase, with the transitional mechanisms having a consultative/advisory status, but eventually accepted a transfer of the relevant power.

The disagreements in Working Group Two proved insurmountable. They dealt with the core of the difference between the ANC and Government. However, the structure and proceedings of Codesa, referred to above, submerged this fundamental disagreement in a tangle of differences over process.

The ANC and its allies are committed to principles of democracy as universally understood, including specifically: that rights should be vested equally in citizens regardless of political belief, religion, ethnicity, race or sex; that political power should not be unrestrained but subjected to checks and balances; and that, while minorities should be protected, within the constitutional parameters ultimately the will of the majority should prevail.

Perceptions of substance inevitably influence process. Hence the ANC wished these principles to be reflected in the constitution-making process itself. The constitution-making body should be democratically elected. While provision could be made for special majorities on specific matters, the decision-making process should reflect the electoral strength of the parties. Minorities had a significant role to play as the opposition. While the ANC was open to accepting constitutional provision for government by a coalition in the interim, it could not accept this as a provision in the final constitution.

The NP and its allies, on the other hand, articulated a different conception of democracy in which power is shared among representatives of groups. Originally these groups were racially defined and exclusive power was entrenched in the white group. Notwithstanding the NP's claim to having moved away from apartheid and made a rhetorical commitment to democracy, the party has not abandoned the power-sharing concept. Its groups are no longer explicitly defined in racial terms, but are described as political minorities.

Hence, the NP wanted the constitution to be agreed to by consensus among the leaders of political parties without taking into account the level of support they might enjoy, as was the case in Codesa. It also proposed that, regardless of the level of support of parties, they should be entitled to govern through power-sharing executives in the interim and final constitution of South Africa. As all parties would share power, there was no role for an opposition.

When pressured to give way on a democratically elected constitution-making legislative assembly, the NP sought to place restrictions on the decision-making process. It wanted Codesa to agree to detailed constitutional principles which would bind the elected body, making it simply rubber stamp agreements previously reached at Codesa. It further tried to curb the capacity of the elected body to make decisions by requiring unreasonable majorities and subjecting it to a veto by a Senate, of regional representatives. Winning elections would not be important, as every party receiving more than 10% of the vote would be entitled to an equal number of seats in the Senate. Inevitably, it was christened the 'House of Losers'.

The overlap of substance and process resulted in different interpretations of the breakdown of Codesa. According to the Government and much of the white-owned press, the break was caused by quarrels over the powers of the constitution making body such as the majority necessary for approval of the constitution and the Senate veto. For the ANC, however, the break came following a reluctant acknowledgment that the NP was not really committed to democracy but wished instead to introduce a system that would ensure its continued presence in government irrespective of its electoral support.

It could be argued that the ANC should have recognized from the outset that De Klerk had never committed himself to what he calls 'simple majoritarianism'. Further, in the all-white referendum held while Codesa was in session, he campaigned on the principle of power-sharing. The ANC failed to come to terms with this until the very final moments of Codesa II, possibly in the belief that De Klerk's statements were directed to the right wing and to his white supporters.

It has also been argued that the NP shifted its stance in the midst of the negotiations. It entered into Codesa with the objective of trying to influence the final constitutional structure and preserve some role for whites. It saw its power base as the white electorate. In March, De Klerk called an all-white referendum to secure a mandate to continue negotiations. The substantial majority by which the negotiating process was endorsed was seen as an endorsement of the NP. Combined with media reports about the alleged lack of support of the ANC among the Coloured and Indian minorities, the disintegration of the ANC structures and disunity in its ranks, the NP began to think that it could win an election. It therefore began a two-track strategy: conceding the principle of an elected constitution-making body with the hope of emerging as the major party, and simultaneously safeguarding its interests by trying to curb that body's decision-making powers.

More recent developments suggest that the NP is trying to put together an alliance which can win elections. To gain support it is playing on ethnic factors, and advocating autonomous regions. This is a major shift. Historically, the NP has acted to reduce powers of the provinces and to centralize government functions since it came to power in 1948.

For its part, throughout the negotiations the ANC proceeded on the basis that the NP was persuadable. Concessions had been made on the assumption that there would be agreement on objectives and hence it was possible to compromise on the mechanisms to achieve those objectives. With the failure to agree, all compromises were withdrawn. Hence, none of the proposals that had been agreed in the working groups, including the mechanisms for the transition and the interim government were put forward for adoption by Codesa II.

This crucially important. For, in the absence of agreement on the constitution-making process, implementation of the transitional arrangement would have trapped the ANC in a power-sharing interim government of indefinite duration. It would thus share responsibility but have little power — any

changes in existing policies would require the approval of the
NP, and the constitutional arrangements could not be changed
easily or quickly. There is good reason to believe that this was
the conscious intention of the NP.[4]

Initially the Government failed to grasp the significance of
the cause of the breakdown at Codesa. It focussed on the
question of whether a 70% or 75% majority was needed for
adopting a constitution. As an inducement, it offered to
immediately introduce legislation to give effect to the
transitional arrangements, paying no heed to the ANC's position
that all agreements were conditional on the whole. There could
be no partial implementation.

At Codesa II it was agreed that the Management Committee
should continue to meet and try and resolve the outstanding
differences. However, within weeks the whole exercise was
closed down and the ANC suspended even its bilateral talks
with the government until a list of demands was met. Though
these were itemized under 14 specific headings, at stake was the
issue of agreement on the concept of democracy, and
government action to release the remaining political prisoners
and bring an end to violence.

During the negotiations, evidence of the involvement of the
Security Forces in the violence mounted, as did the casualties.
Every week brought new revelations. The names of those
involved reached up to the highest levels. But there was no
credible explanation for De Klerk's failure to act. The massacre
at Boipatong proved to be the last straw. A number of residents
testified that police vehicles brought the attackers from the
hostel, and many others reported the failure of the police to act to
prevent the massacre or to take prompt action to round up the
perpetrators.

Government complicity in the violence was manifested by:
the failure to act against those who were involved; the delay in
acting on recommendations of its own judicial Commissions,
such as the Goldstone Commission; the insistence that the police
investigate the charges against themselves; and the maintenance
of special forces and mercenary units made up of Angolans,
Mozambicans and Namibians.

The ANC had appealed for international monitors to be sent

to South Africa in April. Boipatong provided the stimulus for the international community to act — with the UN Secretary-General sending a special representative, followed by UN monitors as well as others from the Commonwealth, the EEC and OAU.

Having called off all constitutional discussions, the ANC and its allies embarked on a mass action programme. 'Struggle' and involvement of the masses were always referred to as necessary counterparts to negotiations. However, this had not always been the practice. As a result, there was considerable disquiet about the negotiations among ANC members and its wider constituency. There was concern that the ANC might be trapped into a process from which it could not extricate itself, or might make unacceptable compromises. Some of the problems referred to above appeared to have been perceived at the grass roots at a very early stage.

The decision to break off negotiations proved to be very popular and no doubt was a significant factor in the success of the mass action campaigns. The mass response cannot be explained away as a consequence of ANC 'intimidation'. How can 4 to 5 million people be intimidated into taking simultaneous action?

Acknowledging widespread support for the ANC's position, the government has conceded ground on a number of issues. It has accepted an international presence in South Africa, though it continues to try to limit the scope for independent action by the monitors or observers. Announcements have been made about a restructuring of the police force, of independent investigation teams etc. But those who have been implicated in the violence and the assassinations remain in office. One had to wait to see if De Klerk was ready to abandon the weapon of violence, or whether he still wished to use it to destabilize the country and to limit the capacity of a democratic government.

The NP also shifted on the constitution to some extent. The ANC's recent acceptance of the shift in regard to the constitution-making body, however, may be over-optimistic. Nothing the government has said or done suggests that it has abandoned its objective of power sharing. On the contrary, it continues to mobilize support on precisely that premise.

The Government is also faced with deadlines of its own. The economy is deteriorating. No investment can come in until there is some certainty and stability. The international community, including De Klerk's friends, can no longer be fobbed off with statements of good intent. As time passes the government nears the end of its term of office under the present constitution. The NP faces the prospect of having to call another all-white election, which it has publicly said it will not do. As a way of pressuring the ANC into entering an interim government before there is clarity about future arrangements, the government intends to introduce legislation for the transitional mechanisms.

The ANC, aware that the Government desperately needs to demonstrate that negotiations are in motion, must exact a high price for re-entering the process. It has called for action to back the Governments' stated intention. However, unless the issue of power-sharing versus democracy is resolved, there will be a further breakdown. Unless the ANC can prove that negotiations will deliver positive gains, the popular disenchantment with the process will grown, and a resumption of talks will prove more difficult.

The ANC leadership is committed to negotiations, but on the ground the message is quite clear: Not at any price.

NOTES

1   The trade unions have been accommodated through the establishment of a National Economic Forum. Women are still not adequately represented in the process.

Despite agreement on a Declaration of Intent that included a commitment to the establishment of a democratic, non-racial, *non-sexist* South Africa, parties did little to include women in their delegations. The ANC, which had taken very strong positions on both the need for the broadest participation in constitution making, and on the emancipation of women, did not include a single woman with full delegate status. After protests at the absence of women, Codesa agreed to establish a Gender Advisory Committee, with responsibility for examining the gender implications of the terms of reference of the working groups and the recommendations. Initially, this was considered to be a sop to the women. It was only after the Committee began its work, that there grew an appreciation of what was involved, e.g., the definition of political intimidation was expanded to include issues such as sexual harassment. The potential of public education about gender issues was restricted, however, when Codesa II failed to agree and the full report of the committee was not debated.

2   The ANC's National Working Committee now schedules its weekly meeting for Wednesday.

3   Each working group had lengthy terms of reference and a range of issues to address. Briefly: Working Group 1 dealt with matters pertaining to the creation of the climate for free political activity and the role of the international community; Working Group 4, with the re-incorporation of the TBVC territories; and Working Group 5, with time frames and necessary legislation.

4   In the draft document placed before Working Group 2 there was no reference to a Senate, while the words Parliament and National Assembly appeared to have been used interchangeably. Initially, the Government delegation tried to suggest that this variation arose from careless drafting. When, however, an amendment was tabled in an attempt to secure a uniform usage, the government revealed for the first time, that while the National Assemblyw was correctly assumed to be the constitution-making body, the use of the word Parliament encompassed a second house, namely the Senate with veto powers. Had this amendment not been moved, would the Government have revealed its intention at Codesa II, or would it only have owned up after the document had been accepted?

2

The Last Trek?
Afrikaners In Transition To
Democracy

Hermann Giliomee

Introduction

In the literature there is an accepted wisdom that there is no
precedent for an undefeated minority voluntarily negotiating
itself out of power. The perception has been that the Afrikaners
represent a particularly intransigent minority whose position of
privilege in the state, Calvinist beliefs and apartheid dogma rule
out the possibility of voluntary surrender or even of power-
sharing. The chapter *Broedertwis* discusses the underlying forces
which brought about a decisive shift away from Afrikaner
domination in the late 1960s. This chapter looks at the evolution
of National Party policy with regard to a negotiated settlement
from the mid-1980s to the beginning of 1992. It will show that
while the NP embarked on negotiating itself out of the position
of sole control over government it still wishes to retain on behalf
of whites and possibly also other minorities a substantial share of
power in a post-apartheid state and economy.

NP Constitutional Thinking, 1986-91

Although the NP in its Federal Congress of 1986 accepted the
principle of one nation and a common citizenship for all South

Africans (outside the 'independent' homelands) the leadership for more than three years played around with models still closely resembling apartheid thinking. The core idea was that the constitution would be based upon groups as building blocks. While the state no longer insisted on defining the groups, it had the duty to protect these groups after they had been formed on a 'voluntary' basis. It was not clear what the dynamics of such a process would be, but it was obvious that the government had racial or colour and not ethnic or religious groups in mind. To take the 'racial sting' out of the system, the government was prepared to allow an 'open' group for people who did not feel at home in the group to which they had been designated through race classification. The government's proposals further provided that each group had to be able to exercise self-determination for their 'own affairs' and a form of power-sharing and consensus for 'general affairs'. This system had to be structured in such a way that the domination of one group by another was impossible. If consensus could not be achieved, deadlocks had to be resolved through outside mechanisms created in the constitution.[1]

By 1989 the NP leadership realized that these proposals had little chance of acceptance by any black leader with a respectable constituency. Virtually unanimously, black leaders demanded that a future constitution had to be negotiated by all political parties and that this process could not start without the release of the political prisoners and the unbanning of the liberation organizations.

In the course of 1989 a fundamental reassessment started to occur in the ranks of the NP and Broederbond leadership. Particularly revealing of the ferment are two Broederbond documents which were circulated in mid-1989. The one document under the heading *Political Values for the Survival of the Afrikaner* takes as its starting point that the survival of the Afrikaner is coupled with the survival of the white man and that the basic conditions of such survival had to be formulated.

The document emphasized that maintaining the status quo or a further consolidation of power in white hands was no longer an option. The exclusion of effective black sharing in the political processes at the highest level had become 'a threat to the survival of the white man'. There could no longer be a white government and the head of government did not necessarily have to be white.

The document equally stresses the need to ensure that white control is not replaced by black control. Consequently, the system had to be restructured in such a way that one group could not dominate the other. Population groups had to retain 'self-determination' and the system had to be devised in such a way that it could not be changed without the approval of the majority of the whites.

Implicitly accepting that black support was essential, the document draws an important distinction between constitutional demands which were desirable and those which were essential for the meaningful future existence of the Afrikaner and the white man. It pointedly added : 'We must guard against endangering the future of the Afrikaner as such by over-accentuating preferences and desirable aspects'. While separate residential areas might be desirable they were not a condition for Afrikaner survival. And while ethnicity was 'a reality' in identifying groups it did not 'imply the absoluteness of group rights'.

The document reflects a growing awareness of the need to articulate universal interests and needs. It stated that a good government was one which governed in the interests of all its subjects. While language and cultural rights were prerequisites for Afrikaner survival they had to be propagated in such a way that they were supported across colour lines. Ultimately, the most important prerequisite for Afrikaner survival was the acceptability of a new constitution for the majority of the population. In drawing up a constitution it was necessary to include groups 'which through their non-participation or exclusion can cause a new constitution to fail'.

In a concluding passage the document highlighted the future political shift of the Afrikaners from ruling group to minority group:

> A test which we should set for the acceptability of a system must always be: what will be in our interests in the event that we end up in the opposition seat? Furthermore, we must also realize that humanly speaking there are simply no guarantees. The greatest risk that we are taking today is not taking any risks. The will to

survive as Afrikaner and our faith and energy will serve as our greatest guarantee.

Should the Afrikaner not succeed through its own creative power to bring about negotiated structures which are strong enough to accommodate the conflicting powers in the country, it is inevitable that structures will be forced upon him in which he has no share at all. This will make self-determination impossible.[2]

Another document which the Broederbond circulated at the same time takes up some of the same theories and introduces new aspects. The constitution, which has to be the product of an evolutionary constitutional process 'had to protect individual rights and accommodate groups based on free association'. It was important to the Afrikaner 'that he alone or together with others with whom he wishes to associate are entitled to protection as a group'. The component parts of the constitution would be groups which would choose their own representatives. These component parts had to be guaranteed autonomous decision making over their own affairs and representation in the general affairs legislature and the executive. The groups as component parts, however, had to realize that they could not survive in isolation and that there was a need to develop cross-cutting loyalties and symbols to develop a sense of national unity.

This document illuminates the uncharted waters in which the Afrikaner leadership now found itself. After outlining the constitutional options it posed some questions (without answering them). They included the following :

- Would an approach rigidly based on race be accepted by blacks and the international community?

- Was it desirable to divide whites into several ethnic groups and where did the coloured people fit in?

- Should the Afrikaners participate as an ethnic group or as part of the white racial group?[3]

In the light of these uncertainties, De Klerk during his first few months as leader in 1989 stressed the need for negotiations in which every party presented its viewpoint but strived to reach consensus. At the same time, however, he left no illusion about the NP's bottom line. He rejected 'typical majority domination which would turn South Africa into a Zimbabwe or Nigeria'. Whites were not prepared 'to be suppressed in the land where they became free'. Black majority rule 'or any form of majority rule will sound the deathknell to South Africa'. Domination of whatever kind had to be eliminated through a system of co-government which was based on groups but which removed the privileges and disabilities which were historically tied to group membership. Since the presidency was so closely associated with the domination of one particular group, De Klerk wanted to depoliticize it and reduce its powers as part of a process of establishing a system which desired to achieve 'a balance of power'.[4]

NP Strategies — the Transition and Beyond

The expressed constitutional policies of the NP offer only a partial glimpse of the way the De Klerk leadership hopes to secure Afrikaner survival during the transition and beyond. While safeguarding material interests is obviously a main objective, the NP elite does also have ideal goals and needs which go beyond the material existence of its constituency. These goals and needs cannot be reflected accurately in constitutional documents: they have to do with the desire of people to belong to a collectivity, to be considered justified in what they and their ancestors have done and to have a significant role in the future evolution of their country, not as individuals but as part of a group. The NP leadership wants, to use the words of Dickie-Clarke, construct 'a changed Afrikaner view of social reality which arises out of the interplay between the now different material conditions and interests on the one hand and the new "content" or means of satisfying ideal interests on the other'.[5] Survival has to be reinterpreted and this redefinition has to be given currency among the rank and file. Gerrit Viljoen was engaged in this task when he stated in March 1990:

> [We] who want change want it exactly because we realize that our survival depends upon orderly change. . . . We must see that

change is inevitable and can be made in such a way that does not
put our existence as a nation at stake. . . . [The] whole approach of
government is to shift the emphasis from race to the quality of
government and the broadening of democracy in spite of the
risks.[6]

There are basically three options before the De Klerk government
in the politics of the transition period. They are: an elite
settlement, white group veto, and power sharing with the
balance of power temporarily tilted in NP favour. Each will now
be considered in turn.

An Elite Settlement

The idea of an elite settlement was widely floated during the first
few months after the unbanning of the liberation organizations.
Both the NP and ANC leadership privately claim that the other
side approached it to conclude a deal. What would such a
settlement entail? It presumably meant the suspension of
parliament and a government of national unity headed by the
NP and ANC which would rule until the time was considered
ripe for carefully staged elections which the NP and ANC would
fight as an alliance.

This idea of an elite settlement started to fade from the end of
1990. It is easy to see why. Firstly, disunified elites elsewhere in
the world are motivated to seek settlements because, as a recent
study put it, 'no single faction has been a clear winner and all
factions have more nearly been losers'.[7] Although it suffered
reverses in the late 1980s, such as having to withdraw its bases
from Angola and losing its Soviet sponsorship, the ANC did not
consider itself to be losing after its unbanning. It was, on the
contrary, coming home and starting a new round of the struggle.

Neither did the NP leadership consider itself as going down.
Internal resistance and sanctions exerted constant pressure but
they failed to achieve the fundamental requirement for a
substantial shift in power: a crack in the regime. No significant
section within the ruling bloc went outside for support.[8] In
making his decision in late 1989 to unban the liberation
organizations, De Klerk did not act at the behest of business or
religious elites but on the advice of his security advisors, who felt

that the ANC had been sufficiently weakened to be a containable force. Furthermore, there was no immediate economic crisis confronting De Klerk, after some dark days in mid-1989 when the foreign reserves ran very low.

A second reason why an elite settlement did not come about in South Africa is the relative lack of autonomy which the NP and ANC elites have from their followers. In Latin America, successful transitions from authoritarian rule occurred in countries where the elites enjoyed considerable autonomy from mass followings and pressures.[9]

The degree of autonomy which the ANC leadership enjoyed while still in exile or in prison decreased considerably as the movement established itself in the midst of the people. From the grassroots Mandela came under severe fire for contemplating talks with Buthelezi, suspending the armed struggle, and negotiating with the regime. De Klerk, on the other hand, could only count on a limited brief from his followers: he could negotiate the sharing but not the transfer of power. The most fundamental difference between the transition in Latin America and South Africa is that the government in South Africa is elected by a constituency which has a long tradition of democratic (white) politics and which has formidable resources to impose its will upon the process both during and after the transition. De Klerk has always known that he would need the consent of his people and that this could only be obtained through persuasion. Gerrit Viljoen summarizes the main lessons the leadership of the NP and ANC have learnt in this regard as follows :

> The ANC ran into two obvious cases of difficulties: one, when they suspended armed action without the necessary pre-consultations; and the other one, at the beginning of last year, was when they formally accepted the concept of a multi-party congress, again, apparently without making sure their support base was fully with them.

> We have experienced the same with regard to our support base, which we've been losing to a certain extent to the extreme right wing: and we realize that we have been remiss in the last couple of months in not giving enough attention to communication and keeping people informed as to what is going in, why it is necessary, and so on.[10]

Compared to Latin America the transition in South Africa has, at this stage at least, a much more open and democratic nature. In a recent survey of the Latin American literature, Peter Smith pointed to the undemocratic features in virtually all the Latin American transitions: during the process the military elites continued to wield enormous influence, the Left emasculated, with the result that electoral contests were tepid, fail-safe affairs; and there was tacit censorship with some areas such as the redistribution of income simply not open to public debate.[11]

Consider the stark contrast with South Africa. Given the overlapping membership of the South African Communist Party (SACP) and the ANC, De Klerk never really had the option of banning the Left and restricting the public debate. Neither could he impose censorship or other security measures in view of the fact that the lifting of American sanctions would have been blocked by a suppression of civil liberties.

Furthermore, successful elite settlements are usually concluded either within a year at the utmost or not at all. In the course of 1991 it became clear to government that the ANC would continue to resort to mass mobilization, which it regards as inimical to an elite settlement; Mandela, on the other hand, was alienated by the revelations of government funding of Inkatha and his suspicion of the involvement by a 'third force' in the township violence.

A White Group Veto

When the government unbanned the liberation organizations on 2 February 1990, its own constitutional thinking was remarkably vague. In the same week Viljoen remarked that in ten years the NP would not likely be in control of government. He added that by then one would not have a single party in the government but a coalition. He added that his imagination 'would have to be very heavily taxed' to see a NP-ANC coalition.[12] In May 1990 Viljoen declared that the government would not seek to thwart the will of the majority; however, it wanted minority protection because majority rule in itself did not guarantee democracy.[13]

The idea of group or minority protection was at first essentially cast in terms of a white veto which in turn presupposed the classification of a white group. In the course of the next months, the NP steadily retreated from this concept. It first dropped the idea of racial classification. Then it drew back from the idea of group or minority rights as a permanent principle. It now argued that accommodating minorities was instrumental to building a new inclusive South African nation in which everyone felt secure.[14] By September 1990 Viljoen in his words had acquired a 'new vision'. In terms of this the NP had abandoned the idea of groups as such being represented and making claims; instead minority groups had to articulate their values and interests through a party or alliance representing minorities. It was accepted that the more support such an alliance could demonstrate at the polls the more effective it would be.[15]

The De Klerk leadership was pushed from different quarters in this direction. As far as its own constituency was concerned the evidence was unambiguous that it did not have any confidence in minority protection. In a poll conducted in April 1990, 81 percent of the NP (and 89 percent of Afrikaners) indicated that they 'not at all trusted'[16] the ANC promise not to allow black domination over whites. Since the NP leadership was not making decisions on behalf of itself it had to find a solution which it could sell to its constituency.

The ANC also rejected minority or group rights. Initially, a measure of ambiguity existed. In Mandela's Memorandum from Prison he stressed the idea of a compromise between two political issues: the demand for majority rule and the insistence of whites on 'structural guarantees that majority rule will not mean domination of the white minority by blacks'.[17] Since his release from prison Mandela has conveyed two different messages. On the one hand he rejected group or minority rights on the grounds that 'any form of racialism is a formula for disaster' and because it implied that 'white South Africans do not yet trust us'.[18] In Mandela's view the anxiety of whites would abate once they were aware their individual rights would be protected by a bill of rights.[19] While the ANC would not protect white privileges it would put 'civil and political rights — as well as some cultural and economic rights — beyond the reach of the temporary majority'. They would be guaranteed as core or fundamental human rights.[20] Apart from Mandela, a leading ANC intellectual, Pallo Jordan, also attacked minority rights. In his view they would thwart nation-building by providing a cloak for the continued propagation of racism and the entrenchment of white wealth and privilege.[21]

On the other hand, Mandela has also suggested ways of accommodating minorities which go beyond upholding formal individual rights. In a speech, significantly delivered at the University of Stellenbosch, Mandela elaborated on the structural guarantees he had in mind.

> Of course, the principle recognized in all democratic countries is that the political party which gets the most votes forms the government and there is no reason why we should not observe that principle here. But all principles, democratic or otherwise, must be applied in accordance with our background: it may not be enough to work purely on one-person one vote, because every national group would like to see that the people of their flesh and blood are in government.[22]

In an interview with Stanley Uys, Mandela returned to this theme:

> [We] have to make sure. . . that the ordinary man . . . must look to our structures and see that as a coloured man I am represented, I have got Alan Boesak there whom I trust. And an Indian must also be able to say: 'There is Kathadra — I am represented. And the whites must say: there is Gerrit Viljoen — I have got representation . . . ' It may well be that we have to consider very carefully how the principle of one-person, one-vote should be applied in the light of our situation especially in the first few years of democratic government . . . It is a situation also of doing something to show that the system has got an in-built mechanism which makes it impossible for one group to suppress the other.[23]

But also this issue is surrounded by ambiguity. At times the ANC leadership seems to favour a meritocratic or a co-optive approach. Mandela has mentioned as a future cabinet minister someone like van Zyl Slabbert who has no significant Afrikaner support base.[24] At the same time, the ANC leadership in organizing its own structures, has favoured a form of proportional allocation of positions according to the size of the population group. In addressing the ANC Western Cape Congress Mandela urged delegates to elect an executive which reflected the composition of the population of which coloured people formed 54 percent, blacks 25 percent and whites 21 percent.[25] At the same time, however, Mandela has insisted that South Africa must show the world a new form of democracy in which all forms of factionalism and regionalism have been eliminated.[26]

Some commentators have argued that it is in the best interests of whites to accept the ANC's non-racialist approach and to eschew any form of minority guarantees or over-representation. Allister Sparks has observed that nothing would be more calculated to build anti-white feelings and that the best security of whites 'lies in the satisfaction of black aspirations and their own economic indispensability in achieving that'.[27] Lawrence Schlemmer responded that this view had 'a certain smell of the now thankfully dying tradition in Africa that one had to suppress or incorporate opposition in the search for "nation-building" and unity'.[28] This is not the place to enter into this debate, except to note that the NP leadership over the short to medium term is committed to rejecting a political order in which minorities would have to make themselves politically as invisible as possible.

Power Sharing

The power sharing plan which the NP leadership has adopted to present to its constituency contains three strategic elements. First, it promises continuity. The leadership told its followers that it was in the process of initiating far-reaching changes without, however, allowing constitutional continuity to be jeopardized. 'In our thinking', Viljoen declared in March 1990, 'a complete cut, a complete break in history would be unacceptable'.[29] Initially, senior cabinet ministers were reluctant to decry apartheid except as a policy which did not work.[30] Lately, De Klerk has called it an 'inhumane policy',[31] but added that change would take place without endangering the 'values and achievements of communities and individuals of the past and our dreams and future plans'.[32] As a symbol of continuity the NP leadership chose to maintain not the official anthem or flag, but Afrikaans as an official language which it presents as a non-negotiable issue. This underlines Horowitz's comment about language as a potent symbolic issue linking 'political claims to ownership with psychological demands for the affirmation of group worth'.[33]

Second, it has adamantly refused to consider 'simple' majority rule. This is partly justified on survival grounds — it would in the leadership's perception be 'the end' of Afrikaner history[34] — and partly for technocratic reasons: there was no possibility of the NP handing over the reins of power 'to one or other potentate or group with no experience of governing a sophisticated country'.[35]

To achieve its stated objective of securing a balance between the power of the numerical majority and the protection of minorities the NP proposes a whole range of measures:

- Minorities must be over-represented in the presidential college, cabinet and the upper house of parliament: no effective decision could be taken without their concurrence.

- The constitution (and not parliament) would be sovereign and an independent judiciary would be able to 'test' parliament's legislation and protect individual rights as enshrined in a bill of rights.

- Parliament should be able to control the cabinet more effectively.

- Powers should be devolved to the regions as far as possible.

- In metropolitan areas room should be allowed for local communities identified on non-racial grounds to deal on their own with community matters including aspects of culture and welfare.

- A double vote for property owners in municipal elections.

- Maintenance of professional standards in the civil service.

- An army which would be loyal to the constitution rather than the government of the day.

Third, the NP from the end of 1990 started to project itself as a winning party which would remain part of the power structure for a long time. In October 1990 Viljoen declared at the Cape NP congress for the first time that in terms of his 'new vision' a multi-racial alliance based on moderate values could beat the ANC in an election.[36] At the same congress NP cabinet ministers expressed the view that the abolition of statutory discrimination would remove the main cause of the hate and the bitterness of the past and provide the basis for a 'new broad South Africanhood and common loyalty'.[37]

In the course of the next year the NP's confidence grew. De Klerk spoke of the NP's having 'a hand on the tiller' of government for 'a very long time' to come.[38] In words reminiscent of Dirk Mudge in South West Africa, De Klerk declared that the white minority was free 'to join and form majorities based on common values and interests. We are once again capable of joining the global majority which advocates the same basic economic and constitutional principles.'[39] As its party slogan the NP has chosen 'Build a nation', which it propagates with an emphasis on continuity. At an annual general meeting of the Afrikaans publishing house Nasionale Pers, Viljoen spelled it out in the following terms:

> Like the National Party, Nasionale Pers through the years has given broader expression to the concept of nationalism. Initially it was concerned with nationalism in which the Afrikaner people's interests were paramount, in the course of time it became a broader nationalism which embraced both language groups of the white nation. Since the 1980s the concept of nationhood has broadened to include coloured people and Asians and today we are grappling with the difficult task to build an all-embracing and inclusive sense of nationhood which in its diversity includes the black peoples (volke) and communities as fully-fledged citizens of the new South Africa.[40]

However, the NP was only too aware of the general scepticism outside party ranks about its ability to defeat the ANC in an election. Consequently, it has continued to hold open the possibility of forming a ruling alliance with the ANC, provided it sheds its links with the SACP. In November 1990 Viljoen declared that no one could ever say categorically that he would never co-operate or consider an alliance with another party. 'If a party adjusts its policies and/or principles in such a way that it becomes acceptable to one, it creates a new situation in which one has to reconsider one's options.'[41]

Against this background the NP has so far succeeded in taking a strong majority of whites along in its goal of negotiating a power-sharing constitution. The Conservative Party received a resounding thrashing in the referendum of March 1992 because it held up no credible alternative for establishing stability in the country. Another reason was that the NP had managed to present the power-sharing option as a fail-safe affair: even if it went wrong the government and the state at large had the power to redirect the process. Some cabinet ministers even turn the CP's accusations of selling-out around, and accuse the rightwing of being *bangbroeke* (scaredy pants).[42]

An Evaluation of the Process

There are three basic problems with the constitutional process in South Africa. Firstly, the more the NP manages to assuage white fears the less the prospect of the ANC willingly accepting a power-sharing constitution. This raises the spectre of a permanent paralysis in a future government. Democratic theorists have argued that if the outcome of the political game is not the periodic awarding of effective authority to one group, unstable and irresponsible government rather than democracy will result. Leaders of the poorer section of the population will be unwilling to demand sacrifices from their followers because they are not really in the position to deliver substantial material rewards.

While the ANC is prepared not to insist on a classic majoritarian form of government, it demands effective power for the majority. In its view the urgent task of transforming society makes it imperative that the majority's capacity for action cannot be constrained beyond certain limits.[43] The NP's plans are obviously designed for a transitional period of ten years in which South Africa can develop the basic requirements for a genuine democracy of which the most important is the existence of at least two parties which can alternate as the ruling party. The ANC might be prepared to buy a transitional constitution if it can be clearly marketed as such and does not extend beyond, say five years. However, this is anathema to the NP which fears that after the expiration of the period all checks on the majority would be swept away.

Second, there is the problem of resolving the ancient question of *cui bono*? Terry Karl has observed that the issue of 'who benefits?' from democracy has been singularly problematic in Latin America where the pattern of dependent capitalist development has been especially ruthless in its historic patterns of exploitation.[44] No easy solution for the problems of widespread poverty is possible: indeed what often has happened after a pact between competing parties is a significant trade-off between a form of democracy (usually consociationalism) on the one hand, and equity on the other. The same problems and prospects exist in South Africa. What aggravates matters here is that the government has traditionally accorded a misplaced emphasis on the needs of the affluent, who enjoy political power, rather than the poor. Furthermore, the poor in South Africa are particularly badly off. A recent study notes: 'if recorded income were distributed as in the US (not a country with a highly egalitarian distribution) the income of the poorest 15 million people in South Africa (40 percent of the population) would be about 70 percent higher than it is'.[45] A new government which redistributes only marginally will face continuous resistance; one which redistributes liberally will run into the problem of a flight of capital and skills that could endanger the prospects for stability and democracy.

Finally, unresolved political and economic problems could trigger a debilitating fight over the national culture and educational system. There have been calls from the ANC's cultural desk for an assault on all aspects of 'apartheid culture'. While apartheid culture has never been defined such calls raise the possibility of conflict over matters such as literature and language. It may embroil Afrikaans, which presently enjoys the status of a Most Favoured Language.[46] While he personally took the trouble of learning Afrikaans in jail, Nelson Mandela has warned that a great mistake would be made if special status and protection is demanded for Afrikaans.[47] The teaching of history in schools is another area where conflict can erupt. There has been a demand from some Afrikaner educationalists that sixty-odd percent of the new syllabus should be considered as a nation-building core but that the rest should be devoted to own-group education for those communities who wish to exercise that option. This has been attacked on the grounds that this would result in a policy of special rights and privileges for the Afrikaners.[48]

To the extent that the political and economic problems remain unresolved, core aspects of Afrikaner identity such as language and history could increasingly become vulnerable.

Conclusion

The transition of the South African state towards an inclusive democracy did not follow on the collapse of the state or the economy. The NP leadership is in the process of negotiating the most blatant privileges of whites away but it insists that some identity issues could not be compromised. Like other ethnic groups in divided societies Afrikaners value power not for purely instrumental reasons but as an end in itself and as confirmation of ethnic status. The demand of the NP leadership is for some form of power-sharing for Afrikaners and other minorities which would assure them of not being dominated by non-members of the group. Whether this demand is compatible with the ANC's insistence on majority rule, only the future can tell.

Notes

1   N.J.J. Oliver, 'Constitutional Policy of Mr F.W. De Klerk', unpublished paper prepared for the Democratic Party. This and other study documents by Prof Olivier provide valuable insights

into NP thinking during the second half of the 1980s.

2   'Political Values for the Survival of the Afrikaner', unpublished
     document of the Afrikaner Broederbond, July 1989.

3   *Die Volksblad*, 20 June 1989, *Dokument van Broederbond*.

4   Transcript of TV interview, 14 May 1989. See also speech in
     House of Assembly Debates, 23 May 1989.

5   'Ideological Misconceptions of Afrikaner values', *South Africa
     International*, July 1981, p.291.

6   *Sunday Star*, 17 March 1990.

7   Michael G. Burton and John Higley, 'Elite Settlements', *American
     Sociological Review*, 1987, vol.52, p.298.

8   Adam Przeworski, 'Some Problems in the Study of Transition to
     Democracy' in Guillermo O'Donnell et al, eds., *Transitions from
     Authoritarian Rule: Comparative Perspectives* (Baltimore: John
     Hopkins, 1986), p.56.

9   Burton and Higley, *Elite Settlements*, p.301.

10   *Financial Mail*, 27 March 1992, Special Report on Codesa, p.72.

11   Peter Smith, 'Crisis and Democracy in Latin America', *World
     Politics*, 42, July 1991, p.610.

12   *Cape Times*, 7 February 1990.

13   *Argus*, 11 May 1990.

14   *Argus*, 10 May 1990.

15   *Argus*, 12 October 1990.

16   N.J. Rhoodie, 'Survey-based indicators of black and white
     perceptions of socio-political change in South Africa', in D. J. van
     Vuuren, et al., eds., *South Africa in the Nineties* (Pretoria: HSRC
     Publishers, 1991), p.537.

17   *South*, 25 January 1990.

18   *Argus*, 7 May 1990.

19   *Cape Times*, 9 February 1990.

20   *Cape Times*, 13 May 1991.

21   I discuss this in greater detail in 'Building a new nation:
     alternative approaches' in Fanie Cloete, ed., *Policy Options for
     South Africa* (Pretoria: HSRC Publishers), 1991, pp.65-86.

22   *Argus*, 18 May 1991.

23   *Argus*, 18 July 1991.

24   See also the comment of Walter Sisulu who tried to assuage

Afrikaner fears by pointing to the Afrikaners the ANC respected. He mentioned Beyers Naude and Bram Fischer and added: 'We judge a man on his ability.' *Die Burger*, 19 October 1989.

25   *Rapport*, 29 September 1991.

26   *The Argus*, 26 February 1990.

27   *The Star*, 4 September 1991.

28   Lawrence Schlemmer, "The National Party Constitutional proposals", *SA International*, 22 (October 1991), p.68.

29   *Sunday Star*, 17 March 1990.

30   *Sunday Star*, 17 March 1990.

31   *Die Burger*, 12 November 1991

32   *Die Burger*, 22 November 1991

33   Horowitz, *Ethnic Groups in Conflict*, p.222.

34   *Sunday Star*, 17 March 1990.

35   *Argus*, 25 May 1991.

36   *Argus*, 12 October 1990.

37   *Die Burger*, 9 October 1990.

38   *Cape Times*, 8 May 1991.

39   *Die Burger*, 22 November 1991.

40   *Die Burger*, 27 July 1990.

41   *Argus*, 15 November 1991.

42   Hernus Kriel in *Cape Times*, 15 February 1991.

43   Stanley Uys, 'Can a democratic constitution take root in South Africa?', *South Africa International*, 22 (1991), p.85.

44   Terry Lynn Karl, 'Dilemmas of Democratization in South Africa', *Comparative Politics*, 23 (1990), p.13.

45   Economic Policy Study Group, *Is South Africa a Rich Country?* (Johannesburg, 1991) p.5.

46   The term is that of Neville Alexander.

47   Nelson Mandela and Hein Willemse, 'Fitting in Afrikaans, *New Era*, (Spring 1991), p.16.

48   Peter Kallaway, 'Education and Nation-building in South Africa in the 1990s', paper presented to the UCT African Studies Seminar, 28 May 1991.

3

The State, Politics and Violence 1989-91

Joan Wardrop

Introduction[1]

The period since State President FW De Klerk came to power in September 1989 can be divided into a number of phases defined by the policy strategies of the National Party government which De Klerk leads.

1. an early phase in which De Klerk moved to consolidate power within the National Party and made some minor concessions to the Mass Democratic Movement;

2. the period from 2 February 1990 (when De Klerk made his 'landmark' speech opening the Parliament) until the end of July 1990;

3. July 1990 to July 1991, during which a number of apartheid laws were repealed and the townships of the Rand in particular were subjected to extreme levels of violence;

4. July 1991 to November 1991, the post-Inkathagate period, during which the process of negotiation between the government and liberation movements slowed, and the violence became more random and arbitrary; and

5. The period of the Codesa talks, accompanied by violence and destabilization of the Rand townships and Natal.

This chapter uses current media reports to follow developments in these phases, the primary aim being to assess the underlying thrust of the De Klerk reform process. In the late 1980s, the liberation movements in South Africa shared an expectation that the apartheid system would eventually crumble and, in the process, demolish white control of the economic, social and political life of the country. The developments surveyed in this analytical chronicle indicate that this may be a flawed expectation. It is possible to conclude that, throughout the period surveyed, the National Party (NP) government was pursuing a carefully-calculated strategy to retain power, not only in the short term but also in the 'new South Africa' after the constitutional negotiations have been concluded and a universal franchise has been achieved.

The Background to De Klerk's Ascension

The last years of the PW Botha presidency saw considerable unrest domestically and the imposition of wide-ranging sanctions through the United States' Comprehensive Anti-Apartheid Act (CAAA), the Commonwealth and the European Economic Community. While the unrest in the townships (along with South Africa's foreign adventures in Namibia, Angola and Mozambique) ensured that the security forces were kept fully occupied, the sanctions affected imports and exports, foreign debt renegotiation and trade credits.

The unrest was handled by the Security Forces under the aegis of the State of Emergency legislation (imposed 1985-86) and the Internal Security Act (1982) which proved very effective in confining the domestic disturbances to the townships. There was a substantial fiscal cost but this was absorbed by a white population which had been the subject of extensive campaigns by the government over a long period of time to convince it of the threat to national security posed by township activists. In real political terms, the civil unrest posed more of a difficulty internationally through the gradual isolation of white South

Africa economically and culturally. To a certain extent it proved possible to limit the international community's knowledge and awareness of what was occurring within the townships through the increasingly severe media restrictions imposed under the Emergency legislation but by the late 1980s the weight of the evidence already gathered by the international media and by diplomatic representatives was so substantial that increased levels of sanctions and boycotts were imminent. On the domestic front the problem could be contained, but internationally the problems for South Africa continued to multiply.

Sanctions in particular were beginning to cause substantial problems. Import substitution was practiced (through such entities as SASOL and its oil substitutes), middlemen were used to bust sanctions, and a positive policy of encouraging consumers to choose not to participate in import consumerism was adopted. Indeed, in some ways, sanctions were psychologically helpful to government policy makers who could call on the historical images of the siege and the laager, and who could reinforce these images with a sense of the justice of white South Africa's position and the dangers that faced the country from the marxist threat both internally and externally, as well as the threat posed by the misguided policies of western 'liberal' governments.

Pretoria could just cope with domestic unemployment (which was then occurring principally in the black community and therefore was not a major factor politically) and also with disinvestment by foreign companies (which tended to sell out to South African-based companies or simply to move to neighbouring countries such as Swaziland). The greatest problem was the clampdown on revolving credit facilities for international trade and the foreign debt balances which by 1988-89 were reaching dangerously high levels.[2] The international financial community was reacting to unsatisfactory investment conditions in South Africa, caused both by the sanctions imposed from outside and by the domestic unrest. In effect these were combining to make the South African economy a difficult investment proposition. Business confidence domestically was falling, the formal-sector was stagnant and the inflation rate was rising.

After PW Botha fell ill in early 1989, he resigned the leadership of the National Party (NP), although he retained the State Presidency, and in the subsequent election for the leadership the NP rejected the Foreign Minister Pik Botha as too liberal and another contender, Chris Heunis, as too close to the State President. The final ballot was fought out between two conservatives, FW De Klerk and Minister of Finance, Barend du Plessis. Although FW De Klerk had not been part of the securocrat establishment, he had a considerable reputation as a hard-line NP conservative through his role as NP leader in the Transvaal and was noted for his robust use of the cultural icons of the Afrikaners in his speeches. In 1982, for example, he had declaimed that:

> Although there are no direct links between the South African situation of today and the battle of Blood River in 1883, the country must adopt the discipline, faith and decisiveness of the Voortrekkers in Natal. We have three choices. We can abdicate, sit and wait, or we can do something. Our moment of truth has come. We must act, plan diligently and work together to take democratic decisions.[3]

De Klerk Consolidates Power

Bringing such sentiments to higher office, De Klerk took over as State President after the general election of September 1989 and in his first few weeks in office gave the appearance of no more than a minor re-evaluation of PW Botha's policies. Some marches by the Mass Democratic Movement were permitted, for example, but there was no substantial indication that the government might be rethinking its position until October when the Commonwealth Heads of Government Meeting (CHOGM) convened in Kuala Lumpur. One of the major agenda items for CHOGM was the ratchetting-up of sanctions as part of a planned series of phases designed to increase pressure on South Africa. In a move which rather stole the thunder of CHOGM, Pretoria announced that renegotiation of part of the international debt had been achieved and that a number of political prisoners including Walter Sisulu were to be immediately released.[4]

This action set a pattern for the following period in which

gains in the international arena were achieved by Pretoria while concessions were made towards 'normalization' domestically. In one sense this first concession was a holding action, allowing some sense of optimism that some measure of reform might be achieved but sending a signal also that change would not come quickly. It could also be read, however, as the first step in a carefully-calculated scenario designed to eliminate sanctions, defuse the internal unrest, and re-create the South African polity while yet preserving a manageable level of political power for the Afrikaner. An additional factor, as Hermann Giliomee argues in the previous chapter, was that 'a window of opportunity' had been revealed to the South African leadership by the very rapid changes in the USSR and Eastern Europe in the last half of 1989 which presented opportunities for new ways of thinking about the structural problems South Africa was facing.

Since the first release of prisoners the government has pursued a course of action which sends very mixed messages domestically but fairly consistent messages internationally. In fulfilling the specific conditions of the CAAA in particular, significant legislative reform has been undertaken.[5] Political prisoners have been released and exiles allowed home, while on the other hand government ministers and spokesmen have resisted demands to begin to rectify the deficits for the majority population in areas of social spending such as education, power supply and health services.

February 1990 and its Aftermath

The political changes substantially began on 2 February 1990 when, in a 'landmark' speech opening the Parliament, De Klerk announced the unbanning of the African National Congress (ANC) along with a number of other liberation organizations, lifted a number of the emergency restrictions such as those on media reporting of emergency incidents, and decreed 'a new dispensation' which would include a democratic constitution based on a universal franchise.[6] Eleven days later, Nelson Mandela was released from 27 years of imprisonment.

This was the starting point for the De Klerk government's overt strategy of engaging the ANC and other organizations in discussion about the shape of the 'new South Africa' and the transitional mechanisms through the so-called 'talks about talks' which during 1990 produced two major agreements, the Groote Schuur Minute (May), and the Pretoria Minute (August). Further, the government began to move towards the dismantling of the apartheid legislation, with the first step being the repeal in June 1990 of the Separate Amenities Act which for 37 years had provided the legislative underpinning for the separate and unequal provision of public amenities according to racial group.

In response to what seemed to be a willingness on the part of the NP government to move towards reform, the ANC after a lengthy internal debate announced the suspension of the armed struggle on 7 August 1990. Already however there had been ominous signs that the endemic violence of Natal/KwaZulu was about to erupt in the townships and squatter camps of the Reef when, in an incident on 22 July, 27 people were killed at Sebokeng in a clash between supporters of the Inkatha Freedom Party (IFP) and the ANC. The continuing violence in Natal/KwaZulu and the Transvaal has been the underlying counterpoint of the period since February 1990 and has severely strained relations between the ANC and the government because of the numerous allegations of involvement of members of the security forces in instigating violent incidents.

On 27 June 1991, in partial fulfilment of his pledge to remove the legislative underpinning of apartheid, the State President signed eight Acts of Parliament, repealing many of the 'pillars of apartheid' including the Group Areas Act (1966), the Land Acts of 1913 and 1936 and the Population Registration Act (1950).[7] At least 22 Acts of Parliament and literally hundreds of by-laws and provincial ordinances which were part of the apartheid legislation remain on the statute books, however, including the Electoral Act (1979) which created separate franchises for whites, Coloureds and Indians, but no franchise at all for blacks; the General Pensions Act (1979) which provides for differential allocation of pensions according to racial group; and the Defence Act (1957) which provides for white-only compulsory military service.[8]

In international terms, this partial repeal of the 'pillars of apartheid' had the effect desired by the National Party since, despite the reservations expressed by Nelson Mandela about the speed at which the international community was moving to remove sanctions, the US almost immediately lifted the sanctions it had applied through the CAAA.[9] The beneficial effect of the release of prisoners, the return of exiles and the repeal of legislation, was however somewhat mitigated by the revelations during July 1991 of government funding of the Inkatha Freedom Party and its activities (and also of covert funding of some parties during the Namibian elections and allegations made about the involvement of members of the security forces in the ongoing township violence).[10] Although an All-Party Conference was finally convened in November 1991, much of 1991 was marked by open suspicion on the part of the liberation movements about the government's intentions. The rate of prisoner releases and the return of exiles were slow and, despite the Patriotic Front and the National Peace Accord, there was no relief from the 'cycle of violence' which De Klerk had described on 2 February 1990.

In the meantime, the white South African polity altered in very significant ways. The more conservative elements of the traditional National Party constituency moved towards support for the Conservative Party (CP) and some moved even further right to the Afrikaner Weerstandsbeweging (Afrikaner Resistance Movement) and the other right-wing parties which support the notion of a Boer homeland. Members of these non-parliamentary political organizations feel betrayed by the National Party. In the words of CP member Dr W J Snyman, those who remained members of the National Party after 2 February 1990, 'already stand apart from the nationalism of the Afrikaner people. In short, these are the so-called Afrikaners who no longer regard themselves as bound by the Covenant of 1838.'[11]

On 30 Aug 1990 it was announced, in a major turnaround, that the NP would become non-racial. Early in June 1991, *The Saturday Star* reported on plans by the NP to construct an 'alliance of moderates' or 'Christian Democratic Alliance' to defeat the ANC when elections finally take place.[12] While this seemed at the time to be improbable, within a few days, the Minister of Constitutional Development Gerrit Viljoen was saying that the NP was no longer interested in functioning, 'on the basis of representing a minority, however defined. . . . We accept the need for the formation of a broad political movement, including alliances with other parties, which works on the assumption that it can be a majority movement. This is not wild, naive optimism.'[13]

Indeed it was not, since a Gallup Poll conducted in June 1991 indicated that the NP could expect 6% of Africans to definitely vote for it in an election and a further 40% were possible NP voters. Amongst white voters, 42% were 'definite' NP voters with a further 31% being potential supporters. Interestingly, 4% of whites would vote for Inkatha with 45% perhaps voting for it or 'feeling quite good about' it.[14] Concrete signs that major changes in the NP's own perceptions of its catchment area were under way had already occurred in May 1991 when twenty five former Labour Party members and two members of the President's Council became the first Coloured members of the National Party and were followed by more of their numbers over the next month.[15]

This was a clear threat to ANC ambitions to form the first 'non-racial' government in the new South Africa and was the basis for a number of statements by senior ANC personnel. In July, at the ANC conference in Durban, Nelson Mandela announced that ANC membership had grown to 700,000 but that relatively few White, Coloured or Indian members had been recruited and that the 'ANC had to ask itself frankly why' this was the case. 'In this context we should not be afraid to confront the real issue that these national minorities might have fears about the future.'[16] In his opening speech to the ANC's Western Cape conference in October 1991, Mr. Mandela further warned that 'The NP is challenging us in our own constituency, and it is making an impact. Unless we get involved in house to house campaigning, we are working on an illusion'.[17]

Despite the ANC's comparatively low membership figures, and its lack of success with the Coloured and Indian groups, however, a Gallup poll in June 1991 indicated that 68% of Africans definitely would vote for the ANC if there were an election and a further 12% would perhaps vote for it. Inkatha was completely rejected on principle by 62% of urban Africans and only 3% said they would definitely or perhaps vote for it although 4% of whites would definitely vote for it, with more than 30% saying they felt 'quite good' about it and 15% perhaps voting for it. The Pan Africanist Congress (PAC) received 7% of African definite support with a total potential vote of 48%.[18]

The white polity further changed as a result of the 17 March referendum called by De Klerk in the aftermath of a major defeat of the National Party by the Conservative Party in the Potchefstroom by-election in February 1992. The referendum, based on the limited franchise permitted under the 1984 Constitution, asked white South Africans to vote on whether or not the De Klerk reform process should continue. In a result which clearly surprised even the NP strategists, an overall majority of 67% was achieved. While this gave De Klerk a genuine mandate to continue the process of change, it had the side effect of further marginalizing the Democratic Party, many of whose voters now were clearly looking to the National Party. As the NP became more centrist, a number of the so-called 'left-wing' MPs of the Democratic Party split with the party to sit as Independents representing the ANC in the Parliament.

Codesa Talks Begin

Despite the diversions of the whites-only politics, the establishment of the Convention for a Democratic South Africa (Codesa) which first met in plenary session in December 1991 provided some measure of participation in the political process for both the ANC and many smaller groupings which previously had been totally excluded from the political process. Codesa operated through five working groups charged with negotiating specific issues such as the question of the reincorporation of the so-called 'independent homelands'.

The post-referendum political scene was dominated by the attempts being made by both the ANC and the NP to expand the limits of their traditional constituencies, by the continuation of the Codesa talks, and by the National Party's continued attempts to involve the ANC in a form of 'power-sharing'. This had an obvious downside for the ANC since it would become associated with the legacies of apartheid policies such as the education, employment and health crises, and the violence in the townships, while having little real power under such a system to rectify any of these major problems.

The Violence

De Klerk's 2 February 1990 speech acknowledged that South Africa was caught in 'a cycle of violence'.[19] In its most acute, and noticeable, form, this was manifested in Natal/KwaZulu beginning in 1985-86.[20] Similar patterns of violence appeared in the townships of the Rand in 1990. This might be said to have begun with the deaths of 27 people in a clash between ANC and Inkatha supporters in Sebokeng on 22 July but it was not till the second week of August that the violence became a nightly reality for township residents. The full meaning of the deaths at Sebokeng had not at that early stage become apparent. Indeed, it was during the first week of August, in a gesture of reconciliation, that the ANC decided to suspend the armed struggle. By 16 August, however, the death toll in the Reef townships, particularly Katlehong, Vosloorus, Thokoza and Soweto, had reached 159, thousands of people had fled their homes looking for sanctuary and the armed attacks on trains carrying commuters which still continue had begun. The following weekend saw 123 people die within 48 hours and a total death toll for the week of more than 400 with the circle of violence spreading out to neighbouring townships such kwaThema, Kagiso, Daveyton and Tembisa. The government acted under the Public Safety Act (1953) and declared 19 magisterial districts (including 27 townships) as unrest areas.[21] The violence cost many more hundreds of lives over the following months and there were a number of increasingly desperate calls by ANC grass-roots activists for the leadership to re-activate its armed wing Umkhonto weSizwe (MK) as a self-defence organization within those townships worst hit by the nightly rounds of attacks.

This prolonged outburst of killing is often explained by the media as a simple tribal conflict between Xhosa and Zulu, as the type of 'black-on-black' violence which it is alleged is endemic in much of Africa south of the Sahara, and which, in some minds, makes 'tribalism' a fatal flaw for African democracy. At a slightly deeper level of analysis, it has been argued that the 'township violence', as it has come to be called, should be understood as a straightforward struggle for future political power in the 'new South Africa' between two principal opponents, the African National Congress (ANC) and the Inkatha Freedom Party (IFP).[22] According to this relatively clear, if rather simplistic, line of argument, aims and purposes are discerned and the violence then relegated to a category of explainable and understandable jockeying for power such as occurs, overtly or covertly, in any political system. Doubts about the validity of this analysis increased as more evidence became available about the motivations and mentalities which underlie this prolonged outbreak of extreme levels of killing and destruction of property and ways of life. A third explanation, which alleges that the government is directly or indirectly involved in instigating or at the least permitting the violence to continue, must also be considered. That there is a widespread public perception within South Africa that this is the case is indicated when even elements of the centrist media such as *The Star* (Johannesburg) charge that the South African Police's 'reputation as impartial upholders of law and order is in tatters'.[23]

Supporting evidence comes from eyewitness accounts, from media representatives who have witnessed attacks (and in some cases caught them on film), or who have interviewed survivors or participants, from representatives of monitoring groups such as the Human Rights Commission, Lawyers for Human Rights, or the Black Sash, evidence from legal cases or enquiries, and circumstantial evidence.

The accusation made by such organizations is that the government had been indulging in a version of *realpolitik*, of pragmatic undermining of the power base of its principal opposition, the ANC, through destabilization of its potential and natural constituency in the townships by creating conditions in which it is not only made obvious that the ANC cannot protect the people of the townships from random and arbitrary attack, but also in which it is made difficult if not impossible for the ANC to recruit large numbers of new members. The former secretary-general of Inkatha, Oscar Dhlomo warned in August 1990 that there was a deliberate policy of 'ethnicising political differences' on the part of political leaders. In broad terms, Dhlomo was pointing to a process of using migrant workers, the hostel-dwellers, many of whom are Natal Zulus in origin, against the more 'urbanized' Xhosa township residents.[24] The level of violence subsequently escalated, with more than 3,000 deaths since July 1990, caused in various ways.[25]

The types of intervention alleged to have been made by the security forces (including the SAP), and other, more shadowy organizations, can be divided into a number of categories.

Accusations of heavy-handedness by the police

This could almost be called a 'traditional' category since this type of allegation is not new and indeed numbers of such accusations have been proved to have foundation in both court cases and special inquiries during the last decade. Into this category fall those incidents of heavy-handedness by the police or security forces in dealing with demonstrations or civil unrest in which civilians were injured or killed. Often assaults, thefts and rapes have occurred in the course of purported police investigations or searches within the townships.[26] Such occurrences have been part of life in the townships for more than thirty years and present little that is novel in their structures or processes. In response to questioning in the Parliament, the Minister of Law and Order, for example, gave the following figures:

Table 3.1
Convictions of Members of the South African Police: Offences of Violence

Offence	1987	1988	1989	1990
Murder	3	22	27	11
Culpable homicide	19	28	31	24
Culpable homicide (motor collisions)	11	20	14	11
Assault (grievous bodily harm)	86	119	136	77
Common assault	345	420	338	295

The Minister noted the 'drastic decrease in 1990', but further remarked that:

> the situation is still not satisfactory, and to the Commissioner, the South African Police and myself it remains totally unacceptable. Steps are being taken to make members aware of this unacceptable state of affairs, to warn them against such deeds and the committing of such deeds, as well as to impress upon them the fact that it has a negative influence on the positive image the South African Police are striving at.[27]

In April 1991 the Minister announced that eighty-seven people had died while in police custody during the twelve months to February 1991. In May he stated that while nearly R900,000 had been paid in compensation to victims, only four police officers (of 372 convicted) had been dismissed as a result.[28] Such cases contributed in no small measure to a climate of distrust of the SAP which threatened to make many areas ungovernable. After a massacre involving at least seventeen deaths and twenty-nine serious injuries in an attack on two buses near Pietermaritzburg in February 1991, for example, seven local residents gave 'sworn statements that they were assaulted and almost set alight by policemen who demanded the identities of the perpetrators of Sunday's bus ambush'.[29]

In July 1991 the judge in the so-called 'balaclava' trial in Natal questioned the actions of the police in not obtaining a warrant to search particular premises and permitting about ten balaclava and camouflage-clad armed men illegally to enter the premises during the search. The judge remarked that there appeared to have been no hindrance to the obtaining of a warrant.

> 'The reason I stress this is that it appears, certainly in Natal, that police regard (the) provisions of the Criminal Procedure Act as having been abrogated by disuse. It is time that they became aware this is not so. . . .'

> He warned that if the police continued to ignore the law, public policy could well demand that the courts rule as inadmissible any evidence obtained in such a search.[30]

Police partiality/bias — 'standing by'

Police partiality in what was referred to as 'the previous era' came to be openly acknowledged by ministers such as Adriaan Vlok who, however, claimed that:

> We have lived through an era and the President started with a new concept on the 2nd of February . . . .Many people have that perception [of political actions by the SAP] . . . I have never denied that the police in the past era were involved in party politics . . . we stopped this . . . policemen are not allowed any longer to play on the political, the party political field . . . .[31]

Nonetheless, reports and allegations continued of police either standing by while murders were committed in the Reef townships or even actively assisting the attackers in various ways. In Swanieville, a declared unrest area, on 12 May 1991, for example, twenty-eight squatters were killed, thirty injured and eighty-two shacks burnt down in an attack by more than 900 Inkatha supporters wielding rifles, guns, pangas and spears. Allegedly, police arrived during the attack but stood by and then escorted the Inkatha supporters back to their hostel. Police claimed that the reason they had not intervened was 'that the attack took place during a shift change', even though the attack lasted more than three hours.[32] In this case, Inkatha actually claimed responsibility for the massacre. It was, Inkatha stated, a revenge attack for the deaths of two Inkatha supporters in the nearby hostel on the previous night.[33] This pattern of police assistance for the attackers seems to have been repeated in Boipatong two months later when police arrived more than an hour after residents had telephoned for help. Then, allegedly, they escorted the attackers, estimated to number more than 300, still carrying AK-47 rifles, pangas, knobkerries and spears, back to KwaMadala hostel. The intention of the attack seems to have been to create a climate of fear. Only one person was killed but there was considerable damage to property.[34]

Indirect police involvement and 'Inkathagate'

Prior to July 1991 there had been many indications that Pretoria's relationship with Mangosuthu Buthelezi went far beyond

support in his role as Chief Minister of KwaZulu. The actual
extent of the government's support for the Inkatha Freedom
Party however has been the subject of much debate. Inkatha
members were, on many occasions, permitted to demonstrate in
the townships and even in central Johannesburg carrying
'traditional weapons'. For more than a century, the Natal Code of
Zulu Law had prohibited Africans from carrying any 'cultural'
weapon but in August 1990 an amendment to the Code officially
permitted the carrying of such weapons.

This was in a sense a recognition of the status quo: more than
a thousand Inkatha supporters had marched through central
Johannesburg on 22 June 1990 armed with assegais and
knobkerries.[35] The amendment was clearly discriminatory, in its
impact since Inkatha members (who are overwhelmingly Zulu)
were permitted to carry dangerous weapons if they accorded
with 'traditional Zulu usages, customs or religions' while non-
Zulus were not. The amendment was challenged in the Supreme
Court in June 1991 on these grounds with the argument that 'the
exception was aimed at giving legal justification to police refusal
to disarm Inkatha members when they attended gatherings
carrying dangerous weapons'.[36]

There seemed to be evidence of continued partiality or bias
in the government's thinking on the subject when the Law and
Order Minister, Adriaan Vlok, announced on 16 April 1991 that
carrying pangas, bush knives and axes 'in conflict situations' was
henceforth banned but refused to consider the inclusion of
traditional weapons in the ban.[37] In May De Klerk agreed with
Nelson Mandela to ban all 'traditional weapons' other than sticks
and assegais in 'unrest areas'. Two days later Vlok banned the
possession of implements that could be dangerous weapons,
while still excluding ceremonial battle axes and spears from the
ban.[38] Later in the month an agreement on restricting the
carrying these weapons in unrest areas was reached between De
Klerk, Buthelezi and the Zulu king, Goodwill Zwelithini. As a
result on 22 May spears and assegais were forbidden to be
carried in unrest areas unless at traditional cultural gatherings
(for which advance notice had to be given).[39]

Central Johannesburg was clearly not an 'unrest area' on 14
September, the day that the National Peace Accord was signed,

when more than 2,000 Inkatha supporters armed with metal pipes, spears and knobkerries surrounded the Carlton Hotel where the talks were taking place. Mangosuthu Buthelezi's explanation was that his supporters were spontaneously paying tribute to the king, Goodwill Zwelithini.[40] In June 1991, the *Star* reported that the 'KwaZulu police are issuing weapons permits for rifles and permits to Inkatha supporters'. The Legal Resources Office in Durban

'was told the KwaZulu government was issuing G3 rifles and other guns to chiefs and headmen . . . some of the guns were being carried by Inkatha supporters at marches and rallies . . . none of the strict security checks carried out by the South African police when issuing weapons licences are put into effect'.[41] The KwaZulu government had also abolished three provisions in the law on dangerous weapons since the previous November with the effect of reducing sentences for violent offences. Buthelezi confirmed that the SA Police were supplying G3 automatic rifles to Inkatha personnel.[42]

Over a period of several years, a number of members of Parliament had tried to get detailed information concerning the government's links with Inkatha from the State President, the Minister of Defence and the Minister of Law and Order through Parliamentary Questions, but had been consistently denied information on the grounds that to deliver it would 'defeat the purpose of lawful actions and also the rightful, legal protection of security information as contemplated amongst other things, in the Protection of Information Act, 1982'.[43] In 21 June 1991, Defence Minister Magnus Malan was asked a series of questions in the Parliament concerning the relationship between the SADF and Inkatha, including whether the SADF had 'financed and supplied weapons to the Inkatha Freedom Party'. The minister replied that he would not order an investigation of the allegation 'because it is devoid of all truth'.[44]

Less than a month later, the *Guardian* (London) and *Weekly Mail* (Johannesburg) jointly published documents detailing payments by the security police to Inkatha to organize rallies and demonstrations at the time of the release from prison of Nelson Mandela. One of these, the King's Park rally in Durban on 25 March 1990 was closely followed by a vicious outbreak of

violence which became known as the Maritzburg War, while the
other in November 1989 was also followed by a very steep
increase in the number of unrest-related deaths in Natal.[45] The
State President then admitted secret government funding of only
four organizations, including the Inkatha-linked union Uwusa.[46]
Subsequent revelations showed that the list of secretly-funded
organizations was rather longer and included the conservative
National Students Federation.[47] Claims were also made by
former security and intelligence officers that Pretoria's secret
support for Buthelezi and Inkatha dated back to Inkatha's
foundation in the mid-seventies.[48]

The revelations clearly damaged the government, not least
because the unanswered questions about the secret use of
taxpayers' funds in the pursuit of questionable ends eroded the
newly-won and very precarious gains the National Party had
made in attracting support for its policies among former
supporters of the Democratic Party.[49] On the other hand, there
may have been some gains for De Klerk inasmuch as the post-
'Inkathagate' Cabinet shuffle enabled him to sideline Defence
Minister Malan who had represented the unreconstructed and
verkrampte securocrats in the inner circles of the government and
party since De Klerk assumed power. Malan was replaced by the
younger Roelf Meyer who has no significant military
background and who, while in no way being *verligte*, has a quite
different and more open style than that of Malan.

Further revelations emerged during August concerning
military training by the SADF of Inkatha members. De Klerk had
claimed that the squads were trained as bodyguards for
KwaZulu leaders, but members of the group of 150 Inkatha
personnel to which he referred in this denial claimed that they
had been trained in offensive guerrilla warfare in Namibia
(Caprivi Strip) prior to independence. They then returned to
KwaZulu where a number participated in clandestine attacks on
Inkatha's political opponents in KwaZulu and Natal. The SADF
admitted that 'security-directed' training of Inkatha personnel
had indeed been carried out in the Caprivi Strip and has now
acknowledged the existence of at least one training camp in
Natal.[50]

The saga of the links between Inkatha and the government

had its occasional moments of farce. The *New Nation* reported on 13 July 1991 that Inkatha's Youth Brigade had issued a press statement denying any association with the SAP — a statement which was sent out on a fax machine belonging to the security police.[51]

The 'Third Force'.

The existence of a 'third force' has been much discussed within South Africa. There have been hundreds of allegations that whites participated in attacks on township residents and hostel dwellers. The *Star* reported on 5 September 1990 that armed whites participated in an attack on Sebokeng hostel which led to eleven people being shot by the SADF.[52] That the idea of a 'third force' has been taken seriously by some elements within the government is demonstrated by De Klerk's statement in September 1990 that 'small groups had organized to kill people at random and that there `might be a yet unknown group which has decided to misuse the general state of unrest and violence in these specific areas to derail the negotiation process'.[53]

Nelson Mandela charged in September 1990 that the violence was being instigated by a 'third force operating in this country, a third force which is backed by the same security forces which are supposed to maintain law and order in this country. These are the people who are shooting and killing our people.'[54] His based his argument on the accumulating evidence of 'black men with white hands' involved in attacks, and on the evident disparity between the amount of force being used and the capability of Inkatha to mount such attacks unaided outside its own territory in KwaZulu/Natal.[55]

Such suspicions have been reiterated in many quarters, although another argument has been put by the Independent Board of Inquiry into Informal Repression (IBIIR). It gave no credence to the idea of a third force, 'but did not rule out the involvement of "certain elements within the Government" in efforts to destabilize the ANC'.

At the same time the IBIIR found that:

> Hundreds of township dwellers on the Reef [had] fled their homes
> as a result of escalating Inkatha Freedom Party intimidation since
> March. . . . Many workers had also been intimidated into cancelling
> their membership of trade unions affiliated to the ANC-aligned . .
> . (Cosatu) . . . Inkatha supporters were charging R20 to R100 a
> month 'protection fee' from township families, saying they would
> be excluded from Inkatha attacks if they joined up.[56]

By the time of the IBIIR statement, even comparatively
conservative newspapers were printing speculation about the
existence of the third force:

> It is significant that witnesses to the attack [a train massacre in
> which seven people died] said the attackers 'did not say a word'.
> Was it because they could not speak any of the black languages or
> that they could not speak Zulu and if they tried to speak, it would
> punch holes into the 'Inkatha theory'? Do we have a Renamo-type
> operation here?[57]

Police statements about a shooting in central Johannesburg in
which three people were killed and eight wounded seemed to
bear out the involvement of whites in such assaults. A white
woman made a statement which was taken very seriously by
police that she had seen both white and black men in the
attacking minibus and that five pedestrians had been forced into
the vehicle after it had stopped alongside her. She was shot after
she was seen by one of the minibus passengers and later died in
hospital.[58] In July the police began an internal investigation into
allegations that members of the security forces were involved in
the killings of 5 ANC members at Ndaleni township.[59]

Widely-published statements by former SADF officer Nico
Basson in June and July 1991 alleged that 'a "substantial number"
of senior army personnel are considering coming forward with
information about covert actions aimed at destabilizing the
African National Congress, its allies and black townships'.
Basson further charged that the SADF was purchasing AK-47s in
Mozambique and passing them on to Inkatha.[60]

The Government and Violence

Continued high levels of violence posed an obvious threat to the process of political reform and the orderly transition to a new, non-racial constitution. It is not so clear that the De Klerk government regarded violence as an unmixed blessing.

A number of observers have seen a correlation between peaks in the township violence and
1) attempts made by non-government organizations to bring about peace accords; and
2) times of some significance for the government (such as De Klerk's trip to Europe in October 1990, when Parliament opened in January 1991, and in June 1991[61]).
For example, actions by the Inkatha union Uwusa in September 1991, when the National Peace Accord was being discussed, resulted in a number of deaths and injuries to bystanders and members and officials of the major umbrella union organization COSATU.[62] At the same time, three men, who could not be identified with either the ANC or Inkatha fired on Inkatha members going to a rally in Thokoza on the East Rand. Twenty three men were killed and many others injured. The violence spread rapidly to neighbouring townships and then to Soweto with a death toll of more than 100 by the end of the week.[63] Earlier in the year, a local peace accord in Alexandra was torpedoed when a number of people were killed in battles between hostel dwellers and squatters.[64] On 29 January, Mandela and Buthelezi reached a national agreement.[65] Within 24 hours at least eight people died and dozens were critically injured in an attack at Umgabagaba in Natal, while within the next few days at least eleven people died in political violence in the township of Bekkersdal.[66]

A report on the violence issued by the International Committee of Jurists in January 1991 stated 'that the SAP helped Inkatha by turning a blind eye to violence by its members against the ANC'. Africa Watch also accused the security forces of fostering political violence.[67] A few days later, Lawyers for Human Rights alleged police partiality and active police 'participation in attacks by Zulu-speaking men on Phola Park squatter camp residents'.[68] The independent Community

Agency for Social Enquiry (CASE) released a study in October 1991 covering the first year of the Reef violence which examined 'thousands of newspaper reports' from across the spectrum of print media, as well as figures compiled by monitoring organizations such as IBIIR, HRC, Centre for Applied Legal Studies and Lawyers for Human Rights.[69] These organizations had been able to allocate responsibility in 257 acts of violence (out of 601 incidents involving 2271 deaths of whom 87% were not identifiable members of political organizations). 'Of these Inkatha (IFP) had been reported as responsible in 51%, the South African Police (SAP) in 23%, and the ANC in 4% of cases while the SAP was recorded in 46 reports as "actively colluding with IFP supporters in acts of violence and aggression"'.[70]

The South African Police responded directly to the CASE study by releasing a media statement which sought to prove, somewhat unconvincingly, that CASE had not used 'any scientifically recognized method to come to all the conclusions and assumptions published in the report'.[71] The SAP found that in 143 out of 643 cases it examined between 2 February 1990 and 31 July 1991, 'both the aggressor and target were . . . politically connected. An analysis shows that 40% of the attacks were carried out by Inkatha-members/supporters, 56% by ANC-members/supporters and 5% by PAC/AZAPO-members or their supporters.'[72] In 12% of the cases where only the aggressor was identified as being politically connected, 12% were Inkatha while 86% were ANC. Somewhat ingenuously the SAP claimed that it 'has never refused to investigate any allegations levelled against it. It is, however, a rule of law in our justice system that all accused persons must be fairly treated and afforded the opportunity to explain his or her actions in court.'[73]

The SAP conducted internal investigations of particular complaints from time to time. In September it acknowledged that 24 police officers were then under suspension, facing charges from assault to murder.[74] These investigations usually came about after prolonged pressure by human rights organizations. A number of deaths of young men and boys from Khutsong at the Welverdiend police station, as well as accusations of torture of suspects over a period of 18 months for example, resulted in the appointment of such a unit in July 1991. Numbers of the witnesses who had given sworn statements concerning alleged torture and killings at Welverdiend were subsequently shot by police in other incidents.[75] Police continued to use considerable levels of force in township areas, even settlements which have not been declared 'unrest areas'. On 19 August a 14-year old school student was shot dead at Sakhile township during a protest over occupation of a school building in the township. 'Police spokesman Captain Oosie van Niekerk admitted police had used live ammunition on stone-throwing pupils. Five others were injured.'[76] On 13 October, an ANC youth leader was shot in the back by police in Diepkloof, Soweto. In the four days of protests that followed the police used both birdshot and live ammunition against school students within school grounds in a number of locations in Soweto.[77]

In April 1991 De Klerk announced 'the establishment of a standing commission to investigate, combat and identify the perpetrators of politically-inspired violence and intimidation'.[78] It has not proved successful, so far at least, in identifying the perpetrators of violence or bringing them to justice. Nonetheless, a major stumbling block to the success of the National Peace Accord signed by the government, ANC and Inkatha on 14 September 1991 was the lack of a structure for the automatic external investigation of complaints against police or the SADF. While 1989-91 saw some intermittent improvement in the standards adopted by government-appointed inquiries, in general inquiries have acted to exonerate government agencies of involvement. Nonetheless, the cycle of violence continues, amid continuing suspicion concerning the attitude of the NP government towards the violence.

Two thousand years ago, the Roman politician and writer Cicero (who himself discerned the value of assassination as a political weapon) argued that in order to read a political situation the observer must ask 'cui bono?'. 'Who gains' is a useful question to ask about the violence in South Africa's townships.

Conclusion

Despite all De Klerk's rhetoric about transferring power, it can be argued that the ruling regime decided on a course which it perceives will allow it to maintain dominance of the 'new South Africa'. It pursued reforms demanded by the international community but it did not move decisively to rectify the historical deficits of social spending in areas such as health, education or housing which have been responsible for the creation of vast inequities for the majority population. The spread of the KwaZulu/Natal inter-communal violence to the overpopulated townships of the Reef has had disastrous effects on township dwellers' perceptions of the likelihood that they will be secure in the 'new South Africa'. Informed observers continued to believe that the government was not displeased with such developments. It may be argued that the National Party leadership deliberately aimed to create conditions in which it could represent itself to a newly enfranchised black electorate as the only possible government for a country with significant economic and security problems.

Notes

1   In gathering material and preparing this chapter I have had the assistance of the School of Social Sciences, Curtin University, the Indian Ocean Centre for Peace Studies, Stephen Heyns, Sheila Suttner and Jennifer Weir. Their assistance is very gratefully acknowledged.

2   The amount outstanding was over $US21 billion at the end of 1988. *Sunday Star*, 10 September 1989 quoted in *Race Relations Survey 1988-89* (Johannesburg, SAIRR, 1989), p.xxvii.

3   Quoted in *Weekly Mail*, 18-24 August 1989, p.2.

4   J. Wardrop, 'Continuity and Change in South Africa and in South Africa's Relations with its Neighbours', in R. Bruce, ed., *Changing Prospects for Peace in the Indian Ocean Region* (Perth: IOCPS, 1992).

5   H. J. Cohen, 'Looking forward to a new South Africa', statement before the Subcommittees on Africa and on International Economic Policy and Trade, House Foreign Affairs Committee, Washington, D.C., 31 July, 1991.

6   Republic of South Africa, *Debates of Parliament (Hansard)*,, hereafter referred to as *Hansard* , 2 February 1990, cols.1-15.

7   *Citizen* , 28 June 1991, p.7.

8   *Weekly Mail* , 23-29 August 1991, p.13.

9   On 10 July 1991; transcript of news conference held by Herman Cohen, Assistant Secretary of State for African Affairs.

10   See for example the reservations expressed by Cohen in a statement before the subcommittees on Africa and on International Economic Policy and Trade, House Foreign Affairs Committee, Washington D.C., 31 July 1991.

11   *Hansard* , 5 February 1990, col.93.

12   Reported in *SA Barometer*, 21 June 1991, p.179, and 19 July 1991, p.211. The hypothetical alliance was to include the almost-defunct Democratic Party, Inkatha, the Zion Christian Church and 'homeland' leaders.

13   *Sunday Times*, 23 June 1991, p.2.

14   *Star*, 3 July 1991, p.11; *Citizen*, 3 July 1991, p.8.

15   *SA Barometer*, 24 May 1991, p.147; 7 June 1991, pp.162-163.

16   *The Citizen*, 3 July 1991, p.8.

17   *Weekly Mail*, 4-10 October 1991, p.17.

18   *Star*, 3 July, 1991, p.11.

19   See, for example, De Klerk's opening speech to Parliament, *Hansard*, 2 February 1990, col.15.

20   The death toll in Natal/KwaZulu during this period is impossible to establish with any real accuracy, but figures for 1990 supplied by the Minister of Law and Order indicate that 782 people died in Natal and 353 in KwaZulu during that year, *Hansard*, 21 March 1991, cols.729-730.

21   *SA Barometer*, 27 August 1990, p.242.

22   There have also been outbreaks of violence between supporters of the ANC and the Pan Africanist Congress (PAC), see for example *SA Barometer*, 22 June 1990, p.162.

23   13 September 1990 cited in *Who is murdering the peace? C.A.S.E. research statistics* (Johannesburg: CASE,1991), p.8.

24   *Weekly Mail*, 17-19 August, 1990, p.1.

25   'Between January and April 1991, 28 percent of all violent deaths were caused by firearms, mostly AK-47s, 22 percent by incendiary devices and 18 percent by knives, spears, pangas and other sharp instruments. During the same period 26 people had been necklaced.' South African Institute of Race Relations analysis, cited in *SA Barometer*, 7 June 1991, p.162.

26   See, for example, *Hansard*, 12 March 1991, cols.444-445.

27   *Hansard*, 22 March 1991, cols.743-744.

28   *SA Barometer*, 26 April 1991, p.114 and 7 June 1991, p.162.

29   Ibid, 1 March, 1991, p.49-50.

30   *Weekly Mail,* 5-11 July 1991, p.2. Evidence was given by a police officer that the balaclava-wearing men formed part of the South African Police Task Force and that they were only in the district for a week 'for a particular task'.

31   *Agenda,* SABC, 21 July 1991.

32   *SA Barometer*, 24 May 1991, p.147.

33   *Weekly Mail,* 17-23 May 1991, pp.1-2.

34   Ibid, 19-25 July 1991, p 6.

35   *SA Barometer*, 6 July 1990, p.178.

36   *Star*, 25 June 1991, p.2, and 26 June 1991, p.7.

37   *SA Barometer*, 26 April 1991, p.114.

38   Ibid, 24 May 1991, p.346.

39   Ibid, 7 June 1991, pp.161-162.

40   Ibid, 27 September 1991, p.292.

41   *Star*, 23 June 1991, p.9.

42   *SA Barometer*, 19 July 1991, p.209.

43   *Hansard,* 5 March 1991, cols.294, 310-311, and 12 March 1991, cols.435-438, 441-442.

44   Ibid, 21 June 1991, cols.2089-2090.

45   The death count in such incidents in Natal in October 1989 was 176. This rose to 212 in November and 210 in December, reaching 353 in March and 286 in April before declining again to 125 in May; *Weekly Mail,* 26 July-1 August 1991, p.5.

46   At a much-delayed press conference on 31 July, ten days after the reports had been first published.

47   A spokesman for the State President denied secret funding of the NSF but within only a few hours the NSF itself as well as the Department of Law and Order made a public admission that such funding had taken place;*Weekly Mail,* 9-15 Aug.,1991, p.4.

48   *Weekly Mail,* 19-25 July 1991, pp.1-3, 26 July-1 August 1991, p.1-5, and 2-8 August 1991, pp.1-4; *Guardian,* 20 July 1991, p.1.

49   Perhaps his most inventive response was to say that a statement he made on 13 June that the government had not funded political parties was not applicable because Inkatha was a cultural organization at that time, not a political party; *SA Barometer*, 2 August 1991, p.227.

50   *Weekly Mail*, 21-27 September1990, and 9-15 August1991, pp.1-3.
        Former Captain Dirk Coetzee (now in exile in London) has
        alleged that the destabilising violence and the alleged
        involvement of the third force is not understandable without an
        understanding of the security culture of South Africa's police,
        special branch and military. He alleges that the Koevoet counter-
        insurgency unit used in Namibia was formed with a core of
        Zulus from Natal and that this core, with their weaponry were
        brought back to SA after independence for use in Natal and the
        Reef townships. Similarly he alleges that the military covertly
        used soldiers trained with Renamo in the townships; ibid, p.19.

51   Members of the Inkatha Youth Brigade (IYB) have been deeply
        implicated in the Reef violence. IYB leader Themba Khoza (the
        so-called 'Lord of the Rooidoeke') for example was one of 137
        Inkatha members arrested by the SAP after allegations that he
        had been at many violent attacks including the 5 September
        attack on Sebokeng hostel, *Weekly Mail*, 7-13 September 1990, pp.
        1-2; *SA Barometer*, 14 September 1990, p.258.

52   *SA Barometer*, 14 September 1990, p.258; *Weekly Mail*, 7-13
        September 1990, p.1, reported that the assault was carried out by
        'four white men wearing balaclavas and long khaki coats and
        carrying firearms. There were over 100 black men in the group
        wearing overalls and the red headbands that characterise
        Inkatha supporters'.

53   *Weekly Mail*, 21-27 September 1990, p.1.

54   Ibid, 21-27 September 1990, p.1-2.

55   In early May Musa Myeni, head of public relations and
        international affairs for Inkatha, rather unrealistically threatened
        'to deploy 100 000 fighters in Soweto and another 150 000 in other
        townships around Johannesburg' unless the ANC brought an
        end to the fighting within a week; *SA Barometer*, 24 May 1991,
        p.145.

56   *Star*, 26 June 1991, p.3.

57   Ibid, 27 June, 1991, p.24.

58   *SA Barometer*, 28 September 1990, pp.275, 281.

59   Ibid, 21 August 1991, p.226.

60   Ibid, 21 June, 1991, p.179.

61   CASE, *Who is murdering the peace?*, p.4.

62   *Weekly Mail*, 6-12 September 1991, p.8.

63   Ibid, 13-19 September 1991, pp.1-5.

64   *SA Barometer*, 29 March 1991, pp.80-81.

65   Signed in Durban, the so-called Royal Hotel Minute covered the
        violence in both Natal and the Transvaal and called for the
        consolidation and implementation of 'existing agreements such
        as the Lower Umfolozi Peace Accord'; *SA Barometer*, 15 February
        1991, p. 33.

66   Ibid, 15 February 1991, p.34.

67   Ibid, 1 February 1991, p.18.

68   In September, 1990; ibid.

69   CASE, *Who is murdering the peace?*, p.1.

70   Ibid.

71   SA Police Public Relations, Pretoria, 28 October 1991, p.1.

72   Ibid.

73   Ibid.

74   *SA Barometer*, 27 September 1991, p.293.

75   *Weekly Mail*, 5-11 July 1991, p.6. Five police officers were
        suspended on 29 July, and another ten during August; *SA
        Barometer*, 16 August 1991, p.242, 30 August 1991, p.259, 13
        September 1991, p. 273; *Hansard*, 21 March 1991, cols.729-732.
        See also the charges laid against members of the SAP and SADF
        'in connection with unrest in the Pietermaritzburg district from 1
        January 1990' up to 31 May 1990: 4 charges of murder; 3 charges
        of attempted murder; 2 charges of kidnapping; 1 of damage to
        property; 2 of assault and 1 of arson; *Hansard*, 13 June 1990,
        col.1783; see also the series of official complaints laid against
        members of the SADF during 1989 as a result of actions of troops
        in townships, *Hansard*, 6 June 1990, cols.1667-1668. On March,
        1991, Minister for Law and Order, Adriaan Vlok, said 'the SA
        Police should not be accused when things go wrong. Place the
        blame where it belongs, and not on the SA Police;' *Hansard*, 5
        March 1991, col.293.

76   *Weekly Mail*, 23-29 August 1991, p.8.

77   Ibid, 18-24 October 1991, p.5.

78   *SA Barometer*, 26 April 1991, p.114.

4

The Commonwealth and Peacemaking in South Africa

Deryck Schreuder

'. . . the Commonwealth must remain ready to assist the negotiating process in ways that would be found helpful by the parties concerned'.

The Harare Communique, October 1991.

'. . . no outsiders, but South African themselves, can resolve the problems facing this country'.

South African Foreign Affairs Minister,
'Pik' Botha, 12 July 1992.

Introduction

Even in the terrible African drought of 1991-92, the jacaranda trees of Harare blossomed with spring colour as we came to Zimbabwe for the Commonwealth Summit. A certain tone of hope also surrounded the peacemaking process in the region: 'the cry for freedom, as well as the cry for justice, stops at no border', President Robert Mugabe declared in his opening address to the Commonwealth Heads of Government Meeting (CHOGM) at the start of this international meeting, on 16 October 1991 in Harare.

As you stand on Zimbabwe soil, only a stone's throw away from
South Africa, the world expects us to spare no effort in helping to
achieve an outcome there, which will being comfort to the
oppressed people of South Africa. We have a duty to be for South
Africa what the Lusaka CHOGM in 1979 was for the then
Rhodesia.[1]

This might have seemed an unusual call and claim for
international action — not least since South Africa had 30 years
previously left the Commonwealth: in 'the triumph of
Commonwealth expulsion', Verwoerd's phrase as he returned
from the 1961 CHOGM and launched both the beginnings of the
era of high apartheid and the isolated era as 'polecat' of the world
community of states. Under the banner of *'In God ons glo'* (in
'God we trust') the Republic of South Africa headed out into the
stormy seas of international criticism, and, increasingly, of
isolation. This at last severed connections to the British Crown,
Empire and Commonwealth of Nations, going back to the 1910
'Union of South Africa' as one of the four settler 'Dominions' of
Pax Britannica. Indeed, a connection that eventually stretched
back to the early nineteenth century and the coming of British
rule to the sub-continental region as successor to the Dutch-East
India Company at the Cape.

Mugabe was striking a representative and resonant tone in
Commonwealth ideology and history. Although it was true that
South Africa and the Commonwealth had taken diametrically
divergent paths since 1961, a very particular relationship of
concern and commitment had grown up over those decades, so
that 'Commonwealth' often seemed as much about South Africa
as if the repugnant state still remained as a rejected yet obdurate
member of the 'club'. Where the Commonwealth had become
ever more representative of a decolonizing world of mass
nationalist movements, especially in the Third World, so
reflecting exactly a changing pluralist international order, the
Republiek van Zuid Afrika had answered decolonization with its
policy of apartheid and a minority white regime, dominated by
Afrikaner nationalist ideology and representative of narrowing
ideas of ethnic purity and race classification. 'South Africa' was
to be for 'Europeans', the descendants of white migrations since
1652, while the majority of 'Non-Europeans' as an 'indigenous

people' were to find their political destiny in designated 'home-land' enclaves — 13 scattered rural regions which had about them the character of labour reservations for the refugees of a dislocated and conquered peasantry.

The struggle against the politics and privations of apartheid had been led by internal South African movements until their suppression in the 1960s, when external agencies took up the cause of democracy and liberty for all South Africans. The Commonwealth, especially its Third World members, had become increasingly involved in that campaign. The results had been uneven, and often seen by cynical observers to produce more unity and focus for the disparate international organization than actual change in South Africa. But there was no doubt that Commonwealth politics contained deep commitments towards shaping a new South Africa. Each CHOGM following 1961, and especially those in the 1970s, had seen advocacy of peaceful change, coupled increasingly with actual proposals to invoke international opinion and finance to pressure that process along.

The CHOGM in Harare stood at the apogee of that history, coming as it did after the historic decisions of the De Klerk government to begin a process of engagement with African nationalist forces, towards what was hoped to be peaceful change in the Republic. Nelson Mandela's appearance at the CHOGM summit as guest of President Mugabe, following his release from 27 years of imprisonment, symbolized the new 'moment'. Mugabe himself declared:

> Since our last meeting in Kuala Lumpur, the struggle for a free and democratic South Africa has attained new heights. South Africans are now talking to each other. A positive start has been made. Our decisions and deliberations on South Africa should bring hope to the oppressed and encouragement to the Government of South Africa. We must assist the South Africans to embark without further delay on negotiating a new Constitution based on universally shared democratic principles.

This chapter reviews the process of Commonwealth involvement which had led up to the Harare Summit, and it considers in detail the Commonwealth anticipation later in 1991 that it would play a constructive role in the South African peace process. I conclude with an attempt at a realistic assessment of how far that ambition was realized. The Commonwealth was clearly eager to extend its role as an agency of change in South Africa. But to what extent has it been able to be an 'honest broker', between government and African nationalist parties, in the struggle towards creating the constitutional settlement which would usher in the interim administration and mass democracy? Will the Commonwealth indeed play a key role in facilitating the rise of a New South Africa, following its recent history of commitment to destroying apartheid and promoting peaceful change?

An African Summit: CHOGM in Harare, October 1991.

The Commonwealth involvement with the South African question is broadly related to its commitment to principles of democracy and non-racialism. But it is also more closely related to Commonwealth membership itself: the great majority of members have thrown off their prior colonial status within the British empire and have strongly identified with the liberation struggle against white minority rule in South Africa. Apartheid was the last standing edifice of colonial, exploitative, alien rule in the Third Wold. Moreover, as Africa's 'Deep South', it stood as an affront to the dignity of all Africans, and as such called for the extension of the politics of de-colonization through all appropriate agencies.

The Commonwealth was a prime agent for those political pressures, not least because of the strongly African character of the organization. This can be illustrated both by analyzing Commonwealth membership and its agendas of concerns. But it can also readily be found in the working of the Harare CHOGM. The Commonwealth was very much 'at home' in the great continent.

Not only are 14 of the 50 members of the Commonwealth drawn from the African states, but nearly 50% of the African population reside in Commonwealth nations (over 230 million people). In addition, 9 of the 17 least developed countries of the Commonwealth (with less than US$500 per head p.a.) are African societies — with some like Tanzania (at US$120 per head p.a.) even more disadvantaged than a poor Asian state such as Bangladesh. Commonwealth policies and programs reflect these African realities, both in terms of strength in membership and population, as well as in the shared need for general development and infrastructure services.

Table 5.1
The African Commonwealth (14 of 50 Commonwealth member states)

	Population, millions (1989)	GNP per Head (US$)
Botswana	1.217	$940
Gambia	.848	230
Ghana	14.425	380
Kenya	23.277	380
Lesotho	1.722	470
Malawi	8.230	180
Namibia	1.300	2440
Nigeria	113.665	250
Sierra Leone	4.040	200
Swaziland	.761	900
Tanzania	25.627	120
Uganda	16.772	250
Zambia	7.837	390
Zimbabwe	9.567	640
Total	229.236	

Source: compiled from*The Commonwealth Today* (London, October 1991), pp.18-19, using figures from World Bank.

Harare highlighted the African character of the Commonwealth. President Mugabe was in the Chair, and in his presentations to fellow 'Heads' of Delegations, he adroitly linked the general Commonwealth concern to those of Africa today. The new Secretary-General of the Commonwealth was the immensely able and urbane African diplomat Chief Emerka Anyaoku of Nigeria. He came to his first CHOGM, in his new office, with a clear set of policy priorities that included a commitment to

ensure a continuing Commonwealth role in the South Africa
settlement — while also determining to enshrine aspects of
human rights and democratic freedoms in the principles of
Commonwealth membership and practice. The newest
Commonwealth member, Namibia, was welcomed from Africa,
and its own plural democratic practices were much praised.
Elections in Zambia were pending, and a Commonwealth
monitoring group was then preparing to oversee the polls which
were to bring about the fall of President Kaunda, who had been
in office continuously since decolonization in 1964. Interestingly,
Mozambique attended as an observer state, and its role in
Southern African peacemaking, its problem with regional
refugees, and its deep problem with civil war and poverty, were
subjects of considerable discussion.

More broadly, Africa was a crucial feature of the major
general issues agenda of the Commonwealth debates on
agricultural development, the environment and national
heritage, youth, sport, education, the control of drug trafficking,
the liberation of women and the awesome problem of AIDS in
the modern world. Debt remission proposals from the British
delegation — following up the noted Trinidad and Tobago
terms, and looking forward to the meeting of the Group of 7 —
also had considerable potential for many African economies
within the Commonwealth. Empire had gone from Africa, but
Commonwealth very much remained.

A Southern African Summit

The agenda of the Harare CHOGM brought these several African
factors together and made it into not least a regional conference
on peacemaking and change in the Southern African context.

Symbolically and appropriately, this Summit was being held
in the capital of the most significant of the 'Front Line' African
states which had been most directly engaged in the long struggle
against Apartheid — a member of SADCC, a nation in which a
successful war for liberation was still a vivid memory, and an
independent state where independence had been prominently
facilitated by Commonwealth diplomacy, including

prominently that of Australia. The Zimbabwe peace settlement of 1981 was in fact still very much in the mind of delegates of this CHOGM as a piece of 'Commonwealth lore', showing how the organization could use its good offices in a negotiating and diplomatic manner to assist in the troubled politics of decolonization and transfers of power from minority regimes to popularly elected governments.

Harare also pushed to centre stage the charismatic Nelson Mandela, who carried with him not only the huge moral authority of a prophet of anti-apartheid liberation, but who also symbolized a South Africa before apartheid and within the Commonwealth. 'We never left', Mandela is said to have remarked from the perspective of the ANC and African nationalism when the question of a New South Africa's possible re-admission to the Commonwealth was raised. Certainly, Mandela was claimed by the Commonwealth Heads as a comrade in the politics of liberation, and as the kind of leader they wished to see at the head of that New South Africa.

In the immediate politics of 1991 Mandela was also present so that CHOGM Heads could consult on the evolution and potential ending of Commonwealth sanctions against South Africa. By the time of Harare, the Foreign Ministers Committee on South Africa (CFMSA) had met at Delhi in May (1991) to consider what steps should be taken in the light of the reforms of the De Klerk administration in a momentous year. That meeting, of the CFMSA Committee, had recommended a major principled step in the adjustment of the sanctions following a 'programmed management approach . . . linking any change in the application of sanctions to the taking of real and practical steps to end apartheid'. Some commentators wondered aloud whether the major African Commonwealth states would press for a harder line than the British delegation, thus raising the possibility of another notorious separate final communique, as at a previous CHOGM. Mandela had a range of confidential talks with all the parties concerned, and at times looked and sounded like one of the Commonwealth 'Heads' of delegation.

A fascinating question hung over the Harare CHOGM. Might a South African government delegation also be invited to join the discussions, so fulfilling the aspiration of certain

delegations to press further the 'honest broker' role of
Commonwealth in the peace-making process? Indeed it was
even rumoured that one 'HOD' — President Kaunda of Zambia
— had urged that an invitation be offered for an official South
African presence at the informal weekend retreat, held at the
Victoria Falls in the middle of the Summit. Presumably the
retreat would have provided the best possible conditions for
private discussions, outside the range of media and a heavy
presence of officials.

It came to naught. The HODs proceeded to discuss the
easing and adjustment of sanctions on their own, and to focus
their enthusiasm for brokerage activity on a possible mission by
the Secretary-General to South Africa itself. While careful to
declare that 'the terms of a constitutional settlement were for the
people of South Africa to determine', the Commonwealth Heads
remained committed to regional peacemaking, through the
office of Chief Anyaoku, 'in order to explore with the principal
parties concerned ways in which the Commonwealth would
assist in lending momentum to the negotiating process' (Section
20 of the final Communique). Apartheid was to be ended by the
politics of conciliation, if not of constructive engagement.

South Africa in and out of the Commonwealth: the Long Road to 1991

The CHOGM of 1991 was very much aware that this was the 30th
anniversary of the South African departure from the
organization. The sense of history was essentially related to the
fact that change was under way, the region had been
transformed by decolonization since the 1960s, and that South
Africa's republican path leading away from the Commonwealth
in 1961 could be coming full circle, with the tantalizing promise
of major change in a post-apartheid 'New South Africa'.

The ghosts of 1961 were accordingly part of the politics and
myth-making of 1991. The official handbook, *The Commonwealth
Today* , published by the Information Division of the Secretariat
in October 1991, declared that 'South Africa was forced to leave
[the Commonwealth] in 1961 by other members' opposition to

apartheid'. That view fitted well with the orthodox view of the Commonwealth challenge to apartheid. But in fact the inside accounts of that crucial 1961 CHOGM in London — based on recently available memoirs and state papers — shows that the leaders of the Commonwealth went to considerable trouble in an attempt to keep South Africa *in* the organization, even as a republic. That diplomatic persuasion, which aimed at getting the Verwoerd government to 'soften' its race policies, was led by the British prime minister, Harold Macmillan, and also by Robert Menzies of Australia: the Menzies Papers and his Memoir, *Afternoon Light*, reveal the long-term efforts made by the Australian leader both to ease South African intransigence and to persuade fellow Commonwealth leaders to abide by a principle of non-interference in the politics of other member states.

The South African delegation refused to give an inch in its devotion to apartheid principles and policies, so confirming the inflexible line taken in Verwoerd's replies to Menzies in a lengthy private correspondence before the 1961 CHOGM. African member states did not automatically challenge the diplomacy of private persuasion. Indeed, it is remarkable how long this early version of 'constructive engagement' endured — until the South African themselves wrecked the strategy. Verwoerd's steely resolve, and foreign minister Eric Louw's style of diplomacy, ultimately infuriated other Commonwealth leaders — especially those from Africa and India — as well as the other potential new members from the Third World, as decolonization broke empire into independent Afro-Asian states. If South Africa had then not withdrawn its application for membership as a republic — following its own 'whites' only referendum and republican declaration — it could have been a fatal moment in the emergence of the modern Commonwealth.

Just as the 1991 Harare meeting came at a crucial time, the 1961 CHOGM stood at an historical cross-road for the organization. Harold Macmillan's famous 'Winds of Change' speech, given to the combined Houses of the South African parliament in February 1960, had excellently represented the trends in international politics of the era as Asia, and then Africa, experienced the processes of decolonization from imperial powers. The British were committed to a liberal Empire-

Commonwealth of inclusive membership. All the former colonial territories were to be called and all were to be chosen.

Macmillan's Cape Town speech had flattered White South Africa by referring to Afrikaner nationalism as the first of the African nationalisms. By inference the South African leaders should appreciate the force of nationalism in the continent at large, and also the aspirations of its own black citizens. But the South Africans took an exclusive view of nationalism: their sense of nationality was informed by a devotion to ethnicity that ultimately could not be reconciled with a pluralist vision of a decolonizing world. They effectively took themselves out of the Commonwealth as its changing membership threatened their domestic arrangements. The white state would secure its power by the social engineering of apartheid, based on the spatial division of the nation which declared Africans to belong in tribal 'homelands'. Here was South Africa's perverse vision of decolonization and the transfer of power. They put themselves outside a multi-national, multi-racial Commonwealth by shaping their own region on principles which were the antithesis of that pluralistic process of liberation.

South Africa's departure eased the Commonwealth's move from old 'Club' to new association, largely Third-World in character, with a notable African content (11 new members came from Africa in the 1960s alone). Conversely, the principles promulgated by the new Commonwealth sharpened the South African resolve to build the walls of apartheid against that kind of world. A curious dialectic therefore existed in the growth of both Commonwealth and apartheid. It was expressed in the politics of nationalist aspiration — white and black — and it was also exhibited in the increasingly conflicted relationship of a non-racial new Commonwealth focussing much of its collective action against the ethnic purity policies of apartheid.

Indeed, the Commonwealth increasingly involved itself over the next 30 years in three significant challenges to apartheid. There was the challenge to promote multi-racialism in South Africa. There was the challenge to bring the processes of decolonization to Southern Africa, including a transfer of power in the mandated territory of South West Africa, then under firm apartheid rule. And there was also the challenge to bring a new stability to the region at large — both militarily and economically as the effects of apartheid policy came to destabilize and skew the development of the surrounding states of southern and central Africa.

That last challenge involved actions within Africa itself, in which several major initiatives can be identified. First, there were the processes of change which saw the UDI state of 'Rhodesia' transformed into Zimbabwe. The UDI declaration itself (November 1965) had appalled the Commonwealth: it appeared to be the reinstitution of colonialism, rather than a declaration of independence from the metropolitan state. A white majority regime, led by a settler farmer, Ian Smith, had effectively seized power, and now stood defiant against African nationalism and the international community. Military action was considered, in various strategic forms, by the Harold Wilson Labour Government of the United Kingdom, but abandoned. Even a Liberal Party proposal to cut key rail and road connections in a bid to force capitulation was rejected. A fifteen-year conflict began in central Africa as African nationalists launched their own armed struggle against the UDI Smith regime, leading to more than 30,000 casualties of a bitter and vicious rural war. The Commonwealth pursued its campaign through a special CHOGM, appropriately in Africa (Lagos) in January 1966, when it launched an interesting initiative — a Sanctions Committee, which later became the Commonwealth Committee on South Africa, and which both monitored the UN sanctions being developed against rebel Rhodesia, and also pointed the way to the later Commonwealth sanctions strategy against apartheid. In addition, a training programme was begun which educated future Zimbabweans outside Smith's state: over 4000 benefitted from this practical aid. Through the 1970s, Commonwealth involvement in the various initiatives to end white minority rule in Rhodesia continued, culminating in the Lusaka Accord of 1979. This provided the grand plan taken up by the British authorities to achieve a cease fire and bring together the leading players in the Lancaster House negotiations. Commonwealth observers monitored the first democratic, non-racial elections in Zimbabwe, leading to the 1980 victory of Robert Mugabe's liberation movement.

A second, highly significant area of Commonwealth involvement in peacemaking within the region, concerned what later became the republic of Namibia. In the form of 'South-west Africa', the territory had been under Mandate to the Union of South Africa since the Versailles Settlement of 1918. It was a Mandate South Africa declined to relinquish as part of African decolonization. The Commonwealth became involved through its general support of African liberation from colonialism, and specifically through support of the crucial UN Resolution 435 of 1978, which had proposed a blue print for self-government. Once again, as in central Africa, a liberation war had followed, involving external agencies in Angola as part a of larger Cold War conflict. Only in 1988 did the possibility of a negotiated settlement become likely, and the Commonwealth hereafter played significant roles in bringing 'Namibia' into existence: monitoring elections, providing technical training and expertise for the administrative elite who came to staff the bureaucracy, as well as offering distance education services for exiled Namibians in the surrounding settlement camps, pending independence and a return to their home state. When independence came — on 21 March 1990 — it seemed appropriate that the new 'Namibia' should enter the Commonwealth as its latest African member.

A third major initiative for the region was the Commonwealth role in the creation of SADCC — the 'Southern African Development Co-ordination Conference' — a grouping made up, of eight Commonwealth states most involved in the challenge to apartheid. SADCC aimed to establish programmes which could draw upon Commonwealth resources for such key infrastructure elements as transport and industry, mining and agriculture, education and training. Out of SADCC there grew an even larger Commonwealth scheme extending well beyond the original 8 participating states, to include financial as well as diplomatic commitments to peacemaking. Education was a major focus of support, with schools' programs operating in 6 of the front line states, through which thousands of younger black South Africans were given a broad range of general and technical skills. A range of 'Nassau Fellowships' — initiated at a key West Indian CHOGM (1985) gave support for apartheid exiles to gain further higher education overseas. From 1988 there also existed a very interesting Commonwealth initiative to assist Mozambique with a special fund focussed on economic development and infrastructure growth which was administered through the CFTC (the Commonwealth's technical agency) and supported at a significant level by contributions from 18 Commonwealth states. Mozambique had not secretly entered the Commonwealth, but its difficult position within the overall problems of security and peacemaking in what can be termed 'apartheid Africa' influenced Commonwealth states to include it in regional strategies for Southern Africa as a whole.

Outside these specific, yet wide-ranging regional initiatives, the Commonwealth has been a key player in the international diplomacy aimed at ending apartheid and bringing about a 'New South Africa'. As apartheid itself attempted to tighten its grip on South African society, in the name of a perverted theory of 'parallel development' for rigidly defined race groups, so the Commonwealth was moved by its strongly African and Asian membership to increase its own pressures on the regime itself, not least by drawing ever more tightly the international net of economic and cultural sanctions. Sport was also drawn into the campaign against apartheid. The Gleneagles Agreement of 1977 set codes for contact with South Africa that ultimately proved to be highly effective in isolating the racist practices of the state in its international sporting connections. Combined with financial sanctions, the sporting boycotts came to play a significant role in pressuring white South Africa to enter the negotiating phase of change.

In 1985 the Commonwealth produced an Accord which drew together its stance and policy towards apartheid, a strong declaration of intent to support the peacemaking process. To further that Accord, and in a growing mood of concern over the practises of apartheid and the human costs involved, the Commonwealth decided on a direct approach to the South African authorities through a small but significant mission by several of its senior leaders — quaintly termed the 'Eminent Persons Group'. Chaired by Malcolm Fraser of Australia, and including General Obazanja of Nigeria, it made three visits to South Africa in an attempt to initiate a peacemaking dialogue. The report of these several visits, in *Mission to South Africa* —

published as a Penguin paperback with vivid Malcolm Fraser
photographs of apartheid in practice — revealed the sheer
difficulty of furthering the peace-making process by words
alone.

In many ways, the EPG missions discovered how little the
South Africans had altered since the failure of the 1960/61
diplomacy to move the edifice of apartheid towards 'reform' and
ultimate elimination. Indeed, just to make their resolve plain, the
South African state followed discussions with the EPG members
by staging major military assaults on several front-line states.
The ANC looked ever more to its military wing, while the
Commonwealth itself came to place increasing importance on a
range of sanctions to be applied against South Africa in an
attempt to bring the state to its knees — or at least to the
negotiating table — through financial, trading, sporting,
education and even people-to-people isolating sanctions.
Moreover, the Commonwealth worked hard to stiffen the
resolve of the major UN members, beginning with the USA, but
also including EC states.

A group of seven Commonwealth representatives met in
London in 1986 to further this quest. Despite the dissenting view
of the British conservative government under Mrs Thatcher —
which still preferred constructive engagement by personal
diplomacy to actual sanctions — it agreed to a campaign of
trying to influence the policy of the European states and of the
United States. The Vancouver CHOGM in the following year
accordingly produced the noted 'Okanagan Statement', a
program for action on peacemaking in Southern Africa. It
accepted the EPG's concept of aiming to facilitate negotiation and
affirmed the role of the CFMSA to evaluate and co-ordinate the
pressure of sanctions, while continuing its work in the region by
assisting the frontline states in a variety of infrastructure projects.
To what extent these involved indirect/direct assistance to the
liberation forces in the frontier conflicts became a source of
controversy in countries such as Australia.

It was certainly highly significant that each CHOGM from
New Delhi (1983), Nassau (1985) and Vancouver (1987), through
to Kuala Lumpur (1989) and Harare (1991), had as a first item of
business the progress of peacemaking in Southern Africa, with a

key concern being the role and effectiveness of sanctions as a non-violent means to the ending of apartheid. Commonwealth leaders could accordingly feel a certain gratification when, following the FW De Klerk's accession to power in South Africa (August 1989), the process of internal reform was at last initiated with the 'unbanning' of African nationalist parties, the release of Mr Mandela and other ANC leaders, and the call for a beginning to negotiated change through an interim government and a new constitution (to replace that of 1910, as modified in 1961 and 1981).

But the Commonwealth contribution to this process was actually not pre-eminent in terms of international organizations and member states — despite the sometimes triumphalist claims of certain Commonwealth leaders. In truth, the historical balance-sheet is likely to show that the key forces in moving the South African state to a negotiating stage were the financial sanctions, in which the Commonwealth had been relatively unimportant, and the diplomatic presence of the great powers at the UN, again with little Commonwealth input, given that the United Kingdom was a very reluctant player in the sanctions process. Yet what can be fairly said, is that the Commonwealth was significant in the creation of a climate of opinion which influenced the international community in the adoption of formal sanctions and in the isolating process that made South Africa into the polecat state of the globe.

The fall of the Soviet system and the collapse of international socialism, appear to have been the final elements in the political and economic chemistry that brought into being a negotiating phase of peacemaking in South Africa. But, once again, it could be argued that the Commonwealth had been a vital agency in establishing the notion of peacemaking by negotiation in the region. It was not insignificant that, after his release from detention, Nelson Mandela should pick out certain Commonwealth initiatives and states for appreciative acknowledgement. Also that, at a practical level, he should interact with the Commonwealth over the idea of a graduated removal of sanctions, in return for peacemaking reforms in South Africa itself — in May 1990 he met the CFMSA in Abuja (Nigeria) to discuss the notion, something then repeated at a more advanced stage at the Harare CHOGM in October 1991.

Sanctions and Peacemaking

Thus the Harare Declaration represented the fruition of a long history of Commonwealth pressure on apartheid. Yet it was also a document for the moment. Apartheid was no more than partially ended; Nelson Mandela came to Harare as a free man but a man without civil rights. Reform and change had begun in South Africa — partly through the ending of 'petty apartheid', partly through the state simply recognizing that it has ultimately failed to regulate inter-group relations. But that 'beginning' had been both dramatic and modest. Some commentators saw the De Klerk initiatives as part of a 'strategy' to secure white authority through complex constitutional arrangements of 'power-sharing', rather than a simple decolonizing 'transfer of power'. More still, the means and mechanisms by which this peacemaking would take place were still uncertain at the time of Harare. Commonwealth leaders therefore remained concerned to use such leverage as sanctions provided to move along the peacemaking process, and to find ways in which the Commonwealth could play a brokerage role in the actual negotiating events and councils from which a new South Africa might emerge.

Three levels of sanction mechanisms were now identified as Commonwealth peacemaking initiatives appropriate to the changing political environment within South Africa. Following the principles agreed at the early (May) CFMSA in Delhi, there was to be a 'reward' for the De Klerk administration at least embarking on a reform process. South Africa was to come in from the cold of international relations with the ending of all people-to-people sanctions, including the re-establishment of air links and sporting contacts. The Harare Declaration (Section 22, 'Sanctions') explained its general approach:

> Heads of Government expressed the hope that the stage would be reached when the situation in South Africa would justify reconsideration of their sanctions policy against South Africa. They recalled that the purpose of sanctions had always been to

bring about a peaceful end to apartheid through the promotion of negotiations between the Government and the acknowledged representatives of the black majority. In recognition of the crucial role sanctions had played in bringing about the changes thus far, they agreed to continue to use effective forms of pressure to assure a successful final outcome to the conflict in South Africa. Accordingly (subject to the proviso in the following paragraph) they endorsed the programmed management approach, elaborated by the Commonwealth Committee of Foreign Ministers on Southern Africa, linking any change in the application of sanctions to the taking of real and practical steps to end apartheid.

A conditional 'stage two' easing of economic sanctions was foreshadowed, subject to satisfactory progress in negotiated change in South Africa: or as the Declaration put it, 'when appropriate transitional mechanisms had been agreed', enabling 'all the parties to participate' in those internal negotiations. Financial sanctions, and the arms embargo, were to be kept in place, pending agreement on the negotiated test of a 'democratic constitution'. The British prime minister, now Mr John Major, dissented from this timetable of leveraged peacemaking, and stressed instead the importance of immediate re-investment in South Africa, to spur economic growth and job creation as a basis from a new order of South African society.

Section 22 of the final Harare Communique also detailed this ongoing Commonwealth involvement with change in the region.

- the arms embargo, applied by the United Nations and supported by a variety of specific Commonwealth measures, should remain in force until a new post-apartheid South African government is firmly established, with full democratic control and accountability.

- the most demonstrably effective of all sanctions — financial sanctions — including lending by international financial institutions such as the IMF and World Bank — should be lifted only when agreement is reached on the text of a new democratic constitution, unless a contrary recommendation is made by agreement at the proposed All-Party Conference, or by an interim government.

- other economic sanctions, including trade and investment measures, should be lifted when appropriate transitional mechanisms have been agreed which would enable all the parties to participate fully and effectively in negotiations;

- people to people sanctions, namely consular and visa restrictions, cultural and scientific boycotts, restrictions on tourism promotion and the ban on direct air links should be lifted immediately in view of progress made in overcoming obstacles to negotiations and the need to give external support and encouragement to democratic anti-apartheid organisations in South Africa and to permit free interaction with them. The ban on air links would be lifted on condition that South African Airways (SAA) and other South African airlines proceed with appropriate affirmative action programmes.

The caveats which the British expressed on this approach were still emphatic, but they were now expressed in more diplomatic language. Gone was the heyday of Thatcherism, and now a more progressive view of peacemaking and economic growth in South Africa was offered.

The British Prime Minister stressed the importance of foreign investment in restoring growth to the South African economy and the need for decision now if the current economic decline was to be halted in time for the inauguration of South Africa's first majority government. It is for this reason that, while agreeing with the lifting of 'people sanctions' and the maintenance of the arms embargo, he did not agree with the recommendation of the Committee, on the time scale for lifting economic and financial sanctions.

There was to be no separate communique to embarrass the Commonwealth and lessen the impact of its peacemaking work.

The same careful diplomacy marked the resolution on the tendentious issue of sporting contacts. Hence the Heads, apparently easily, resolved to end isolation, subject to particular reforms.

Heads of Government were encouraged by the recent considerable progress in the evolution of a unified and non-racial sports movement in South Africa and welcomed the decision of the International Olympic Committee to grant recognition to the National Olympic Committee of South Africa. They agreed to continue to encourage these developments and, where appropriate, to provide assistance, they stressed the need for each sporting code to provide assistance to sportsmen and women disadvantaged by apartheid. They agreed that restrictions in respect of a particular sport be lifted when the following criteria have been met:

- the formal endorsement of the achievement of unity by the appropriate representative non-racial sporting organization in South Africa;

- readmittance to the relevant international governing

- agreement of the appropriate non-racial sporting organization within South Africa to resume international competition.

Yet beyond the past and present role of the Commonwealth at Harare, there was also a certain searching for future roles. The Secretary-General seemed determined to see the Commonwealth adopt a new set of principles, to take the organization into the 1990s and beyond, just as the Singapore Declaration had earlier (1971) attempted to reflect a new, post-colonial Commonwealth. Indeed, Chief Anyaoku was plainly concerned to find a broad role for Commonwealth post-apartheid: human rights, good government and economic development were therefore prominent among a new set of minimum goals for the international organization whose usefulness has often been questioned, not least in an environment of many international and regional organizations in global politics.

The unfinished business of apartheid and the enduring commitment of many Commonwealth members to see through the peacemaking process — perhaps even the diplomatic atavism of Commonwealth initiatives involving South Africa — also appeared to ensured continuing involvement in the region. The return of a new South Africa to the Commonwealth as a full member deeply attracted some African members, who saw it as a logical recognition of common regional interests. Out of sentiment, the Old Dominions and the UK, however, saw a certain fruition in closing the circle on the 1961 departure.

For a variety of reasons, therefore, the HOD's at Harare agreed on the interesting sentence in the final communique which very much looked to shaping a future history in declaring that the Commonwealth 'must remain ready to assist the negotiating process in ways that would be found helpful by the

parties concerned'. What would this mean in practice? Some
thought it pointed to a new EPG, this time acting in a broker's
role. Others thought more modestly and focussed on the
emissary role of the Secretary-General, a hope which came closer
to reality in the year immediately following the Harare CHOGM.
Almost immediately after the summit Chief Anyaoku proceeded
to South Africa , and talked with all the main parties in the
evolving negotiating peace process. He was then able to report
in detail to the ten members of the curiously named HLAG — the
Commonwealth High Level Appraisal Group which had been
created at the 'K-L' summit, to consider the future of the
Commonwealth.

The result has been interesting. The Commonwealth has
very closely monitored the peacemaking process in South Africa,
and the Secretary-General has subsequently made several visits
to South Africa, expressing deep concern at the growing violence
in the nation, apprehension at the collapse of the Codesa talks,
and willingness to play any intermediary role requested. But
there is, so far, no sign that Commonwealth initiatives have had
any appreciable effect on South African developments. Chief
Anyaoku has been politely received by the De Klerk cabinet and
warmly welcomed by the ANC. Commonwealth observers have
been included in the Codesa process.

There the Commonwealth initiatives end. A role as honest
broker is clearly not practical politics: South Africa has
determined to solve its own negotiating settlement. And yet
what is also striking is that the Commonwealth is *not* necessarily
the preferred international agency to facilitate peacemaking
when the internal parties concerned have come to the painful
view that an external monitoring element is needed in the
conflicted public scene of South Africa. It is to the United
Nations that South Africa has lately turned when exploring
possible international monitoring and investigation of the
escalating violence.

Mediating or Meddling?

Why is this? The short answer is that the South African
government holds to the view that, if it has to accept

international involvement in the peacemaking process, then it will engage with the major international organization: the United Nations. South Africa sees no special relationship with the Commonwealth of Nations — despite the Commonwealth's self designated role, its African composition, and the Union of South Africa's Commonwealth membership over the 50 years 1910-61. Indeed, the National Party Government of South Africa has, since its 1948 accession to power, held a sceptical if not hostile view of the Commonwealth. The very African membership of the Commonwealth, which attracts the ANC, naturally repels the South African government. Finally, since the US commitment to 'constructive engagement', and the fall of the Soviet Bloc, South African external relations have increasingly been built on bilateral relations with the United States in its now pre-eminent role in the international arena. The Commonwealth hardly seems pertinent in that reading of global politics, while the United Nations has been the focus of international action, notably in the Middle East and Eastern Europe. Even the Organization of African Unity (OAU) has more meaning for a potential new South Africa than the defunct Commonwealth linkage and involvement.

This perspective does not, of course, fully reflect all the current external views about mediation in South African peacemaking. International commentators have pointed to four major organizations who could be expected to play a significant role in any external peacemaking, or peacekeeping role, in an increasingly unstable South Africa: the United Nations, the Commonwealth of Nations, the Organization of African Unity, and the European Community. Diplomats within each organizations have followed the South African reform and negotiating process with close attention to the common problem of how the constitutional settlement might be rescued from a conflicted local political environment of stalemate and violence. Such urgent discussions, and the projection of possible plans for international mediation, have been somewhat melodramatically presented by the South African press, ever sensitive to the role of outsiders in regional peacemaking. The *Weekly Mail* of 10 July 1992 reported on these diplomatic developments in a dramatic article headlined

International Beehive Ready to Swarm

Hundreds of would-be peacemakers are on standby around the world, ready to swarm into South Africa to avert further confrontation between the government and the African National Congress.

Four key organizations which span the globe are urgently consulting on how best to co-ordinate roles for the teams of fact-finders, observers, monitors and intermediaries they hope to send here. (p.3)

One option canvassed in the press in mid 1991 was a *combined* diplomatic mission, which could draw from the differing strengths of the various organizations, with the Commonwealth acting as the experienced African peacemaker. Another proposition focussed on Commonwealth and OAU peacemaking with the UN and EC devoting their energies to restoring the internal negotiating processes.

None of these elaborate diplomatic ideas came to immediate fruition. And even the offer of Commonwealth Secretary-General Chief Anyaoku, to send an immediate team of experts led by 'eminent persons', with policing and military resources, to work in with the South African Peace Accord arrangements, was not implemented. The South African administration had no intention of allowing an alternate source of authority to determine the political environment and security of the country. Chief Anyaoka, and UN Secretary-General Boutros Boutros-Ghali, remained at arms-length from the actual dynamics of South African politics as the winter and the violence of mid 1992 deepened.

However, it was the escalation of that very violence, the tragedy of events such as the Boipatong massacre, the suspicion of government complicity in the inter-ethnic conflict, leading to the ANC withdrawal from the Codesa process, which finally forced the De Klerk administration to accept the 'indignity' of help from external agencies. To some degree, the dramatic involvement of the UN organization in later July (1992) at the behest of the South African themselves, was actually an expansion of a practice already set in motion — the use of outside experts as 'observers' and 'advisers' in several peacemaking internal organizations. Codesa itself had included invited international observers, while the Goldstone Commission of enquiry into police actions had come to include jurists, police officers, even academics, from interested foreign nations, including notably those in the Commonwealth. At the core of the matter was the determination of the De Klerk cabinet to limit external involvement in domestic peacemaking to observation and analysis, rejecting all offers from honest brokers, facilitators and intermediaries. Equally significant, the ANC took a different position, seeing the involvement of a major international body as bringing crucial pressure to bear on the government by exposing its partisan security actions and also by providing a peacekeeping force for the urban areas. This very difference between Government and ANC deeply complicated the potential role to be designated by or for the agencies of the international community. As the *Weekly Mail* rightly commented, in the midst of the uncertainty after the Boipatong killings and funeral:

> A major difficulty seen by international authorities is that De Klerk and Nelson Mandela expect different things from the international community. De Klerk would want it to urge the ANC back to Codesa; Mandela would want it to condemn the government's handling of the security situation and its perceived attempts to perpetuate white supremacy in new constitutional forms (10-16 July 1992).

In the end, however, it was the sheer scale of violence and the destabilization of South Africa which forced the issue of outside involvement in the peacemaking process. The Government and the ANC had reached a standoff. The former could not or would not control the security forces and the violence; the latter refused to negotiate with a state regime which it declined to trust, but in a situation in which it was still committed to a negotiated settlement. A battle of rival memorandums, putting the case for Government and then the ANC in the week of 6 July 1992, brought South Africa to the edge of political chaos. Mandela rejected a formal meeting with De Klerk to re-open discussions, and it was left to lower level contacts between Roelf Meyer (Constitutional Development Minister) and Cyril Ramaphosa

(ANC Secretary-General) to look for a way out of the impasse. In answer to Mandela's charge to De Klerk, 'to find a way within yourself to recognize the gravity of the crisis', Meyer now offered softer words, remarking that 'the ANC has raised a number of matters of justifiable concern to all parties'.

The practical effect of these discussions was to move South Africa closer to some kind of external mediation which could break the impasse and avoid catastrophe. De Klerk still declared emphatically that the Government would 'discharge its duty at all costs and would not allow South Africa to slide back into isolation and helpless stagnation'.[2] 'We face a few difficult weeks ... But the Government will not sit in a corner, cry, worry, stagnate'. The ANC declared, in response, that the crisis was of the Government's own making. Not only were they implicated in the violence, but as Mandela said in his letter to De Klerk, they refused to negotiate for a democratic South Africa — by constantly focussing on the short-term transitional arrangements which could entrench National Party control. Mandela's challenge was blunt: 'There is a way forward. It depends on how the NP Government responds to our efforts to break the negotiations deadlock and takes practical steps to end the violence.'

With both major 'parties' locked in this public conflict, the international community, through the United Nations, now offered its good offices. There was to be a debate at a special sitting of the UN Security Council at which all major players could put their views about what form mediation might take. Neither Government nor ANC rushed to this option, but it was a way out at a point of public impasse. The US Assistant Security of State for Africa, Herman Cohen, liaised with the Government and ANC in the hurried preparations for the UN debate scheduled for Wednesday 15 July 1992 in New York. 'Mediation could get talks going' declared the South African press, as much in hope as assurance.[3] Simon Barber reported in his 'Washington letter', on 14 July, under the headline 'UN can provide support for the right options',

> The UN Security Council meets tomorrow to help South Africa out of its current impasse. To most of the permanent members ... this

> is not a proper use of the Council's time. Unlike the Balkan crisis, South Africa's problems do not constitute a threat to international peace.
>
> Nonetheless, if UN Secretary-General Boutros Boutros-Ghali and the permanent members can keep their heads . . . this week's seminar should prove a valuable exercise. With all nineteen Codesa members, plus nine African foreign ministers deputed by the OAU, having the right to speak, the superficial theatre will be unedifying. Beneath the surface, however, important business should be transacted.[4]

And so it was. By the following week, and after a most extraordinary session of South African politics being played out live on international television from the UN Headquarters in New York, a 'peace mission' was launched, headed by the former US Secretary of State, Cyrus Vance.

His charter was to make recommendations to 'assist in bringing an effective end to violence and in creating conditions for negotiations leading towards a peaceful transition to a democratic, non-racial and United South Africa'. More immediately and practically, as one news correspondent pointed out, the Vance mission was intended 'to produce proposals enabling stalled constitutional negotiations to resume, without loss of face by the main players'.[5]

The effort of having to accept external aid had a certain salutary impact on the politics of negotiation in South Africa. The major players all claimed to have influenced the 'success' of involving the UN, but the reality was both more complex and more of a lesson in how not to resolve the process of peacemaking. Under the ironic heading of 'A drama for heroes', one South African newspaper cut to the heart of the matter.

> South Africa's political leaders disgraced themselves before the world with their partisan, confrontational rhetoric at the United Nations Security Council. The unanimous decision of the Council to send a special envoy to South Africa to help restart talks should be seen as an humiliation. . .[for all] who have played self-interest above national interest so hard that they have had to admit the need for outside help. But the intrusion of the UN envoy nevertheless marks a new beginning of sorts. Regardless of kudos, it is the needed moment for reflection. . . What South Africa wants urgently, whether the UN envoy is breathing over its shoulder or

not , is to get to grips itself with the scourge of violence and to show an open-mindedness on constitutional options.'[6]

The people of South Africa waited for that resolution to its deep divisions and inequalities as the winter of 1992 progressed.

A Lesson from History?

Perspective is very hard to establish with processes which are still in motion.   But recent events in South Africa involving external agency in the evolution of peacemaking do appear to suggest the importance of a certain 'lesson' from contemporary history.

The transfer of power from colonial to indigenous rulers has become a key feature of this aspect of international history since the Second World War.   And that process has rarely been accomplished in a completely peaceful manner.   But it was invariably more orderly and more controlled in certain political environments.   Perhaps the decisive feature of these successful 'demissions' of power was the degree to which the imperial or metropolitan authorities could negotiate their withdrawal, by timetable, in favour of a national movement which had coherence and legitimacy in the eyes of the citizenry.   In effect, nationalists then speedily became rulers as previous rulers became the departing guests.

On the other hand, this scenario worked least well, and often involved greatest conflict and violence, when there was no dominating external power, and no unified local nationalist power.   A worst-case scenario usually involved a pluralistic colonial society, constituted of normally several nationalist or ethnic parties, but also settler and migrant communities. Whether it was Kenya or 'Rhodesia', Algeria or the French Pacific settlements, the Belgian Congo or Dutch Indies, a simple historical rule stood out: a peaceful decolonization seemed impossible when the metropolitan power was challenged by its own migrating populations overseas, previously its local collaborative agents of empire.

South Africa appeared to be a compound expression of this historical experience. It had enjoyed self-government since 1910, when its own form of 'decolonization' had effectively removed the 'imperial factor' from local politics. Thereafter it was impossible for any simple transfer of power to take place from European power to local mass movement. The capacity of the imperial authorities to maintain stability, law and order, through the contested politics of change, was long gone from the South African environment. Any change here would have been negotiated and implemented by entirely local forces. Moreover, there has been every sign that the intention of the National Party Government was not to engage in a transfer of power, as a declining force: but rather to devise a 'sharing of power' on terms which should be as advantageous as possible for the European population who claimed South Africa as 'home'. The contest for power could not be regulated by any external agency. The challenge for South Africa, the Government and the liberation forces, was to make this political dispensation in a way satisfactory to its contending groups. And also to implement that process of fundamental change in peaceful ways for all its peoples.

Codesa has symbolized that aspiration to shape a democratic society for South Africans by South Africa. But whether that ideal of peacemaking can contain the forces engaged in the struggle for South Africa is an open question. It may well become necessary, as the recent UN involvement demonstrated, for international agencies to assist the peacemaking process. The UN 'fact-finding' mission suggests a basis for further involvement.

More broadly, since its 1961 departure from the Commonwealth, the international organization had 'played a leading role in the international campaign against apartheid', as the Harare Communique suggested in section 9 of its October 1991 text. 'Now that the goal is closer than ever before, heads of Government consider ways in which the Commonwealth should continue to play a significant role in progress towards a non-racial democratic South Africa'.

That role could include a range of duties, from monitoring an electoral process, to involvement in the emergence of a New South Africa. The Commonwealth itself might even be strengthened by the return of South Africa to membership. In an era involving such momentous events as the ending of the Soviet system, the potential emergence of a new democratic South Africa seemed not utterly impossible. But much still depends on the actions of the domestic forces in the region, coupled perhaps with realistic or appropriate support from external agencies — such as that of the Commonwealth.

As this volume goes to the press, that very issue has been brought into sharp focus by the further violence in the Ciskei on 8 September 1992. At least 28 people were been shot dead as the Ciskei Security forces opened fire on a peaceful ANC march of 60,000 protesters in the town of Bisho in the Eastern Cape. Senator Evans, as Australia's foreign minister, expressed the horror of the international community when he remarked 'this is a massacre that is to be added to that ever-growing list, including Sharpville and Boipatong, and is a direct and inevitable backlash of the oppressive apartheid system'. The Australian Government looked to the South African administration 'to quickly take action to ensure those responsible for the killings are brought to justice'.

But he also, significantly, argued that the tragedy demonstrated the necessity for a really effective international observer presence within South Africa. 'United Nations observers are to take up their task this week and we're presently discussing with the Commonwealth what we might appropriately do by way of supplementary exercise in that respect'. Prime Minister Paul Keating underlined Australia's willingness to act as 'peacekeepers', within an international initiative under United Nations or Commonwealth auspices.

The awesome African drought continues to haunt the region, with hope resting in especially good spring rains. Peacemaking also awaits on its own spring of human magnanimity and reconciliation. In the words of one shocked editorial, on this peacemaking process, 'The agony of South Africa, it would seem, has only just begun'.[7]

Notes

1   This paper based on researches conducted while I was attending the 1991 CHOGM in Harare, Zimbabwe. Unless otherwise

indicated, quotations from CHOGM events and speakers are drawn from *The Harare Communique, October 1991*, and *The Commonwealth Today* (October 1991) by the Commonwealth Secretariat. For the history and dynamics of the Commonwealth I have drawn especially from: W.D. McIntyre, *The Commonwealth of Nations: Origins and Impact, 1869-1971* (Minneapolis: University of Minnesota Press, 1977) and *The Significance of the Commonwealth, 1965-1990* (Basingstoke: Macmillan, 1991); William Dale, *The Modern Commonwealth* (London: Butterworths, 1983), M.M. Ball, *The Open Commonwealth* (Durham, N.C: Duke University Press, 1971) and P.B. Harris, *The Commonwealth* (London: Longman, 1975). Margaret Doxey has written an incisive account of the workings of the international organization in *The Commonwealth Secretariate and Contemporary Commonwealth* (Basingstoke : Macmillan, 1989) as well as a shrewd assessment of its effectiveness in *The Commonwealth in a Changing World* (Canadian Institute of International Affairs, 1992). The major changes in the membership and politics of the organization are excellently documented in the *Surveys of Commonwealth Affairs* by Nicholas Mansergh and J.D.B. Miller, (London: Oxford University Press, 1952, 1958, 1964, 1974). South Africa's dramatic impact 'in' and 'out' of the Commonwealth can be traced in TRH Davenport, *South Africa: a Modern History* (London: Macmillan, 1991); F. Hayes, 'South Africa's departure from the Commonwealth, 1960-61' *The International History Review*, II, 3 (July 1980) pp.453-84; Stephen Chan, 'The Commonwealth as an international organization: constitutionalism, Britain and South Africa, *The Round Table* (October 1989) 312: 393-412; and O. Akinrinade,"Africa and the Commonwealth, 1960-80', *Round Table* (January 1989) 309: 33-53. The EPG Report has been published as *Mission to South Africa* (Harmondsworth: Penguin, 1986). For the Australia's contribution to the Harare CHOGM, see D.M. Schreuder, 'The Commonwealth Connection: a contemporary history and prospect', in *Diplomacy in the Marketplace*, edited by J.R. Angel and R. Boyce (Melbourne: Longman Cheshire, 1991).

2   *Natal Mercury*, 10 July 1992.

3   Ibid.

4   Ibid, 14 July 1992..

5   Arlene Getz, in *Sydney Morning Herald*, 22 July 1992.

6   *Weekend Mercury*, 18 July 1992.

7   *Canberra Times*, 9 September 1992.

5

Explaining the Death Throes of Apartheid

Norman Etherington

Success has a thousand fathers; failure is an orphan.

Introduction

A wag has remarked that in ten years time it will be impossible to find anyone in South Africa who ever supported apartheid.[1] The epidemic of amnesia sweeping the subcontinent today resembles the miraculous disappearance of French Nazis after the Allied liberation — there were no collaborators; everyone fought with the Resistance. Diverse champions, personal, economic and technological, claim to have slain the dragon of apartheid. Two remarks by ex-President Ronald Reagan on the reasons for the collapse of Soviet communism could readily be adapted to South African circumstances. When asked to name his greatest achievement, he replied with a boyish grin, 'Some folks say I won the Cold War'. On another occasion, Reagan attributed the fall of communism entirely to the silicon chip. At one end of the spectrum, the emergence of a New South Africa is credited solely to FW De Klerk; at the other end, to electronic transfers of capital. Although historians are notoriously reluctant to offer authoritative accounts of current events, the searchlight of historical perspective can help to distinguish improbable propositions from plausible ones.

Commentators on South African affairs frequently fall into a fallacy akin to what historians of the United States call the doctrine of American exceptionalism.[2] The fallacy is to exempt South Africa from patterns of causality that rule elsewhere in the world. It has been around for a long time, epitomized in such expressions as 'complex South Africa', 'puritans in South Africa', 'a chosen people'. Believers in South African exceptionalism employ the doctrine not only to differentiate local racism from racism in North America and defunct settler colonies elsewhere, but also to wall South Africa off from the rest of the African continent. A witty scholar has ridiculed the tendency to draw a 'boerewors line' (after boerewors, a South African sausage favoured at weekend barbecues), at the Limpopo River, because 'they do things different up north'. In the rest of this chapter, which attempts a preliminary sorting out of explanations currently being offered for the death of apartheid, strenuous attempts will be made to avoid South African exceptionalism and to ignore the boerewors line. Under no circumstances should this essay be mistaken for a potted history of the recent past. It aims to trace patterns of causation, not to supply a panoramic sweep.

FW De Klerk as Liberator

Admirers of the reforming State President reach for the top shelf when they search for historical figures who brought about comparable changes from within a power structure. De Klerk is Disraeli leaping in the dark, De Gaulle making peace with Algeria, Lincoln freeing the slaves. Another frequently drawn comparison, likening De Klerk to Mikhail Gorbachev, is a good test of the premise that a single human being can engineer a revolution from the top, because the two statesmen are exact contemporaries. The comparison is appealing in many ways. Each astounded the world by presiding over fundamental changes in systems which had been widely thought to be impervious to change except through invasion or violent revolution. Each was subjected to vilification by hardline conservatives and undercut by elements within the police and

security forces.   Each saw national unity threatened by a
Pandora's box of murderous ethnic nationalisms.   Each helped
pull armies away from debilitating campaigns beyond national
frontiers: Gorbachev in Afghanistan, De Klerk in Angola.   Each
watched with dismay as his state lost the ability to rule in vast
regions of the country.   Each vigorously promoted the virtues of
a competitive market economy.   Each man presented the illusion
of working hard to put himself out of a job.

It is striking, however, that neither man garbs himself
rhetorically in messiah's robes.   Each has steadfastly maintained
that necessity was the mother of his alleged inventions, and
insisted that he could no more stand against the forces of change
than Canute could command the waves.   These claims should
not be lightly dismissed as false modesty.   Neither Gorbachev
nor De Klerk stepped onto the world's stage as a prophet from
the   wilderness.   Gorbachev   had   for   decades   served
unobtrusively among the band of brothers who filled the top
posts in the Soviet bureaucracy.   De Klerk possessed all the usual
attributes and attitudes of the Afrikaner *nomenklatura*.   When
they embarked upon new paths, they moved as leaders of packs,
not as lone wolves.   Attempts to turn the clock back by picking
off the leaders failed because most of the state apparatus stood
firmly on the side of change.   This was notably the case with the
attempted coup against Gorbachev.   In South African politics it
might be said that De Klerk only came to power because the elite
group would no longer tolerate the obstinacy of his predecessor,
PW Botha.   It is not a denial of the contingent ability of
individuals to affect the course of history to observe that the
celebrated reformers to whom Gorbachev and De Klerk are often
compared were also cogs in larger machines.   Disraeli's 1867
Reform Bill extended a franchise which Gladstone was sure to
have amended when the Liberals took office.   De Gaulle came to
power in 1958, only because the faltering coalitions of the Fourth
Republic had failed to deal with the intractable war in Algeria.
Lincoln's Emancipation Proclamation was the result, not the
cause of the war waged over structural disparities between
North and South.

It is also worth noticing that De Klerk fans punctiliously
observe the boerewors line when comparing their idol to other

national leaders. No one likens him to Kenneth Kaunda or Daniel arap Moi, African politicians who have also reluctantly trod a path towards multi-party democracy. Still less do they admit comparisons with Angola, Zaïre or Liberia where loss of control over opposition forces and internal security forces has recently brought about dramatic changes. Movements away from state ownership and towards free markets have been as marked under black African leadership as under 'enlightened' Afrikaners. If De Klerk, as an individual, is credited with the leading role in bringing change to South Africa, then his black brothers north of the Limpopo must be equally assigned niches in the post-apartheid pantheon of African heroes. Scholars less entranced with Carlyle's Great Man theory of history will look beyond individuals when they seek to explain the simultaneous outbreak of democracy and free-market capitalism along the road from Cape to Cairo.

The End of History in Africa?

Francis Fukayama achieved instant international celebrity in 1989 by propounding the thesis that history, conceived by Hegel as the dialectical struggle of opposing ideas, had been brought to an end by economic development. Fukuyama sees liberal capitalism's victory over Soviet-led communism as only part of a larger world-wide movement toward democracy. He has lately applied his theory to the collapse of apartheid in an article written for the South Africa Foundation's journal,*South Africa International*.[3] Although his original thesis stressed the triumph of liberal capitalism as an idea, there is a materialist ghost in his Hegelian machine. The article on South Africa puts a heavy emphasis on forces of production. Urbanization, education, and the growth of a large middle class are, for Fukuyama, the universal harbingers of democracy. In South Africa he finds these three factors operating among Afrikaners over the last fifty years:

> . . . there is no question that economic change provides a very helpful environment for liberal democratic ideas to take hold. Middle-class societies with large numbers of college-educated,

urban professionals — those we have learned to call 'yuppies' in the 1980s — simply have a different type of politics than uneducated and illiterate smallholders in predominantly agrarian societies. In the latter, it is possible for authoritarian rulers to mobilize poorly educated followers into armies or death squads...

It is precisely the transformation from smallholder to yuppie that has occurred within South Africa's Afrikaner community over the past forty years. The unbanning of the ANC did not undermine the political base of the National Party among whites; if anything, De Klerk's support among whites is higher than it was when he first came into office. This indicates that he was not simply leading Afrikaner opinion by his surprising moves, but reflecting it as well.[4]

Thus, in Fukuyama's reading of South African history, the Afrikaners become again a chosen people — chosen not by God but by the marketplace. At first sight, this seems a breathtaking inversion of the ancient hope of British liberalism that capitalism would eventually wear down the Afrikaner's reactionary devotion to eighteenth-century ways of life. On reflection, however, it can be seen that Fukuyama restates rather than rejects the liberal paradigm. Capitalism is still the agent of change. The Afrikaners are acted upon rather than acting.

There has been a rash of similar analysis lately. Fukuyama is merely one in a chorus line of commentators congratulating capitalism for its victory over apartheid. RW Johnson of Oxford recalls that 'the struggle between Afrikaner nationalism and big business raged for decades, never achieving more than an uneasy truce'.[5] Michael Christie, Director of the Washington D.C. office of the South Africa Foundation, pronounces that 'apartheid collapsed because it was morally bankrupt and because it could not resist modernization or the will of black South Africans to break it', a will that Christie attributes to the urbanising effects of modernization.[6] Smirking behind such analysis is a jibe at scholars of the early nineteen seventies who used arguments from history to show that capitalism and apartheid made congenial bedfellows.[7] See, say the neo-conservative political commentators, we were right all along.

It is worth pausing for a moment to reflect on this claim, not because old scores need to be settled, but because there are implications for the future. Twenty years ago, attempts to argue that the requirements of capitalism were functionally and efficiently met by the apartheid state were condemned by liberals and conservatives as vulgar economic determinism. Paradoxically, Fukuyama, the professed champion of ideas, makes economic determinism respectable again on the right. To be sure, he cautions that 'economic development does not bring democracy . . . in an automatic or deterministic way' but he clearly believes that, in the last analysis, economic development dooms certain sorts of political regimes. In the long run. There's the rub. Fukuyama does not revisit the rose-coloured world of WW Rostow's *Stages of Economic Growth*. Liberty with affluence is not the certain destiny of every society which takes a first step onto the upward escalator of development. There must be urbanization, education and the growth of a substantial middle class. The attainment of those conditions among Afrikaners brought De Klerk and Codesa. But what kind of regime can we expect if majority rule brings government by an urbanized African electorate deficient in education and led by an anaemic middle class?

This is the pessimistic stinger in the tail of the upbeat message that democracy follows the flag of untrammelled capitalism. Fukuyama worries about the ANC.

> A good deal of the blame must be laid at the door of the ANC, which by promoting 'armed struggle' in decades past under slogans like 'liberation before education' sought to undermine the authority of local officials and to make the townships 'ungovernable'. By providing ideological sanction to what eventually became simple criminal behaviour, the ANC helped create a monster that it is no longer able to control, and with which it will have to deal once it comes to power.[8]

Irony is heaped upon irony. Township struggle, abetted by exiled ANC leadership, is blamed for threatening, not praised for advancing, the cause of democracy. Reversing his earlier argument that state sponsorship of Afrikaners during their transition from poor yokels to verligte yuppies made democracy possible, Fukuyama insists that any similar state-sponsored redistribution to blacks will wreck the country by wrecking the economy. If whites are not persuaded to stay by gutting the

economic clauses of the *Freedom Charter*, South Africa will be 'on
the road to becoming a Zambia, Zimbabwe, or Tanzania'.[9] In
that case, 'the end of history' in Africa will be like its beginning,
before the energizing advent of colonial rule.[10]

With this dire warning Fukuyama invokes the old nightmare
that Africa will cross the Limpopo and destroy the world the
settlers made. This fear is exacerbated in a dark prognosis lately
sketched by Samuel Decalo.[11] As a specialist in West African,
francophone politics working at a South African university,
Decalo is in an excellent position to view the continent as a
whole. However, his work on 'The Process, Prospects and
Constraints of Democratization in Africa', strictly observes the
boerewors line. There is no suggestion that De Klerk's
innovations might be causally or morphologically linked to
democratising commitments recently taken by more than half
the other sub-saharan African states. Indeed, South Africa is
only mentioned once, in an oblique reference to the ANC as a
'would be late-comer to the Marxist fold'.[12] Decalo is fairly
vague on the reasons for the simultaneous outpouring of
enthusiasm for multi-party systems. He thinks the Eastern
European example had something to do with it, as did the
withdrawal of Soviet assistance and pressure from Western aid
agencies. But apart from those external factors, Africa is trying
democracy out of sheer desperation because nothing else has
worked in this worst of all possible regions. In a grippingly
pessimistic conclusion with clear implications for South Africa,
Decalo doubts that democracy will take permanent root in such
uncongenial soil.

> Some countries — the more important ones, or those with greatest
> value to the world — are likely, with continued neo-colonial
> bondages and external aid keeping them in line, to surmount the
> 'obstacles' posed by democracy, developing relatively stable
> multiparty systems. But it is hard to escape the conclusion that
> many other African states, in the absence of constant munificent
> benefactors (and when the global fervour with 'democracy
> possibly goes out of vogue?) will be seen as a bad bet and let loose
> to drift their own way, backsliding into political strife, social chaos,
> single-party and military rule.[13]

This glum prophecy lends support to the conservative policies recommended to South Africa by Fukuyama. Slash government spending, clamp down on inflation, resist demands for welfare spending from the poor, open markets to the world, cut foreign debt, and the country *might just* maintain a semblance of democracy under black rule.

The People as Liberators

The left offers a parallel for each of the conservative explanations canvassed above. Each explanation likewise carries with it a hoped-for vision of the future. The leftwing version of heroic leadership , lacking a De Klerk, casts the township masses in the role of self-motivating liberators. This does not deny the importance of Nelson Mandela, a charismatic politician who does not suffer by comparison with any of the African leaders who spearheaded drives to independence in the nineteen fifties and sixties. Nkrumah, Kenyatta and many others did some time in what used to be called the University of Gaol, but none can match Mandela's miraculous feat of emerging after twenty-eight years with his charm and political savvy intact. There are two main obstacles to fixing on him as his people's liberator. The first is that De Klerk released him from prison when the revolution was already under way. The second is that most of the shine has worn off the image of charismatic African leadership in the course of the last thirty years.

Township masses make a plausible and attractive collective hero. Revolutionary spirits cherish a people's rising. Decades before Marx and Engels fluttered with hope at the sight of the Paris commune, Ledru-Rollin caught the ideal in an aphorism. 'I must follow them, for I am their leader'. The kind of spontaneous, creative violence Frantz Fanon celebrated in *Wretched of the Earth* appears to many observers to have energized the school children of Soweto in their 1976 protests. Those with a biblical cast of mind can recall with equal satisfaction Isaiah's prophecy that when lions lie down with lambs, 'a little child shall lead them'. This line of thought can, without straining, trace a direct line of descent from the Soweto protests through exile camps and the ungovernable townships of the eighties to the new order emerging in the nineties. And if the masses could make their own revolution against such a determined adversary, they can be counted on to resist future regimes who may try to oppress them or sell them out.

Alternative explanations of urban protest are put forward from diverse quarters. As we have seen, Fukuyama justifies his suspicion of the ANC by blaming its leadership for closing schools and inflaming townships, thereby creating 'a monster that it is no longer able to control'. The ANC would reject the charge stated that way, but would not wish to disclaim any role in promoting protests of the past. They want to be seen as leaders.   Definite conclusions about the causes of urban resistance over the last two decades can only be formed after painstaking empirical research. Although the evidence so far available is fragmentary, Shula Marks and Stanley Trapido have made an attempt to bring together new scholarship on this subject in the March 1992 number of the *Journal of Southern African Studies* .

The studies in their collection generally run counter to the idea that a single set of causes or leaders connect resistance movements since the nineteen fifties. Nozipho Diseko shows that the South African Students' Movement, which came to prominence at the time of the 1976 Soweto uprising, had only tenuous links to Black Consciousness, the ANC or the PAC.[14] According to Howard Barrell, events in Soweto challenged, rather than fulfilled ANC expectations, thereby provoking a major rethinking of strategy in the organization.[15] Even after that review, the ANC was caught by surprise when the UDF sprang into being in 1983.

Did the UDF, then, supply the brains behind the township violence over the next few years? The South African state thought so, but Jeremy Seekings' research indicates otherwise.[16] When the UDF attempted to steer or inspire localized revolts, it was subjected to state repression so intense that it lost all capacity to play a central coordinating role. Alexandra is a case in point for Charles Carter.[17] Although revolutionaries of various colours claimed to have helped transform near anarchy into organized cadres, the image of a community in rebellion was more powerful than the reality. Kumi Naidoo's study of 'youth resistance' in Durban likewise finds a complex cocktail of chemicals reacting with each other to produce a localized urban explosion.[18] No one party or leader can claim responsibility for the widespread disturbances. Nor did the people of various communities act magically in concert. Different things happened in different places at the same time.

Taken together, the studies brought together by Marks and Trapido do not disprove the hypothesis that people acted to liberate themselves. However, questions remain. Why did oppressed communities rise in the nineteen eighties and not before, when conditions for revolt were equally propitious? South Africa's horrendous statistics on poverty, disease and economic stagnation mock the idea of a 'revolution of rising expectations'. None of the interpretations so far considered explain the timing of events.

A New Phase in the Development of Capitalism in Southern Africa?

Although Fukuyama, Merle Lipton, RW Johnson and others consider the case now proved that apartheid was incompatible with the needs of business, less conservative students of the South African political economy do not admit to having been wrong. The thesis that the South African state continually adjusts itself to the needs of capitalism is not necessarily undermined by the events of the last twenty years. During the nineteen seventies dramatic developments in the world economy altered the environment in which South African business and the state operated. Gold went on a roller coaster ride after the demise of the Bretton Woods agreement. While OPEC oil shocks initially sent the price of gold into orbit, stagnation in other commodity prices and changes in gold mining technology destabilized the South African economy. By the mid-nineteen eighties scholars writing within the political economy tradition were saying that the state had been driven into a cul-de-sac.

One of those writers, Fuad Cassim, set out the essence of the case in 1988.[19] In addition to being hit by a general recession affecting the world's commodity producers, South Africa was handicapped by 'a specific structural malady of the its economy which was characterized by low productivity, growth and investment,' as well as the adoption of specific policies recommended to the government by the IMF.[20]   Financial deregulation in 1983 caused a massive currency devaluation. Interest rates, inflation and debt all moved in ways that imposed massive hardships on the poorest sections of the population. It was not the political agitation of the ANC or anyone else that made townships ungovernable:

> Against this background of deflationary policies, it becomes easier to understand why the Vaal Triangle erupted in September 1984 and unrest spread throughout the country.   Political 'ungovernability' was, in fact, preceded by economic mismanagement or rather lack of management and guidance. On 20 July 1985, the government declared a State of Emergency, and as investors began switching funds out of South Africa, imposed a debt freeze and a two-tier exchange rate.   At the same time, resistance in the country reached a new stage.   Though it has become fashionable to blame political events for the debt crisis, the economic developments outlined must be seen as interacting and intensifying political instability.

This sort of analysis takes De Klerk at his word when he claims to have no choice about bringing an end to apartheid; just as it takes seriously statements made by his predecessor, PW Botha, about the need to 'cross the Rubicon' and 'adapt or die'. The dire economic consequences of Botha's reversal of course eventually made his removal a necessity of state. So long as the townships could not be brought under control, investors withheld their capital and the devalued Rand imported inflation which, as part of a vicious circle, further exacerbated hardship in the townships. Confidence could only be restored if the government could find partners who possessed credibility in the townships. Hence the release of Mandela and the other dramatic developments of 1990. Following the same line of thinking, the future looks grim for any South African government that fails to beat inflation, attract investment and maintain real wages — a tall order indeed. Democratization will be merely the first step along a new and rugged road.

On the surface, this leftwing economic explanation resembles older analyses which linked state action to the needs of capital. However, there are important differences. The models devised by Harold Wolpe and others twenty years ago recognized that reliance on export of minerals and crops was a fact of life, but they otherwise paid little attention to external factors. Explanations for shifts in state policy were sought in the realms of production rather than exchange. South Africa was treated as an exceptional case on the African continent: the only country that had built a national economy relatively free of colonial domination from Europe. Segregation/apartheid was seen as an arrangement which conformed to the internal dynamics of a system independent enough to be said to be taking its own 'Prussian path' to modernization. In contrast, Cassim's evaluation of the economic forces fracturing the apartheid state emphasizes the critical role play by external forces: world commodity prices, the IMF, G7, European and American banks, international capital transfers.

Other scholars working on organized labour have also drawn attention to the critical importance of international economic developments. However some important recent scholarship points out that the trajectory of legal unionism in South Africa cannot be considered in isolation. Gay Seidman's comparative study of organized labour in South Africa and Brazil finds many parallels.[21] Dave Cooper extends the comparison to Chile and Argentina, concluding that complicated interactions between local and external forces led both to the toleration of unions by 'bureaucratic authoritarian' regimes and to their later politicization.[22]

In these attempts to link internal developments to international developments there is the germ of an explanatory framework which breaches the boerewors line and can link democratization in South Africa to similar movements in the rest of Africa and on other continents.

Explanations which Link International Forces to Democratization

In the long run it seems likely that the most convincing explanations for the South African Revolution will combine internal and external factors. F. van Zyl Slabbert, maverick politician and former leader of the Progressive Federal Party, has lately compiled one such explanation in the form of a list.[23] In addition to factors already noticed (urbanization, black unrest, personal leadership), he counts among the most important internal factors, population growth and expensively replicated social service and bureaucratic apparatuses. Slabbert divides external pressures into two categories, planned and unplanned.[24]

Unplanned	Planned
Changed relations between US and USSR	Conclusion that the war in Angola was untenable
Collapse of Eastern Europe	Withdrawal from Namibia
Decline of South Africa's share of world gold production	Sanctions
Decline of Africa as an area of geo-political influence	

Aside from changes in gold production, the items on both lists are closely related. Without the collapse of the Soviet Union and Eastern Europe, superpower competition for influence in Africa, including support for the war in Angola, might well have continued. Sanctions could never be truly effective so long as Western strategic planners feared that the demise of apartheid would strengthen Soviet influence in Africa. The end of communism blew an enormous hole in the ideology of white minority rule, invalidating most publicly acknowledged reasons for maintaining a large defence force. It fatally undermined the longstanding policy of treating the ANC as a Soviet surrogate at the same time that it cast doubt on the ability of the ANC to maintain the armed struggle.

The collapse of communism has had equally dramatic and related consequences for other African countries. Free guns are no longer on offer to sustain repression and rebellion. It will, of course, be some time before existing arms cease to make life miserable in the Horn of Africa and other notorious battlegrounds.[25] Nonetheless, the ability of anti-democratic regimes to make power grow from the barrels of guns is greatly curtailed. Attempts, such as Fukuyama's, to explain democratization on the basis of ideas, technological change and demographic shifts have much more trouble linking events in different parts of the African continent. It is clearly not the case that urbanization and yuppiedom have led the charge towards multi-party democracy. Any analysis that ignores the influence of Western Europe and America will be seriously deficient. Beginning with Henry Kissinger's tenure at the State Department, 'Constructive Engagement' was the cover for supporting anti-communist white minority regimes without openly flouting the principles enshrined in the US Constitution.[26] Support for dubious characters such as Mobutu could be justified, not only by the old axiom that 'he may be a sonofabitch, but he's our sonofabitch'. but also by the so-called 'Kirkpatrick doctrine', which held that capitalist dictatorships could revert to democracy while communist ones could not. The US no longer has a pressing need for any sonofabitch in Africa and the Kirkpatrick doctrine has gone through the paper shredder. Western lending agencies now have the luxury of adding democracy to the list of conditions they impose on African borrowers.

Towards a Multi-factor Explanation for the Fall of Apartheid and the Spread of Democracy in Africa

Even before scholars break into the archives, it seems possible to outline a historical explanation for events that takes into account most of the factors outlined above.

Such an explanation might begin by noticing that all attempts at economic nationalism and autarchy came under extreme pressure in the nineteen seventies. It became less and less possible for any national economy to function as a stable, self-contained entity. International currency markets, floating exchange rates, and new technologies for moving capital back and forth across state frontiers defeated the best efforts at control, even by the Soviet bloc. At the intellectual level, 'the boys from Chicago' and other theorists of economic deregulation had great success in reviving nineteenth-century ideals of an integrated world economy based on peace and free trade. They seized control of the commanding heights of finance capital from which they made offers that could not be refused by mendicant states. As South Africa was buffetted, along with the rest of the continent, by disastrously altered terms of trade, the government accepted a set of neo-classical prescriptions for recovery which were at war with fundamental concepts of apartheid: privatization, deregulation, free movement of labour, less state intervention, and 'level playing fields'.

Even before adopting new-look economic policies, the state had been losing the battle to maintain influx control. In the nineteen eighties it ceased to try. Urban populations soared. In other circumstances, the restoration of economic freedom to Africans might have boosted growth and won the support of a burgeoning black petty bourgeoisie. But as the Rand plummeted on international currency markets, inflation soared. Workers' wages bought less, and life for the unemployed became intolerable. The school children of Soweto had shown in 1976 that the will to resist with physical force had not been permanently crippled by the apparatus of extreme repression imposed after Sharpeville. Violence broke out again as the hardships associated with the new economic order bit in the townships. Although the violence can not, on the evidence presently available, be attributed to leadership from any single political organization, it was neither anomic nor politically innocent. Slogans, demands and banners of the period attest to people's awareness of the potential for the UDF, ANC and other banned organizations to take leading roles in bringing about change. Important elements among the white population, including commercial leaders, began to look to the exiled ANC as an organization with whom they should learn to do business.

The state, however, hesitated at the very brink and behaved as though it were seeking to repeat the successful repression of the nineteen sixties. Armoured columns in the townships, destabilization campaigns in neighbouring countries, arrests and banning orders became the order of the day. These measures produced mixed results. International outrage was expressed in predictable places but did not succeed in significantly tightening sanctions over the objections of the British and American governments. The Americans continued to cooperate with the South African government behind the scenes to carry on the war in Angola. Unlike the sixties, however, repression succeeded neither in crushing open resistance nor in restoring economic stability. Negative growth, inflation and currency problems persisted. Anxiety grew in government circles as important foreign debts came up for renewal.

At about the same time it was becoming apparent that the communist regimes of Europe and the Soviet Union were in equally serious trouble. Aid from socialist countries to African regimes and resistance movements slowed to a trickle. Then, in 1989, the Soviet empire commenced falling apart. Not just South Africa but the whole of sub-saharan Africa was profoundly disturbed by these events. What van Zyl Slabbert calls 'the decline of Africa as an area of geo-political influence' meant that African states who wanted outside capital had to compete for it without the advantages formerly available to those who lined up with one side or the other in the Cold War. South Africa's forces of production dwarf those of other African countries but the combination of stagnation, urban unrest, international sanctions and currency instability made her look little more attractive to overseas investors. The Americans showed evident impatience to see the Angolan conflict settled. It is no more surprising that De Klerk chose this moment, the beginning of 1990, to look for credible black partners who might help salvage the fortunes of the South African state. The character of township violence a few years earlier made it plain that the ANC would have to be a candidate for that role. It was no accident that at about the same time other African regimes embarked on experiments in democracy, which they hoped might make them look like more normal, attractive places to do business.

The kind of account sketched here allows some place to all the factors surveyed earlier in the chapter. It cannot pretend to be definitive, inasmuch as it guesses about some things which can only be gradually tested as evidence now hidden becomes available. It is as remarkable for what it leaves out as for what it includes.

For example, the day-to-day ebb and flow of politics hardly figures. To the very end of the drama, liberalism has been a bit player on the South African political stage — a buzzing gadfly among the lumbering major actors. The hope cherished by the inventors of parties called liberal and progressive, that the good sense of the their ideas would gradually permeate the community, has not been fulfilled. In 1990 the National Party leadership took a flying leap beyond Helen Suzman, Alan Paton and all the other liberal gradualists of times past. The rise of the United Democratic Front was certainly a major event of the eighties. In retrospect, however, it is hard to say that the UDF played a crucial role in pushing the state towards the precipice. It could be said its campaign to discredit the Tricameral Parliament replayed conflicts of the past more than it paved the way to the future. The Tricameral Parliament was one more in a long series of attempts by the ruling regime to divide and rule its opponents with a device that could be dressed up and presented to the world as an extension of democracy. The UDF, like the Black Sash before it, sprang up to denounce the latest constitutional contraption as a fraud. When the townships spun out of control, the government seized the opportunity to hit the UDF with the customary weapons: banning orders, mass arrests, detentions without trial. To seasoned observers of the South African scene, the sense of déja vu was overwhelming.

This time, however, the crackdown did not work. The disappearance of television cameras from the townships did not stop other countries from reporting on the crisis and the harsh measures fruitlessly imposed to deal with it. Nor did the disappearance of known UDF leaders lessen international pressures at the time the country's debts had to be rescheduled to avoid a default. The stalemate was only broken when De Klerk and the ANC agreed to negotiate. After the Codesa talks began, neither side found much room to manoeuvre. Early in the process, it appeared that the National Party was making the running while De Klerk strutted in overseas capitals and the ANC leadership appeared to be losing touch with an impatient and desperate rank and file. The killings at Boipatong provided an opportunity for the ANC to restore the balance of power and to drive wedges between De Klerk, the security forces and the fast-declining power of Buthelezi's IFP. The ANC leadership was back in the streets but carefully refrained for calling for renewed sanctions or severing sporting ties. It remained firmly committed to an orderly transition. So did De Klerk, with a very nervous eye on the immediate unfavorable reaction of financial markets. Internal forces in South Africa continue to make their own history, but not in circumstances of their own choosing.

Notes

1   A remark echoed by Shula Marks and Stanley Trapido, 'Introduction', *Journal of Southern African Studies*, 18 (1992), 2: 'already it is difficult to find members of the National Party who ever believed in apartheid'.

2   Ian Tyrrell, 'American Exceptionalism in an Age of International History', *American Historical Review*, 96 (1991), 1031-55. See also the replies and discussion in the same volume.

3   F. Fukuyama, 'The Next South Africa', *South Africa International*, 22 (October, 1991), 71-81.

4   Ibid, p.72.

5   R.W. Johnson, writing in *The Times*, reprinted in The Australian, 20 March 1992.

6   *South Africa Foundation Review*, 18 (March, 1992), 4.

7   A good recent summary of some of that controversy is to be found in Christopher Saunders, *The Making of the South African Past* (Cape Town: David Philip, 1998), pp.167-91.

8   Fukuyama, p.74.

9   Ibid, p.79.

10   Ibid, 'sadly it would appear that colonialism, far from having been responsible for Africa's poverty, was in fact a major source of skills and infrastructure, and that the region has become worse off economically the further from colonialism it gets'.

11   Samuel Decalo, 'The Process, Prospects and Constraints of Democratization in Africa', *African Affairs*, 91 (1992), 7-35.

12   Ibid, p.8.

13   Ibid, p.35.

14   N. J. Diseko, 'The Origins and Development of the South African Student's Movement(SASM): 1968-1976', *Journal of Southern African Studies*, 18 (March 1991), 42.

15   H. Barrell, 'The Turn to the Masses: the African national Congress' Strategic Review of 1978-79, *Journal of Southern African Studies*, 18 (March 1991), 72, 85.

16   '"Trailing Behind the Masses": the United Democratic Front and Township Politics in the Pretoria-Witwatersrand-Vaal Region, 1983-84', *Journal of Southern African Studies*, 18 (March 1991), 93-114.

17   'Community and Conflict: the Alexandra Rebellion of 1986', *Journal of Southern African Studies*, 18 (March 1991), 115.

18   'The Politics of Youth Resistance in the 1980s: the Dilemmas of a Differentiated Durban', *Journal of Southern African Studies*, 18 (March 1991), 143-65.

19   Fuad Cassim, 'Growth, Crisis and Change in the South African Economy', in J. Suckling and L. White, eds., *After Apartheid, Renewal of the South African Economy* (University of York and London, 1988), 1-17.

20   Ibid, 7-8.

21   Gay W. Seidman, 'The Emergence of Political Unionism in Brazil and South Africa,' *South African Sociological Review*, 3 (1990), 3-18. She extends these themes in a forthcoming book.

22   Dave Cooper, 'Locating South Africa in the Third World: Comparative industrialization and Political Trade Unionism in South America', *Social Dynamics*, 17 (1991), 1-40. For more on political trade unionism, see the final chapter in this book.

23   Frederik van Zyl Slabbert, 'The Basis and Challenges of Transition in South Africa: A Review and a Preview', in *Transition to Democracy, Policy Perspectives 1991* (Cape Town, 1991), 1-13.

24   Ibid, 8-10.

25   Preston King's *African Winter* (Harmondsworth: Penguin, 1986), details many links between arms supply and African misery.

26   Although the phrase 'Constructive Engagement' originated with Chester Crocker in the Reagan administration, the policy it denoted can be traced back at least to Kissinger. See Paul Rich, 'United States Containment Policy, South Africa and the Apartheid Dilemma', *Review of International Studies*, 14 (1988), 179-94.

6

The Origins Of Ethnic Violence In South Africa

Shula Marks

Introduction

In 1981, with a degree of prescience the historian can only envy, Anthony Smith wrote:

> In every continent and practically every state, ethnicity has reappeared as a vital social and political force. The plural composition of most states; their policies of cultural integration; the increasing frequency and intensity of ethnic rivalries and conflicts and the proliferation of ethnic movements; these are the main trends and phenomena which testify to the growing role of ethnicity in the modern world.[1]

A decade later, the world is awash in a veritable sea of warring ethnicities — from Azerbaijan to Zaghreb, from the Armenians to the Zulu: the alphabetical symmetry is irresistible. Daily our papers are filled with stories of Serbs and Croats killing one another in Yugoslavia, and Zulu and Xhosa apparently doing the same thing in South Africa. People who have lived side by side for decades have suddenly taken to hating and killing. And in all these cases, journalists are wont to describe these events as the emergence of long-held animosities and innate identities which inevitably rise to the surface when a coercive state finally loosens its hold. It is what one might call the genie in the bottle theory of ethnicity. The genie is there all the time, but only escapes when you uncork the bottle. This has its variant in the oft-repeated explanation of what is happening in South Africa as black on black violence or atavistic tribal conflict between a Zulu Inkatha and an allegedly Xhosa ANC. Yet the reality is far more complex and historically specific than these simple stereotypes allow, and, as we shall see, in South Africa at least, ethnic explanations by themselves have only limited value.

Assessing the Violence

In South Africa, over the past half dozen years, some 6000 people have been killed in internecine warfare in the province of Natal, ostensibly between members of the Zulu cultural organization, Inkatha, and its political opponents, although the vast majority who have been killed, injured and displaced from their homes have been ordinary members of the community. There the battle has been between Zulu-speakers, over the soul of the Zulu and what constitutes Zulu-ness: in much the same way as there have been struggles between Afrikaners over the soul of the Afrikaner and what constitutes Afrikanerdom. In July-August, 1990, the battle was taken from Natal to South Africa's industrial heartland, where more than 500 Africans were killed in a matter of days. Since then what amounts to a war against the black urban community on the Rand has been waged and another 2-3000 Africans have lost their lives; the bloodletting continues. Clearly both the violence and the form it has taken demand explanation. Quite apart from the sheer horror and suffering it inflicts, the warfare has threatened at times to throw off course the delicate negotiations between the government and the ANC over a constitutional settlement; it has weakened the ANC and is likely to endanger a stable post-apartheid government. And there are those who believe that this is its main purpose.

Although the allocation of responsibility for these events is a matter of controversy, it seems clear that Inkatha supporters, mobilized around a specific Zulu ethnic identity, have been the source of most of the aggression. This is true both in Natal where the work of a variety of church-attached monitoring groups has shown this to be overwhelmingly the case, and on the Rand, where a study based on a content analysis of media reports across a broad political spectrum showed that Inkatha supporters were the aggressors in 51 per cent of attributable incidents of violence between July 1990 and July 1991. This was ten times more often than the ANC at 4 per cent. And by far the largest number of dead — 87 per cent — were 'ordinary members of the community'.[2] These figures may be spuriously precise; they are unlikely to be totally wrong as an indication of trend.

Through all this there have been persistent claims of police collusion in the violence from ordinary township residents, independent church monitoring groups, human rights lawyers and the ANC, and, according to the CASE investigation, the security forces were held responsible in nearly a quarter of the episodes reported. Until very recently, the police in Natal have been noticeably and notoriously reluctant to act even when there have been court injunctions against senior members of Inkatha for multiple murders; in Natal and on the Rand they have appeared on the scene to escort Zulu *impis* into safety after their murderous assaults on shantytown dwellers and township funeral vigils.[3] Over the past few months, the evidence of state collusion in the violence has mounted: in the European summer of 1991, conclusive evidence was published showing that the government had been funding Inkatha for a number of years (perhaps since its inception) and had continued to do so even after the unbanning of the ANC.[4] There is further evidence that this continued a full ten months after De Klerk assured parliament that it had been ended.

There is little doubt, then, that the violence in the townships of Natal and the Rand *is* being and has been fomented by elements in the army and the police. As Dave Everatt argues, `the aim seems to be to destabilize black South Africa life and to prevent the establishment of a normalized political climate.'[5] And the state president does not seem particularly perturbed: bloodletting on this scale among whites would almost certainly have seen far more concerted efforts by the state to bring matters to a halt. Nelson Mandela is surely correct to say that black lives are still held cheap in South Africa — and that as head of state De

Klerk bears the responsibility, whether it is because he actually approves of state involvement in the violence or because he does not have sufficient control over the police and army to do anything about it. After all, if more than 3000 white citizens had been killed in communal violence over fifteen months, the government of the day would undoubtedly be called to account. Some Nationalists may well hope to take advantage of the violence to weaken the ANC deliberately in the run up to non-racial elections; at least until Inkathagate there was also talk of an electoral alliance between the National Party and Inkatha, although this seems less and less likely. The strategy of destabilization is one the South Africans adopted in Namibia at the time of the elections in order to weaken SWAPO; it should not surprise us if it is being used within South Africa.[6] But it is a very dangerous game to play.

At one level the violence has clearly been between members of Inkatha, the Zulu National Cultural Movement, founded by Chief Mangosuthu Buthelezi in 1975, and members of the non-racial democratic organizations, the Congress of South African Trade Unions (COSATU), the United Democratic Front (UDF) and, since 1990, the African National Congress (ANC). Yet in both Natal and on the Rand, as Lauren Segal has recently reminded us, such explanations may be imposing `an official sounding order on the overwhelming confusion and horror of the violence' where in fact there is no such coherence: only a 'shifting assortment, a "kaleidoscope" of explanations . . . the human face of violence is far more diffuse and complex than most media and political accounts portray'.[7]

Moreover, important as the concrete evidence is of SADF and police culpability in fomenting the political violence, this does not fully explain its nature, form or timing. The security forces are watering a ready-made field. The field was ploughed and the seeds of the violence were sown by the apartheid state, and — ironically — were fertilized by its very disintegration.[8] South Africa was a very violent society long before the current wave of killings hit the headlines, and apartheid has been a major source of this violence. In all parts of the world rapid industrialization and urbanization have led to massive social dislocations. These are powerful and painful processes not captured by the bland term 'modernization'. In South Africa, where whites have been the beneficiaries, and blacks have borne the burdens, these processes have been made even more disruptive and traumatic through the destruction of social support systems as a result of the migrant labour system and the uprooting of communities in the name of a myriad racial laws and regulations. Apartheid has created a veritable laboratory for violent behaviour, but this violence has always afflicted the unprotected black communities to a far greater extent than it has the white population, which has traditionally been protected by the state and by their residential segregation from the worst of its impact.

For both black and white the psychological toll of these processes has been immense over the past hundred years. But while the racial form that capitalist development has taken in South Africa has offered blacks impoverishment and all-pervasive humiliations in daily life, it has afforded whites an almost unlicensed domination. The results can be seen in the Republic's inordinately high rates of physical violent crime: murder and robbery; capital punishment, and the brutal flogging of rural labour; domestic, industrial and motor accidents; alcoholism, drug abuse, suicide and divorce are all symptoms of a disordered society. As Neil Andersson and I have remarked elsewhere, 'these phenomena are not simply isolated aberrations; they combine to form a matrix of cultural violence which is integral to continued social inequality in South Africa.'[9]

Much of this violence is gender-specific; with a few exceptions, the violence is perpetrated by men, both white and black. And while most of the political violence is probably directed by young men against young men, every day violence against women — rape, assault, witchcraft accusations — is also extremely high: and this too is structural, related to the nature of the wider society. Mamphela Ramphele's work in the hostels of Cape Town has shown how in a situation of powerlessness, black men take out their frustrations and aggressions on the only people lower in the pecking order than they are — black women. Cathy Campbell, who has looked at the gendered nature of violence in Natal, also argues, 'that the ability of men to control women and the use of violence to ensure this control is the one area where not only has the power of working class men not been threatened by racial capitalist society, but [has] actually been reinforced by it.'[10] And Albie Sachs has recently remarked that, 'patriarchy is likely to outlast racism in South Africa.'

None of this is particularly new — but this high level of violence, family breakup and frustration forms part of the essential backdrop to the contemporary situation. Faced with intense social problems, there is a ready recourse to violent 'solutions'.   Nevertheless, overtly political violence between blacks in South Africa is relatively new and entered a new phase over the past decade, the decade of reformism, as street battles between police and people became commonplace in the industrial heartlands, as the youth responded to calls from the ANC to render the country `ungovernable', and as warlords began to mount their onslaught against the communities who refused to acknowledge their power in Natal.

And this shift, this escalation of violence may, as Doug Hindson and Mike Morris have recently pointed out, have as much to do with the disintegration of apartheid as with apartheid itself. For them, 'the harsh reality is that racial, ethnic and class antagonisms held in check under classic apartheid have resurfaced in the climate of [economic] liberalization and deracialization'. The irony is that apartheid which spawned so much of the violence also held it in check. With the collapse of apartheid and 'the changing role of the state has come an ever increasing level of social chaos . . . . The disintegration of apartheid has been accompanied by, and given rise to, a variety of economic, social and political processes which shape the contours of the violence: rapid urbanization, increasing class differentiation, struggles between geographically and socially distinct urbanizing communities over scarce residential resources, and major political struggles between competing power centres.'[11]

In many ways it can be argued that the newly unleashed political violence all over South Africa has resulted as much from the insecurities — and unfulfilled but suddenly no longer wholly unattainable aspirations released by reform — as by apartheid itself: the massive influx of people into shacklands around the cities with the repeal of the pass laws at a time of economic recession and massive unemployment, the power vacuum as old lines of authority have broken down and have to be reasserted, and the defiance of the gerontocracy as young people came to assert their political agency.

Thus another major cause of the violence has been generational divisions, witnessed for example in the rise of vigilantes in the Cape townships and in some of the struggles on the Witwatersrand. In a situation of rapid social change in which the power of adult men in the family is being constantly eroded, both by their lowly position in the race and class hierarchy and with the growing number of female-headed families, high rates of unemployment and the 'catapulting' of the youth into political prominence, it is hardly surprising perhaps that a reassertion of the power of the 'fathers' should characterize not only tensions in family life but also so many of the street struggles in South Africa. So we have *witdoeke* — white head-banded vigilantes attacking 'comrades' in Cape Town, and *rooidoeke* , red head-banded vigilantes acting against 'comrades' in Natal and on the Rand.[12] But the former have not taken an ethnic form, and the latter have. Generational conflict has long been one of the idioms of African politics: it is now being played out in a new and deadly fashion.

And this serves to alert us to the reality that material and political conflicts are always played out in a cultural idiom, and these have their own regional specificities. Culture, as Stuart Hall and others have reminded us, is not only 'the way the social relationships of a group are structured and shaped . . . it is also the way these shapes are experienced, understood and interpreted'. It is materialised in 'patterns of social organization' and internalized through the institutions and experiences of daily life.[13] Thus, the very terms ANC/UDF/ 'comrades'/ *amaqabane* on the one hand, and *Inkath a* and *amatheleweni* on the other, encapsulate 'maps of meaning', clusters of attributes in the minds both of those who identify themselves in this way and in those of their opponents. The labels go far beyond what we usually consider political allegiance, to encompass urban and rural values, styles of language and dress. Membership means being a part of the 'culture' or sub-culture of the groups involved, rather than merely signifying adherence to a political programme: hence the inability, which many observers have noted with bewilderment, of many of the members of both movements to specify 'the national policies and leaders of the organizations they are killing and dying for'.[14]

In all this conflict ethnicity has been a relatively insignificant apolitical force until comparatively recently. This is not to say that people do not have an ethnic consciousness: an awareness of being Zulu or Xhosa, or Sotho or Tswana. Migrants to cities all over the world have used ethnic strategies of survival and solidarity — and South Africa is no different. From at least the 1920s, black workers from the same areas, even the same villages, have clustered together to form new ethnically-based associations in the cities, to find jobs, to find housing, to find company, to find burial. And these associations could at times be used for other purposes of mobilization — whether as in the case of the 'Amarashea' or 'Russians' from Lesotho who terrorized the Rand in the 1940s and 1950s or for more political purposes, as in the case of the Mpondo young men's association, the Indhlavini, which provided a network for the mobilization of mineworkers at the time of the 1946 strike. The Sebatakgomo movement which provided a network between town and countryside for Pedi migrants to the Rand, and which was a major means of ANC mobilization in the Northern Transvaal in the 1950s is another example.[15]

Origins of Ethnic Consciousness

To reiterate, what is striking about black South Africa is how relatively insignificant ethnicity has been — except in Zululand-Natal — and even there it is complex — as a salient cultural/political category. This is all the more surprising when one considers the enormous investment of the state in utilizing ethnicity in order to divide and rule: perhaps because the attempts have been so blatant that they have debased the currency. Thus, the reinforcement, manipulation and construction of ethnic identities have been at the heart of segregationist policies of the state before 1948 as they have been central to its apartheid policies since. Crucial to the latter was the so-called Bantu homelands policy whereby a form of local 'independence' was granted to politically manageable, ethnically defined rural 'homelands' under chiefly control. In the 'independent homelands', or 'bantustans' as they are derided by their critics, the state gave ethnicity a new reality by providing material incentives for ethnic identification: a platform and 'perks' for local politicians; an infrastructure of control involving compliant chiefs and headmen, paid for by the state; a local police force; access to jobs in the bureaucracy and business opportunities for the small middle class — all this on the basis of their ethnic affiliation. In the Bantustans as in the urban areas, welfare was allocated through ethnic networks, either refurbished or even newly invented for the purpose. Housing was distributed on a supposedly ethnic basis and all forms of representation were linked to ethnic ties. 'Bantu education' ensured that schooling was duly ethnicized; Radio Bantu — a much understudied phenomenon — inculcated similar messages; and the state also directed its attention to the black intelligentsia, through the provision of separate ethnic universities — and even separate ethnic Nursing Councils and Nursing Associations in the Bantustans.

In all its attempts to ethnicize politics, however, the state was only partially successful. At one level, state discourse probably did alter people's perceptions, often in unforeseen ways, and this could include an acceptance of the state's ethnic categorizations which were in turn taking up and manipulating existing popular perceptions and identifications, especially in rural areas. It would be amazing if it had not done so — and the legacy may well continue to bedevil post-apartheid South Africa. Yet, for the permanently urbanized, the towns, especially on the Witwatersrand, constituted a remarkable melting pot, and have done so for the best part of a hundred years. And although there were undoubted ethnic tensions in the urban areas, often expressed over access to jobs and women, and voiced in negative stereotypes of 'the other', apart from on the mines (which had made use of ethnicity for purposes of social control in specific ways which I have not time to consider here), this was rarely expressed in overt physical conflict.

Indeed, in the late 1970s with the resurgence of trade union organization on the Rand it seemed as if ethnic tensions even among migrant workers, who were most steeped in rural and parochial values, were being overcome. Thus in a sociological investigation of metal-workers on the East Rand, the sociologist Ari Sitas concluded that the rapid unionization amongst migrant workers on the East Rand had transformed worker consciousness, cutting across regionalism and ethnicity, so that migrant hostel dwellers were in the vanguard of the strike wave there. Yet, but a decade later, the East Rand hostel dwellers are in the forefront of the ethnic violence.[16] Clearly the genie in the bottle argument, the argument of innate tribalism, cannot hold. As Barrington Moore has reminded us:

> Culture or tradition . . . is not something that exists outside of or independently of individual human beings living together in society . . . . The assumption of inertia, that cultural and social continuity do not require explanation, obliterates the fact that both have to be recreated anew in each generation, often with great pain and suffering . . . . To speak of cultural inertia is to overlook the concrete interests and privileges that are served by indoctrination, education and the entire complicated process of transmitting culture from one generation to the next.[17]

Undoubtedly there are real ethnic identities to be mobilized — elements of language and kinship and custom which are deeply ingrained and powerfully felt, and which can be drawn on by politicians and culture brokers. How and why ethnicity remains a powerful way of doing so has in part been explained by Raymond Williams:

> . . . we are in fact aligned long before we realise we are aligned. For we are all born into a social situation, into social relationships into a family, all of which have formed what we can later abstract as ourselves as individuals. Much of this formation occurs before we can be conscious of any individuality, Indeed the consciousness of individuality is often the consciousness of all those elements of our formation, yet this can never be complete. The alignments are very deep. They are our normal ways of seeing the world. Of course we may become intellectually aware that they are not normal in the sense that they are universal. We come to recognize that other people live differently, were born into different social relationships, see the world differently. Yet still, at certain deep levels . . . . our own actual alignment is so inseparable from the constitution of our own individuality that to separate them is quite impossible.[18]

But these subjective alignments are never innocent, are never simply the ideas and sentiments imbibed with our mother's milk. They are constant constructions and reconstructions in the present as elements of our individuality are posed and juxtaposed in our effort to make sense of, survive in, an ever shifting world; and they are frequently assisted by powerful messages from politicians, media and state as well as, in the South African case, various individuals determined to sow dissension in the community.[19] We all have multiple identities which get called to duty in different contexts, together or singly. Eddie Webster's account of the life story of the Zulu migrant, Mandlenkosi Makhoba, simultaneously foundry-worker, trade unionist, Inkatha founder member, and now subsistence farmer in Kwazulu illuminates the point beautifully.[20] Which one is salient and is called into service at any particular time is the result of multiple determinations.

Inkatha, Buthelezi and Zulu Ethnicity

Why then has the ethnic card been played with such devastating success by Inkatha in Kwazulu-Natal, and then taken on to the Rand? What is peculiar about this region, that has led to so successful an ethnicization of politics. The first point to make is perhaps a simple demographic one. At seven million the Zulu are the single largest 'ethnic' group in South Africa today, with relative linguistic and cultural homogeneity. This has clearly provided Buthelezi with the incentive to engage in the form of ethnic politics played with such success by the Afrikaner nationalists of the 1930s and 1940s. With a decentralized federal state and proportional representation he has everything to play for if, like the Afrikaners of a previous generation, he can get the Zulu to identify first and foremost as Zulu — not as Africans, or as workers, or as social democrats, but as 'Zulu'. Thus, ever since the resurgence of African opposition in the early 1980s, Buthelezi has attempted to assert Inkatha's political hegemony among the Zulu, and to do so like the Afrikaner nationalists, by fanning the fears and discontents of a people undergoing all the strains of rapid impoverishment and urbanization in order to mobilize the

Zulu around an ethnic identity.

Again, in itself this is inadequate to explain the whole story. After all, other Bantustan leaders have attempted to mobilize equally impoverished populations along ethnic lines — but without the same degree of success. What is it that differentiates Inkatha and Kwazulu? An article by the Indian historian David Washbrook may hold some of the clues.[21] In this Washbrook explores the application (and limitations) of Wallerstein's world system theory as applied to India and the ways in which South Asia's modern history has been moulded by forces associated with a capitalist world system. He argues on the one hand that in India the culture of the protonationalist elite became imbued with what he, like Wallerstein, terms the '"the ideology of Hegemonic Universalism" which emerged out of the Western Enlightenment' so that most of its nationalist leaders identified 'freedom with nation state formation in a   way that was originally and uniquely Western' and subscribed to 'the truths that were discoverable by positivistic social science and to the ideals of progress, especially in the material domain, envisioned by industrialization'. In other words, the Indian elite subscribed to the vision of redemption through capitalist development. Yet, he argues, it was not only South Asia's

> perceptions of the future that were hijacked by modernity. It was also, and perhaps more crucially, its perceptions of the past. All theories of progress and development view history teleologically and are inclined to define the future, which they venerate, against denigrated caricatures of the past, or 'tradition', which they abhor.

This caricature of the past, 'universalism's distorted version of traditional, has become the basis of mass identity in South Asia'. Of course, popular versions of the past have little relationship to anything that actually existed in the eighteenth century or before. 'If not in its ability to commit the majorities of society to "modernizing" progress', concludes Washbrook, 'then in its ability to imprison the pasts, from which they gain their identities, in rigid, irrational and changeless structures, the culture of hegemonic Universalism has become unquestionably dominant over the society of contemporary South Asia'.

What Washbrook and Wallerstein have called the ideology of hegemonic universalism is pretty close I think to what Philip Corrigan has recently termed 'occidentalism' — 'a way of seeing, saying and showing the world (historically and contemporaneously) .... not only as a view *from* the west, but as a viewpoint, a standpoint, a set-up imposed on those countries, peoples, and geographies not conceived as in/of the West. Occidentalism is about cartographic orthogonality — how maps display untruths, not accidentally but systematically.'[22] Central to this cartographic orthogonality is the concept of 'tribalism', a concept which partially enables the hijacking of the past in order to blur the contradictions of the present in order to stake a claim to the future.

It is, I believe in this double hijacking — of the future and of the past — that the origins of Zulu ethnic violence in contemporary South Africa lie. Let me expand and explain: In South Africa the notion of 'tribalism' follows much the same trajectory as 'traditionalism' (indeed that word is also used) in India, and has the same function of locking people into a static, simplified, brutalized version of the past. This was par-excellence the function of the segregationist and apartheid state. And no group has been more locked into this colonial version of the past than the Zulu with their 'proud military history'.

Originally simply one of the small, closely related chiefdoms in the coastlands of South East Africa, the Zulu rose to prominence in the second and third decades of the nineteenth century, under their revolutionary leader, Shaka, who became king of the Zulu people in 1816, by conquering their neighbours.[23] Crucial to the later history and image of the Zulu was the co-incidence that it was during Shaka's reign that white traders from the Cape Colony arrived in Natal, harbingers of the missionaries, settlers and colonial rulers who were to establish themselves between the Tugela and Umtamvuna Rivers in the succeeding two decades. As Carolyn Hamilton and Daphna Golan have pointed out in rather different ways, it was during this period that the mythology of Shaka and the mighty Zulu military machine was produced both by African communities and the literate whites who encountered them, for their very different purposes, and provided some of the raw material for the Inkatha version of Zulu history and its heroic picture of Zulu manhood.[24] Moreover, although Natal became a British colony in 1843, north of the Tugela River, Zululand remained independent of white rule until 1879, periodically inspiring fear among white settlers with their collective memories of Zulu might. This was reinforced in 1872 when Cetshwayo became king, and was believed by many to be restoring Shaka's 'military machine'. The Anglo-Zulu war of 1879 with its initial Zulu victories further confirmed this stereotype, of utility both to the settlers and to the Zulu themselves. The image of the Zulu as a powerful 'warrior race' thus became crucial to later Zulu self-representations, drawing both on settler and imperial imagery and on popular memory.

At the same time, for much of the nineteenth century the colonial state south of the Tugela in Natal was extremely weak, and was forced to come to terms with the existing structures of the African chiefdoms. As I have argued elsewhere, the British colony of Natal provided a model in the twentieth century for broader South African policies of segregation and later apartheid.   Thus, in the absence of administrative or financial resources, Africans were constituted into 'tribes' and governed through chiefs appointed by the government. African customary law — as interpreted by the colonizers — was recognized and the British governor took the position of 'Supreme Chief', with powers over the African population that were supposedly modelled on those of the Zulu kings. The material basis of this system were reserves set aside for the sole occupation of Africans, some one-eighth of the land area of Natal. At the time these lands were regarded as adequate, although even then the missionaries argued that they were 'fit only for the eagle and the baboon'. In the twentieth century they became increasingly overpopulated, and land shortage fuelled so-called 'faction fights' between chiefdoms and fractions of chiefdoms which had been given a continued reality by their recognition by the colonial state. And, after its annexation by the British in 1879, similar policies were applied to Zululand, north of the Tugela.[25]

Initially Africans in Natal appear to have acquiesced in colonial rule. So long as they had access to land, Africans had little need to work on the white-owned sugar plantations that had become the most important sector of the colonial economy by 1860. As a result Indian indentured labourers were brought to Natal in large numbers: by 1900 they slightly outnumbered the number of white settlers. Despite the increasing involvement in the world economy of both white settlers and black peasants, these policies tended to conserve — albeit in deformed ways — rather than to restructure African social forms. The result was to perpetuate parochial group loyalties and residual land claims. Helen Bradford has put it characteristically succinctly in her admirable *A Taste of Freedom*:

> ... it was hard to improve on the South African prescription for people to seize hold of parochial identities for political purposes. Take a tract of land containing a multiplicity of heterogeneous precapitalist societies in which production is deeply integrated with territory, kinship, language and political authority. Let the boundaries of the country as whole and the reserves in particular be 'jerry-built by imperialism'. Add mine magnates and traditionalist blacks striving with uneven success, to preserve older social formations. And then insert petty bourgeois nationalist politicians, striving to 'stitch together' alliances and rally constituencies. [26]

And nowhere has this 'prescription' been followed more closely than in Natal-Zululand. This means, as Professor Michael Whisson has recently suggested, that today

> what in other, similarly deprived areas like the Cape Flats, Soweto or the peri-urban slums of Latin America erupt as gang fights for turf and racket control, in Zululand [sic. Kwazulu] are articulated into the clan identity of everyone in the region.

There was, however, another card which the Zulu had up their sleeve, another reason why ethnicity was to have greater resonance there than elsewhere. The existence of a cohesive kingdom, under threat from the mid-nineteenth century, and under a king who claimed to represent all the people, probably gave the Zulu a capacity for constructing a nationalist identity which was not matched in the rest of South Africa. As Eric Hobsbawm has remarked, 'in one way or another, membership of an historical state, present or past, can act directly upon the consciousness of the common people to produce proto-nationalism . . . . The potential popular appeal of a state tradition for modern nationalism is obvious'. This, then, was the great advantage the Zulu had over the other ethnic groups in South Africa. It was also the advantage that the first Inkatha movement founded in the early 1920s had over other ethnic associations which flourished in South Africa in the 1920s and 1930s as a response to the segregationist policies of the state, the migrant labour system and the activities of ideological brokers. The history of their kingdom, and its ethnic symbolism, provided a ready and rich resource for the culture brokers of the twentieth century. So rich a resource was it that Africans in Natal, who had never formed part of the Zulu kingdom, who had actively resisted it or had served in colonial armies fighting it, came to identify with it as a an alternative to colonial oppression. To quote Helen Bradford once more: 'In Natal in particular, the ruins of South Africa's most powerful precolonial kingdom [has] haunted the present.'[27]

Origins of the first Inkatha

Natal's attempts to destroy the Zulu monarchy as the pivot of Zulu national unity, even after Natal became part of the Union of South Africa in 1910, merely served to increase its legitimacy in the twentieth century. A new Zulu ethnic identity was forged based on the reinterpretation of past history, and 'custom'. This new Zulu nationalism was not an unmediated transmission of innate and immutable past values and culture, however. The rich historical and cultural tradition of the Zulu did not in itself predict that a Zulu ethnic nationalism would be constructed, although it undoubtedly assisted its creators who formed the first Inkatha movement in the early 1920s and the Zulu Cultural Society which followed on its demise in the 1930s. Ironically, the first Inkatha was created jointly by Natal African Christians many of whose forbears had fled persecution in the Zulu kingdom in the nineteenth century; by the Zulu Royal Family, anxious to mobilize popular support in order to gain state recognition; and by white ideologues of segregation. For the latter, now that the Zulu kingdom had been destroyed, a refurbished traditionalism based on the monarchy was seen as a bulwark against the more radical class-based and nationalist politics, such as, for example, those of the Industrial and Commercial Workers Union which spread like wildfire amongst the dispossessed peasants and labour tenants of Natal in the late 1920s, or the less radical but still pan-South African African National Congress in the interwar years. The conversion of the Communist Party of South Africa in the late 1920s to working amongst African peasants and workers further roused the anxieties of South Africa's white rulers.

G N Heaton Nicholls, a prominent Zululand sugar planter who was also one of the key ideologues of segregation, saw the issues clearly. He urged the state to recognize the authority of the Zulu king, in order to 'stem the tide of tribal disintegration' and prevent 'the evolution of a native proletariat'. As he wrote in May 1929, 'We must come back to the real issue of tribal life — communalism — a very different thing to communism. If we do not get back to communalism we will certainly arrive at communism . . . . We cannot long continue as a white aristocracy or black proletariat . . . . We end ultimately in the not too distant future in the class war'. In the 1930s Heaton Nicholls was a close ally of the Zulu Cultural Society, and persuaded the Department of Native Affairs to fund its activities to the tune of £250 a year — not a vast sum, but substantial enough and indicative of where its sympathies lay. Neither the state recognition of the conservative role that can be played by Zulu cultural nationalism nor its funding of Zulu ethnic endeavours is new.

Yet at a time of growing dispossession and exploitation, many people turned to the Zulu Royal family precisely because of the state's refusal to recognize the King's powers — despite the efforts of Heaton Nicholls and the Zulu Society. Through their allegiance to the Zulu Royal family, they expressed their resentment against white rule: the king was to be their redeemer, representative of an heroic past in strong contrast to their impoverished and humiliating present as farm labourers and miners and 'houseboys'.

Zulu ethnic nationalism was never uncontested, however, whether in the 1920s and 30s or later. Many of the same socially disruptive forces which led the more conservative intelligentsia to construct Zulu ethnic nationalism were responsible also for the rise of more radical pan-South African movements, which found a ready constituency in Natal although they all had to come to terms in different ways with a powerful undertow of Zulu cultural identity. Even in the 1950s, when the ANC expanded to claim the allegiance of a far wider constituency in Natal for the first time, there were tensions, particularly over the ANC's non-racial policies and its collaboration, born in 1949 in the midst of a dangerous anti-Indian riot, with the South African Indian Congress. Nevertheless, for much of the 1950s Natal was firmly in the ANC fold, under the leadership of the Natal-based Chief, Albert Luthuli. The Zulu Cultural Society died when it backed the wrong incumbent to the chieftaincy, and even support for the monarchy dwindled once the apartheid state handed the king a poisoned chalice by recognizing him.

Buthelezi, the ANC and the revival of Inkatha

Since the 1950s, several processes have intensified the struggles in Natal. Many of the social dislocations of the interwar period have been greatly exacerbated by the state's policies of apartheid between 1948 and the early 1980s. In the 1960s and 1970s, these involved even greater control over African influx into the urban areas, the extension of the migrant labour system, and, in 1972, the establishment of Kwazulu as a 'Bantu homeland' (or Bantustan). This gave the inchoate but still pulsating Zulu cultural nationalism a territorial base even if the highly fragmented Kwazulu state relied on South Africa for more than three-quarters of its revenue and most of its investment. At the same time it also gave its political leaders powerful material resources and patronage. These were particularly important at a time when in other ways Kwazulu, like the other Bantustans, was quite incapable of providing subsistence for the vast majority of its inhabitants. As elsewhere in the South African periphery, dire poverty and dependence had led to and been aggravated by the constant drain of the able-bodied and energetic from the rural areas to South Africa's white-controlled mines and farms and industries, whose wealth has been built on their labour.

Nowhere was the space provided by the state's Bantustan

policies more inventively used than by Chief Mangosuthu Buthelezi, who became Kwazulu's first and only Prime Minister. In 1975, at a time when the ANC and other radical non-racial political organizations were banned, Buthelezi, cousin of the Zulu king, grandson of Cetshwayo's Chief Minister, and Prime Minister of Kwazulu, filled the political vacuum by resurrecting the Inkatha Zulu Cultural National Movement, with the covert support of the ANC. Combining an appeal to the heroic reconstructed Zulu past and the colours, songs and slogans of the 1950s ANC, he used his Kwazulu base and resources to build up his constituency.

Initially Buthelezi was brilliantly successful in working within the system, while distancing himself from it. This did not — perhaps could not — last long, however. By 1979 he had broken with what he now termed contemptuously 'the ANC in exile', while portraying himself as the true heir to its legitimate tradition. To survive as Bantustan leader with state patronage he had little option but to oppose the armed struggle and the ANC's sanctions campaign. Buthelezi now came to project himself nationally and internationally as the 'moderate' leader whom local whites and international capitalists could trust — and fund. Between 1979 and 1985, the dramatic resurgence of the trade union movement, the rise of the non-racial UDF and of its aggressive youth constituency, sharpened and radicalized politics and challenged Buthelezi's claims, driving him back on his local constituency and its ethnic symbolism. Opposed for the first time, Inkatha rapidly acquired a reputation for violent action, against students, workers and community leaders, while the Chief himself uttered veiled threats against his critics. With his close ties to business, Buthelezi was particularly angered by the launch of the COSATU in Natal in 1985 and the violence escalated. With the unbanning of the ANC in February 1990 it reached a new pitch of intensity, as the Zulu people now had to chose among competing loyalties, contrasting definitions of Zulu-ness.

In his attempts to mobilize his constituency, Buthelezi laid great stress on Zulu history — with frequent invocations of the Zulu past in Inkatha rallies and political events — and on traditional virtues embodied in the *'Ubunthu-Botho'* (Good

Citizenship) school syllabus.[28] This like the Charter of the Zulu Cultural Society in the 1930s stresses the need for discipline and obedience from the youth, and deference from women. Playing on gender and generation insecurities, *Ubunthu-Botho* provides an ethnic ideology and a vision of a social order calculated to appeal to older men from the rural areas who feel most threatened and alienated by the corrupting ways of the town and of the disrespectful *amaqabane*.

Yet there is an ambiguity at the heart of the discipline of the elders, for in the current civil war, Buthelezi cannot ignore his youthful constituency. On the contrary, the Inkatha Youth Brigade has always been his direct responsibility, and he claims it is now the largest section of the Inkatha Freedom Party.[29] And, as Segal points out, in the hostels it is the young workers who have taken the lead in organising the violence, and that this has 'to some extent upset the gerontocratic order' which previously provided the organising principle of the hostels.[30]

Contradictions and countercurrents

There is an even greater contradiction at the heart of Inkatha's espousal of 'tradition'. To return to Washbrook: Buthelezi's espousal of 'traditionalism' is not simply a caricature of the past, it also serves to disguise the radicalism of his espousal of free enterprise in the present, and the consequences of his alliance with the state and capital. By the late 1970s he had emerged as the most articulate black protagonist of capitalist development, wooing the international business community and persuading some of its more maverick millionaires to fund him. Over the past decade Kwazulu has been the site of some economic development — an economic development which has intensified the stratification of the local populace into a small select band associated with the top echelons of Inkatha and Kwazulu who have managed to accumulate considerable wealth through their ties with the bureaucracy, through sugar farming and the Kwazulu Development Corporation, and a vast mass of people who are being marginalized and displaced by the same processes of 'enterprise capitalism' — and who are finding their way into the burgeoning squatter camps around the towns of Natal and into the hostels of the Rand.[31] The enterprise capitalism which Buthelezi applauds has thus involved the breaking up of community in Natal and Kwazulu through, for example, the allocation of communally held lands for individual tenure; together with drought it has led to the accelerated proletarianization of its inhabitants over the past decade to such an extent that Durban and Pietermaritzburg are amongst the fastest growing urban areas in the world.

Thus the current processes of urbanization, as Doug Hindson and Mike Morris argue, have been accompanied by 'massive social dislocation, upheaval, violence and heightened political conflict', as people struggle over 'the distribution and control of the resources necessary to support city life: employment, land, housing and services'. 'Ultimately', they say, the turmoil in the townships of Natal 'is part of a much wider struggle over the country's wealth: who owns and controls it and how it is distributed'.[32] How better to blur the explosive consequences of this class formation and potential class conflict than in the time honoured way of calling for a cross-class Zulu identification — and blaming the increased impoverishment of the Zulu not on apartheid, or the accumulating ventures of the home-grown new middle class — but on the youth, the ANC and the unions, whose calls for boycotts and sanctions and strikes undoubtedly deprive frequently unconsulted migrants of vitally needed employment, and not surprisingly rouse their anger.

Thus the most desperately impoverished of South Africa's black population — the migrants living in the anomic hostels on the Rand — have been enlisted in an all-out war on neighbouring squatter camps through appeals to their Zulu identity and their ancient military glory on the one hand, and in an onslaught against the political programme of the ANC and the unions on the other. For those caught up in the struggle, the battle has seemed necessary to protect what little they had.

There can be little doubt that the ethnic nationalism being mobilized by Buthelezi and fomented by elements in the state is of grave importance for the future stability of a post-apartheid South Africa, despite the fact that the unbannning of the ANC, the violence and the evidence of state support may well have eroded Inkatha's support over the past few months.[33]   The complexity of these events warns, however, against their easy labelling as some kind of return to an atavistic past. Zulu history enters the current configuration of events as an invented and reworked past, not an accurate portrayal of 'what happened'. Behind the violence lie not deep cultural or psychological traits but the intensification of rural poverty, migrancy, unemployment and urban overcrowding; that it takes an ethnic form is the result of the consistent working and reworking of ethnic divisions and the deliberate glorification of Zulu military 'traditions' by politicians and culture-brokers, both black and white. As everywhere, the ethnicizing of political conflict and its eruption into brutal killing is a product of present interests not of past culture.

Notes

1   A.D. Smith, *The Ethnic Revival* (Cambridge, 1981), p.12.

2   Community Agency for Social Enquiry, *Who is Murdering the Peace? C.A.S.E.Research Statistics*, (Johannesburg: Case, 1991), p.1. The research was compiled by David Everatt.

3   International Commission of Jurists, *Signposts to Peace. An Independent Survey of the Violence in Natal, South Africa* (London, 1990).

4   This was reported extensively in the press at the time, but see, for example, Allister Sparks, 'F W Must Have Known of Secret Funding', *Reality*, September 1991, pp.15-16.

5   CASE, *Who is Murdering the Peace?*, p.2.

6   This draws on the evidence of former SADF Major Nico Basson, who admitted to being in charge of these operations. According to Basson, the whole Namibian exercise, which also involved the illegal funding of anti-SWAPO parties was a 'trial run for a similar but more elaborate campaign to destabilise the ANC' and enabled the NP and its black allies to win the first post-apartheid election. (See Allister Sparks, 'F W Must have Known', p.16.) See also *Weekly Mail*, 4-10 October 1991, p.3, where Basson is cited as saying 'the deployment of former Koevoet and South West African Territory Force men [in South Africa] formed part of a concerted strategy carried out by the special forces of the SADF and the SAP'. See also 'Namibia. Report of a visit by Peter Pike, MP, John MacDonald, QC and Alison Harvey from Sunday 28th

May to Friday 2nd June, 1989'. I am grateful to Alison Harvey for a copy of this report.

7　　See L. Segal, 'The Human Face of Violence. Hostel Dwellers Speak', Project for the Study of Violence, Seminar Paper no.6, Sept. 1991; See also S.Stavrou and A. Crouch, 'Violence on the Periphery: Molweni', unpublished paper presented at the Twentieth Annual Congress of the Association for Sociology in South Africa (University of Witwatersrand, July, 1989), who also argue that the political definitions are too clear-cut and that these identities cohere around different factions in a struggle for scarce material resources, rather than out of the different ideologies of the organizations per se.

8　　For a development of this argument see M. Morris and D. Hindson, 'Political Violence and Urban Reconstruction in South Africa', unpublished paper for Economic Trends Meeting 7th July 1991. I am grateful to Mike Morris for sending me this paper.

9　　N. Andersson and S. Marks, 'The Epidemiology and Culture of violence' in A. du Toit and C. Manganyi, eds., *Political Violence and the Struggle in South Africa* (London: Macmillan, 1991).

10　　See C. Campbell, 'Learning to kill? Masculinity, the Family and the Current Political Violence', paper presented to the Conference on Violence, St Antony's College, Oxford June 1991; forthcoming, *Journal of Southern African Studies*.

11　　Hindson and Morris, 'Political Violence and Urban Reconstruction'.

12　　See C. Campbell, 'Learning to kill?'

13　　John Clarke, Stuart Hall, Tony Jefferson and Brian Roberts, 'Introduction' in Stuart Hall and Tony Jefferson, eds., *Resistance through Rituals. Youth Subcultures in Post-war Britain* (London, 1975), 10-11.Cf., speech of Buthelezi in 1975 before the KwaZulu Legislative Assembly:

'In other words, all members of the Zulu nation are automatically members of Inkatha if they are Zulus. There may be people who are inactive members as no one escapes being a member as long as he or she is a member of the Zulu nation' (Kwazulu Legislative Assembly Debates, vol.5: 134, cited in Gerhard Maré, 'Tradition and control', p.5).

14　　Hindson and Morris, 'Political Violence and Urban Reconstruction'. They argue that this renders the political explanation of the violence used by many of the participants themselves problematic. Segal, 'The Human Face of Violence' and Stavrou and Crouch, 'Violence on the periphery' make similar statements. I find it less puzzling.

15   See, for example, W. Beinart, 'Worker Consciousness, Ethnic Particularism and Nationalism: the Experience of a South African Migrant, 1930-1960' in S. Marks and S. Trapido, *The Politics of Race, Class and Nationalism* (London, 1987); P. Delius, 'Sebatakgomo: Migrant Organization, the ANC and the Sekhukhuneland Revolt', *Journal of Southern African Studies*, 15 (1989), pp. 581-616.

16   A. Sitas, 'African workers' Responses on the East Rand to Changes in the Metal Industry', Wits. Ph.D. 1983, cited in Segal, 'The Human Face of Violence'. Segal proceeds to show how and why this changed in the mid 1980s, as the unions came to be led by urban-based trade unionists who were less sensitive to the needs of the hostel-dwellers, and as the migrants themselves came under pressure from the huge number of unemployed kin who made the hostels their first port of call in search of work on the Rand. Her work, based on interviews with nineteen Zulu hostel-dwellers, informs much of my analysis.

17   Barrington Moore, *Social Origins of Dictatorship and Democracy. Lord and Peasant in the Making of the Modern World* (Harmondsworth: Penguin, 1967), pp. 485-6.

18   Raymond Williams, *Resources of Hope: Culture, Democracy, Socialism*, ed. by R. Gale (London: Verso, 1989). Williams is writing of course of the alignment and commitment of the writer — but this is equally true of the people of Natal who are trying to make sense of lives being disrupted by the forces of modernity — and who return to these subterranean, subliminal alignments to enable them to do so.

19   Hence the many rumours and forged pamphlets, attributing warlike motives to the ANC and deliberately spread in the hostels.

20   E. Webster, 'Taking Labour Seriously', paper presented to the annual conference of the African Studies Association of Australia and the Pacific, Perth, December 1-4 1991.

21   'South Asia, the World System and World Capitalism', *Journal of Asian Studies*, 49 (August 1990), pp.481-2.

22   'Occidentalism: from Montaigne to Trink-Minh-ha, via Fanon and Foucault', a summary version of Professor Corrigan's inaugural lecture, 'The Necessity for Historical Sociology' given at the University of Exeter, 19 April 1991. I am grateful to Professor Patrick O'Brien for a copy of the lecture.

23   There is a lively controversy in South African historiography at present on the reasons for the rise of Shaka Zulu, but this need

not detain us here. See, for example, J. Cobbing, 'The Mfecane as Alibi: Thoughts on Dithakong and Mbolompo', *Journal of African History*, 29 (1988), pp.48-519; J. Wright, 'Political Mythology and the making of Natal's mfecane', *Canadian Journal of African Studies*, 23 (1989), pp.272-91; E. Eldredge, 'The Mfecane reconsidered: the origins of violence in South Africa, ca 1800-1830', and C. Hamilton, 'The Character and Objects of Chaka: a reconsideration of the making of Shaka as Mfecane "Motor"', both in *Journal of African History*, 33 (1992), pp.1-63.

24   Hamilton, 'The Character and Objects of Chaka'; and D. Golan, 'Inkatha's Uses of History', *History in Africa*, 18 (1991), pp.113-26.

25   This paragraph and what follows draw heavily on my 'Patriotism, Patriarchy and Purity: Natal and the Politics of Zulu Ethnic Consciousness', in Leroy Vail, *The Creation of Tribalism in Southern Africa* (London, Berkeley and Los Angeles, 1989), and *The Ambiguities of Dependence. State, Class and Nationalism in Early Twentieth-century Natal* (Baltimore and Johannesburg, 1987).

26   *A Taste of Freedom. The ICU in Rural South Africa 1924-1930* (New Haven and London:Yale University Press, 1987), p.96.

27   Bradford, *Taste of Freedom*, 100.

28   Golan, 'Inkatha', pp.115, 122.

29   Address of M.G. Buthelezi to the Inkatha Youth Brigade, 'Peaceful change through negotiations and tolerance or chaos and conflict through violence and intimidation', Ulundi 24 Aug 1991.

30   Segal, p.10.

31   This is based on D. J. Tilton, 'Writing the script for the future. Inkatha and the role of development in KwaZulu', D. Phil. Oxford, 1991. The inference is mine. Although development aid from international donors has not been vast, given the dire poverty of Kwazulu, its impact is considerable, and there has been some trickle-down effect: the patronage it has made possible is one of the reasons why Buthelezi has been able to maintain some of his support, especially among older women in the rural areas.

32   Doug Hindson and Mike Morris, 'Class Differentiation, Political Conflict and State Reform: a Study of Black Urbanization in the 1980s', unpublished proposal, 1990.

33   Last year Buthelezi was alleged to have about 7% of the popular
        vote nationally; recently it has been put at 3-4%. Poll figures in
        South Africa are notoriously unreliable for all kinds of reasons;
        but they are useful in suggesting at least an order of magnitude.

7

Sons of Shaka, or Sons of Umslopogaas?

James Shuttleworth

Introduction

This chapter explores the construction of the Zulu as a 'warrior people'. It begins by contrasting two Nguni-speaking peoples — the Zulu and the Xhosa — and asks why these closely related societies have acquired such very different public images. The question is of more than merely academic historical interest. A certain set of assumptions about the ethnic singularity of the Zulu lies as the basis of Inkatha's political claims. While not denying the importance of historic memory to those people who identify themselves as Zulu, this chapter argues that the emergence of the Zulu and Xhosa as two very different historical entities is largely a product of white culture. Some key white culture brokers have assisted in the manufacture of an image of the Zulu which has until recently been of evident utility to white interests at the expense of black South Africans. Through constant reiteration and 'feedback loops', images generated by white writers have been fed into the self-conscious identity of ethnic Zulu.

Inkatha has become the model for rapid political growth and effective organization that other 'homeland' leaders have tried to emulate. However these other leaders have failed to achieve MG

Buthelezi's international prominence. Despite the resources and authority of the Bantustan system which they, like Inkatha, have at their disposal, they lack Inkatha's sizable and devoted following. The ethnic identities, myths and traditions that the other 'homeland' leaders possess do not appear to have the same resonance with Africans elsewhere in the subcontinent. When leaders of the Ciskei faced a crisis of legitimacy during the late 1970s and the 1980s they attempted to develop loyalty to their administration by promoting a sense of ethnic nationalism. Despite the most determined efforts, Ciskeian national consciousness failed to take root and the regime was forced to fall back upon brute repression to achieve its aims.[1] Compared to Inkatha, all other attempts to establish ethnic nationalism in other 'homelands' must be deemed to have failed.

Why do some ethnic nationalisms thrive while others refuse to take root? AD Smith's study of ethnicity suggests that the more striking and well known an ethnic group's identity and myths are, the greater the chance that it will survive and endure; conversely, the more shadowy and obscure its identity and myths, the less vivid its sense of uniqueness and the greater its likelihood of dissolution.[2]

The important point about ethnic, as opposed to other kinds of groupings is the rationale that sustains the sense of group uniqueness. That rationale is to be found in the history of the group and above all in its myths of group origins.[3] However, it is not common descent that is the basis of ethnic attachments; rather it is the myth of a common and unique origin in time and place that is essential. Like those of most ethnic groups, the Zulu's boundaries of ethnicity have been very fluid and the people who have come to make the inhabitants of Kwazulu have diverse origins. But, without a sense of common origins and history, however garbled or mythical, no ethnic community can subsist.[4] The so-called Shakan revolution and the rise of the armed Zulu Kingdom have provided the myths of ethnic origin used by Inkatha.

The 'great man' history of Zulu oral traditions (praise poetry) as well as the work of a number of scholars from the western tradition concentrate upon Shaka as the founder of the Zulu Kingdom. In many ways Shaka personifies the myths of Zulu ethnic origin. According to these myths it was Shaka's military innovations which allowed the Zulu Kingdom to rise and dominate neighbouring black societies. Shaka is said to have modified the Nguni throwing spear into a shorter weapon to be used like a bayonet rather than flung. He is credited with the development of the large cow-hide shield used by Zulu impis. The age-mate system of regimentation and practice of delayed marriage are often claimed to have been Shaka's inventions. The 'typical' battle formation shaped like a charging buffalo with the main body of the impi constituting the chest and the two flanks, the horns, is likewise attributed to Shaka's genius. In addition to its claims of descent from the great founder, Inkatha has been able to invoke a striking array of ethnic symbols from the old Zulu Kingdom, including the monarchy, politico-religious traditions and festivals as well as the 'warrior' tradition of tremendous spectacle. However, the sorts of traditions used so effectively by Inkatha in the Kwazulu-Natal region are not absent from the historical experience of other 'homelands'.

A Warrior People? Representations of Zulu and Xhosa

The Xhosa, like the Zulu, are an Nguni-speaking people. They have military traditions, oral poetry and ritual very similar to those of the Zulu. Many of the traditions which are central to the appeal of Inkatha's ethnic identity were also features of the Xhosa past. The spectacle and rituals of the Zulu, so vividly celebrated by some western writers can also be discerned in Xhosa military traditions. Like the Zulu, the Xhosa believed all human activities and especially war were influenced by magic.[5] Xhosa war doctors would administer medicines derived from the bodies of fierce animals such as snakes and bulls, that would help the warriors in battle. As with the Zulu, these medicines were rubbed into incisions made in the body. Every healthy adult male was a warrior in Xhosa society and war played a prominent role in Xhosa history.[6] Oral traditions enshrined the deeds of war heroes; and warriors often assembled at the Great Place to feast, dance and compose praises. Like the Zulu, at the scene of a battle Xhosa warriors would respond to the exhortations of their leaders by chanting and striking their shields with spears.

Many features of warfare that are often attributed to Shakan innovation were common to most Nguni-speaking peoples — including the Xhosa. The short stabbing spear, which has taken on the significance of Excalibur in the myths of Zulu ethnic origin, was used by the Xhosa, and became their most effective weapon against the European invaders during the Frontier Wars.[7] The Xhosa battle formation of central mass flanked by wings was the equivalent of the famous charging buffalo formation of the Zulu.[8]

The Xhosa can point to a much longer record of military prowess than the Zulu. However, during their long history of conflict with European settlers, the Xhosa modified traditional Nguni methods of warfare and at times completely abandoned them. To resist European domination they developed guerilla tactics.[9] They gradually learned to avoid open resistance and to conceal themselves in bushes and kloofs, only leaving cover to harass the enemy's rear guard. Like so many guerillas since, they were expert at living off the land and developed systems of spies to gather information and used signal fires to pass information between scattered war-bands. They used firearms when they had them, but more often relied upon spears, and at times stones and agricultural tools became weapons. During the Fifth Frontier War (1818-1819), Nxele invaded the colony and attacked Grahamstown itself. The success of Xhosa guerillas forced the British to recruit Khoi and Mfengu auxiliaries and to adopt Xhosa tactics. The seventh Frontier War (also known as The War of the Axe, 1846) saw Xhosa guerrillas virtually prostrate the British. Sandile was forced to pull back on the brink of victory in order to avoid the famine that the British army's scorched earth policies threatened to produce.

Thus the Xhosa proved to be at least as capable as the Zulu of standing up to the technological superiority of the Europeans. There is evidence that the Zulu began to adopt similar tactics following the invasion of the Zulu Kingdom in 1879.[10] However, it is the Zulu tactic of charging into guns that is emphasized in ethnic myth. The fiercest battles fought by the Xhosa were against European invaders. In contrast, the Zulu army of mythic memory concentrated its efforts on dominating neighbouring black societies. There is little doubt that Xhosa military traditions and history of guerilla warfare could could have been a potent source of pride for black South Africans. Why then, has emphasis upon the Xhosa war leaders of old like Nxele and Sandile in the Ciskei and Transkei not achieved the same success as Inkatha's ethnic mobilization in Kwazulu? Why have no Xhosa leaders attained the fame of Shaka, Dingane or Cetshwayo?

It may be, as Jeff Peires suggests, that attacks by dispersed Xhosa war-bands do not capture the imagination as does the massed rush to victory of the Zulu at Isandhlwana.[11] However, it is more a matter of emphasis and of the ways that these events have subsequently been portrayed, than any intrinsic qualities of the events themselves which have commanded the attention of subsequent generations. The tragic and self destructive events of the Xhosa cattle-killings (1856-1857) cannot explain the failure of attempts at ethnic mobilization amongst the Xhosa of Transkei and Ciskei. In other societies, it has often been just this kind of tragedy which has provided the powerful symbols around which ethnic mobilization has taken place.[12]

Construction of Knowledge about the Zulu

So, how are we to explain that the image of the Zulu as a proud and disciplined warrior race has been projected around the world while the military traditions of the Xhosa and other have been ignored and forgotten? One vital difference between the two groups is the way their pasts have been portrayed by white culture. White culture has perpetuated myths of Zulu military superiority while Xhosa military traditions have been virtually ignored. It should come as no surprise that white culture should glorify images of the Zulu, as a black nation that preyed upon and dominated other black nations, while the Xhosa, waging a guerilla war upon white invaders, have been ignored. World capitalism in general and white South Africans in particular have had very little interest in glorifying black guerilla fighters.

On the other hand, various white groups have had a direct interest in promoting an image of Zulu military superiority. Nineteenth century accounts detailing the events surrounding the rise of the Zulu Kingdom emphasized violence and depopulation of Natal. Those who first wrote about the consolidation of Shaka's Kingdom and the accompanying violence known as the *mfecane* were the very traders, settlers and missionaries whose material interests were served by such an image of the Zulu. As Julian Cobbing has pointed out, the timing of this alleged depopulation of Natal, just prior to the white invasion of the area, is no mere coincidence.[13] White settlers and traders in Natal who were interested in establishing rights to large tracts of land in Natal also had an interest in propagating an empty land myth. Their claims to land were strengthened by the story that Natal had been cleared of population by Shaka's impis. Settlers also used the story to justify domination of the African population. The coming of white rule, they could claim, had inaugurated an era of peace and stability which attracted black 'refugees'.[14]

Evidence is mounting which suggests that the cause of conflicts in African societies during the early 1800s was not expansion of the Zulu Kingdom, but 'the imperialist attentions of mercantile and early industrial capitalism'.[15] Demands for labour and cattle stemming from the Delagoa Bay region, the Eastern Cape and raiding bands of armed Griqua horsemen accelerated the series of attacks and counter-attack known as the 'mfecane'. Cobbing believes literate whites used the documents to provide themselves and their Griqua raiders with an alibi. The Zulu became the scape-goat for violence which emanated from capitalism's demands for labour and cattle.[16]

At times Cobbing appears to get carried away with the significance of his work as a metaphor for the causes of black of black violence in the late twentieth century and occasionally his arguments fly in the face of empirical evidence.[17] However, despite this, and an occasional tendency to treat black people as passive objects in need of whites to initiate action, Cobbing's work throws an important new light on the rise of the Zulu Kingdom. Regardless of whether the 'mfecane' is a complete myth that should be abandoned, or has some basis in historical reality, the relevant point for this chapter is that the image of the Zulu as an all powerful, all conquering warrior race is shown to have a long pedigree in the minds of self-interested white traders and settlers.

Missionaries fed another stream into the production of knowledge about the Zulu. In the early decades missionaries had very little success in their attempts to convert the Zulu. Most Zulu commoners were not eager to join the capitalist political economy that the mission stations represented, nor did they rush to become Christians. Zulu kings opposed conversion because it meant the withdrawal of converts' labour power from the kingdom, their services from the army and their allegiance from the Zulu state.[18] Disappointed and embittered missionaries mounted a public campaign designed to encourage British intervention in the affairs of the Kingdom. They portrayed the Zulu as warlike savages and a threat to the white settlers of Natal.[19] Tales of dark and bloody deeds inside the Kingdom emanated from missionary sources.

The central role played by the Zulu in Afrikaner myths of ethnic origin has also helped to perpetuate exaggerated pictures of the the 'warrior people'. These myths emphasize that adversities faced on the frontier forged the Afrikaner national character. A crucial element in these frontier experiences are the Zulu. Portrayal of the Zulu as a serious military challenge is indispensable. These myths demand images of the Zulu as a bellicose race with tremendous military skills. The massacre of Piet Retief and Blood River are portrayed as central tests faced by the Boers on their journey. It was by facing and defeating the challenge of the Zulu at Blood River that gave the Boers 'access to the promised land'.[20] Myths surrounding the assegai and Zulu military virtues have been as important to Afrikaner nationalists in the past as they are now to Inkatha ideologies.

The Anglo-Zulu war of 1879 changed some of the ways whites perceived the Zulu. Three main views developed during and in the years following the war. First, there was the view of the Zulu 'devised by imperial agents in South Africa to justify their invasion of the Zulu Kingdom'.[21] This drew heavily upon the images and history which land hungry settlers and embittered missionaries had presented over the previous half century. A second view was championed by Bishop Colenso of Natal and those who opposed the invasion of Zululand. While they aimed to rebut the charges of murder and atrocity against King Cetshwayo, they did little to debunk Zulu military prowess. The third, and most important view as far as this chapter is concerned, was activated by the Zulu victory at Isandlhwana. Press reports of the victory fired the reading public's imagination — especially in Britain. Russell Martin points out that after this opening phase of the war 'respect and even admiration were now expressed for the military qualities of the Zulus who had measured themselves against British might and not been found wholly wanting'.[22]

In the decades following the war the image of the Zulus as heroic savage warriors that had been popularized by the press, was taken up and elaborated upon by the novelist H Rider Haggard, who had lived in Natal during the eighteen seventies.

Fiction and the Zulu

Haggard's enormously popular work celebrated Zulu military virtues, bravery, discipline and sense of duty, as well as what he saw as their savage and sensual culture. His portrayal of Zulu society is a world 'in which all taboos are abolished. Incest, polygamy, cannibalism, nudism, necrophilia, patricide, fratricide and general homicide are everyday occurrences'. In these romances "the beasts Victorians feared to encounter in themselves could be contemplated at a safe remove".[23] The narrator and namesake of *Allan Quatermain* explains the appeal that the Zulu of Haggard's imagination possess as follows:

> No man who has for forty years lived the life I have can with impunity coop himself in this prim English country, with its trim hedgerows and cultivated fields, its stiff formal manners and its well dressed crowds. He begins to long — ah, he longs! for the keen breath of the desert air; he dreams of the sight of Zulu impis breaking on their foes like surf upon the rocks, and his heart rises in rebellion against the strict limits of civilized life.[24]

The Africa of Haggard's imagination provides a contrast to the order and restrictions of 'civilized' England. It is a wild and alien landscape where anything is possible. The Zulu characters as inhabitants of this terrain represent that side of Haggard's psyche which longs to escape an existence where the rules of 'civilized' conduct have been laid out like so many hedgerow bordered fields.

In *Allan Quatermain* Haggard introduced his most famous Zulu character — Umslopogaas. Umslopogaas is the real hero of this adventure.[25] This 'great warrior of royal blood' lives only for the fray. He possesses super-human martial skills, stamina and bravery. All other Africans pale by comparison. The narrator tells his readers that he was 'in his own savage fashion, the finest general I ever knew'.[26] All these characteristics make Umslopogaas the personification of Zulu martial virtue and traditions. On the old warrior's death Haggard pays to him what to Haggard (in many ways the quintessential Victorian Englishman), must be the ultimate tribute: 'We had only done our duty, as is the fashion of both Englishmen and Zulus to do.'[27] The irony here is that in *Allan Quatermain* the Zulu military traditions, personified in Umslopogaas, have been harnessed to serve the ends of his white masters. That irony will not be lost upon close observers of Inkatha.

Haggard's romances entered the market place when, for the first time in history, a mass reading public existed. Haggard's portrayal of the Zulu has a parallel in the images of the Plains Indians which emanated from the United States. At around the same time Umslopogaas, Blood River and Isandhlwana filled the pages of Haggard's novels, the myths of the 'savage' plains 'tribes' like the Sioux and their Battle of Little Bighorn were being portrayed in a plethora of pulp fiction. Just as the Sioux leader Sitting Bull toured the capitals as part of 'Buffalo' Bill Cody's Wild West Show, so troupes of Africans billed as 'Zulu warriors who had fought at Isandhlwana' toured Britain exhibiting their martial skills and re-enacting attacks.[28]

These parallel myths about Plains Indians and the Zulu have entered the mainstream of twentieth-century popular culture. Through the print and electronic media Haggard's portrayal of the Zulu as 'the bravest savages in the world'[29] whose motto was 'kill till you are killed'[30] has become almost universally known. These endlessly recycled images fulfil white fantasies of black savagery and concurrently advance the interests of whites at the expense of black South Africans. EA Ritter's *Shaka Zulu* is a striking example of how the Haggard tradition lives on. Ritter describes the book as a biography and claims it is based upon oral tradition.[31] However, his explanation of how these sources were transmitted to him is less than convincing. The book dwells upon superstition, witchcraft, torture, slaughter and Zulu sexual practices. He tells his readers that Zulu warriors possessed

> a profound knowledge of female physiology... and they were past masters in the delicate art of pre-coition excitation or lover play. [Shaka we are told] ... was as outstanding in love as battle ... [able to impart] full satisfaction to all his partners [and able to] ... deflower a reasonable number ... in the first three hectic days of his sexual marathon ...[32]

To Ritter the *impis* form a picture "of sinister military beauty".[33] His many battle scenes glory in Zulu savagery.

> The gaping wounds caused by the broad Zulu blades practically drained the Ndwandwe corpses of their blood, which, with the Zulu quota, was now flowing or in pools in the confined area of the fighting, and its odour intoxicated the fighters.[34]

These descriptions do not resemble any of the known oral sources. What they do resemble is Haggard's fiction and they seem to be designed to titillate readers with a fantasy of black savagery.

Films such as *Zulu, Zulu Dawn* and the television series 'Shaka Zulu' have multiplied the impact of the stereotype on the mass consciousness. Cy Endfield's films present striking portraits of the Zulu en masse — portraits that call to mind Haggard's intoxicating imaginings.

> It was a splendid sight to see them their assegais glittering in the sunlight as they rose and fell above their blackshields, their war-plumes bending upon the wind, and their fierce faces set intently on the foe, while the solid earth shook beneath the thunder of their rushing feet.[35]

Bare-breasted maidens and brave warriors shaking the earth with 'tribal' dancing also mimic Haggard. *Zulu* depicts a small group of whites isolated from outside help who must defend themselves against a vast horde of black 'savages' in order to survive. The analogy with the way white South Africa has often depicted itself as an outpost of 'civilization' fighting against the forces of violence and chaos is obvious. The attitude to race relations in South Africa presented in *Zulu Dawn* is a more ambiguous one. Early in the film Cetshwayo addresses a gathering of his warriors and explains to them that they are about to go to war in order to protect the fruits of their labour from the English invaders. The clear intention here is to point out that we are not dealing with mindless savagery. The Zulu are fighting to protect their way of life. However, in both film and book form, *Zulu Dawn* celebrates a paternalism most black leaders would reject.[36]

Buthelezi played the role of his ancestor Cetshwayo in *Zulu* and Endfield dedicated *Zulu Dawn* to 'a great man and a dear friend, Chief Gatsha Buthelezi'. Buthelezi's willingness to ignore the subtexts and other objectionable aspects of these works may be due to his enthusiam for their glorification of Zulu military traditions and the Zulu ethnic past as well as for their emphasis on his own special relationship to that past. Buthelezi's rather precarious position in relation to the portrayal of the Zulu past by white culture was highlighted by his response to the South African Broadcasting Corporations television series, 'Shaka Zulu'. This truly dreadful series depicts all the bloodlust, superstition and savagery of Haggard's novels. Initially, Buthelezi seems to have found the series an embarrassment and publicly attacked it both for portraying Shaka as a bloodthirsty tyrant and for distorting Zulu history. However, he was not willing to completely disassociate himself from the series, because, despite its glaring flaws 'Shaka Zulu' worked as a powerful endorsement for the Kwazulu leadership.[37]

All the myths of Zulu ethnic origin are vividly portrayed in the film. Single-handedly Shaka reshapes Zulu warfare. The success of his innovations is dramatically depicted in battle scenes where the Zulu impis easily defeat their neighbours who cling to pre-Shakan methods of war. This portrayal of a glorious, if rather bloody, Zulu past was of evident value to a political organization like Inkatha which draws so heavily upon the symbols and traditions of the ethnic past as a means of mobilizing support. Buthelezi, who traces his ancestry back to Shaka on the maternal line, could not resist the opportunity of riding on the dramatic success of this vivid recreation of the life of the founder of the Zulu Kingdom.[38]

It would be difficult to think of an ethnic nationalism which has a set of images and myths at its disposal that are more striking and well known than those of Inkatha. However as recent investigation of the Zulu past by Cobbing, John Wright and others has demonstrated, these images of the Zulu as an all conquering warrior race are only very loosely based upon any historical reality. Rather, these images have largely been created and perpetuated by whites to serve white interests, usually at the expense of the interests of black South Africans. These images were performing similar functions in the 1980s.

Every time Buthelezi or King Goodwill Zwelithini uses a Pretoria-sponsored rally to glorify Zulu military superiority and appeal for loyalty from 'the sons of Shaka', they are using these images which were originally crafted to serve white interests. Inkatha, we have lately learned, has been paid by white South Africa to conform to their stereotypical version of black savagery. Zulu ethnic nationalism is being used to legitimate an Inkatha leadership which has been prepared to collaborate with a regime that has denied people virtually all rights of citizenship upon the grounds of skin colour. Ethnic symbols and loyalty are used to mobilize impoverished Zulu-speaking peasants and migrant workers and to encourage them to attack those who carry out rent and consumer boycotts, strikes and other forms of resistance. Every time an Inkatha *impi* dresses in leopard skins and, using 'traditional' weapons, carries out such attacks, it provides ammunition for those who wish to demonstrate that handing the country over to black majority rule can only lead to 'inter-tribal' war and that white rule must be preserved in order to keep the 'tribes' apart.

Notes

1   Anonymous, 'Ethnicity and Pseudo-Ethnicity in the Ciskei' in L. Vail, ed., *The Creation of Tribalism in Southern Africa* (London, Berkeley and Los Angeles, 1989), pp.395-410.

2   A.D. Smith,*The Ethnic Revival*, (Cambridge, 1981), p.65.

3   Ibid, p.65.

4   Ibid, p.67.

5   J. B. Peires, *The House of Phalo: A History of the Xhosa People in the Days of Their Independence*, (Berkeley: University of California Press, 1982), p.136.

6   Ibid, p.138.

7   Ibid, p.141.

8   Ibid, p.138.

9   For a more detailed account of Xhosa guerilla warfare upon which the account in this paper is based, see ibid, pp.139-160.

10   E. Unterhalter, 'Confronting Imperialism: the people of Nquthu and the invasion of Zululand' in A. Duminy and C. Ballard, *The Anglo-Zulu War New Perspectives* (Pietermaritzburg: University of Natal Press, 1981), pp.103-104.

11   Peires, *The House of Phalo*, p.160.

12   A good example of this phenomenon is found amongst the Sioux in the United States. In 1891 Sioux warriors rode to their deaths against the United States army believing they would be protected from bullets by their 'Ghost Shirts'. The tragedy of the 'Ghost Shirt Religion' is a central image in Sioux ethnic mobilization.

13   J. Cobbing, 'The Mfecane as Alibi: Second Thoughts on Dithakong and Mbolompo', *Journal of African History*, 29 (1988), p.488.

14   J. Wright, 'Political Mythology and the Making of Natal's Mfecane', *Canadian Journal of African Studies*, 23, (1989), p.277.

15   J. Cobbing, 'The Mfecane as Alibi', pp.488-489.

16   Ibid, pp.492-496.

17   A good example of these features of Cobbing's work is seen in ibid, p.510, where he insists upon implicating the trader Henry Francis Fynn in Shaka's assassination by Dingane's supporters. As Cobbing admits there is no direct evidence for this and it is safe to assume that black Africans are just as capable of committing deeds both good and bad as whites are. Few would

dispute the existence of fratricidal tendencies amongst Zulu princes and these tendencies reach legendary proportions in Zulu oral traditions. See for example C. de B. Webb and J.B. Wright, *The James Stuart Archive*, Vol.4, (Pietermaritzburg: University of Natal Press, 1986), pp.93-96. Zulu folklore suggests that these fratricidal squabbles continued even after death. Shaka and Dingane returned to Zululand from 'the world below' in the form of big snakes to continue their struggles. It is said they were fighting ' because one had killed the other in the world above'.

18   N. Etherington, *Preachers, Peasants and Politics in South East Africa, 1835-1880: African Christian Communities in Natal, Pondoland and Zululand* (London: Royal Historical Society, 1979), pp.74-83.

19   R. Martin, 'British Images of the Zulu C.1820-1879', unpublished Ph.D. thesis (Cambridge, 1982), p.226.

20   M. de Villiers,*White Tribe Dreaming, Apartheid's Bitter Roots*, (MacMillan of Canada, 1987), p.13.

21   Martin, 'British Images of the Zulu', p. 253.

22   Ibid, p.285.

23   N. Etherington, *Rider Haggard*, (Boston: G.K. Hall, 1983), p.50

24   Haggard, *Allan Quatermain*, (London:Target paperback, 1980), p. 9.

25   Ibid, p.253. Ironically Haggard's model for Umslopogaas was a Swazi.

26   Ibid, p.64.

27   Ibid, p.249.

28   Martin, 'British Images of the Zulu', pp. 279-280.

29   Haggard, *Allan's Wife*, (London, 1920), p. 71.

30   Ibid, p.92.

31   E. A. Ritter, *Shaka Zulu* (Middlesex, 1987), p. 401.

32   Ibid, pp.220-222.

33   Ibid, p.177.

34   Ibid, p.158.

35   Haggard, *Allan's Wife*, p.87.

36   The paternalism in *Zulu Dawn* comes in the form of an implied need for whites to help raise blacks to the level of 'white civilization'. The implication is made through the device of the 'Sikhali Horsemen'. The Sikhalis are Africans who have been educated by missionaries and trained by the British Army. They have proved to be competent soldiers and as Endfield puts it

have 'long ago earned full membership in the society which had modelled their behaviour and beliefs'. C. Endfield, *Zulu Dawn*, (London, 1979), p.277. The Sikhalis' commander and the symbol of white paternalism is played by Burt Lancaster in the film. He is a character of considerable sympathy and the only white in the film who displays any real understanding of Zulu society. He tries to convince his superiors that the Zulu would rather avoid war, so they can carry out the agricultural activities upon which their survival depends. However the extremist white supremacists, represented by the British high command, push the Zulu too far and war results. The Sikhali, their commander and hence all the good work that has been done to 'civilize' these 'natives' is wiped out in a holocaust of black violence at Isandlwana. This kind of paternalism provides support for so-called positive apartheid. This is very evident in the book form where there are strong contrasts between various groups of Africans. For example, the clumsy clown-like Basutos, who have deserted their 'traditional' lifestyle, but have not yet received the benefit of white civilization, compare very unfavourably with the disciplined and competent Sikhalis and the graceful magestic Zulu who cling to their 'traditional' ways. Ibid, p.68. The implication for modern South Africa is clear — blacks need to be raised by white leadership before they are ready for entry into 'white' civilization and until then, they are better off clinging to their 'traditional' ways.

37   C.A. Hamilton, 'A Propositional Gambit: Shaka Zulu and the conflict in South Africa', *Radical History Review*, 44 (Spring, 1989), p.26.

38   Ibid, p.27.

8

Broedertwis: Intra-Afrikaner conflicts in the transition from apartheid 1969-1991

Hermann Giliomee

Introduction

One the most striking features of the contemporary scene in South Africa is the political overreach of Afrikaners, currently forming approximately eight per cent of the population. Afrikaners are in a predominant position in the cabinet, the top levels of the central state bureaucracy, the state television and radio, and the senior officer corps of the security forces. By the end of the 1980s the ruling National Party was still effectively an Afrikaner party which retained many of the ethnic linkages forged in its rise as an ethnic mobilization movement. A study showed that on economic issues the government was far more responsive to Afrikaner institutional pressure and lobbying than to representations from English big business or blacks.[1] Managerial positions in the para-statal sector remained largely an Afrikaner preserve. As recently as 1986 a study described the South African state as the Boereplaas (literally the Afrikaners' farm).[2]

In pursuing negotiations the NP leadership is still strongly motivated by the goal of securing the survival of the Afrikaners.[3]

A negotiated settlement in South Africa will, to an important extent, depend on the ability of Afrikaners to adapt to a major curtailment of their overreach through redefining their ethnic identity and claims. This chapter will discuss the general debate on the transmutability of ethnic groups before proceeding to an analysis of the Afrikaner Broedertwis — the quarrel between 'brothers' over the group's identity and interests.[4]

Modernization, class and ethnicity

During the 1960s and 1970s the debate on ethnicity was dominated by modernization theorists who tended to see a person's ethnic identity as being subordinate to his/her class concerns. What interests us here is not the perspectives of these theorists on the origins and growth of ethno-national movements but their conviction that modernization undermines ethnic identities and loyalties. They argue that once the the goals of ethnic mobilization have been achieved, the primordial identifications of old become dysfunctional as people increasingly focus on their respective class interests. At this stage modern, overarching identities and a common consumer culture are supposed to replace the old, obsolete ethnic identities. Writing within this tradition, Heribert Adam observed of contemporary Afrikaner society: 'It has yet to be proven anywhere that a BMW-owning bureaucratic bourgeoisie with swimming-pools and servants readily sacrifices the good life for psychologically gratifying ethnic affinities.'[5]

Like modernization theorists, Marxist analysts see ethnicity as subordinate to larger economic forces and conflicts in society. In the Marxist perspective capitalism breaks down ethnic barriers and distinctions and assimilates nations. If a mobilization of ethnic power does occur in societies well advanced on the modernization road it is attributed to 'backwardness' or to the manipulating powers of class elites using ethnicity to advance their own particular goals.[6] In South African historiography Dan O'Meara has taken Marxist theory further by attempting to show how organized class forces in Afrikanerdom under the banner of the NP forged an alliance to construct the apartheid state which temporarily resolved the accumulation crisis of the 1940s. By the early 1980s, however, with modernization of the economy and society much further advanced, the alliance had become unstuck. As O'Meara puts it, Afrikaner unity had become an obstacle to the accumulation of capital by Afrikaner 'Hoggenheimers' and it 'was sacrificed on the altar of "Total Strategy" and the unity of the capitalist class'.[7] This chapter will discuss O'Meara's interpretation at some length as a critique of the approach of both modernization theorists and Marxists to the problem of the persistence of political ethnicities.

From the start of the 1970s the modernization and Marxist perspectives have been challenged by what can be called the conflictual modernization paradigm. Its perspective is radically different: far from softening ethnic conflict, modernization tends to aggravate it as individuals from different ethnic groups vie for political status and political power. Walker Connor has argued that modernization theorists have greatly exaggerated the influence of materialism upon human affairs and in doing so have ignored the powerful emotional bond of ethno-nationalism. In his view ethnic groups are often prepared to make large material sacrifices in order to retain some form of autonomy which gives them freedom from domination by non-members.[8] In similar fashion Donald Horowitz has urged scholars to look beyond materialism and focus on the collective drive for social status and power. This drive is particularly strong in divided societies where an individual's status is inextricably linked to the status of his/her ethnic group. Power is not only sought as a means to secure tangible goods (as is the case in homogenous modern societies) but also for confirmation of ethnic group status. In Horowitz's terms: 'The fear of ethnic domination and suppression is a motivating force for the acquisition of power as an end. Broad matters of group status regularly have equal or superior standing to the narrow allocative decisions often taken to be the uniform stuff of everyday politics'.[9]

Writing about minorities in Eastern Europe, George Schöpflin also makes the point that material concerns are not decisive. In his view ethno-nationalism is a political category which derives from cultural rather than economic concerns. It leads to a form of politics in which the community 'relies on its culture as its storehouse of moral precepts, or set of rules by which it determines its moral universe and defines what behaviour is right and wrong'.[10] To regard culture only in terms of its outward manifestations such as language, symbols and consumer habits is to misunderstand the dynamics of ethno-nationalism.[11] Culture must be defined as the sum total of the subjective perceptions in a community; the rules by which it orders its life; its sense of a common past and a shared future and its socially constructed picture of the world.

There is yet another perspective which must be considered. This is a view which looks beyond class struggles and economic conflict to incorporate the specific role of the state. In a comparative study Stanley Greenberg sketched a compelling picture of states which maintained racial and ethnic divisions long after they were no longer functional to the classes which had originally demanded their statutory imposition.[12] Theda Skocpol introduced the concept of state autonomy which she describes as the capacity to formulate and pursue goals that are not simply reflective of the demands or interests of social groups, classes or society. In the collection *Bringing the State back In*, Skocpol and her co-editors note that social identities can depend on the strategies of 'hegemonic states' that have the motivation and capacity to structure or restructure the patterns of group formation in society.[13] In the case of South Africa the apartheid state long had a motivation to preserve Afrikaner political unity as one of its main bases. However, as competing political claims intensified, the state developed an interest in transcending a narrow identification between the state and the Afrikaner group. To a large extent the division of the 1980s between Afrikaners in the NP and those in the Conservative Party (CP) turned on the question how explicitly state power could be used to protect Afrikaner identity and interests. This has given rise, as we shall see, to sharply conflicting conceptions of Afrikaner identity and interests.

This chapter addresses the various perspectives discussed above. Its emphasis will be equally on change and continuity. On the one hand ethnic identities are situational: they adapt to changing circumstances and in the process are recreated.[14] On the other hand ethnic identities cannot simply be discarded as easily as one would in changing sports clubs. Ethnic identities are difficult to change not only because ethnic leaders cannot simply turn the tap off at will but because an ethnic identity is also defined by out-groups. A history of colonial conquest and of apartheid, which was administered by Afrikaner bureaucrats, have produced strong views among the various black groups about Afrikaners. In many social distance evaluations Africans consistently rate Afrikaners at the furthest extreme of all the outsiders. Horowitz calls the location of Afrikaners on the furthest end of the Xhosa response scale in a study of Soweto matriculants 'truly extraordinary'.[15]

Given the Afrikaner leadership's manipulation of ethnic identities in the apartheid system, it is doubtful whether black groups would be persuaded by a sweeping redefinition of the concept of Afrikaner by Afrikaners themselves. To the extent that ethnic identities are other-defined as well as self-defined, the scope ethnic entrepreneurs have for redefinition may be considerably smaller than modernization theorists commonly think.

The following sections will trace the evolution of Afrikaner identities accompanying major political shifts and schisms in Afrikaner ranks over the past twenty-five years. The discussion will focus on the main assumptions of the theories under discussion. In particular it will critically review the assumption in modernization and Marxist literature that it is conflicts over class and other material issues that cause the schisms and allow the business class to play a decisive role in imposing their class interests upon politics.

From Unity to Schism: the NP Splits of 1969 and 1982

At its apogee in the 1960s, apartheid drew Afrikanerdom together in a tight political unit. The apartheid system greatly enhanced the cultural distinctiveness and common interests of Afrikaners. Controlling the state offered Afrikaners vast opportunities to catch up economically with the English-speaking white group. To mention just one indicator of the economic advance: Afrikaners in white collar occupations (as distinct from those in blue collar or agricultural occupations) rose from 29 per cent in 1946 to 65 per cent in 1977.[16] Political unity, economic affluence and cultural chauvinism enabled Hendrik Verwoerd as leader to present the Afrikaners as a unified, classless democracy and himself as the articulator of the ethnic consensus.[17] Nevertheless shortly after Verwoerd's death in 1966 the verkramp/verlig struggle broke out, leading to the expulsion from the NP of the most prominent verkramptes (archconservatives) under Albert Hertzog and to the founding of the Herstigte Nasionale Party.

The verkramp/verlig split

As we have seen, modernization and Marxist literature considers ethno-nationalism as increasingly dysfunctional once a certain stage in economic development has been reached. From a Marxist dimension O'Meara has argued that the root causes of the verkramp/verlig split should be sought in the fact that by the mid-1960s the two Afrikaner-controlled conglomerates, Sanlam and Rembrandt, had so expanded their base in industry and mining that they were now in effect independent of Afrikaner agricultural capital which originally had launched them. The split was thus essentially a struggle between the verkramptes, who fought to preserve the alliance of 1948, dominated by the interests of farmers and the petty bourgeoisie,on the one hand, and, on the other, the new aggressive class of verligtes who sought political influence in the Transvaal in order to adapt the ideology and policies of Afrikaner nationalism to the changing social composition of the volk.

Part of O'Meara's argument rests on his contention that the financial interests particularly around Sanlam founded the NP in the Cape Province 'and always dominated it', Sanlam also controlled the major Afrikaans publishing house Nasionale Pers (which publishes the most influential Afrikaans daily, *Die Burger*). In O'Meara's account Sanlam from the mid-1960s began to co-operate closely with Anglo America Corporation in an alliance of monopoly capital. As spearhead of the *verligte* campaign for reform, Sanlam articulated the capitalist demand for a more mobile, better trained African labour force as a prerequisite for renewed economic growth.[18]

It can be categorically stated that for most of those statements not much, if any, evidence exists. Sanlam was founded after the Cape NP and never controlled it. Neither did it dominate Nasionale Pers. In 1969 Sanlam held 16.8 percent of the total shareholding but because company rules decreed that no single shareholder could cast more than 50 votes it controlled only one per cent of the votes. Piet Cillié, editor of *Die Burger* from 1954 to 1977 and chairman of Nasionale Pers since 1977, commented , 'In my experience the Sanlam directors on the board always shared the political loyalties of the other directors, which included senior NP politicians. They did not try to push any political line or exert any political influence which was different from that of the other directors.'[19]

Afrikaner business leaders such as Anton Rupert and Andreas Wassenaar, who headed up Rembrandt and Sanlam respectively, were not conspicuous in public for calling for reforms such as the easing of labour curbs on blacks. Rupert largely restricted himself to propagating the economic development of the homelands while Wassenaar attacked the financial profligacy of the state. Both enjoyed a good relationship with Verwoerd's successor, B J Vorster. To verkramptes who suspected them of exerting a 'leftist influence' Vorster replied that he considered them as 'good Afrikaners'.[20] If he gave a hearing to them it was because they served the common ethnic cause, not because they might withdraw their political support from the party. The influence of business leaders was limited because Vorster always tried to balance the different interests of Afrikaners in order to preserve party unity.

This is not to say that economic conflicts were absent in the Afrikaner ethnic alliance. There was intense economic rivalry between Nasionale Pers and the Transvaal-based Afrikaans publishing houses. To an important extent the *verkramp/verlig* struggle was triggered by the decision of Nasionale Pers in 1965 to publish a national Sunday newspaper, *Die Beeld*, in Johannesburg. However, this intra-Afrikaner 'press war' was more significant for being a reflection of the larger ideological battles among Afrikaner nationalists and between the Transvaal and Cape wings of the NP than for the relatively small economic stakes involved.

In fact, the *verlig/verkramp* struggle was more about symbolic and status issues than economic conflicts. In the latest analysis of the battle, the first one based on extensive primary sources, the following main points of contention are highlighted: multi-racial sport, black diplomats, the NP policy of (white) national unity, (white) immigration, 'excessive' spending on black homelands and the retention of 'petty apartheid'. An issue such as the freeing up of black labour did not figure prominently, either in the disputes of the 1960s or early 1970s between *verligtes* and *verkramptes* or in the dialogue between the business class in general and government.[21] Had black labour been a pressing issue it would have been reflected in the debates of the Prime Minister's Economic Advisory Council (EAC). This was not the case. A prominent Afrikaner asserted in 1977 that 'the English-speaking private sector has been heavily represented in the EAC right from the start in 1960. Right through that decade they never presented a convincing case for the need to train and develop blacks, or for housing and so on, beyond expressing their opposition to certain laws such as the Physical Planning Act.'[22]

At the very core of the struggle was a battle among Afrikaners about the purpose of the state and about the goals of Afrikaner nationalism. Until the mid-1960s the NP generated its fervour from politicising the ties of kinship and a distinctive religion, culture and language. Once the ideal of a republic had been realized the NP leadership's attention began to shift to the task of building up the state. While the state's purpose was certainly to protect the culture and status of Afrikaners as a group it had to meet many other pressing demands of which some required that the nationalist rhetoric and the specific favouring of Afrikaner interests be toned down.

In a 1971 analysis Sam Nolutshungu perceptively captured the essence of the conflict:

> The *verligtes* and *verkramptes* represent two inherent contradictory tendencies of exclusivism and accommodation within the nationalist Afrikanerdom ... While the *verligtes* see themselves as whitemen (as well as Afrikaners) the *verkramptes* see themselves as Afrikaners first and last and insist that it is their detailed dissimilarity from other white groups in Africa which accounts for

their survival in a hostile Africa.[23]

Juan Linz has recently remarked in a general context that primordial ties constitute a weak and uncertain basis for the creation of an independent nation-state. Ethno-national movements as a result invariably display a shift from an ethnic to a territorial conception of nationhood.[24] The same can be said of Afrikaner nationalism. Vorster was the first Afrikaner nationalist leader to accept that it was impossible for the movement to press for the increasing Afrikanerization of the state or to seal Afrikaners off as a separate ethnic entity. In future Afrikaner nationalism had to be content with the gains it had made and to seek new allies with people sharing the same land. One of Vorster's first moves was to suppress an inquiry Hendrik Verwoerd had launched into ways in which the economic predominance of the Anglo American Corporation could be curbed. To survive, the increasingly embattled apartheid state had to align English-speaking whites, and English big business in particular, behind the state and the NP government.[25]

Verligtes also began to attack Verwoerd's idea of a 'white nation' protected by a 'white state' in a 'white land'. In its place they developed a sense of 'territorialism', firstly for whites and secondly, albeit very tentatively, also for the Coloured and Indian groups for whom no separate 'homelands' were available. While the idea of a white nation was still a racist concept, the idea of a territorially-based community relied on a voluntaristic definition. It certainly did not mean the end of discrimination but at the very least it implied the acceptance into a wider political community of people who were not white and of the idea that they had legitimate claims on the state. Compared to Verwoerd, Vorster was much more explicit in stating that there were no 'inferior people' in South Africa.[26]

While Vorster was emotionally strongly committed to party unity, he realized that a rigid apartheid system was not compatible with building a strong state and winning broader support for the Afrikaner-dominated state. He made a major break with his predecessor when shortly after assuming power in 1966 he privately told a group of Nationalist parliamentarians that apartheid was longer to be considered as a goal in itself. It was merely a means to protecting the Afrikaners' position. Vorster's words were recorded as follows:

> 'No, you have got it all wrong. The cardinal principle of the NP is the retention, maintenance, and immortalization of Afrikaner identity within a white sovereign state. Apartheid and separate development is merely a means to achieve and to perpetuate this. If there are other and better methods to entrench it then we have to find those methods and continue with them.'[27]

Despite the cautious nature of these shifts Vorster had to face some formidable opposition. One of the chief ideologues, Broederbond chairman Piet Meyer, advocated undiluted Afrikaner hegemony and the 'Afrikanerization' of the English-speaker. The goal, in Meyer's terms, was that the latter 'will integrate his ideals and life style with those of the Afrikaner, that he will adopt Afrikaans history as his own and that he will accept Afrikaans as his national language'.[28] As cabinet minister, Albert Hertzog, told Parliament that the defense of the white nation and civilization could only be entrusted to the Afrikaners who, unlike English-speakers with their liberal beliefs, subjected themselves to authority and were prepared to use stringent security measures.[29] *Verkrampte* parliamentarians and newspaper editors constantly reiterated the theme that Afrikaners could only maintain themselves as a group 'through isolating themselves by maintaining the borders of their race, culture, religion, morals and language'.[30] To be an Afrikaner, someone had to subscribe to a Calvinist and conservative world view.

Vorster counter-attacked after realizing that these chauvinist appeals were aimed at undermining his leadership position. He bluntly told Meyer and his supporters at Broederbond meetings that he had no intention of 'cheating' the English-speakers whose support could not be dispensed with. In public he attacked the verkramptes by saying that white unity was threatened as much by people who considered themselves 'Super Afrikaners' as by jingoes.[31] *Verligtes* strongly rallied behind Vorster in this vital ideological struggle. In a key speech, HB Thom, chairman of the important Broederbond front, the Federasie van Afrikaanse Kultuurverenigings (FAK), exhorted Afrikaners to establish contacts across language and colour borders. In his words, 'the

gates of the laager have to be thrown open: our Afrikanerhood
must be extended fearlessly'.[32]

The *verligtes* finally managed to win this ideological battle
but remained deeply divided over future courses of action,
confirming the point Linz made that ethno-nationalism by itself
does not provide a clear basis for political action. A study
undertaken in the mid-1970s showed that for most Afrikaners an
ethno-cultural awareness was closely tied to a determination to
maintain Afrikaner, and large white, economic and political
privilege.[33] For the leadership it was virtually impossible to
disentangle the cultural and other identity concerns, which it
wanted to maintain, from the explicit privilege from which it was
slowly retreating.

The split of 1982

The party of the verkramptes, the Herstigte Nasionale Party and
other far rightwing parties, never attracted more than 15 per cent
of Afrikaner support at the polls. It represented an ethnic
splinter, not a split. Afrikaner political unity was finally
shattered in 1982 when AP Treurnicht and sixteen Nationalist
MPs broke away to form the Conservative Party. NP Afrikaner
support plummeted from over 80 per cent in the 1981 election to
under 60 per cent in the 1987 election.

In analyses informed by Marxist or modernization theory it
has been argued that this split was brought about by the growing
crisis of capital accumulation since the early 1970s and the labour
reforms introduced since 1979 to remove the restrictions on
African labour. O'Meara argues that with PW Botha's ascent to
power Afrikaner capital had established its political dominance
in the party, and was supported by other bourgeois
organizations and institutions and the army. This shift in class
forces in the NP was resisted by a coalition of farmers who had
not yet made the transition to highly mechanical production, the
lower levels of the Afrikaner petty bourgeoisie and the less
skilled white workers.[34]

Craig Charney also tries to give a distinct class character to
Afrikaner politics and its divisions. Charney writes that white
wage earners defected to the CP because of their discontent with

wage trends and labour policy. White support for the NP and CP among farmers tended to divide according to scale of enterprise (large versus small farms) and market (domestic versus export). Charney further argues that the NP remained organically linked to the NP. Afrikaner private business supported the NP because their interests were different from that of English-speaking capitalists. As Charney formulates it:

> Even much of Afrikaans private business, structurally often the weak relation of its English competitors, remains dependent upon state patronage, protection or non-intervention.   In the case of Afrikaner finance capital, Volkskas still has many state accounts, while Sanlam would lose a lot of insurance business if state medical and pensions schemes were established. Nor should the importance of state orders for Afrikaner industrial undertakings be minimized.[35]

There can be no argument with an attempt to connect political developments in Afrikaner society to larger social processes at work. The Afrikaner unity of the 1950s and early 1960s was made possible by the high economic growth which enabled the leadership to provide substantial protection to the 40 per cent Afrikaners who by 1960 were still in blue collar and other manual occupations. This unity came under strain in the 1970s because apartheid failed to stop the vital manufacturing sector from becoming increasingly dependent on black workers. Between 1960 and 1980 the number of white workers in this sector rose by 75 per cent from 208 900 to 357 700 while the number of Africans jumped by 140 per cent from 314 000 to 772 000. In the thirty years since 1950 the number of Coloured people employed in this sector more than trebled from 73 810 to 241 900 in 1980. From the start of the 1970s whites on the lower levels of the labour market again had to face competition from workers who were not white. In the countryside the position of white farmers declined as the government cut back on subsidies and as producer prices failed to keep up with sharply rising producer costs.

However, the attempts of O'Meara and Charney to connect these economic developments directly to divisions in Afrikaner ranks are problematic. There is no evidence that the richer farmers supported the NP while the poorer farmers voted for the CP. Neither can Afrikaner business's alignment to the NP be explained in class terms. Since the early 1970s the state has been careful not to give preference to Afrikaner capital over English capital. In the early 1980s, when Charney did his study, it was English firms like Anglo Vaal and Barlows, who benefited enormously from the state's expansion of the armaments industry. If Sanlam was worried about state pension schemes so were its English competitors. And as far as banking was concerned, Pieter Morkel, managing director of Volkskas in the early 1980s, presented this view of the relationship between finance capital and the state. 'Most of the state's business was done through the Reserve Bank.When the state placed business with private banks it was done without preference for any particular bank. State business was an insignificant proportion of the overall business of Volkskas.'[36]

No study has yet been done of the correlation of party preference and class. However, if income is taken as an important indicator of class, it is clear that no close correlation exists between party preference and class. In Table 8.1 the support for the CP and NP across Afrikaner income groups is given in response to the question: 'For which party would you vote if a House of Assembly election was held in your constituency?'

Of the Afrikaners who indicated their party preference in the 1983 poll, 60% support the NP and 19% the CP; the corresponding figures in the 1992 poll were 46% and 41%. In March 1992 the NP and the CP drew largely the same support from the high (over R6000 per month) and the middle income (R3000-R6000) groups in the Afrikaner community. Between 1983 and 1992 the proportion of NP support which came from low income Afrikaners (below R3000) dropped by half but during the same period the proportion this group comprised in Afrikaner society declined by 28%. The NP now shows a growth of support in the middle category while the CP's support in all three categories has remained the same.

Table 8.1
Party Support of White Voters According to Household Monthly Income, March 1983 and March 1992

1992	Total	High	Middle	Low
All whites	3515	32%	50%	18%
Afrikaans	2228	31%	51%	18%
NP	1028	35%	52%	13%
CP	904	31%	49%	20%
English	1287	34%	48%	18%
NP	592	32%	48%	18%
DP	329	28%	47%	24%

1983	Total	High	Middle	Low
Alll whites	2007	34%	43%	23%
Afrikaans	1160	30%	45%	25%
NP	697	32%	41%	26%
CP	222	31%	50%	19%
English	844	38%	41%	20%
NP	175	34%	40%	25%
PFP	330	45%	36%	18%

Note: In both tables the figures in the second column show the distribution of whites according to income group; those in the third line, that of Afrikaners and the fifth line that of English-speakers. To identify trends it is also important to take into account how support for parties deviated from the average percentage or total. If this indicator is used it becomes clear that in 1983 the NP support among low income Afrikaners was above average and in 1992 below average.

Source: Market and Opinion Surveys, Rapport, March 1983 and unpublished poll data, 1992. Table drawn up by Frans Badenhorst of the polling firm.

There are some other differentials that can be noted. Overall the CP's support is stronger in the rural than metropolitan areas but this differs from region to region. The CP performed particularly well in rural constituencies where maize farming predominates. This can be explained in two ways. On the one hand the government cut back severely on subsidies and price support for maize farmers, while on the other hand PW Botha in the early 1980s alienated delegations from those farmers in a particularly damaging way. There is no similar explanation for the NP's loss of support of stock farmers in the northern districts of Transvaal. There is also an important age differential. In the 1992 poll the NP was supported by only 29% in the age group 16-24, against the CP's 54%, showing the conservative influence of the Afrikaans schools and military service.

A study by Lawrence Schlemmer of white support for the NP used different criteria but came to a roughly similar conclusion. It reveals that the party's support is inclined towards the lower socio-economic levels.[37] Far from being the party of the bourgeoisie the NP throughout the 1980s tried to balance the concerns and interests of the different income groups. For its part the CP from the start presented itself as the 'NP-in-exile', eschewing working class or populist appeals and concentrating on ethnic symbolism and status concerns to mobilize support. In the run-up to the split of 1982 Treurnicht and other parliamentarians on the conservative wing of the NP initially tried to rally support by attacking the labour reforms of 1979, which allowed blacks to train for skilled work and form trade unions. However, they soon dropped it, sensing that the labour issue did not provide enough of a base for an alternative party.[38]

As in the split of the late 1960s, the schism which occurred in the early 1980s was not in the first place about class issues but about different approaches to Afrikaner survival and conflicting strategies to maintain Afrikaner power. The CP and other rightwing Afrikaner parties and movements insisted on an aggressive Afrikaner nationalism which used party, government and the state to back up Afrikaner claims ranging from the right of Afrikaners to their own fatherland to the protection of white jobs. Within the rightwing, however, there were pronounced differences about strategy and goals. Within the CP some favoured a much reduced Afrikaner volkstaat (ethnic state) which Afrikaners could control but the majority wanted to base their state largely upon the territory of the current Republic (excluding the homelands) and endorsed the party policy of building an amalgamated white nation under Afrikaner leadership. For this reason the party continued to recognize English as an official language and sought English-speaking support. By contrast, the HNP, the para-military Afrikaner Weerstandsbeweging and several splinter movements wanted to uphold the 'purity' of the Boer or Afrikaner people and insisted that Afrikaans be the only official language.

For its part the NP, since the mid-1970s, increasingly fell back on a defensive nationalism which sought allies across the racial divide. The developments which brought pressure to bear on the NP included the collapse of the colonial regimes to the north of the country, the Soweto uprising of 1976, increased labour strife and a much more militant new generation of blacks. A key turning point in the shift from aggressive to defensive nationalism was the state's failure to enforce in Transvaal black schools the policy that children had to receive instruction in Afrikaans in 50 per cent of the subjects not taught in the mother tongue. This is widely considered to be the trigger of the Soweto revolt of 1976.[39]

In the aftermath of the Soweto revolt the defensive nationalism gave expression to fumbling attempts to master the art of minority-group politics. In this politics apartheid was, in the words of Broederbond chairman, Gerrit Viljoen, an 'open-ended method or road in the goal of retaining the Afrikaners' national identity'. In his view the 'excessive and artificial' statutory protection was something of the past: the time had come for a 'much more dangerous, more risky and less protective phase of our survival'.[40] Instead of maintaining the myriad of apartheid laws the NP leadership now saw its main task as that of building a strong state and mobilizing support for a free enterprise system which could underpin the state.[41]

In 1978 the editor of *Die Transvaler*, Willem De Klerk (brother of the politician FW), could still tell a foreign correspondent that minority group politics for the Afrikaners as a group was out of the question because 'this country is ours'.[42] In public, however, *verligte* intellectuals no longer depicted South Africa as a 'white state' but as a 'multi-national state' in which Coloured people and Indians 'were fully-fledged citizens'.[43] In 1979 Gerrit Viljoen wrote in the FAK journal, *Handhaaf*, of all the 'binding elements' which connected the Afrikaner people with other peoples: in the case of the Coloured people there was the common language of Afrikaans and with people across the racial spectrum a shared Christianity and 'attachment to free enterprise, democracy and republican independence'. He concluded:

> Our identity is not monolithic but is comprised of a complex of components of which many overlap with components in the identity of other peoples (volke) and groups. . . . The unity or separateness of our Afrikaans identity must not make us blind or averse to the commonalities which we share with the identity of other volke.[44]

Triggering the NP split of 1982 was an editorial in the NP's propaganda sheet in which the editor, Jan Grobler, emphasized the 'reality' that whites, Coloured people and Indians inhabited 'one geographic area'. Grobler argued that it was only logical that there could not be more than one government in the same land. The rightwing leader, Andries Treurnicht, immediately objected. To him it implied the quite unacceptable idea that Coloured and Indian ministers would co-govern him and all other whites.

Grobler did not respond by pointing out that the NP's constitutional plan made it impossible for Coloured and Indian ministers to wield effective power over whites or that it excluded blacks. Instead he asked Treurnicht how he responded to the idea that 'we at any price align the Coloured people as a bloc of 2,5 million people behind the whites to broaden our own power base and thus avoid turning them over to a black power situation'.[45] Treurnicht was unimpressed: in his view both the symbols as well as the substance of Afrikaner power had to be retained.

In the course of the 1980s NP-supporting Afrikaners developed a dual conception of the state. On the one hand there was a strong tendency among them to regard the state as what Gagiano calls a Boereplaas. State symbols, and cabinet ministers were seen as Afrikaner symbols and ministers as 'their' ministers. A survey of students at the University of Stellenbosch found a strong presumption that Afrikaners had the prerogative to rule South Africa for themselves (and for others). At the same time, however, they had increasingly come to accept the state as being multi-racial and inclusive. They saw the Coloured and Indian Houses of Parliament, the homeland leaders (particularly Mangosuthu Buthelezi) and English-speaking business leaders as part and parcel of the state with which they identified, defending it against sanctions and other forms of external pressure, and against subversion by internal enemies. Afrikaner students indeed saw white radical student bodies or the English-language press in a much more negative light than supportive black leaders or organizations.[46]

The split between the NP and CP has often in the press been presented as one in which the CP represents the true nationalist party, monopolizing all the old ethnic symbols while the NP is seen as a technocratic party aiming at preserving middle class privilege and skills. It is true that the NP underwent a major shift away from the idea of a territorially-based white nation. It is captured by Schlemmer in describing the party at the time of the 1987 election:

> While the white 'nation' under the leadership of Afrikaners remains a guiding political motive, the ideal of a correspondence between 'nation' and 'territory' has been abandoned. The dominant theme is that of interdependent national groupings within a common territory, combined with the relatively restricted aim of a preservation of 'own' areas in the form of (some) segregated white suburbs.[47]

On the other hand, as the studies of Gagiano show, there was no real disagreement between the NP and CP in the 1980's about the basic goal of retaining a vital role in managing the existing state and through that ensure Afrikaner survival. In a survey of white student attitudes towards public authority (taking in the security services, the state president, parliament and the public service) the big difference is between Afrikaner and English-speaking students, not between NP and CP supporting Afrikaners (see Table 8.2).

In the same survey a composite index was built from several
views towards the legitimacy of state institutions, support for the
security services, repression potential of respondents etc. It
found no marked difference between Afrikaner supporters of the
two parties. Some 70 per cent of Afrikaners were strongly
attached to the state against less than 30 per cent of English-
speakers.[48]

Table 8.2
Sympathy/antipathy towards public authority.

	NP	CP	English-speaking whites
Very sympathetic	35	12	3
Sympathetic	53	59	19
Apathetic	10	27	38
Unsympathetic	1	2	33
Very unsympathetic	0	0	9

Source: Gagiano, 'Ruling Group Cohesion', p.196, and
unpublished poll data.

During the 1980s the essential difference between NP and CP
supporting Afrikaners was not over the basic goal of defending
the state but the best strategy for doing it. The CP wanted the
state to be openly biased in favour of Afrikaners and whites as a
whole; the NP by contrast considered Afrikaner survival to be
best secured by making the state more neutral and drawing
'responsible' blacks into the state bureaucracy and political
system.

Some analysts argue that in the course of the 1980s the NP
had passed beyond the stage of ethno-nationalism and was only
clinging to a corrupt 'racial [i.e. white South African]
nationalism'.[49] Studies based on original research painted a
picture of the NP which differs strongly. What emerged is a party
whose primary base was still an ethnic one. In public,
particularly during election times, the NP partly disguised its

ethno-nationalism to attract English-speaking support. However, the government remained in many ways an Afrikaner government.

A study conducted in the second half of the 1980s found that elites in government considered Afrikaner business organized in the Afrikaanse Handelsinstituut (AHI) to be twice as influential as the Urban Foundation (the lobby of big business) in economic policy-making. On social issues the Afrikaans churches were perceived to be three times more influential than the UF. On socio-political issues the Afrikaner Broederbond was considered to be the most influential (38 per cent 'much influence'). It was followed by the Dutch Reformed Church and AHI to which 32 per cent and 30 per cent respectively ascribed much influence as against 11 per cent and 1 per cent who thought Inkatha or the SA Council of Churches respectively had much influence.[50]

The Afrikaner socializing agencies and the ideology of Afrikaner ethno-nationalism remained intact. Cabinet ministers stayed on as members of the Broederbond. The FAK, which acted as the front organization of the Broederbond and as co-ordinator of cultural associations, continued to stress a racial definition of Afrikaners. Indeed the FAK, which was aligned to the NP, persisted in refusing to throw membership open to black or brown Afrikaans-speakers.[51]

Afrikaner nationalism maintained its sway over the school and university education of Afrikaners. Several studies found that the Afrikaner youth at schools and universities were firmly locked into the grid of the communal institutions which bound together Afrikaner society. In a study of history textbooks in use in secondary schools in 1980 and 1981 the following were two of the twelve 'master symbols' which appeared repeatedly: 'The Afrikaner has a special relationship with God', and 'South Africa rightly belongs to the Afrikaner'.[52] Another study, undertaken in the mid-1980s, found that Afrikaner youth showed a strong intolerance towards protests against the state which was expressed in a belief that the black revolt of the mid-1980s was caused by intimidation and instigators, that black political violence was not justified and that the state acted properly in suppressing it. In 1989 a nation-wide study 75 per cent of Afrikaner student respondents indicated that they would resist physically an ANC government or emigrate for political reasons. In responses to these questions there was such a difference between Afrikaner and English-speaking white students that one is led unescapably to the conclusion that ethno-nationalism was still very much alive.[53]

Transition to an inclusive democracy

The NP abandonment in the early 1990s of the last pillars of statutory apartheid and its acceptance of negotiations with the liberation movements was a watershed event in the history of Afrikaner nationalism. Was it brought about by white middle class concerns or did the consideration of Afrikaner ethnic survival play the decisive role? In interpreting the shift the historian George Frederickson comes close to reducing everything to a single factor when he observes that it was 'economic sanctions that, more than anything else, brought the government to the bargaining table in the first place'.[54] This is a one-sided interpretation which reflects the continuing influence of modernization theory.

A study of NP leadership thinking during the years 1986 to 1991 reveals a rather more complex picture in which calculations about long term Afrikaner political survival figured much more prominently than pressing economic concerns. There appear to be three main considerations in the thinking of the NP leadership in moving from apartheid to negotiations. In the first place there is the recognition of a shifting power balance. In the medium to long-term, exclusive Afrikaner and larger white domination was untenable as the capacity of blacks to resist or circumvent the apartheid system grew in proportion to the increase of their numbers, skills and power. De Klerk has understood, much better than his predecessor, that Afrikaners, and the larger white group, have a much better chance of striking a bargain now than if they waited a further ten years. He put this succinctly in a speech at a Nasionale Pers function shortly after legalising the liberation movements: 'We have not waited until the position of power dominance turned against us before we decided to negotiate a peaceful settlement. The initiative is in our hands. We have the means to ensure that the process develops peacefully and in an orderly way.'[55]

The NP leadership came to accept that apartheid failed to provide any reliable allies, a point vividly driven home by the 1976 and 1984-86 political uprising and an escalation of 'political' strikes by increasingly militant black trade unions. The state and Afrikaner domination of the state were starkly exposed by the lack of an ideology which could project state power as in the general interest. This was apparent even in the case of the most likely ally across the colour lines, the Coloured people. PW Botha had thought that they would settle for the sectional advantage they had over blacks and for the symbolic participation they enjoyed in the Tricameral Parliament. He only succeeded in raising a storm of protests when he exclaimed in the 'Coloured' house in 1987: 'Let me tell Hon. members something now: if it were not for the very Afrikaner and the National Party the Coloured population would not be in the privileged position it is in today.'[56]

Second, the NP leadership accepted that economic stagnation made it imperative to find a political solution. This is not to the place to analyze in detail the effects of sanctions but a few comments are in order to put the issue in some perspective. Sanctions had a definite, if complex, impact. In 1988 and 1989 senior cabinet ministers both in public and in private interviews insisted that sanctions made it more difficult to break finally with apartheid, lest they appeared vulnerable to foreign pressure. After the government did indeed break with apartheid some senior party spokesmen acknowledged the contributing role of sanctions, and added that the economy had been bled white.[57] In a 1989 survey of attitudes of private and public sector white elites in which NP supporters predominated more than 60 per cent felt that international pressure and sanctions would force the opposing parties to negotiate.[58]

Is this a typical case of double-talk of a governing elite under severe and contradictory pressures? There is indeed an element of this. It obviously suited the government in the late 1980s to appear resolute in the face of foreign pressure but to pretend now that there was no alternative than a fundamental revision of course. However, momentous decisions cannot be reduced to the

double-talk of politicians for short-term gain. If one wants a
structural explanation it is useful to start with the work of Lipton
on how apartheid over a long period was shaped.

Lipton shows that the NP constituency over a period of forty
years invariably tried to push the costs of apartheid on to the
shoulders of others (usually blacks). When that became
impossible it insisted on modifications of apartheid. But there
was one area where this did not apply, namely security. As
Lipton formulates it: 'People were willing to sacrifice their
economic interests and ethnic preferences if their security (the
safety of themselves, their families and their property, and of
institutions which safeguarded them) was perceived as
threatened'.[59]

Was the pressure of sanctions so severe by the end of the 1989
that material considerations forced the government to accept the
demands of its opponents internally and abroad? If this had been
the case one would expect the private sector, which was most
directly affected by sanctions, to have been critically involved in
pushing for the necessary socio-political changes to bring
sanctions to an end. Yet this is not the case. A comprehensive
study on the subject found that English-speaking business
leaders were left outside the circles where socio-political policy
was discussed. The Afrikaner business leaders did have access
but held no political views independent from those expressed by
the Botha government at the end of the 1980s. By and large
business leaders had learnt to live with sanctions — the way PW
Botha wanted them to do.[60]

This brings us to the third major cause of the government's
fundamental revision of course, namely the dramatic changes in
the international context towards the end of the 1980s. It is most
unlikely that the government would have moved towards
negotiations had the international climate remained as
unfavourable as it perceived it to be. In government circles the
perception existed right up to the last half of 1989 that no
settlement with the ANC was possible as long as it was strongly
backed by the Soviet Union. As late as September 1989 De Klerk
sent word to his brother to stop talking to the ANC. In his view,
this movement could never have a role in negotiations. Informal
talks with the ANC by South Africans hoping to act as third

parties in De Klerk's words 'played into the hands of forces who are geared towards destabilizing South Africa and destroying the good order'.[61] The government was also worried about its ability to negotiate a settlement if the USA only pressurized the government and not the liberation movements as well.

In the last months of 1989 the international climate changed dramatically in the perception of the De Klerk leadership. For the first time it considered negotiations a viable option. The crucial developments were the severe internal troubles the Soviet Union was experiencing and the end of the Cold War. The Soviet Union indicated that it favoured a peaceful settlement in South Africa and that it was up to the South Africans themselves to reach accommodation. In the government's perception the ANC without Soviet backing was a containable force. At the same time the government was heartened by a clear statement of the US government towards the end of 1989 that it would put as much pressure on the white power structure as on the black majority to engage in fruitful negotiations and that it would criticize the first party to move away from these negotiations.[62]

In sum, then, it was a complex of interrelated factors which combined to bring about the demise of statutory apartheid. While one should not underrate the sustained pressure of the ANC and affiliated organizations, it should be emphasized that the government never considered the state to be seriously threatened; nor did it ever perceive a transfer of power to be imminent. Regardless of whether these perceptions were rooted in reality or not, the government moved into the transition firm in its conviction that the outcome of negotiations would strengthen the existing state. In a rare interview, Niel Barnard, head of National Intelligence, revealed that when the government embarked on secret talks with Nelson Mandela in 1988 the latter acknowledged that the ANC did not have the military capacity to force the government into a corner. Barnard described the decision to start negotiations in the following terms: 'What happened now represented an act of volition on the part of the government. Without being with its back to the wall it decided to take the political initiative.'[63]

Within the cultural elite of Afrikanerdom a similar fundamental re-evaluation of strategy was occurring. A

Broederbond document of 1989 illuminates the shift. Headed 'Political Values for the Survival of the Afrikaner', it argued that the exclusion of effective black sharing in the political processes at the highest level had become 'a threat to the survival of the white man'. There could no longer be a white government and the head of government did not necessarily have to be white.

The document reflects a growing awareness of the need to articulate universal interests and needs. It stated that good government was one which governed in the interests of all its subjects; and while language and cultural rights were prerequisites for Afrikaner survival they had to be propagated in such a way that they were supported across colour lines. Ultimately the most important prerequisite for Afrikaner survival was the acceptability of a new constitution for the majority of the population.

In a concluding passage the document highlighted the future political shift of the Afrikaners from ruling group to minority group:

> A test which we should set for the acceptability of a system must always be: what will be in our interests in the event that we end up in the opposition seat? Furthermore, we must also realize that humanly speaking there are simply no guarantees. The greatest risk that we are taking today is not taking any risks. The will to survive as Afrikaners and our faith and energy will serve as our greatest guarantee.[64]

Closely echoing these words Gerrit Viljoen stated in March 1990:

> [We] who want change want it exactly because we realize that our survival depends upon orderly change. . . We must see that change is inevitable and can be made in such a way that does not put our existence as a nation at stake. . . [The] whole approach of government is to shift the emphasis from race to the quality of government and the broadening of democracy in spite of the risks.[65]

Viljoen added that 'a complete cut, a complete break in history would be unacceptable'. Hence the NP's refusal to consider 'simple' majority rule. This is partly justified on survival grounds — it would be in the leadership's perception 'the end' of Afrikaner history[66] — and partly for technocratic reasons: there was no possibility of the NP handing over the reins of power 'to one or other potentate or group with no experience of governing a sophisticated country'.[67] To emphasize its commitment to continuity the NP leadership has all along insisted on the retention of Afrikaans as official language and the enactment of the new constitution by the Tricameral Parliament.

Within the Afrikaner state and cultural elite the decision to abandon apartheid and negotiate a democratic order triggered a re-evaluation of Afrikaner identity. Just before De Klerk's speech of February 1990 the FAK journal, *Handhaaf*, which reflects Broederbond thinking, tried to present sensible Afrikaners as those who rejected, on the one hand, the rightwing with its violent schemes and, on the other, those on the left who wished to make a radical break with the past and 'wanted to consider themselves not as Afrikaners but as Afrikaans'. (As a cultural concept Afrikaans embraces Afrikaans-speakers of all groups).[68] In mid-1990 *Handhaaf* published a significant contribution by the Pretoria linguist VN Webb which reflected the new political course signalled by De Klerk. He proposed a break with the old conception of Afrikaners and of ethnicity which spoke of a people united by a common historical, racial and spiritual bond. Instead ethnicity should increasingly be considered as 'a set of strategies for obtaining resources which people need in changing economic and political circumstances, and through which one can still gain access to the riches of the land'. In meeting novel demands for survival the Afrikaners have to develop a new form of ethnicity. Webb wanted the Afrikaans language to be elaborated and become the symbol of a new socio-cultural identity with different norms, values, attitudes and convictions.[69]

In polls taken in 1970s a majority of Afrikaners had indicated that they considered an Afrikaans-speaking Coloured as an Afrikaner. Several Afrikaans writers and academics propagated a non-racial definition of Afrikaner identity. However, the Afrikaner political and cultural elite long resisted an inclusive definition of the volk or the kind of approach towards ethnicity which Webb's article reflects. Leading Coloured intellectuals also rejected any identification with Afrikaners.[70] The radically changed political circumstances of the early 1990s have forced the Afrikaner cultural elite to re-open the issue. This time there was much greater support in elite ranks for the non-racial definition which they as late as January 1990 had attacked as 'leftwing'.

The search for political allies has prompted the NP leadership to reject the racial definition of Afrikaner identity. A revealing Parliamentary debate on this issue took place a few days after a large number of Coloured MPs had crossed the floor to join the NP. In a speech to a joint sitting of Parliament AP Treurnicht insisted on the traditional, exclusive definition of the Afrikaners. The following exchange took place:

Barend du Plessis: Are those Hon. [Coloured] members sitting there not Afrikaners?
Treurnicht: No, the Afrikaner people have been known for more than two and a half centuries as the Afrikaans-speaking whites of South Africa. . .
Du Plessis: Who spoke Afrikaans first?
Treurnicht: Go and ask Adam Small [a Coloured intellectual] and others whether they are members of the Afrikaner people. . . These people said a number of years ago they were not. The hon. member must not try to integrate another community in order to strengthen their party.
F W De Klerk: I am also a member of that [Afrikaner] people.
Treurnicht: [It] is possible to come across a member of a people who renounces the right of that people. . . What sort of compatriot is that?
Du Plessis: I asked him [Treurnicht]. . . whether there were Afrikaners in the [Coloured] House of Representatives. . . I want to ask the Hon. Leader of the Official Opposition [Treurnicht] why he says they are not Afrikaners. They speak the way we do. They believe the way we do. They live the way we do. Why does he say they are not Afrikaners? He says he is not a racist.
Treurnicht: You are naïve!
Du Plessis: There is only one variable which remains and that is the colour of the skin: Is it correct that it is only the colour of the skin that remains?

Treurnicht: No.[71]

What we have here is a political realignment between the NP and a Coloured party prompting a redefinition of Afrikaner identity. It is still restricted to political elites and is rejected by the CP on the one hand and by 'Coloured' intellectuals on the other. It nevertheless shows the considerable distance the NP elite has travelled since the late 1960s when Treurnicht's definition held sway among it.

Conclusion

In the case of the Afrikaners, modernization theorists were wrong to assume that ethnic identity would wither way. The political schisms in Afrikanerdom were not in the first place triggered by material conflicts waged along class lines but by symbolic issues which brought to a head intra-Afrikaner conflicts about the best ways of ensuring Afrikaner survival. However, the theory has validity if it is taken to mean that modernization brings about a change in values. Most prominent in the Afrikaner case was the acceptance of the norm of non-discrimination and a rejection of explicit racism which was gradually incorporated as a value in the Afrikaner culture, or at least of most of those who support the NP.

This does not mean that the conflictual modernization paradigm is wrong in stressing the importance of group status or pointing to the unlikelihood of an ethnic identification being easily replaced by an identification with the state. The Afrikaners represent a rather special case where a minority ethnic group took possession of the state and strongly began to identify with it. This state was the Boereplaas but it was also considerably more than that. It assumed a growing measure of autonomy as it had to mediate and adjudicate between ethnic groups and classes and had to adjust apartheid to stem South Africa's exclusion from the international state system. The core state remained dominated by Afrikaners but the extended state with its black bureaucrats and policemen was a multi-racial one which the Afrikaners could not control by pretending to be a people apart or refusing forever to share power. Rather than to dominate the black groups the NP leadership in the 1980s came to believe that it should seek freedom from domination by non-members, which according to Connor is the core demand of ethno-national groups throughout the world.[72]

The decision to start negotiations with the ANC was once again influenced more by political than material considerations. A poll of white South Africans revealed that only 15 per cent believed they would be better off in the 'new South Africa'.[73] Why then negotiate? On the one hand there was the desire to remain part of the Western world and to be seen as upholding its values. On the other hand it was a question of survival — both Afrikaner survival and that of the wider white community. The NP leadership believes that white domination of the economy, military and bureaucracy provides a secure framework in which the ANC could be drawn into the political and bureaucratic structures of the state without that leading to a fundamental change in the character of the state. A successful transition to majority rule will largely depend on whether an Africanization of the state will come about in a gradual and unthreatening way.

*A earlier version of this chapter appeared in African Affairs.

Notes

1   A.Y. Sadie, 'Regerings en sake-elites se persepsies oor die invloed van die Suid-Afrikaanse sakesektor op openbare beleidsformulering', Ph.D. dissertation, University of Cape Town, 1991.

2   J. I. K. Gagiano, 'Meanwhile back on the "Boereplaas"', *Politikon*, 13 (1986), pp.3-21.

3   Interviews with senior cabinet ministers and Western ambassadors stationed in South Africa, 1990 and 1991. That a bond, albeit a tenuous one, still exists among Afrikaners on different points of the political spectrum is evident from the remark of the para-military Afrikaner Weerstandsbeweging leader, Eugene Terre'Blanche, to a liberal Afrikaner, van Zyl Slabbert: 'Although I think you are naive, I accept you as an Afrikaner. I accept you want the best for your country'; Graham Leach, *The Afrikaners: Their Last Trek* (London: Macmillan, 1989),

p.282. Although there were growing signs towards the end of the 1980s of Afrikaner identity being redefined in non-racial terms this chapter still uses the prevailing definition of the Afrikaners as people of European descent who identify with Afrikaner history and destiny.

4   For an excellent survey, see Saul Newman, 'Does Modernization Breed Ethnic Conflict?', *World Politics* 43 (1991), pp.451-478.

5   Heribert Adam, 'Cohesion and Coercion', in Hermann Giliomee and Jannie Gagiano, eds., *The Elusive Search for Peace: South Africa, Israel and Northern Ireland* (Cape Town: Oxford University Press, 1990), p.236.

6   Stanley B. Greenberg, *Race and State in Capitalist Development* (New Haven: Yale University Press, 1980), pp.5-28, 405-410. See also John Schwarzmantel, *Socialism and the Idea of the Nation* (Hemel Hempstead: Harvester Wheatsheaf, 1991), pp.49-87.

7   Dan O'Meara, *Volkskapitalisme: Class, Capital and Ideology in the Development of Afrikaner Nationalism* (Cambridge University Press, 1983), p.255.

8   Connor sums up his writings with an application to South Africa in `Ethno-nationalism and Political Instability', *The Elusive Search for Peace*, pp.9-32.

9   Donald Horowitz, *Ethnic Groups in Conflict* (Berkeley: University of California Press, 1985), p.187.

10   George Schöpflin 'Nationalism and National Minorities', *Journal of International Affairs*, 45 (1991), p.52.

11   There is a tendency to do this in the work of Heribert Adam and Kogila Moodley. Their belief in the possibility of a constitutional bargain rests upon their perception that whites and blacks share a common South African culture of 'Hollywood soap operas and leisure activities, jokes, tastes and sacred texts'. See their *South Africa without Apartheid* (Cape Town: Maskew Miller-Longman, 1986), p.211. See by contrast the work of Connor, who writes that what really counts is a popularly held awareness or belief that one's own group is unique in a most vital sense. He observes: 'The tangible manifestations of cultural distinctiveness are significant only to the degree that they contribute to a sense of uniqueness'; 'Nation-building or Nation-destroying', *World Politics*, 24 (1972), p.337. David Laitin in discussing the work by Adam and Moodley observes: '...culture has two faces. Looked at from one side, culture is the result of rational individual decisions about membership and inclusion. But viewed from the other side, culture embeds values and guides for moral action...Afrikaner values and beliefs'. See: David Laitin, 'South

Africa: Violence, Myths and Democratic Reforms', *World Politics*, 39 (1987), p.274.

12   Greenberg, *Race and State in Capitalist Development*.

13   Peter Evans, Dietrich Rueschemeyer, Theda Skocpol, eds., *Bringing the State Back In* (Cambridge University Press, 1985), pp.9-20, 254-56.

14   Crawford Young, *The Politics of Cultural Pluralism* (Madison, University of Wisconsin Press, 1976), p.65.

15   Donald L Horowitz, *A Democratic South Africa: Constitutional Engineering in a Divided Society* (Berkeley: University of California Press, 1991), p.69.

16   Heribert Adam and Hermann Giliomee, *Ethnic Power Mobilized: Can South Africa Change?* (New Haven: Yale University Press, 1979), p.169.

17   For a good description of the Afrikaner ethos in the 1960s see Douglas Brown, *Against the World: A Study of White South African Attitudes* (London: Collins, 1966), p.103.

18   O'Meara, *Volkskapitalisme*, pp. 250-54; Dan O'Meara, '"Muldergate" and the Politics of Afrikaner Nationalism', *Work in Progress*, 22 (1982), pp.1-18.

19   Interview with P. J. Cillié, 3 February 1992. In his chairman's address of 1991, Cillié announced that Sanlam had subsequently increased its stake to 28% before reducing it in 1991 to 24.8%. Sanlam did so of its own accord.

20   BM Schoeman, *Die Geldmag* (Pretoria: Aktuele Publikasies, 1980), p.48.

21   J.A. du Pisani, *John Vorster en die Verlig/Verkrampstryd* (Bloemfontein: INEG, 1988), pp.33-55.

22   Anna Starcke, *Survival* (Cape Town: Tafelberg, 1978), p.23. It should be added that an English-speaking member of the EAC responded to this comment with the retort: 'How convincing a case did they want?' At the very least, this demonstrates a lack of cogent arguments and unity of purpose between the Afrikaner business elite and their English-speaking counterparts.

23   Sam Nolutshungu, 'Issues of the Afrikaner "Enlightenment"' *African Affairs*, 70 (1971), p.28.

24   J. Linz, 'From Primordialism to Nationalism' in Edward Tiryakian and Roger Rogowski, eds., *New Nationalisms of the Developed West: Towards Explanation* (London: Allen and Unwin, 1985), p.204.

25   Schoeman, *Die Geldmag*, pp.46-51.

26   P.J. Cillié, *Tydgenote* (Cape Town: Tafelberg, 1980), p.27.

27   Dirk Richard, *Moedswillig die Uwe* (Johannesburg: Perskor, 1985), pp.134-35.

28   J.H.P. Serfontein, *Brotherhood of Power* (London: Rex Collings, 1979), p.238.

29   H. of A. Debates, 14 April 1969, cols. 3876-3884.

30   B.M. Schoeman, (compiler) *Jaap Marais: Stryd is Lewe* (Pretoria: Aktuele Publikasies), p.100.

31   B.M. Schoeman, *Vorster se 1000 dae* (Cape Town: Human and Rousseau, 1974), p.41.

32   Du Pisani, *Vorster en die Verlig/Verkrampstryd*, p.178.

33   A paper by Lawrence Schlemmer cited by Theo Hanf, *South Africa: the Prospects of Peaceful Change* (London: Rex Collings, 1981), p.373.

34   O'Meara, *Volkskapitalisme*, p. 253; O'Meara, 'Muldergate', p. 13. Craig Charney, 'The National Party, 1982-1985', in Wilmot James, ed., *The State of Apartheid* (Boulder: Lynne Rienner, 1987), pp.5-36.

35   Charney, 'The National Party', p.27.

36   Interview, Pieter Morkel, 9 April 1992.

37   Lawrence Schlemmer, 'South Africa's National Party Government', in Peter Berger and Bobby Godsell, eds., *A Future South Africa: Visions, Strategies and Realities* (Cape Town: Human and Rousseau, 1988), p.20. The National Party has continued to balance successfully the interests and concerns of all groups in Afrikaner society and the white group at large. Failure to do so would have meant certain defeat in the general election of 1987 or 1989.

38   Alf Ries and Ebbe Dommisse, *Broedertwis* (Cape Town: Tafelberg, 1982), pp.96-100.

39   For a discussion of the retreat of Afrikaans as a language, see J. C. Steyn, 'Afrikaner-nasionalisme en Afrikaans', in H. du Plessis and L.T. du Plessis, eds., *Afrikaans en Taalpolitiek* (Pretoria: HAUM, 1987), pp.93-100.

40   Gerrit Viljoen, *Ideaal en Werklikheid* (Cape Town: Tafelberg, 1978), pp.95-100.

41   Stanley Greenberg, 'Ideological Struggles within the South African state', in Shula Marks and Stanley Trapido, eds., *The Politics of Race, Class and Nationalism in Twentieth-Century South Africa* (London: Longman, 1987), p.412.

42   Tom Wicker, "'This country is ours'", 26 December 1978, p.A19.

43   Viljoen, *Ideaal en Werklikheid*, p.40.

44   G. Viljoen, 'Afrikaanse Nasionale Kultuurraad', *Handhaaf* (November 1979, p.17.

45   Ries en Dommisse, *Broedertwis*, pp.111-112.

46   I am drawing on Gagiano, 'Meanwhile back on the "Boereplaas"', pp.3-23; 'Ruling Group Cohesion', *The Elusive Search for Peace*, pp.191-210.

47   Lawrence Schlemmer, 'The National Party: Ideology, Aims, Role and Strategy', in D.J. van Vuuren, et. al., eds., *South African Election 1987* (Pinetown: Owen Burgess, 1987), p.57.

48   Gagiano, 'Ruling group cohesion', p.208.

49   Adam, 'Cohesion and Coercion', pp.223-41.

50   Sadie, 'Regerings en sake-elite se persepsies', pp.207-226.

51   For a thorough account see Annelie van Zyl, 'Die Taalpolitiek van die Federasie van Afrikaanse Kultuurverenigings met Spesiale Verwysing na die Tydperk 1976-1986', unpublished MA dissertation (University of Natal), 1990.

52   J. M. du Preez, *Africana Afrikaner: Master symbols in South African School Textbooks* (Alberton: Librarius, 1983), p.6.

53   Gagiano, 'Ruling Group Cohesion', 191-208; Susan Booysen, 'The Legacy of Ideological Control: The Afrikaner Youth's Manipulated Political Consciousness', *Politikon*, 16 (1989) 7-25; Susan Booysen and Hennie Kotze, 'The Political Socialisation of Isolation: A case study of Afrikaner student youth', *Politikon*, 12 (1985) 23-46.

54   George Frederickson, 'African Americans and African Africans', *New York Review of Books*, 26 September 1991, p.38.

55   *Die Burger*, 31 March 1990, p.2.

56   Debates of Parliament: House of Representatives, 1987, col.2286.

57   See for instance the statement by Kobie Coetzee in *Cape Times*, 4 September 1991. In the referendum of 1992 this was a dominant theme of the NP campaign.

58   E.G. Lombard, 'Elite-houdings oor onderhandeling in Suid-Afrika', unpublished MA dissertation (University of Stellenbosch, 1991), p.199.

59   Merle Lipton, *Capitalism and Apartheid: South Africa 1910-1986* (Aldershot: Wildwood House, 1986), p.375.

60   Sadie, 'Regerings en Sake-elite se Persepsies', pp.303-313.

61   Willem de Klerk, *F.W. de Klerk: Die Man en sy Tyd* (Tafelberg: Jonathan Ball,1991), pp.62-63.

62   Richard Dowden, 'West Offers South African Antagonists the Carrot', *Independent*, 31 January 1990.

63   *Die Burger*, 18 February 1992, p.11.

64   'Political Values for the Survival of the Afrikaner', unpublished document of the Afrikaner Broederbond, ca. July 1989.

65   *Sunday Star*, 17 March 1990.

66   Ibid, 17 March 1990.

67   *Argus*, 25 May 1991.

68   *Handhaaf*, January-February,1990, p.12.

69   V.N. Webb, 'Volk, Nasie en Afrikanerdom', *Handhaaf*, June 1990, p.12.

70   See my chapter on Afrikaner identity in *Ethnic Power Mobilized*.

71   Debates of Parliament: Joint Sitting, 20 June 1991, cols.13556-13558, 13651.

72   Connor, 'Ethno-nationalism', p.27.

73   Human Sciences Research Council, *Information Update*, November 1991.

9

Zimbabwe's Response to Change in South Africa

James H. Polhemus

Introduction

There is widespread agreement that significant change is taking place in South Africa. There is less agreement about: why the change is taking place; when it started; how fundamental it is and whether it could still be arrested by a National Party regime bent on preserving the privileged position of whites in a future South African society; what its ultimate outcome will be; and, in particular, what should be done about it. Among the many stakeholders in what is going on in South Africa is the neighbouring state of Zimbabwe. This essay surveys Zimbabwe's reactions to recent changes in South Africa against the background of the relations which developed between the two states during the first decade of Zimbabwe's independence.

1980-1990: Nondestructive Disengagement

When the ZANU (PF) government of Robert Mugabe assumed office on 18 April 1990, the details of its policy on South Africa had yet to be formulated. Land, peace, prosperity and equality had been the major themes in the campaigns of each of the parties contesting the February 1980 elections, which ZANU (PF) won resoundingly. The ZANU(PF) manifesto called for

196

nonalignment and OAU membership, but had nothing to say about the future shape of regional arrangements, even though the threat of South African interference loomed over the election. The foundations of the new state's relations with South Africa emerged in a series of manoeuvrings over the first year or so after independence, and then were to remain basically in place for the following decade.

Although the ZANU (PF) election victory came as an unpleasant surprise for South Africa, which had pinned its hopes on Bishop Muzorewa, at first South Africa could find some comfort in the statements of Prime Minister Mugabe and his ministers. In his first interview with the South African press after his return to what was then Rhodesia to campaign, Mugabe said that while he was 'revolted by apartheid', the struggle in South Africa was largely for the people of South Africa itself, that he would not place his country in jeopardy by offering bases to South African liberation movements, that his government would 'maintain trade relations with South Africa on a realistic basis' and continue to use South African ports and harbours, and that international sanctions against South Africa 'which destroy our own economy will not be acceptable to us'.[1] Similar statements on "good neighbour" relations after the election produced South African press headlines such as 'Amazing Mugabe peace offer to SA'[2] and 'Zimbabwe will keep links'.[3]

Soon, however, relations began to deteriorate, as Zimbabwe commenced to implement what might be termed a policy of 'non-destructive disengagement' from South Africa — disengagement because Zimbabwe sought to the maximum extent possible to disencumber itself from the manifold close links with South Africa which it inherited from the Smith and Muzorewa regimes, links which had been made all the closer by the international sanctions imposed after the Smith regime's unilateral declaration of independence; non-destructive both because Zimbabwe was limited in the extent of its disengagement by the necessity of not destroying itself and because complete disengagement by Zimbabwe would not destroy South Africa.

Disengagement from South Africa proceeded simultaneously on a number of fronts, some more important than others, with differing outcomes. Sporting contacts, an area in which white South Africans seem to be particularly vulnerable, were among the first to go. Linkages in livestock registration and professional associations were severed. Zimbabwe ceased relaying South African Broadcasting Corporation news bulletins. In February 1981 the Zimbabwe government bought out the South African owned shares in Zimbabwe's five major newspapers. Zimbabwe announced its intention to bring to an end the recruitment of Zimbabwean labour for South Africa and Wenala, the recruiting agency, was told to wind up its affairs.

The complexities of the task of disengagement, and the absence of a thought-out policy on South Africa at independence, can be seen in a brief survey of simultaneous developments in two areas of contact between South Africa and Zimbabwe, the exchange of formal representation and tourism.

The one formal diplomatic linkage which Zimbabwe inherited at independence was an exchange of sub-ambassadorial missions, presided over by what were styled 'accredited diplomatic representatives' rather than ambassadors, with South Africa. The South African mission, with a staff of several hundred, occupied five floors of the Sanlam building in Salisbury and Rhodesia maintained an office in Church Square in Pretoria, as well as a consulate in Capetown. When questioned about the future of these arrangements prior to assuming office, Mugabe said 'it is better to leave matters open than to shut doors at this time'.[4] After independence the Zimbabwe flag flew in Pretoria, the South African mission remained in Harare, and there was growing speculation about the future of diplomatic relations, speculation which ended only after several months of manoeuvring. South Africa, ever seeking to build bridges to black Africa, arguing the need to look after 35,000 South African passport holders in Zimbabwe, and having recently launched its campaign for a 'Constellation of Southern African States', was keen to retain or elevate the existing level of representation, but approached the question philosophically. In May South African foreign minister Pik Botha told the South African parliament that there is no reason why 'we in South Africa should insist on a formal Western-type of diplomacy. We don't need to insist that our representatives are called ambassadors'.[5] For Zimbabwe, any official presence of apartheid South Africa was on its face an embarrassment, quite apart from posing a security threat.

Diplomatic relations with South Africa were discussed in the Zimbabwean cabinet early in June 1980. Later in the month Mugabe stated that a decision would be reached soon, but added that 'we will maintain our economic links but there will be no diplomatic ties with South Africa'.[6] He went on to say that he would shortly unveil evidence of a South African plot to bring down his government. He told parliament that there could be no diplomatic relations with South Africa until it 'puts its own house in order and kills the repugnance and revulsion we have to apartheid' but that under the circumstances, 'trade and economic relations are inevitable. According to the extent that it is necessary for it to retain that relationship, my country is prepared to allow representation at that level'.[7]

The first public breach between independent Zimbabwe and South Africa came in July 1980 when Prime Minister Mugabe, making his OAU debut as a head of government, told the OAU Assembly of Heads of State and Government meeting in Sierra Leone that the South African diplomatic mission in Salisbury had been recruiting Zimbabweans for training in South Africa and subsequent infiltration into Zimbabwe to bring down his government. When he returned to Harare he said that the South African mission had been told to 'wind up their affairs, pack up, and go'.[8] South Africa withdrew its senior personnel, but the mission continued to function as before, busily processing a backlog of applications for emigration to South Africa.

By this time South Africa was getting impatient. In a televized newscast in July, Pik Botha said, 'We will not crawl or beg to establish any sort of relations with any country. . . . I will not allow us to be trampled on further. So if Mr Mugabe wants relations he must indicate this now. And if he does not want to indicate this he can stick it in his pocket.'[9]

Nonetheless, South Africa, having abandoned the hope of maintaining a diplomatic mission, continued to press for a consulate general in Harare. In the end, however, it acquiesced to the very low level of representation foreshadowed by Mugabe in June. On 3 September 1980 it was announced in both Harare and Pretoria that accredited diplomatic representatives were being withdrawn with immediate effect to be replaced by trade missions which would also perform consular functions. A few days later, in one last shot which seemed to underscore Zimbabwe's victory in the affair, the acting head of the South African trade mission clarified an earlier statement he had made to the effect that officials of the trade missions would be accorded diplomatic immunity. Rather than 'diplomatic immunity', he explained that they would have 'immunity from civil and criminal jurisdiction', a distinction consistent with Zimbabwe's insistence that it would allow only the bare minimum South African presence necessary for the maintenance of trade.[10] With this, South Africa and Zimbabwe reached a *modus vivendi* on formal representation in each other's capitals which was to remain in place essentially unchanged to the present.

While Zimbabwe was working out its policy on formal representation with South Africa, it simultaneously had to address the question of the future of South African tourism. Historically, South Africans, who required no visas, had been the most numerous tourists to Victoria Falls and other Rhodesian attractions, but the continuation of South African tourism raised certain problems. There were international and domestic pressures and expectations for severing links with South Africa and tourism, apart from ideological objections about an industry which threatened to relegate local inhabitants to a subservient position, when it was not on its face an essential relationship. There was repugnance at having the 'boers' in the country unnecessarily. Moreover, a free flow of South Africans raised questions of security. On the other hand were the interests of Zimbabwe's tourist industry, the increasingly recognized need for foreign exchange, and the fact that tourism is a comparatively labour intensive and clean industry at a time when Zimbabwe faced serious unemployment. Because of these, and perhaps other, contending considerations, the development of policy with regard to tourism from South Africa was an area of dissonance.

Between the election and independence Mugabe said South African tourists would continue to be welcome. In May 1980 Dr Nathan Shamuyarira, a political scientist on the faculty of the

University of Dar es Salaam before becoming Zimbabwe's Minister of Tourism and Information, told the tourist industry that in view of 'diplomatic and political considerations' it was intended to restrict the number of South African tourists to 150,000 per year. In June he told the Senate that Zimbabwe would maintain its tourist traffic with South Africa, but would do nothing to increase it. In July, re-opening the Wankie Safari Lodge before an audience which included a deputy secretary in the South Africa Department of Tourism and nineteen other South Africans, he urged South Africans to come and see developments in Zimbabwe for themselves, saying that South African tourists would continue to be welcome. In August, during National Assembly debate on the annual vote for his Ministry, Dr Shamuyarira agreed that South African tourists were a security risk and said that in keeping with government policy of reducing dependency on South Africa, the number of South African tourists would be reduced to zero, with promotional efforts to attract tourists from elsewhere. An editorial in the *Herald*, the country's largest daily paper, cited Shamuyarira's inconsistencies, noted that there was 'no practical alternative source of tourists in such large numbers', pointed out that a ban on South Africans would 'presumably exclude black South Africans — unless the Government is to make racial divisions — and also many whites and others who do not support the SA Government's policies', and concluded by asking 'What is the Government's real policy?'[11] A few days later Shamuyarira, again in the National Assembly, sought to 'correct' the impression of the previous week by explaining that South African tourists would continue to be welcome, but that they would not be given 'special privileges'.[12] In September full page colour advertisements in South African newspapers declared 'Yes Zimbabwe Welcomes You in a Big Way!' and provided a series of South African addresses for the Zimbabwe Tourist Board.

By this time, roughly coinciding with the *modus vivendi* on the exchange of official representatives, there seems to have been official recognition of the economic importance of South Africans to the tourist industry. Late in September, again in the Senate, Dr Shamuyarira said that his earlier remarks had been taken out of context and that South African tourism would be encouraged. He repeated, however, that an uncontrolled flow of South Africans would present a security risk and, deftly putting the ball in another court, said that a decision as to whether visas would be required for South Africans would be forthcoming from the Minister of Home Affairs — ZAPU President Joshua Nkomo.

The next development in the saga, the adoption of a visa requirement for South Africans, effective 1 July 1981, came not from a Zimbabwean initiative but in reciprocation to a South African visa requirement effective the same day. (Prior to 1 June 1981 South Africa required visas for black, coloured and Asian visitors from Zimbabwe, but not for whites). When the South African decision became known, and along with it the necessity, of a face-saving counter measure by Zimbabwe, rather than rejoicing over the improved security situation, Dr Shamuyarira observed that it would significantly reduce the number of South African tourists.

The representation and tourism issues are illustrative of the difficult, often contradictory, processes by which Zimbabwe worked out its relationship with South Africa in the first years after independence. It is not necessary to trace out other aspects of Zimbabwe's non-destructive disengagement during its first year of independence in the same detail. It is useful, however, to summarize at a more general level some of the major dimensions of Zimbabwe's relationship with South Africa as they evolved shortly after independence and were to remain largely in place, with some fluctuations, until the replacement of PW Botha by FW De Klerk as president of South Africa in the latter half of 1989.

Mugabe had made it clear from the outset that there was no possibility of Zimbabwe imposing trade and transport sanctions against South Africa. At independence South Africa was Zimbabwe's largest trading partner for both imports and exports, and a major source of investment capital. This relationship continued largely unchanged throughout the decade, with South Africa providing some 20% of Zimbabwe's imports and receiving a slightly lesser proportion of its exports.[13] At the same time, Air Zimbabwe continued a co-operative relationship with South African Airlines, and Zimbabwe continued to rely on the two rail lines to South Africa for much of its trade with the non-African world.

Through its membership in SADCC Zimbabwe sought alternative routes to the sea by way of the Beira and Maputo rail lines and the Beira pipeline. In this it was partially successful, so that by the end of the decade perhaps 20% to 30% of its foreign trade was routed through Mozambique, including essential imports of aviation fuel. But the Mozambique routes were unreliable. They suffered from inadequate port facilities in Mozambique and, more seriously, from frequent destruction by the MNR. Inadequate port facilities and the activities of the MNR, backed by South Africa until at least 1986, made it physically impossible for Zimbabwe to shift all its trade to the Mozambique routes, and major exporters, such as those in the economically important tobacco industry, who relied on prompt and careful handling to get their product to market on time and in good condition, were reluctant to abandon traditional routes.

In the effort to protect the routes through Mozambique, as well as to come to the assistance of the Frelimo government, by the latter third of the decade Zimbabwe had committed some 20% to 25% (depending on whose estimates one accepts) of its army to combating the MNR in the Beira and Maputo corridors and beyond. These efforts had variable but limited success, and by the end of the decade the MNR was extending its operations to and occasionally across Zimbabwe's eastern border with Mozambique.

At least twice, in 1986 and 1987, Mugabe pressed for a more complete economic break with South Africa (prompted on one occasion, according to a diplomatic source, by anger at Mrs Thatcher), but each time the economic arguments of the business sector and the majority of the cabinet prevailed.

In terms of formal contacts with the South African government Zimbabwe maintained much greater distance than it did with the South African economy, a position which seems to have been accepted by South Africa. There were occasional efforts on the part of South Africa to induce Zimbabwe to receive the ministerial and presidential visits by South African officials which neighbouring Mozambique, Zambia, Botswana, Lesotho and Swaziland accepted through such blandishments as offering to provide badly needed rail locomotives if a Zimbabwean cabinet minister would come to Pretoria to ask for them, but this Zimbabwe resolutely refused to do. There were official contacts between the governments, but rather than being minister to minister they were trade mission to minister in each country. A South African source in 1988 observed that Zimbabwe was the only country in the region with which South Africa had not had high level talks.[14]

Mugabe had made it clear in 1980 that Zimbabwe would not allow its territory to be used as a launching pad for operations by liberation movements against South Africa. The major thrust of Zimbabwe's support for the liberation of South Africa was carried out in such forums as the Front Line States, the OAU, and the Non-Aligned Movement, in each of which Zimbabwe assumed a prominent role. Nevertheless, both the PAC, with which ZANU had an affinity which pre-dated independence, and the ANC, which was initially suspect in the government's eyes due to its comparable affinity with ZAPU, were allowed to open offices and operate openly in Zimbabwe, holding meetings and issuing statements and publications.

Due to the presence of the liberation movements, and because occasional liberation movement activities in South Africa were interpreted by the South African government as having originated in Zimbabwe, South Africa did not take Zimbabwe's stance at face value. South African espionage and attacks were carried out against the liberation movements in Zimbabwe, with espionage and sabotage activities being uncovered and South African agents put on trial and imprisoned at intervals throughout the decade. In spite, however, of the presence of the liberation movements, and occasional raids and threats of raids against Zimbabwean targets, South Africa appears not to have systematically attempted to subject Zimbabwe to the multiple pressures which induced Mozambique to enter into the Nkomati Agreement in 1984 and which it subsequently brought to bear against Botswana hoping to achieve the same result. There were, however, well-founded suspicions on the part of Zimbabwe in the initial years after independence that, through its recruitment and training of ZAPU elements on South African soil, South Africa was attempting to establish an MNR equivalent in Zimbabwe. For a time there was a good deal of speculation about a 'Super ZAPU' recruited mainly in the refugee camps in Botswana, but this had subsided well before the unity agreement of the two major Zimbabwean parties.

At the level of person to person contacts, after the initial skirmishing over visas in 1980 and in spite of the elimination of sporting links, there was a continuous and substantial two way movement across the border. South Africa was the major source of visitors to Zimbabwe, and the South African trade mission in Harare was said to be the busiest visa office in the world, issuing some 12,000 visas per month for Zimbabweans to visit South Africa by 1988. Much of this two way traffic was economically motivated, particularly on the part of Zimbabwean shoppers in South Africa, but particularly towards the end of the decade Zimbabwe became a venue for meetings between South Africans of all races and others with agenda other than economic. It was remarked that 'the cultural boycott ends at the Zambezi rather than the Limpopo in Southern Africa'.[15]

1990-1991: Limited Re-engagement

Nelson Mandela's release from imprisonment in South Africa on 11 February 1990, although it had been anticipated for months and had been preceded by other significant developments such as the freeing of other political prisoners, the unbanning of the ANC, the PAC, the SACP and some thirty-three other political organizations, and the promised repeal of apartheid legislation following the election of De Klerk on 6 September 1989, marks a symbolic turning point for recent change in change in South Africa. It prompted, among other things, an international debate on the maintenance of sanctions against South Africa.

President Mugabe's immediate response was to welcome Mandela's release but to add: 'Let not those who have been supporters of apartheid, directly or indirectly, now try to deceive us into accepting that what has happened in South Africa is the establishment of democracy. It isn't.'[16] In a rare debate on South Africa, Zimbabwe's parliament promptly moved to adopt a resolution in which it fully supported the President and

1. Expresses its unwavering commitment to the international call for the total dismantling of the evil system of apartheid;

2. Challenges President FW De Klerk to demonstrate his genuine will to change by removing all obstacles his minority regime has placed in the path of majority rule in a free and democratic South Africa;

3. Reaffirms that unless the State of Emergency is repealed and all political prisoners freed and negotiations involving the ANC, PAC and other movements, the authentic representatives of the majority, the South African liberation movements are justified in their pursuit for freedom through their liberation struggle, whether armed, political or economic;

4. Calls for the maintenance and intensification of economic sanctions so far imposed in order to speed up the liberation process.[17]

The dominant theme in Zimbabwe's initial response to the changes in South Africa, symbolized by the release of Mandela, became the campaign against those who thought it was time to lift sanctions against South Africa. This was a campaign which President Mugabe prosecuted systematically over the next eighteen months in his travels abroad, in speeches and interviews in Harare including his opening addresses to Parliament, and in meetings of the Front Lines States, the OAU and SADCC.

A second, less publicized, theme in Zimbabwe's response to changes in South Africa involved efforts to get the rival South African movements, particularly the ANC and the PAC, to cooperate. Here Mugabe found himself in agreement with the ANC and at odds with ZANU's former allies, the PAC. He had hoped to bring representatives of the two movements together in March 1990, on the occasion of Mandela's first visit to Zimbabwe which coincided with a Harare meeting of the PAC. In a public address in Harare Mandela alluded to the example set by the major Zimbabwean parties, and praised Mugabe and Nkomo for overcoming their differences, saying 'that these two men, who just a few years ago were denounced as terrorists by the international press, can lead their people so excellently in the task of nation-building is an example for us in South Africa, who face similar problems, if not worse'.[18] In spite of this opening, Mugabe's efforts were dealt a rebuff by the PAC, which issued a statement rejecting the ANC's stance on negotiations with the South African government. Zephania Mothopeng of the PAC was reported to have snubbed Mugabe's invitation to attend a state dinner in honour of Mandela.[19] Mugabe was openly critical of the PAC, saying that its rejection of negotiations struck "discordant notes" and asking 'When the moment arises, when negotiations could take place, why should we not test the oppressor?'[20]

Subsequently he had more success. He repeated the call for unity at a Front Line States summit attended by representatives of both the PAC and the ANC in Harare in February 1991.[21] In April 1991 he managed to get the presidents and members of the executive committees of the two movements together at a conference in Harare. This concluded with the PAC and ANC agreeing on a call for the election on the basis of universal suffrage of a constituent assembly to draw up a constitution for South Africa and with an agreement to convene jointly a 'Patriotic Conference' of all South African organizations sharing their views as a single Patriotic Front in South Africa in August 1991.[22]

Although Zimbabwe continued the public campaign against the relaxation of sanctions until as recently as August 1991, as the Commonwealth Heads of State and Government Conference approached, the call became more muted, and it is possible to trace a series of events which suggests an alteration to Zimbabwe's stance towards South Africa.[23] This appears to have occurred gradually, and without noticeable public debate.[24]

In July 1990, Zimbabwe lifted the state of emergency which had been declared under the Smith regime and renewed at intervals ever since. This was interpreted as a response to the partial lifting of its own state of emergency by South Africa and to a 'slight thaw' in relations between South Africa and the Front Line States.[25] On 2 November 1990 Zimbabwe announced that a South African spy convicted in 1987 had been granted a free pardon by President Mugabe after serving three years of a twelve year sentence, an act which was said to be prompted by 'the general improvement in the political climate of Southern Africa, including the cessation of hostile acts against Zimbabwe by the South African government'.[26] Later in the month it was reported that Zimbabwe was talking with South Africa about a link with South Africa's power grid in order to share electricity from Cabora Bassa. In June 1991 it was announced that a direct passenger rail service between Harare and South Africa would be opened, supplementing the longer and slower route through Botswana; the train, referred to as a 'trans-Limpopo luxury train' carrying mainly first and second class passengers by contrast with the train through Botswana, made its first trip on 5 October.[27] In June 1991 the Speaker of the Parliament of Zimbabwe opened the session by announcing the presence of 'Dutch Reformed Church students and five Professors from the University of Pretoria and the University of the North' in the gallery, and wished them 'a happy stay in Zimbabwe'.[28] Several weeks later the process was repeated when the Speaker welcomed visitors from the University of Cape Town on a study tour. Given the relative freedom of movement between South Africa and Zimbabwe, the presence of these visitors in the country, and even in the galleries in parliament, was not particularly significant; the welcome they were accorded, however, may have been. Again in June it was reported that Zimbabwe had approached South Africa with a view to renewing the preferential trade agreement dating to 1964, which had lapsed in 1986; in November it was said that negotiations were actually under way.[29] In September it was announced that Zimbabwe would ease visa restrictions on South African visitors, providing multiple entry six month visas, in apparent response to a recent South African decision to offer one year multiple entry visas to Zimbabweans.[30] In October under a front page headline 'SA firms rush for trade fair as ban ends', the *Financial Gazette*, the major privately owned weekly published in Harare, reported 'a tremendous response from South African companies with 27 confirmed bookings so far'[31.] Again in October it was reported that Zimbabwe would join with South Africa in a cartel for marketing ivory.[32] In November it was announced that Zimbabwe would be buying grain from South Africa to deal with a shortfall.[33]

It would be easy to read too much into these developments,

for it is also possible to select other events during the same period which suggest that it was business as usual between South Africa and Zimbabwe. The report of negotiations on renewing the trade agreement between Zimbabwe and South also mentioned that South Africa was using the negotiations to bring pressure on Zimbabwe to change its diplomatic stance. In July, when the Sheraton Hotel in Harare, the venue of the forthcoming Commonwealth Heads of State and Government meeting in October, was bombed, Mugabe is reported to have said that while the culprits were not yet known, every other bombing incident in the past had been the work of South Africa.[34] In August 1991 there was a flurry of press speculation that South Africa had funded the opposition Zimbabwe Unity Movement of Edgar Tekerere, who was known to have made several recent visits to South Africa, along the same lines as recently divulged funding of Inkatha or, more ominously, its earlier funding of the MNR.

Nonetheless, there seemed to have been a perceptible thaw in relations, albeit one which was never announced or debated as such. The diplomacy leading up to the Commonwealth meeting in October would appear to have been a factor. Nine Commonwealth foreign ministers meeting in New Delhi in September, preparatory to the summit, drafted recommendations on removing travel restrictions on South Africa as the first step in reducing sanctions in recognition of South Africa's jettisoning of apartheid legislation and allowing political exiles to return since February. This was reported without comment in the Zimbabwe press.[35] On 9 October when Mugabe briefed the press on the forthcoming Commonwealth meeting he said that the main issue would be the debt crisis and foreshadowed that the summit would not seek to blast South Africa and that for the first time in years the United Kingdom (now under a new prime minister) would not be isolated. He was described as saying that 'sanctions against Pretoria, though necessary, had to be gradually lifted to encourage the South African government to continue with the democratic process and to avoid making them feel that they were being punished and President FW De Klerk feeling that he was a culprit'.[36]

In the event, the Commonwealth Heads of Government

adopted a phased withdrawal of sanctions along the lines foreshadowed. 'People to people' sanctions, including consular and visa restrictions, cultural and scientific boycotts, restrictions on tourism promotion and the ban on direct air links would be removed immediately 'in view of the progress made in overcoming obstacles to negotiations in South Africa'. Arms sanctions would remain until a new post-apartheid government was in place in South Africa. Financial sanctions against lending by international financial institutions would remain until agreement on a new democratic constitution. 'Other economic sanctions including trade and investment measures should be lifted when the appropriate transitional mechanisms have been agreed on which would enable all the parties to participate fully and effectively in negotiations.'[37]

In short, the measures adopted by the Commonwealth Heads of State and Governments, presumably unanimously in accord with Commonwealth practice, coincided fairly closely with the position towards its relations with South Africa which Zimbabwe had practiced for some years, and departed markedly from the position which Mandela had come to the conference to argue.

Conclusion

To date Zimbabwe's response to the geographical accident which places it adjacent to white-ruled South Africa and to recent changes in South Africa appears to have been based on repugnance at apartheid balanced against the dictates of short-term survival rather than on any carefully thought out long-run assessment of national interest. There has yet to emerge a debate on the consequences for Zimbabwe of the emergence of a stable democratic regime in South Africa. At one level, this would represent the realization of an important goal; at another the consequences might well redound to Zimbabwe's disadvantage. A majority-ruled government in South Africa will not in itself relieve Zimbabwe of the festering security problem along its eastern border and along the transport routes to the sea through Mozambique or of the economic and social costs of maintaining its army in the field, for the MNR has long since moved beyond the control of a regime in Pretoria, notwithstanding vestigial support it may derive from South African sources. A peaceful, majority-ruled South Africa is likely to re-emerge as the economic powerhouse of the region, detracting from the role which Zimbabwe has seen for itself within SADCC and making it all the more difficult for Zimbabwe to address its problems of unemployment and slowing development.

Notes

1   Tendai Dumbutshena, 'Mugabe's views on the future', *Rand Daily Mail*, 25 February 1980, p.7.

2   *Sunday Times* (Johannesburg), 9 March 1980, p.1

3   *Rand Daily Mail*, 22 March 1980, p.2

4   *Sunday Times* (Johannesburg), 9 March 1980, p.1.

5   'S.A. Ready to Give Zimbabwe a Chance', *Chronicle* (Bulawayo), 20 May 1980, p.1.

6   *Herald*, 21 June 1980, p.1.

7   *Herald*, 27 June 1980, p.1.

8   *Sunday News* (Bulawayo), 6 July 1980, p.1.

9   *Herald*, 9 July 1980, pp. 1, 2.

10   *Herald*, 6 September 1980, p.2.

11   *Herald*, 18 August 1980, p.6.

12   *Herald*, 20 August 1980, p.4.

13   In 1987 the UK received a larger share of exports than did South Africa.

14   Interview, Harare, September 1988.

15   Interview, Hugh Lewin, Harare, September 1988.

16   BBC, *Summary of World Broadcasts*, 14 February 1990.

17   Zimbabwe, *Parliamentary Debates*, House of Assembly, Vol. 16, No. 66, 15 February 1990, p. 3364.

18   *Africa Report*, May-June 1990, p.36.

19   Ibid, p.37.

20   *Parade* (Harare), April 1990, p.25

21   'SA Freedom Bodies Urged to Unite to Stop Bloodshed', *Herald*,

        7 February 1991, p.1.

22   *Africa Research Bulletin,* April 1-30 1991, p.10089.

23   BBC, *Summary of World Broadcasts,* 19 August 1991, citing Radio
        Tanzania.

24   A possible exception to this is an article which appeared in *Moto,*
        an independent monthly frequently critical of the government,
        which suggested that 'if De Klerk and his regime don't deserve a
        reward for their efforts at dismantling apartheid so far, at least
        they need encouragement and a positive response. . . . What of
        the well-tested old tactic of the carrot and the stick? De Klerk
        could, for instance, have been invited to Harare to meet the
        Frontline Heads of State.'   Makani Kabweza, 'SA, OAU and
        Frontliners', *Moto,* March 1991, p.11.

25   *Africa Report,* September-October 1990, p.7.

26   BBC, *Summary of World Broadcasts,* 5 November 1990.

27   *Africa Research Bulletin,* 16 June - 15 July 1991, p.10451; *Herald,* 7
        October 1991, p.7.

28   Zimbabwe, *Parliamentary Debates,* Vol.18, No.4, 27 June 1991,
        p.98.

29   BBC, *Summary of World Broadcasts,* 9 August 1991, 19 November
        1991.

30   Ibid, 30 September 1991.

31   *Financial Gazette* (Harare), 24 October 1991, p.1.

32   BBC, *Summary of World Broadcasts,* 15 October 1991.

33   Ibid, 12 November 1991.

34   Ibid, 24 July 1991.

35   'CHOGM Ministers for Partial Lift of SA Sanctions', *Herald,* 16
        September 1991, p.1.

36   'CHOGM to Focus on Debt Crisis--President', *Herald,* 10 October
        1991, pp.1, 13.

37   'Club in Accord on SA Sanctions', *Herald,* 22 October 1991, p.1;
        BBC, *Summary*

10

Transition in Namibia, 1989-1990 and the South African Case

Christopher Saunders

Introduction[1]

Whatever the outcome of the transition now underway in South Africa — and historians of the future may look back on it as the single most important stage in an uneven process of transition, in the southern African region as a whole, from white minority and colonial rule to multi-party democracy — it began when a process of transition in neighbouring Namibia was moving towards completion and any understanding of the context of the South African transition must inevitably take account of the Namibian case. Though many references have been made to Namibia as a possible model for South Africa to follow, to date only brief assessments of the Namibian transition have been published, and none of them explains at all adequately why that process was completed in the way it was, or contrasts what happened in Namibia with the process now under way in South Africa. [2]

The two cases are, of course, from many points of view very different, necessarily so when Namibia, though over two-thirds the land area of South Africa, has a population smaller than greater Cape Town. No party outflanked SWAPO, the leading nationalist party, on the left. Its main opponent, the Democratic Turnhalle Alliance (DTA), lacks Inkatha's single ethnic base. In the Namibian case, the transition was from de facto colonial rule to independence, whereas South Africa — whether its present government be regarded as legitimate or illegitimate — is a sovereign, independent state. The question at issue is how power can be shared or transferred within such a state.   As for similarities, and links between the two transitions, there is the central role played by the same South African government — the key South African player in the Namibian transition, Administrator-General (AG) Louis Pienaar, is today a member of the South African government — and the same legacy of apartheid: Swapo deliberately chose the thirtieth anniversary of the Sharpeville massacre as the date for Namibian independence. What was at issue in Namibia before 1990 was not independence alone, but also, crucially, the way it would be achieved and the likely form of post-independence rule. In Namibia, as now in South Africa, the fundamental question was whether racist, authoritarian minority rule could be transformed into some form of liberal democratic rule. [3]

A question on which we can only speculate is the relationship between the two transitions. The same economic pressures on South Africa played a part both in the decision to withdraw from Namibia and to reform internally, though it is generally agreed that the military reverses which the South African Defence Force suffered at Cuito Cuanavale and then in Cunene Province in the first half of 1988 were the single most important factors which pushed the South African government into withdrawal. If there is truth in what President De Klerk has claimed on a number of occasions since he took office — that the origins of the reform process he initiated in 1990 lie as far back as 1986, i.e. well before the decision was taken to withdraw from Namibia — it may be that a secondary consideration in that decision was that the government wished to get rid of that territory as a prelude to internal reform.[4] Or, perhaps, once pushed into withdrawing from Namibia, it decided to use that withdrawal as a trial run for South Africa itself, wanting to see what would happen there before it risked moving towards democracy at home. It has recently been claimed that it was only after a National Party mission to Namibia reported in January 1990 that the Namibian transition had been a success (in the sense that it would produce a government which would pose no threat to South African interests) that the decision was taken to proceed with major reform in South Africa itself.[5] When he wrote his 2 February 1990 speech, President De Klerk must have known that if he was to play an important role at the Namibian independence celebrations seven weeks later, he had first to make bold moves internally. He must also have known that if he did not move internally, pressures on South Africa would inevitably mount following Namibian independence.

Whatever the exact relationship between the transitions, from the perspective of present-day South Africa, the Namibian transition, though it began disastrously, appears to have been remarkably successful. In less than a year, an internationally-monitored election was organized and the Constituent Assembly then elected adopted a constitution for an independent Namibia. The South African transition has been under way for almost two years and the long-promised all-party conference has yet to meet. Continuing violence is only the chief among a number of obstacles in the way of a negotiated settlement and the introduction of a democratic order. That we are still only at the beginning of the South African transition makes a detailed comparison between it and the Namibian case premature, but the Namibian transition, of interest for its own sake, can still provide pointers to the way the South African transition may develop.

Background to the transition

The reasons why the Namibian transition was relatively short, and ended as successfully as it did, lie as much in the years before the formal transition began in April 1989 as in the way the transition itself took place between then and independence on 21 March 1990. To understand the transition, then, it is necessary first to consider some aspects of the earlier history of the Namibian issue. The transition of 1989-90 essentially followed a plan worked out over ten years earlier in negotiations in which the Western Contact Group put proposals before South Africa and SWAPO in turn, which were, after negotiations with each party, accepted and approved by the United Nations (UN) Security Council in September 1978.[6] This plan provided for a three-phase transition: in the first phase, after a ceasefire, steps were to be taken to make possible the holding of a free and fair election: the withdrawal of all but a small South African military force, which was to be confined to base; the release of political prisoners; the repeal of discriminatory laws; the return of exiles and refugees. Then in the second phase there was to be an election campaign, culminating in the election of a Constituent Assembly. In the third, that Assembly was to draft and adopt a constitution and set a date for independence. The Assembly could if it wished — for the plan was silent on this — turn itself into the Parliament of the new nation without a further election.

A second essential part of the plan was that a United Nations Transitional Assistance Group (UNTAG) would monitor the whole process and see that the election was free and fair. But — and this was the crucial concession to South Africa — the South-African appointed Administrator-General (AG) was to continue governing the country during the transition, and be responsible for the maintenance of law and order. At first sight this was a surprising concession, given the illegality of the South African regime in international law and the standpoint of the UN that it was itself the sole legitimate authority in the territory. It was, however, an essential concession to the reality that South Africa occupied the territory and could not easily be dislodged from it against its will, and would not have accepted the plan had it been required to withdraw before the election was held.

The most important addition to the original plan was made in 1982. The so-called Constitutional Principles accepted by the parties that year were deliberately designed to answer South African concerns about a future SWAPO government, in the aftermath of Robert Mugabe's victory in Zimbabwe. These guidelines concerned both the process by which the constitution would be drawn up, and the form of the constitution itself. As regards process, the key provision was that the constitution should be adopted by a two-thirds majority of the members of the Constituent Assembly. The declaration of fundamental human rights which, according to the principles, was to form part of the constitution, provided for protection against arbitrary deprivation of private property and ruled out expropriation of property without just compensation, while another clause concerned fair administration of personnel policy in relation to the public service.[7] These provisions meant that any government of an independent Namibia would be severely restricted in, say, attempting to carry though any programme of nationalization or land reform, or in ridding itself of the 40,000 white civil servants. Whether SWAPO, in 1982 and afterwards, thought it could evade these principles when it came to power is not clear; though never embodied in a UN Security Council resolution, the Secretary-General declared them binding on all parties.[8] (On the eve of the election in November 1989 Pik Botha claimed to have guarantees from the US and UK governments that they would be adhered to.)[9]

In November 1985, in a final agreement on the content of the plan, the parties agreed that the election would be based on a proportional representation system, which would favour smaller parties, rather than the 'winner take all' Westminster system. With that, the plan was said to be complete.

I have considered elsewhere the reasons why the South African government stalled on implementation of the plan for over a decade, and why, in 1988, agreement was reached on implementation.[10] All I shall do here is to point out that, because resolution of the Namibian conflict had become intimately connected to what was occuring in southern Angola, the 1988 negotiations primarily concerned the extrication of the South African forces from southern Angola and the phased withdrawal of Cuban forces from that country. It was fundamental to that deal that implementation of the UN plan would begin, but the plan as worked out between 1977 and 1985 was not modified in any way. SWAPO was not a party to the 1988 negotiations. This partly explains its disastrous decision to send members of its military wing, PLAN, to establish bases in the north as the transition began, a decision which led directly to the deaths of over three hundred of its men at the hands of the security forces in the first weeks of April. In terms of the transition plan, the military conflict was to have ended formally as transition began. When conflict erupted again in April 1989, implementation was suspended; once that conflict was resolved, it got underway

again.[11] However, the crisis exerted a sobering effect on the
parties: it was a reminder of the fragility of the whole process.
South Africa, accused of ruthlessness, was given an excuse not to
demobilize the paramilitary counter-insurgency unit Koevoet,
which had been incorporated in the South West African Police;
SWAPO's international standing plummeted and it was thrown
on the defensive; and the authority of UNTAG, which was
accused of giving in to the South Africans, was weakened. On the
other hand, the very fact that so severe a crisis was resolved
suggested that nothing was likely to prevent the successful
completion of the transition.

Before I consider the transition itself, let me notice that what
happened after April 1989 was also shaped in part by the fact that
a kind of independence for the territory had been on the South
African agenda from the mid 1970s; a broader 'transition' from
South African rule had begun then. The gradual evolution away
from a racial order during the previous decade undoubtedly
helped prevent a mass exodus of whites in 1989: by then a
transitional [sic] government of national unity, which had a
majority of black ministers, had been in office for over three
years, and though it lacked legitimacy, not being elected, it
helped allay white fears of black rule. And the way the UN plan
would operate was fine-tuned during the long period during
which implementation was stalled, though that did not mean
that all its weaknesses had been ironed out.

Much of the language contained in the agreements was
vague, opening the door for differences of interpretation. In
particular, the relationship between the two major authorities in
the transition period, the South African-appointed AG and the
UN Secretary-General's Special Representative (SR), was not
spelled out, and no machinery was provided for mediating
differences between them.   The Western Contact Group
proposals of 1978 merely spoke of UNTAG exercising
'supervision and control' of the electoral process. In 1989 the UN
authorities chose to interpret 'supervision and control' in a
restrictive way, viewing their role as little more than a
monitoring one, in which they reacted to what the
administration did, and employed no enforcement powers.[12]
UNTAG headquarters freely admitted that in the north it was

impossible to supervise adequately the activities of the South West African Police. Though the number of UNTAG police monitors was increased fourfold from the original 360, they were told that they had no powers to intervene, and so were unable to stop breaches of law and order and partisan acts by SWAPOL.[13] Charges of intimidation sent in to UNTAG headquarters in Windhoek from the regional offices were not always followed up.[14]

Another essential element of the plan as elaborated in 1978 was that it contained a timetable for the sequence of events leading to the election of the Constituent Assembly. The timetable provided that that election should take place seven months after the transition began, and despite delays, caused in part by the April crisis, in the repeal of racially discriminatory laws affecting the electoral process, in the return of exiles, and, especially, in organizing the election, the election itself was postponed by only one week. (It could not be further postponed, it was said, because the weather would then be too hot and the coming of the rainy season in the north might make the holding of an election impossible.) The need to keep to a timetable meant that obstacles had either to be resolved within a relatively short period of time, or ignored. Problem cases involving the release of political prisoners, for example, were resolved relatively speedily by an international jurist.[15]

No special interim government was put in place in Namibia during the transition: the Transitional Government of National Unity, which had been installed in office in June 1985, was dissolved before the transition began, and the AG was given full legislative and executive powers, as on a number of previous occasions, and he continued to exercise those powers until independence. It was he who issued the electoral laws and convened the Constituent Assembly.[16] He had, admittedly, to consult UNTAG in what he did, and his draft proclamations providing for registration, for the election itself, and for the convening of the Constituent Assembly were in each case modified after harsh criticism, from UNTAG and various non-governmental monitoring groups.[17] But the SR's objections to what the AG did were by no means always heeded, and while UNTAG, because the UN itself had long given SWAPO a special status, bent over backwards to be impartial, South African partiality to the anti-SWAPO parties was barely, if at all, concealed.

Success, Despite Doubts and Suspected Dirty Tricks

The South African government had long feared that implementation of the plan embodied in UNSC resolution 435 would bring to power a radical government which would be hostile to South African interests and might plunge Namibia into civil war.[18] From the mid 1970s, first the Vorster and then the Botha government had hoped to build up a client party in the territory to which power could be transferred, or which might even win an internationally-monitored election, if one were held. When that strategy seemed unlikely to work, the fall-back was to ensure that if SWAPO did win an internationally-monitored election it would not obtain a two thirds majority. If SWAPO were to win an overwhelming majority, and begin to implement policies the South African government did not like, it had strong cards to play, having a stranglehold over the Namibian economy and the means to destabilize the new regime.[19] Once the decision was taken to withdraw from Namibia, it would seem that South African strategy was, on the one hand, to try to gain as much international credit as possible from allowing the process to take place smoothly, and on the other to try to manage the transition as far as was possible in South African interests, which meant preventing SWAPO from obtaining a two-thirds majority. These aims were often in conflict. Pik Botha's Department of Foreign Affairs wished to create the impression that South Africa was acting strictly according to the rules and entirely honourably, yet we now know, thanks to the revelations that emerged concerning state funding of Inkatha in July 1991, that the cabinet of which he was a member approved covert funding of over R100 million for the anti-SWAPO parties. When it was announced that SWAPO had received 57% of the vote, Pik Botha was very pleased to announce that he had only been one percent out in his prediction.[20] While we know that the government as a whole wanted such a result, we do not know how much it was told about the 'dirty tricks' carried out by military intelligence and other security-related state agencies in order to prevent a SWAPOvictory.[21]

It is impossible to measure the effect on the election of the South African government's funding of the anti-SWAPO parties, contrary to both the spirit of the agreement it had signed with Angola and Cuba in July 1988 and to UN Security Council Resolution 435 itself.[22] Nor is it easy to calculate the impact of the assassination of Anton Lubowski, the leading white member of SWAPO, in September. That was probably the work of the Civil Co-operation Bureau, a secret project of military intelligence, which also employed Nico Basson, who spent lavishly to publicize the claims of maltreatment by SWAPO detainees on their return from SWAPO's prisons outside Lubango in Angola.[23] These actions may have played only a marginal role, if that, in ensuring that the anti-SWAPO parties did obtain a blocking third in the November election. Large sums of South African money had been given Bishop Muzorewa in Rhodesia ten years before, yet Mugabe had won an overwhelming victory. SWAPO's failure to confront the detainee scandal and the tragedy of the missing persons would have cost it many votes whether Basson had taken up the cause or not.[24] Perhaps more important in determining the result of the election were the actions, and non-actions, of the administration in Windhoek.

In terms of a UN agreement — made in 1983 but kept confidential until 1989 — that administration was supposed to be impartial in carrying out its task, acting only as a caretaker and holding the ring while the election took place.[25] Some of its actions after April 1989 may have been the result of bureaucratic incompetence and inertia, and of genuine differences of interpretation of what was required in terms of the agreed transition arrangements, but the administration certainly exploited every opportunity to work to the advantage of the anti-SWAPO parties.

This was seen above all in its failure to demobilize the ex-Koevoet members in the South West African Police, who were widely accused of large-scale intimidation of SWAPO supporters in the north.[26] Even after the UN Security Council in August criticized the failure of the administration to act in this matter, and went on to note that the provisions of the UN Plan 'are not being fully complied with', the AG waited until October, just weeks before the election, to take effective steps to demobilize Koevoet.[27] The SR also urged the AG to dissolve the entire ethnic structure of administration but that was never done, on the grounds that that structure did not 'abridge or inhibit' the objective of a free and fair election. The Chief Electoral Officer appointed by the AG was shown to have been a member of the National Security Council which at a meeting the previous September had discussed how to defeat SWAPO in the election, yet he was retained in his post.[28] Nothing effective was done to make the South West African Broadcasting Corporation change its ways; until the election it continued to demonstrate blatant anti-SWAPO bias.[29] And the election law itself was not promulgated until the middle of October, too close to the election to allow its contents to be widely publicized. Perhaps most extraordinary of all, though without result, the Draft Constituent Assembly proclamation which the AG issued on 21 July said that he was not obliged to give effect to any recommendation it might make; not surprisingly, that provoked immediate condemnation and it was withdrawn.[30] The provision in the AG's law that anyone either born in Namibia or with natural parents born there could vote[31] made it possible for 10,000 ex-Namibians resident in South Africa — more than were needed for a seat in the Assembly — to be bussed back to the territory to register and vote, or be flown to Windhoek for that purpose.

Such actions by the AG led many international observers in the months before the election to doubt whether the SR could possibly certify it 'free and fair'.The Commonwealth Observer Group, one of the most influential of such monitoring teams, reported in October 1989 that the process was 'extraordinarily fragile' and pointed to various ways in which the South African authorities had, in its view, flouted the agreed procedure.[32] Many of the concerns voiced most strongly, however, related to the way the election was being organized; it was feared that for a variety of reasons voters would not be able to cast their votes. But in the event over 97% of the registered voters cast ballots, there were few spoilt papers, and most observers accepted that only a few relatively minor problems — delays in obtaining ballot boxes in certain areas, for example — marred the election itself. So the SR was able to declare it free and fair, and 'a shining lesson in democracy', on 14 November.[33] What had gone before was then largely forgotten. Having won the election, SWAPO was prepared to say that it had been free, if not fair, and it did not alter that assessment even when the South African funding of anti-SWAPO parties was disclosed.[34]

There is no doubt that the administration was constrained to some extent by a concern that South Africa should gain credit internationally from the way it allowed the process to take place, and by the knowledge that the SR was required to declare the electoral process free and fair. On the other hand, it knew that the SR would be under enormous pressure to do that, for there was no question of holding another election, and the UNTAG budget lasted for only a year. In the event, intimidation in the north seems to have been counter-productive; less than a month after the very belated demobilization of Koevoet the people of Ovamboland voted overwhelmingly for SWAPO.[35] Ironically, it may be that had the administration been strictly impartial, the final outcome — the type of government Namibia obtained — would not have been very different.

Drafting the new constitution

While there was an agreed timetable on the run-up to the election, it was not possible to lay down in advance how long the Constituent Assembly would take to draft and adopt the new constitution. In fact, it took only eighty days, in large part because its members wished to achieve independence as soon as possible, and before the last of the UNTAG forces departed from the territory. Suspicions lingered that South Africa, not wanting to see a SWAPO government in office, might still try to delay independence or interfere in the process in some way. Even the DTA members, who were reported by one commentator, rather unkindly, to be 'tired of dancing as South African puppets', made clear that they wanted independence as soon as possible.[36]

The Constituent Assembly was able to work so rapidly

because of the spirit of reconciliation and compromise that prevailed from the first session.[37] The closer SWAPO came to power, the more pragmatic and non-ideological it became. That process was of course helped by the changed world order, with one-party Marxist regimes in Europe and Africa under challenge. As the Namibian people went to the polls, the Berlin Wall fell, and events in Eastern Europe were referred to on a number of occasions in debates in the Constituent Assembly.[38] SWAPO's list of candidates for election had included a number of non-SWAPO people, and when it announced its government-in-waiting in December, it once again included people from outside the party. And when members of the different parties met in the Assembly, they found, to their surprise, that they had interests in common, and that all identified as Namibians.

Not having won two-thirds of the vote, SWAPO had to compromise if lengthy constitutional wrangles were to be avoided. In its final form the AG's proclamation convening a Constituent Assembly did not contain the constitutional provisions of the 1982 principles, but only those concerning process, including the requirement that the constitution should be adopted by a two-thirds majority.[39] SWAPO rejected his proclamation on the grounds that the AG should have no say in how the Constituent Assembly should operate.[40] Nonetheless, at the first sitting it proposed the adoption of the 1982 Principles in full.[41] After that, major differences still remained between SWAPO and its opponents, who wanted a head of state with only ceremonial powers, a parliamentary system, proportional representation, a bicameral legislature and no detention without trial. A Standing Committee meeting behind closed doors resolved many of these differences, and in the end SWAPO was given the executive presidency it wanted, but the president's term was limited to ten years; detention without trial was dropped; proportional representation was adopted instead of the constituency system which SWAPO favoured; and a second chamber was to be established in future to act as a additional check on the National Assembly. On 9 February 1990, the constitution — widely acclaimed as one of the world's most democratic, and an outstanding human rights document[42] — was approved unanimously by the Constituent Assembly.[43]

When the transition began, few had dared hope for such an outcome.

Lessons for the South African transition?

In Namibia, then, there was a long-drawn out interregnum, but a relatively brief formal transition; third-party mediation had secured agreement by the two main players to an agreed formula, including a timetable, in earlier talks; the role of the UN, though much more limited than many wished, was nevertheless, as a monitor, crucial to the outcome.

In South Africa, by contrast, there was no bargain struck before transition began, no prior negotiation except for the talks held between the imprisoned Nelson Mandela and members of the government;[44] and the transition followed no previously agreed formula or timetable (the only 'deadline' is the need for a new constitution to be in place before late 1994, when another election is required for the racist tri-cameral Parliament). There was no agreement from the outset to refer problem cases involving the release of political prisoners to agreed arbitration, with the result that the issue of the release of such prisoners, instead of aiding the process towards negotiations, long hindered attempts to get substantive negotiations going. It seems highly unlikely that any international body — the UN or Commonwealth — will be allowed to monitor the first general election.[45] It is not even clear that there will be an elected Constituent Assembly. While the government says it recognizes the problem of being both active player and neutral referee at the same time, it nevertheless wishes to control events. It argues that the election of a Constituent Assembly would pre-empt the negotiating process, because from its perspective the whole point of negotiation is to produce an electoral system which will not make possible undiluted majority rule, and a Constituent Assembly elected by direct proportional representation would not contain the checks and balances it wants to see written into the new constitution. On the other hand, only an elected Constituent Assembly can legitimate a new constitutional order. Already the government has had to backtrack, allowing the UN High Commission for

Refugees, as in Namibia, to organize the return of exiles, though without conceding a general amnesty, and accepting the need for some kind of transitional arrangements. It may be that something along the lines of the recent proposals put forward by the Democratic Party, themselves influenced by, though in significant respects different from, the Namibian model, will be adopted: that the Codesa talks will agree on basic constitutional principles and procedures; that a constitutional conference will then be elected to adopt a constitution; and that another election will then be held to elect a new government.

Not only has much water still to flow under the South African constitutional bridge; the bridge itself may yet be washed away. Only when, and if, we get to the other side will a full comparison between the South African and Namibian transitions be possible.

Notes

1   I wish to thank the Human Sciences Research Council, which has helped fund the project of which this is a byproduct. The HSRC is not to be held responsible for anything I say.

2   Many articles appeared at the time in such publications as *Action on Namibia, This Week in Namibia, Africa Report, Southern Africa Report.* Some observer groups published post-mortems (for example, National Democratic Institute for International Affairs, *Nation Building: the U.N. and Namibia* (Washington, 1990); Southern African Project, Lawyers' Committee for Civil Rights under Law, *South Africa and Namibia: New Challenges* (Washington, 1990). More reflective assessments may be found in B.Wood, 'Introduction: the UN Plan for Namibia and its Initial Implementation' in *Namibia: Essential Documents of the United Nations Independence Plan, 1976-89* (London, 1989); R. Jaster, 'The 1988 Peace Accords and the Future of South-Western Africa', *Adelphi Papers*, 253 (London, 1990), ch.3; A. du Pisani, 'Namibia: A Nation in the Making', *South Africa International*, 20 (4), April 1990 (virtually identical to his `Mi N!Ore O Namibia' in *Geopolitique et Geostrategie dans L'Hemisphere Sud*   [Reunion, 1990]).

3   For a brief general overview see A. du Toit, 'South Africa as Another Case of Transition from Authoritarian Rule', *Idasa Occasional Papers*, 32 (n.d.[1990?]).

4   In July 1987, P.W. Botha was considering releasing Nelson

Mandela on parole: *Sunday Times*, 24 November 1991.

5   *Southscan*, 6/23, p. 197; *Cape Times*, 27 July 1991; *South*, 14 November 1991: statements by N.Basson re 'Operation Agree'; cf. A. Sparks, 'F W Must Have Known of Secret Funding', *Reality*, September,1991, p.16.

6   One of the clearest accounts of the negotiating process in the late 1970s is Margaret P. Karns, 'Ad Hoc Multilateral Diplomacy: the US, the Contact Group and Namibia', *International Organisation*, 43 (Winter, 1987).

7   UN Security Council Document S/15287: letter dated 12 July 1982 from the Representatives of Canada, France, the Federal Republic of Germany, the United Kingdom . . . and the United States of America to the Secretary-General. See M. Wiechers, 'Namibia: the 1982 Constitutional Principles and Their Legal Significance', *South African Yearbook for International Law*, 15 (1989-90).

8   UN document S/20412 (23 Jan.1989), para 35.

9   *Cape Times*, 7 November 1989.

10 C. Saunders, 'South African Strategy and Namibian Decolonization', paper presented to African Studies Association of Australia and the Pacific Conference, Deakin University, November 1990. See also G. Bender, 'Peacemaking in Southern Africa: the Luanda-Pretoria tug-of-war', *Third World Quarterly* (January 1989).

11 The fullest account available at present is one written to defend the role of the South African and South West African forces: P. Stiff, *Nine Days of War and South Africa's Final Days in Namibia* (new ed., Alberton, 1991).

12 The UN was much criticized for this, for example, by the Commission on Independence for Namibia: see *South Africa and Namibia*, especially p.17.

13 See, for example, C. Thornberry, *Some Thoughts on the First phase of the Namibian Independence Process*, (Johannesburg: S.A.Institute of International Affairs, 1989), p.3.

14 E. Landis, interview with the author, New York, October 1990; B. Carton, 'Dirty Tricks in Namibia: the Voter Registration Drive', Yale University seminar paper, October 1989.

15 Professor Carl Norgaard, President of the European Human Rights' Commission, was appointed by the Secretary-General to advise the SR. See G. Erasmus, 'Namibian Independence and the Release of Politial Prisoners', *South African Yearbook of International Law*, 14 (1988-89); J. Rautenbach, 'Namibia — the

Release of Political Prisoners Revisited', in ibid, 15 (1989-90).

16   *Official Gazette of South West Africa,* 24 April 1989.

17   The opinion of British barrister John Macdonald was that the draft proclamation for the registration of voters was 'deeply flawed' and 'unacceptable as the basis for a free and fair election'; the draft election proclamation was criticized for, among other things, not providing effectively for a secret ballot by the Commission on Independence for Namibia, the National Union of Namibian Workers; the US Commission said the draft Constituent Assembly proclamation would make 'a mockery of the election process': see generally, Namibia Communications Centre, Press Clippings and Other Documents on Namibia (NCC Press Clippings), 15 August 1989.

18   Foreign Minister Pik Botha frequently referred to this possibility: see, for example, his speech on the Recognition of Namibian Independence Bill in *House of Assembly Debates,* 14 March 1990.

19   South Africa had control of Walvis Bay; it had drastically reduced its subsidy to Namibia in 1989, leaving a large budget deficit; there was an R800 million debt which Namibia owed South African financial institutions.

20   Pik Botha, quoted in *Cape Times,* 15 November 1989.

21   The charge that South Africa was trying to rig the election result was dismissed as 'scurrilous and irresponsible' by D. Auret: 'The Settlement Plan for Namibia: a South African Perspective' in M. Hough and M. van der Merwe, eds., *Namibia: Current and Future Prospects* (Pretoria, 1989), p.8. That the Department of Foreign Affairs and Military Intelligence were working to different agendas was seen most clearly on the eve of the election, when Foreign Minister Botha was fed bogus radio messages purporting to come from UNTAG and to concern a build-up of SWAPO fighters on Namibia's northern border.

22   R65 million of the DTA's budget of R72 million came from the South African government, mostly thorugh the Namib Foundation. Some suspected this at the time; others thought the funding came from right-wing groups in South Africa and West Germany. See A. Sparks, 'F W Must have Known', pp.15-16.

23   See especially, N. Basson and B. Motinga, *Call Them Spies — a Documentary Account of the Namibian Spy Drama* (Windhoek, 1989). Basson only became involved in 1989; others had tried to publicize the issue for many years before that. Cf. esp. P.Trewhela, 'Genesis of the SWAPO "Spy-Drama"' and 'SWAPO and the Churches: An International Scandal' in *Searchlight Southern Africa,* 5-7 (1990-91).

24   Cf. Basson and Motinga, *Call Them Spies*. An UNTAG mission
        which went in search of missing persons accounted for all but 315
        persons: 'Report of the United Nations Mission on Detainees', 11
        October 1989, in *Preparing for a Free Namibia: Elections, Transition
        and Independence. The Report of the Commonwealth Observer Group
        on Namibia* (London, 1989), annexure XV. Swapo had grossly
        exaggerated the number of refugees and exiles in presenting
        figures to the UN for aid purposes.

25   Para. 7 of the impartiality agreement of September 1982, which
        was made public in May 1989: 'Informal Check List', given in
        Nation-Building: the U.N. and Namibia, p.115; see also *Washington
        Times*, 14 Feb. 1989.

26   See, for example, *Action on Namibia*, October 1989, pp.8-9.
        Evidence of extensive intimidation was submitted to the
        Commission for the Prevention and Combatting of Intimidation
        and Electoral Malpractices (O'Linn Commission). Koevoet was
        primarily a paramilitary counterinsurgency unit and not
        involved in ordinary policing duties. The AG justified his refusal
        to confine Koevoet to base and to disband it by speaking of the
        threat of another 'invasion' similar to that of April.

27   UNSC Resolution 640 of 1989.

28   D. Lush, 'Namibian Elections — Some Misgivings', *Reality*, July
        1989.

29   The pressure-group NPP-435 monitored the SWABC and
        reported critically on it. Radio was the primary source of
        information for the 60% of the population estimated to be
        illiterate. The print media were as partisan, but there was a range
        of papers, from the pro-Swapo *Namibian* through the pro-DTA
        Republikein and *Times of Namibia* to papers supporting the far
        right.

30   GN 90 in *Official Gazette* 5754 of 21 July 1989. See the analysis by
        G. Dropkin in *Action on Namibia*, October 1989, pp. 12-13.

31   A-G Proclamation 19 in *Official Gazette*, 5740 of 30 June 1989.

32   *Preparing for a Free Namibia*, pp. ix-xiii.

33   Ahtisaari, quoted *Front File*, Dec. 1989, p.5.

34   Hamutenya, quoted *Southscan*, July 1991. Justice Garoeb of the
        UDF said the election had not been free and fair because all
        Swapo detainees had not been able to vote: *Namibia Constituent
        Assembly Debates (NCA Debates)*, 2 vols (Windhoek, 1990), 1:7 (21
        November, 1989).

35   The election results are to be found in, for example, *Nation-
        Building: the U.N. and Namibia*, p.130. Members of Koevoet were

moved to the Western Transvaal in January/February 1990: *Weekly Mail*, 4 Oct. 1991; *Sunday Times*, 6 Oct. 1991, p.11.

36   J. Lindsay, in *Southern African Report*, 5 (1990), p.6.

37   *NCA Debates*.

38   For example, see ibid, p.195.

39   AG Proclamation 62, in Official Gazette 5854, 6 November 1989.

40   Swapo statement, 10 August 1989, in NCC Press Clippings.

41   *NCA Debates*, vol. I (21 November 1989).

42   The constitution is reproduced in *South African Yearbook of International Law*, 15 (1989/90), pp. 301-61. For the making of the constitution, see A. Chaskalson, 'Namibian Constitution', *Monitor*, April 1990; G. Erasmus, 'Die Grondwet van Namibie. International Proces en Inhoud', *Stellenbosch Law Review*, 1, 3 (1990), and for a critical view, Bruce Fein, 'Chinks in Namibia's Constitution', *The Washington Times*, 8 May 1990.

43   *NCA Debates*, vol. 2 (Windhoek, 1990).

44   See, for example, S. Johns and H. Davis, eds., *Mandela, Tambo and the African National Congress* (New York, 1991), p.207 and doc. 43.

45   See A. Johnson in *Cape Times*, 15 November 1989.

11

Making an African Army: the Case of Zimbabwe, 1980-87

Michael Evans

Introduction

The development of Zimbabwe's post-independence army provides an interesting case of how a victorious African revolutionary movement can succeed in balancing ethnic political domination with a significant level of military professionalism. On independence in April 1980, the new state of Zimbabwe inherited three rival armies after a seven year civil war. The Zimbabwe African National Union (ZANU) party led by Robert Mugabe came to power, controlling the strongest political army but the weakest military force.[1] It had virtually no experience of conventional military organization. Seven years later, the Mugabe Government had created a single Zimbabwe National Army (ZNA) which was undergoing one of the most advanced forms of command and staff training in Black Africa. The ZNA was also operating an external task force and had emerged as the dominant military instrument of the Front Line States' diplomatic coalition. In short, the progress of the Zimbabwean Army indicated the ZANU administration's ability to reconcile the often competing needs of ethnic politicization with conventional military capability and reflected its degree of success as an incumbent regime.

To illustrate the process by which insurgent guerrilla fighters were transformed into incumbent conventional soldiers, four phases in the ZNA's development are examined. First, the military policy of the ZANU Government is explained in the context of its attempt to reconcile contending military traditions through a process of army integration. Second, the radically different training roles of Britain and North Korea are discussed. Third, the influence of South African destabilization strategy on the evolution of Zimbabwean military doctrine is assessed. Finally, the ZNA's operational performance — both internally in Matabeleland and externally in Mozambique — is briefly considered to illustrate the capabilities and limitations of such an army as an instrument of state policy.

The Post-Independence Setting: the Military Legacy of the Civil War

The Rhodesian-Zimbabwean bush war ended in a military stalemate. The ZANU Government came to office following a Commonwealth controlled ceasefire and a British supervised election. As Mugabe put it: 'We did not win a military victory . . . . We reached a political settlement . . . as compromise.'[2] The new administration faced the complex problem of amalgamating three mutually antagonistic armies. Each was intact and undefeated in the field; each was different in ethnic composition; each possessed a distinctive military tradition.

The Rhodesian Army

After independence, the regular white infantry and special force units which had served the defunct Smith and Muzorewa regimes were quickly disbanded.[3] But substantial forces remained operational. These included three white-officered *askari* battalions of the Rhodesian African Rifles (RAR) as well as mounted infantry, armoured and artillery units. Black Rhodesian troops were largely recruited from the Karanga, a large Shona sub-group. They were highly trained in counter-insurgency and conventional warfare and many had undergone training in parachute and special force skills. In short, the

Rhodesian Army remained a formidable military organization whose regular structure duplicated that of the British Army.[4]

The Zimbabwe People's Revolutionary Army (ZIPRA)

ZIPRA was the military wing of Joshua Nkomo's Zimbabwe African People's Union (ZAPU). It was a 20,000 strong, mostly Ndebele-Karanga army drawing support from some 20 per cent of the population located in Western Zimbabwe. Largely as a result of its geographical and demographic position, ZIPRA had developed as a mixed guerrilla/conventional force. Operating from Zambia during the 1970s, thousands of ZIPRA recruits had been trained as conventional troops, mainly by Soviet and East German instructors.[5] The ZIPRA High Command led by Lookout Masuku and Dumiso Dabengwa (the 'Black Russian') adopted the so-called 'turning point strategy'. This envisaged a conventional invasion of Rhodesia from across the Zambezi. For this reason ZIPRA's military emphasis was not on guerrilla insurgency — although guerrillas did fight — but on developing a regular army infrastructure.[6]

The Zimbabwe African National Liberation Army

ZANLA was the military wing of the politically victorious ZANU party. It was a 35-40,000 strong, mainly Shona guerrilla army drawing support from some 80 percent of the Zimbabwean population. Using Mozambique as a rear strategic base, ZANLA had executed a *Chimurenga Chechipiri* (liberation war) based on the tenets of Maoist revolutionary warfare. Accordingly, the primary emphasis was not upon military action but on the political mobilization of the peasantry based on strong party-army liaison.[7] Demographic superiority, the use of political commissars and the ability to harness Shona cultural nationalism were the prime reasons for ZANU's election victory.[8] ZANLA forces led by such figures as Josiah Tongogara, Rex Nhongo and Josiah Tungamirai and trained and equipped by such countries as China, Romania and Tanzania waged a war of guerrilla attrition. In strategic terms the ZANLA campaign had advanced to the second stage of Maoist protracted warfare: the stage of revolutionary equalization.[9]   Because of this guerrilla operational mode, ZANLA was, in formal military terms, weak. Unlike the Rhodesian Army and ZIPRA, ZANLA possessed no conventional military organization or capability. It had not, and more importantly, could not vanquish its military rivals. In this sense ZANU was ill-prepared for the military responsibilities of incumbent government. This paradox of political supremacy but military inferiority haunted the ZANU regime. For five years the Mugabe Government sought to correct the imbalance through creating an incumbent military establishment which would be compatible with both ZANU's ethnic political domination and its insurgent ethos. To understand this process it is necessary to consider the revolutionary context of ZANU military tradition since this exercised enormous influence over defence policy in the post-independence era.

Defence Policy and the Revolutionary Context of ZANU Military Tradition

After independence the ruling ZANU party's commitment to creating a single conventional army tended to reflect the experience of revolutionary warfare. The army which finally emerged had a dual character. It embraced both the traditions of a 'regular' professional corps and a guerrilla army with political objectives.   This duality echoed other aspects of the Mugabe regime. In part, it operated though a conventional Westminster parliament and cabinet. On the other hand, much of the political discourse of the government was derived from Eastern European models, including a Central Committee and Politburo. So it was in the army. The idea of 'professionalism' was embodied in training methods taken from the British Army training. At the same time, particular units acquired not only ethnic coloration but also the sort of guerrilla ethos inculcated through the training methods of the North Korean Army.[10]

Zimbabwe is not a Marxist state. Nonetheless, Marxist revolutionary concepts informed the realm of defence policy for many years after independence. Several important features derived from the revolutionary military experience of the 1970s permeated the thought of important cadres throughout the 1980s. One of these was 'the ZANU Idea'. This is an Africanized version of revolutionary war in which Shona cultural nationalism and the legacy of *Chimurenga Chokutanga* (the first war of liberation 1896-97) have been merged with the organizational modes of 'Marxism-Leninism-Mao Tse-tung Thought'.[11] According to the 'ZANU Idea' the guerrilla struggle was a people's storm, a *Gururahundi* in which 'ZANU has become the Zimbabwean people and the Zimbabwean people have become ZANU'.[12] This was to become the slogan of the Zimbabwean Army's North Korean trained units.

Another important influence on military policy during the 1980s was the use of the *Dare re Chimurenga* (ZANU War Council) system developed in the 1970s. The essence of the *Dare* system was to ensure Shona politico-military unity by settling factional strife through arbitration. Mastery of arbitration methods contributed to Mugabe's rise as ZANU leader during the guerilla war. In the 1980s, *Dare* techniques — the use of patronage, co-optation, compromise, pre-emption and elimination — of allies and enemies alike, were successfully transferred by ZANU to manage the military problems associated with wielding power. Both the 'ZANU Idea' and the *Dare* system were the products of an African revolutionary war tradition which was in many respects a world apart from the traditional British concept of 'military professionalism'. It is in this context that the development of the ZNA must be seen.

The Process of Military Integration, 1980-81

The amalgamation of the three rival armies into a single national army took eighteen months and cost Z$378.1 million, about 25 per cent of the Zimbabwean budget. There were three decisive phases in the formation of the new ZNA. These were the creation of the Joint High Command, the introduction of the British Military Advisory and Training Team (BMATT), and the Matabeleland military mutiny of early 1981. By the end of the integration programme in October 1981, the ZANU Government's military position had improved significantly and the politicization of the new national army had commenced.

The Joint High Command (JHC)

At independence, Mugabe's main military concern was to try to camouflage ZANU's weakness. His strategy was to co-opt stronger military rivals into the process of government and integration. This explains why he created a JHC containing representatives of all three armies and why he invited Lieutenant-General Peter Walls, the Rhodesian commander, to oversee the merger operation. The co-option of Walls served to defuse any potential white *coup* attempt. Politically, this move was risky in the long-term, since it made the integration programme dependent upon the white Rhodesian professional officer corps.[13] In retrospect, the Walls appointment is perhaps best understood as a move which bought time for the Mugabe administration to negotiate external military assistance from Britain.[14] Similarly, any immediate ZIPRA threat was pre-empted by making Joshua Nkomo the Minister of Home Affairs. This gave Nkomo control of the powerful para-military police force as well as special access to defence matters through his senior ZIPRA officers on the JHC.[15] In theory, the JHC was supposed to provide the machinery for amalgamation. In practice, it led to stalemate. There was a major disagreement over the force structure for a single national army. In June 1980, the first attempt by Rhodesian officers to integrate ZANLA-ZIPRA forces ended in a ZANLA mutiny which was promptly quelled by Rhodesian *askari*.[16] Subsequently, Walls and many of his officers resigned. But by this time an Anglo-Zimbabwean agreement had been reached and the British Army had replaced the Rhodesian predominance over the merger process.

The Introduction of BMATT

By July 1980, a BMATT of 150 instructors was in Zimbabwe. Why did the ZANU Government request British military aid? The answer seems to lie in the strictly neutral attitude adopted by the Commonwealth Monitoring Force which had supervised the ceasefire in 1979-80. Another factor was the warm personal relationship which Mugabe developed with Lord Soames, the last Governor of Southern Rhodesia, during the same period.[17] To a perhaps surprising extent, ZANU-ZANLA trusted the British to be impartial in military matters. BMATT managed its policy of integration on the basis of operating as an independent agent. Lacking an historical blueprint to work from, the British launched a crash course to create a rudimentary conventional military structure into which thousands of guerrillas could be moved from bush holding camps.[18] By this method, forty-five integrated battalions, or 65,000 personnel were formed into a new ZNA by October 1981. This progress was remarkable since it was seriously challenged by military factionalism and by mutiny.[19]

Factionalism and the Matabeleland Mutiny of 1981

Army integration was accompanied by simmering ZANLA-ZIPRA rivalry which threatened for a time to plunge Zimbabwe into a civil war. Rex Nhongo, the ZANLA commander, was said to believe that Lookout Masuku, the ZIPRA commander was trying to kill him.[20] ZIPRA commanders were bitterly resentful towards a ZANU Government special directive issued in November 1980, which ordered that all field officer commissions be awarded on the basis of parity rather than merit. This decision was made after British Army assessments on merit resulted in the first nine integrated battalions emerging with Ndebele commanding officers.[21] This development was, yet again, an embarrassing reminder to ZANU of the lack of conventional military talent in ZANLA. But worse was to follow.

In February 1981, ZIPRA conventional armoured units stationed in Matabeleland mutinied and attempted to converge on the city of Bulawayo. Here was a direct challenge to the Mugabe regime. Faced with rebellion, Mugabe was forced to rely upon 'Rhodesian' air and ground units to crush the rebels. He was also forced to enlist the support of the ZAPU-ZIPRA leadership to prevent the mutiny from expanding into civil war.[22] He was well served by both parties. The failure of the

1981 ZIPRA mutiny had several important consequences which marked a turning point in ZANU's military fortunes.

First, integration survived the Matabeleland crisis, thus demonstrating that ZNA was durable.   Second, ZIPRA's conventional capacity was destroyed during the confrontation and thousands of ZIPRA soldiers were either disarmed, or, believing they had been betrayed by their leaders, hid their weapons. This fissure between the ZAPU-ZIPRA leadership and many of the rank and file was not unwelcome to an insecure and suspicious ZANU Government.[23]   Third, the ZANU administration was persuaded that it required a special conventional force loyal to the ruling party to end its reliance upon former Rhodesian units — despite the latter's proven loyalty. This was the origin of North Korean involvement in Zimbabwean military training.   Fourth, integration was accelerated. From April to September, 1981, BMATT produced three infantry battalions per month — one Zimbabwean soldier every fifteen minutes.[24] Fifth, in the wake of the ZIPRA mutinies, ZANU announced the formation of a ZNA higher command echelon determined largely by ethnic political considerations and ZANLA dominance. Ethnic parity was, for instance, only conceded at the apex of the ZNA high command. Nhongo became Commander of the Army with Masuku as Deputy Commander. Both men became lieutenant-generals, Josiah Tungamirai (ex-ZANLA) and Jevan Maseko (ex-ZIPRA) became Chiefs of Staff with the rank of major-general. But the majority of the brigadiers and colonels were ex-ZANLA Shona guerrillas. In addition, nearly all of the operational commands were held by ZANU-ZANLA loyalists.[25]

Furthermore, a second army directive was issued by Mugabe. This created two types of commissioned offices for the ZNA: political commissioned officers from colonel and above and field commissioned officers up to the rank of lieutenant-colonel with the latter determined by professional merit.[26] The effect of this cleavage was twofold. First, it concentrated control of the national army in the hands of mainly former ZANLA Shona officers. Second, it shielded the politically commissioned senior echelon from undergoing professional staff training. They were required only to 'attend' an intermediate staff course. Some did, but others, including General Nhongo, went to Pakistan for private training courses. This cleavage was later to cause the ZNA serious operational command and control problems especially in Mozambique.

ZANU's growing ethnic domination of the army also permitted it to strike at its former ZIPRA rivals. In February 1982, the 'discovery' of arms caches throughout Matabeleland, was used to decapitate the ZAPU-ZIPRA leadership in the government and the army. Accused of plotting a *coup*, Nkomo and several co-opted ZAPU ministers were dismissed from office while Masuku, Dabengwa and six members of the former ZIPRA High Command were arrested and tried for treason. Although they were acquitted, they remained in detention where Masuku later died, while Dabengwa was finally released in late 1986.[27] In August 1895, several more former senior ZIPRA commanders serving in the ZNA, were detained on similar charges.[28] These minor purges gave ZANU-ZANLA undisputed mastery over the national army. It was a case of 'MuZANU Chete' (ZANU only). This is not to suggest that there were no senior Ndebele officers left. There were several, but Ndebele advancement in the ZNA came to be determined by the degree of distance between an officer and the ZAPU party. Many senior Ndebele ex-ZIPRA officers were posted to training and service branches as opposed to operational appointments, although again, there were exceptions.[29] The cost of ZANU supremacy in the army was a high one. Throughout 1982, nearly 4,000 Ndebele soldiers deserted from the ZNA and began a five-year insurgent and dissident campaign in Matabeleland.[30] By 1985 then, ZANU-ZANLA the weakest military force in 1980 had successfully imposed its political authority over the ZNA. It was also reversing its conventional weakness. British instructors were producing large numbers of ex-ZANLA Shona Guerrillas as well-trained regular soldiers. In addition, the North Koreans were providing ZANU with special units.

The British Training Role in the Post-Integration Era

During the 1980s, Britain was principally responsible for the professional development of the ZNA. BMATT teams provided the conventional infrastructure required by a modern African army. Great emphasis was placed upon making the ZNA self-sufficient in instructional staff, on officer training and advising on the organization of the Military Academy and the Staff College. The British helped fix the ZNA's strength at 42,000 in 1982. They also helped establish the army order of battle around five infantry brigades supported by armour and artillery units.[31] The conversion of the RAR into a commando regiment, the creation of a parachute group and the raising of a Zimbabwean Special Air Service (SAS) squadron all owed much to the British Army.[32]   In 1986, the ZNA underwent a quantum leap in professionalism when a nine month Command and Staff Course was introduced at the Zimbabwe Staff College. In part, this course was a response to the ZNA's involvement in Mozambique and the problems associated with extended military operations. The Command and Staff course, based on the British Army Staff College, was the equivalent of any such college in the world, and probably unequalled in Southern Africa.[33] To have achieved this standard of professional development after only seven years was testimony to the progress made by the ZNA. Publicly, BMATT Commanders spoke of exceptional, even 'miraculous' results in military advancement since 1980.[34]

Privately, however, there were more cautious sentiments expressed. The British faced considerable difficulties in seeking to 'professionalize' the ZNA.   These difficulties included European ethnocentrism; occasional anti-Western feeling from some senior ZNA officers; and British frustration with a ZNA High Command which was seen as clinging to the ZANLA revolutionary war tradition and impeding good operational practices.   Some British officers were convinced that the professional African officer corps they were shaping in the 1980s was nothing less than the seed-bed for a *coup* in the 1990s which would sweep away Mugabe as Nkrumah had been swept away in the 1960s. Others believed that because of higher command deficiencies the ZNA would remain a 'super *askari*' force.[35] But these criticisms not withstanding, the overall view of the ZNA was still one of guarded optimism with much faith placed in the Staff College.

The Training Role of the North Korean Army in Zimbabwe

The North Koreans were responsible for training special units linked to the Central Committee and Politburo. Why did the Zimbabwean Government accept North Korean military aid? There appear to be several reasons. First, Mugabe clearly shared President Kim Il Sung's interest in the Non-Aligned Movement and seems to have admired Kim's idiosyncratic promotion of revolution in Africa.[36] Second, and related to the above, was Mugabe's interest in Kim's *Juche* (self-reliance) and *Chajusong* (national independence and anti-imperialism) ideology.[37] Mugabe's first overseas visit as Prime Minister of Zimbabwe was to North Korea in October 1980. On this visit to Pyongyang, a treaty of mutual friendship was signed between Zimbabwe and North Korea which appears to have involved a Z$12 million military aid package.[38] Third, were the events of early 1981. The ZANU Government's reliance on former Rhodesian units to quell the ZIPRA mutiny in Matabeleland was undoubtedly profoundly disturbing to many in the ruling party. Redressing military inferiority by forming a special conventional force rapidly trained by the North Koreans was perhaps a strong attraction. In any event, special ZANLA guerrilla cadres were kept outside of the formation of the ZNA during the first half of 1981.[39]

In August 1981, a 106-strong North Korean military team under Major-General Sim Kyon Dok arrived in Zimbabwe.[40] The North Korean Army or *In Min Gun* (People's Army) was at that time the seventh largest army in the world and it was directly controlled by Kim Il Sung's Central Committee and Politburo. It had a distinctive military tradition. The North Korean Army brought several concepts which were adopted by Zimbabwean military units. One of these was the idea of the *Chosen Kyongbidae* (Special Security Corps) which became the model for both the Fifth Brigade and the Presidential Guard Regiment which the North Koreans trained and partially equipped. Both of these units were praetorian in nature. They owed their allegiance to the ZANU party. The Fifth Brigade was, for instance, directly linked to the 'ZANU Idea' and was christened *Gukurahundi* (or

the People's Storm Brigade). It carried a party flag and its slogan
was 'We support the Prime Minister Comrade Robert Gabriel
Mugabe which means support for the whole population'.[41] The
Fifth Brigade numbered some 5,000, was armour-supported and
was commanded by the ZANLA veteran Colonel Perence ('Black
Jesus') Shiri. Both the Fifth and the 3,000-strong Presidential
Guard were incorporated into the ZNA order of battle following
nine months of North Korean training. The latter was wedded to
Soviet tactical doctrine developed during the early 1950s.[42]
When the Fifth Brigade was deployed in Matabeleland in 1983-
84, it created an international uproar and eventually was
withdrawn.[43]   Some elements were retrained by the British.
Other elements became party security intelligence officers within
the ZNA; some went into the air force and still others retained
their links with the North Koreans in the much more successful
Zimbabwe People's Militia (ZPM). The ZPM was based upon the
North Korean theory of the *Nodong Chokwidae* (Workers and
Peasants Red Militia) and copied its *kun* (provincial), *ri* (district)
and *tong* (village) system. The Militia embodied the 'ZANU Idea'
and developed a personality cult around Mugabe which shows
some similarity to that surrounding Kim Il Sung 'the Great
Leader'.[44] The ZPM central training centre was named after
Mugabe. The first ZPM brigade was called the Gabriel People's
Militia Model Brigade.[45] There was even an attempt to render
into Shona the 'Song of Kim Il Sung' with transposed names.

By early 1985 the ZPM was 20,000 strong and had been
absorbed into ZNA Headquarters as an auxiliary wing of the
army and the ruling party. Several militia units were also
deployed into Mozambique.[46]   The North Korean military
influence on the ZNA was mixed. Their training of the Fifth
Brigade was poor and notable for its emphasis upon
indiscriminate aggression. There was, however, more success
with the less operational Presidential Guard and the highly
politicized People's Militia — which in many respects can be
seen as a reserve army closely linked to the ZANU party rural
machine but co-ordinated from ZNA Headquarters. The
appointment in 1984 of the armed services commanders to the
ZANU Politburo was also consistent with North Korean practice
— although it must also be remembered that *Dare* tradition may

also have influenced this decision. Finally, there is some evidence of North Korean involvement in ZANU party intelligence training. By 1986, most North Korean military advisers had departed amidst suggestions that they had become unpopular in Zimbabwean military circles for social and cultural reasons.[47]

South African Destabilization and the Development of Zimbabwean Military Doctrine

Throughout most of the 1980s Zimbabwe suffered from South African destabilization activities. This was due to the ambiguous relationship which existed between Harare and Pretoria. At one level Zimbabwe maintained intelligence and economic relations with South Africa. But, politically, Zimbabwe was at the cutting edge of the ideological cold war being waged against Pretoria.[48] In day-to-day military affairs, however, the hostile realities were muted. Zimbabwe had more of a posture than a policy regarding destabilization. For instance, in all Staff College instruction the enemy was never referred to as South Africa. It was only known by the acronym of 'Antizim'. Military doctrine did reflect common Zimbabwean perceptions about South Africa. These perceptions were largely shaped by government propaganda and the work of Zimbabwean academics and journalists.[49] In the ZNA, perceptions ran from what might be called the 'silver bullet' theory — which postulated an imminent victory for the forces of liberation based on guerrilla warfare and sanctions — to a pessimistic conviction that the South African Defence Force (SADF) was invincible.

The problems of developing threat-assessment in this unstable atmosphere were considerable. The strategic reality for Zimbabwe by 1986 was growing political and military isolation in a region undergoing neutralization and potential devastation at the hands of South Africa.[50] Zimbabwe's external military commitment to Mozambique and internal insurgency in Matabeleland called for the formulation of military doctrine based on a clearly articulated aims. Instead, crisis-management prevailed. For example, no attempt was made to create a Joint

Planning Staff (JPS) to weld operational thinking together. Insufficient numbers of army officers were posted to Defence Force Headquarters (DFHQ) to work with civilian policy-makers in the Ministry of Defence. This resulted in inadequate co-ordination. All of these problems were related to the Zimbabwean Government's apparent determination to centralize military control in the hands of the politically commissioned and hence reliable ex-ZANLA High Command.[51]

Nonetheless, the ZNA muddled through. There was a positive side. BMATT provided sound technical tuition on the SADF down in some cases to unit level. An Anglo-Zimbabwean military planning cell provided tactical scenarios for responding to multiple 'Antizim' threats ranging from airborne incursions to limited invasion.[52] Study of South Africa's Total Strategy doctrine was introduced to military intelligence personnel. The works of leading South African and international scholars were also obtained to provide officers with a multi-dimensional view of South Africa as a complex and deeply divided society incapable of resolving its internal crisis by military force.[53] To sum up, military doctrine was as well developed as could be expected in an army without a defined defence policy.

Operational Performance of the ZNA

After 1982, the ZNA was deployed operationally in Matabeleland and in Mozambique. In both theatres the mode of warfare was counter-insurgency.

Matabeleland

In Matabeleland it is clear from the pattern of army deployment between 1982-87, that the ZANU Government hoped to destroy ZAPU's infrastructure as well as to eliminate Ndebele insurgents. One of the motives for attacking the ZAPU infrastructure appears to have been related to ZANU's drive to create the conditions for installing an eventual one party state.[54] The use of questionable methods and the depredations of the Fifth Brigade have been convincingly documented.[55]   It is perhaps important to emphasize that like all internal security problems, the Matabeleland problem was not amenable to a purely military solution. It took five years for that lesson to be learned in Harare. Matabeleland remained staunchly loyal to ZAPU. The ZNA faced three types of dissidents in the region. First, there was a small minority of so called 'Super ZAPU' insurgents who received some degree of South African aid. This group was magnified by ZANU in its campaign to discredit ZAPU.[56] By far the most numerous of the dissident forces were ex-ZIPRA guerrillas who represented the second type of insurgents. Third there was the pure bandit element. The ZNA contained the insurgency in Matabeleland but it never dominated it. Eventually, a political agreement between ZANU and ZAPU, including an amnesty, was reached in late 1987 which restored peace to the province.[57]

Mozambique

After 1982, Zimbabwe's commitment to protect its transport routes to the sea through Mozambique involved the ZNA in the Front for the Liberation of Mozambique (FRELIMO) war against Mozambique National Resistance Movement (RENAMO). Because Zimbabwe had signed a 1981 mutual defence treaty with Mozambique there was always a fear in some ZNA circles that Zimbabwe would be sucked into an open-ended and unwinnable conflict.[58] Between 1982 and 1985, ZNA forces increased from 1,000 to 7,000. Two railway corridors were created by the Special Task Force (STF): the Beira Corridor and the Limpopo Corridor. Although the ZNA role was mainly confined to defensive patrolling, Zimbabwean special forces did launch large-scale search and destroy operations against RENAMO in Northern and Central Mozambique.[59] Financial restraints, the insistence on trying to control operations from Harare rather than through a forward field headquarters and logistical problems combined to keep the ZNA role limited. The STF commitment was always unpopular amongst many of the troops who often complained of being *hatichada kunyegrera* (literally 'fed up'). The Spillover of RENAMO activities into Eastern Zimbabwe and border refugee problems exacerbated

ZNA problems operationally.[60] Nevertheless, on balance, the ZNA fulfilled an important policy priority for Zimbabwe and other Front Line States by keeping the corridors open: namely defying South Africa's transport hegemony through the deployment of military forces.[61] It was a considerable achievement which helped in the December 1990 Rome Agreement ostensibly aimed at ending the Mozambique crisis.[62]

What Kind of Army?

Armies more often than not reflect the socio-political systems from which they spring. The ZNA's dualistic military character mirrors a dualistic political system. As Zimbabwe utilized both Westminster instruments and ethnically based revolutionary organs, so the army has adopted both regular professionalism and guerrilla modes of politicization. Although there were important professional developments, including a Command Staff Course and British training methods, the revolutionary tradition tended to predominate. This is shown by the formation of the politically commissioned higher command echelon and its control over the more professional field officers. It is important to note the highly centralized nature of the army high command. In structural terms, it is suitable for handling a maximum of 16,000 troops. Currently it controls 47,000 regular soldiers and 20,000 militia — a grand total of 67,000 personnel.[63] The high command is an ex-ZANLA military clique or oligarchy of political and ethnic loyalists closely linked with the ZANU Politburo. Its supremacy is reinforced by party commissars and security officers throughout the army and by balancing special units — the Presidential Guard, the ZPM and the secret intelligence service.[64] Nevertheless the professional field officers are numerous.

What then prevents a clash between the 'politicals' and the 'professionals' in the ZNA officer corps? How is conflict and rivalry resolved? How does the ZNA work organizationally in terms of advancement and promotion? Before considering these questions it is necessary to make three observations. First, in the Zimbabwean military context, politicization and professionalization are not mutually exclusive but tend rather to complement each other. Second, this accommodation is made possible largely because there is no sense of corporate identity within the Zimbabwean officer corps. There exists no sense of historical unity built around a separate, professional and apolitical ethos. Third, the ZANU High Command reflects many of the characteristics of the ZANU Politburo. Although the Politburo is almost exclusively Shona in composition, it is not a monolith. It is a coalition of Shona sub-groups — Zezuru, Karanga and Manyika — whose interests have frequently diverged.[65] Unity has been secured by Mugabe's mastery of *Dare* arbitration techniques and through which factionalism is resolved and patronage equally dispersed. The ZNA mirrors this system of *Dare* centrality through its own methods of patronage and reward.

The ZNA officer corps is overwhelmingly Shona in composition. But it is likewise divided into ethnic sub-groups. Most army officers are either Karanga or Zezuru. Lacking a corporate identity, professionally trained officers often fall back upon their sub-group origin. They attach themselves to an ethnic army *chef* (Portuguese for 'chief', a term picked up from the guerrilla bases in Mozambique during the 1970s) who is in practice, a senior politically commissioned officer.[66] In this fashion Shona officers secure promotion and patronage. The *chef* system embraces mainly ex-guerrillas but former Rhodesian Selous Scouts of Karanga or Zezuru origin have also benefited. Conversely, Ndebele ex-ZIPRA officers tend to rise and fall in accordance with the degree to which they have abandoned allegiance to ZAPU. Through the *chef* system the ZNA has a voice in the Politburo. Again the representation of military interests by politicized commanders in this way works against the institutionalization of 'professionalism'.

In terms of civil-military relations theory, control of the ZNA is subjective and informal rather than objective and bureaucratic.[67] The civil-military system is also 'permeated' through the composition of the Politburo.[68] Ex-guerrillas occupy ministerial posts and former ZNA officers have moved from the military into politics. Senior officers have amassed wealth and property and there is no mandatory term of office for general officers.[69] Consequently, advancement is frequently lateral as well as vertical. Observing the dual military character of the ZNA and the interaction between professionalism and politicization, one senior British Army officer likened the division to that between the American FBI and the Mafia: 'We (BMATT) turn African officers out of the Academy as pure as the FBI but the Mob always gets them in the end.'[70] In conclusion the ZNA does not conform with the classical precepts of military professionalism, simply because the bulk of its soldiery spring from an African revolutionary war tradition. This has been partly influenced by Marxist-Leninist methodology, but is perhaps more decisively shaped by an indigenous African socio-political milieu. In other words Zimbabwe has successfully Africanized its dualistic military heritage.

Conclusion

Problems of welding disparate elements into a unified national army are frequently exaggerated. Although ethnicity and divergent traditions dominated different elements which came together to form the ZNA, the army has survived a number of testing situations without fracturing. South Africa must likewise weld a national and non-racial army from disparate elements after the apartheid regime is swept away. While it would be wrong to draw direct parallels between the present South African defence forces and the old Rhodesian army, or between ZIPRA and *Umkhonto we Sizwe*, Zimbabwe's experience shows that military units with very different backgrounds and training can be made to function as a viable organization.

Notes

1   Officially known as ZANU-PF (Patriotic Front) after 1980, but frequently referred to as simply ZANU.

2   Mugabe interview, *New York Times*, 28 April 1980.

3   L.L. Mathews, 'Zimbabwe', in J. Keegan, (ed) *World Armies* (Detroit, 1983), pp.681-84

4   Ibid.

5   J. Nkomo, *Nkomo: The Story of My Life* (London, 1984), pp.174-75.

6   Interview with Colonel A. Mutinhiri, Director of Army Training, ZNA, 18 October 1984. Mutinhiri was a former member of the IPRA High Command.

7   Interview with Major-General J. Tungamirai, Chief of Staff (Operations), ZNA, 18 September 1982. Tungamirai was ZANLA's Chief Political Commissar during the guerrilla war.

8   For a recent discussion, see P. Pandya, *Mao Tse-Tung and Chimurenga: An Investigation into Zanu's strategies* (Braamfontein, 1988).

9   Interview with Tungamirai, 5 December 1986. See also Pandya, Chapter 21.

10   The ZANU Politburo up until January 1988 contained only one Ndebele member, Enos Nkala, frequently regarded as a 'renegade' figure by many in ZAPU; interview with W. Musarurwa, formerly ZAPU Publicity Secretary, 18 July 1985.

11   Discussion with Tungamirai, 24 October 1986.

12   E. Zvobgo, 'The ZANU Idea', in G. Baumhogger, *The Struggle for Independence: Documents on the Recent Development of Zimbabwe 1975-1980,* (Hamburg, 1984), (7 Vols), Document 28, Vol 2, pp.23-24.

13   Interview with K. Flower, Director-General, Zimbabwe (formerly Rhodesian) Central Intelligence Organisation (CIO), 1964-81, 14 April 1982.

14   Ibid. This interpretation was preferred to the idea of any 'reconciliation' on Mugabe's part.

15   Nkomo did not, however, gain control of police intelligence (Special Branch) which was transferred to the Prime Minister's Office. This weakened the significance of Nkomo's portfolio within ZIPRA; interview with Flower, 14 April 1982.

16   *Herald* (Harare), 5 June 1980. Interview with Brigadier M. Shute, Officer Commanding 1 Brigade (Bulawayo), 18 March 1982.

17   B. Lapping, *End of Empire* (London: Paladin, 1989), pp.574-62.

18   BMATT personnel studied the experience of Carnot in Revolutionary France and of Trotsky in Bolshevik Russia but could find few parallels with Zimbabwean's situation, simply because of the ethnic dimension and the fact that there were three armies involved in the merger progress. Interview with BMATT officers who requested anonymity, 5 April 1984.

19   'Zimbabwe: the Army', *Africa Confidential* 33 (1982), pp.4-5.

20   See the testimony of Lieutenant-General Lookout Masuku in

Herald, 8 and 24 February, and 8 April 1983 during the later ZIPRA treason trial.

21   Ibid.

22   Nkomo, pp.220-223.

23   See the detailed statement by Brigadier C. Grey, a former senior IPRA commander in *Chronicle* (Bulawyo), 8 April 1983.

24   Zimbabwe, Department of Information Press Statement 197/81/SFS, 'Prime Minister's Address on National Army', 16 March 1981.

25   For the list of commissions see *Herald*, 17 April 1981.   For dispositions see Zimbabwe. Office of the Prime Minister Press Statement 1433/82/JS/PR, 'ZNA Senior Ranks and Appointments', 22 October 1982.

26   *ZNA Directive* (Confidential), 5 July 1981.   Copy in author's possession. See also *Herald*, 17 April 1981.

27   See Nkomo, chapter 21.

28   Three brigadiers and a colonel were arrested on the grounds of treason.

29   Two senior ex-ZIPRA officers headed the Directorate of Army Training and an Ndebele colonel was appointed Commandant of the Staff College. In 1989, an Ndebele brigadier commanded the ZNA Special Task Force (STF) in Mozambique.

30   This was the assessment made by Zimbabwean military intelligence. Discussion with Colonel S. Sobusa Gazi, Director of Military Intelligence, 6 June 1984.

31   Much information on the role of BMATT can be found in issues of the monthly *Zimbabwe National Army Magazine* (Harare) especially between 1983-86.

32   See 'New Zimbabwe Order of Battle', in *Armed Forces* (Johannesburg) February 1982.

33   Zimbabwe Staff College. Loose Minute 3/1/10/4 *Directive for Command and Staff Course Directing Staff*, HQ. ZSC.21 January 1986.

34   See the views of successive BMATT Commanders: Major-General P. Palmer, *ZNA Review*, 6 October 1981; Brigadiers E. Jones, *Herald*, 25 February 1985 and R. Hodges, *The Times*, (London), 11 March 1987.

35   Private views expressed to the author by various BMATT personnel.

36   Very little scholarly work exists on North Korean-African

relations. For a rare discussion see P. Chaigneau and R. Sola, 'North Korea as an African Power: A Threat to French Interests', *Strategic Review* (Pretoria: Institute for Strategic Studies, University of Pretoria, December 1986), pp.1-19. Zimbabwe is briefly mentioned in C. Mackerras, *The Democratic People's Republic of Korea in World Affairs* (Griffith University: Centre for the Study of Australian-Asian Relations, Australia-Asia Papers No. 27, August 1984), pp.33-34.

37   In the early years of independence *Juche* in particular was a fashionable subject within ZANU and much discussed in the media. See Zimbabwe. Department of Information Press Statement 79/82/SFS, 'President's Address on Zimbabwe's Relations with the DPRK', 18 August 1982.

38   See the reports in *Sunday Mail* (Harare), 30 August 1981 and *Chronicle*, 31 August 1981 on the military aspects of the agreement.

39   Between 3,500 and 5,000 ex-Zanla guerrillas were brigaded at Tongogara Camp, Chipinge in Eastern Zimbabwe.

40   Zimbabwe. Department of Information Press Statement 629/81/SFS 'North Korean Training Team Here', 14 August 1981. This was a statement by Mugabe.

41   Discussion with ZNA officers, 5 August 1984. For a discussion of the North Korean Army see Keegan, 'North Korea', in Keegan, ed., *World Armies*, pp.338-343.

42   Ibid. Discussion with Brigadier P. Shiri, formerly Commander, Five Brigade, 16 August 1984.

43   The most devastating information can be found in *The Sunday Times* (London), 15 April 1984 and in *The Observer* (London), 15 April 1984.

44   Discussions, ZNA military intelligence personnel.

45   For views on the ZPM see the *Zimbabwe National Army Magazine*, July 1986, pp.24-26.

46   Zimbabwe Defence (Zimbabwe People's Militia) (Non-Commissioned Members) (General) Regulations gazetted by the Defence Forces Services Commission, May 1985.

47   This was the assessment made by Shiri. Another complaint concerned equipment procurement. North Korean equipment was obsolescent.

48   See M. Evans 'The Security Threat from South Africa', in C. Stoneman (ed), *Zimbabwe's Prospects: Issues of Race, Class, State, Class and Capital in Southern Africa* (London, 1988), pp.218-235.

49   See, for example, the somewhat one-dimensional work of D.
      Martin and P. Johnson, 'Zimbabwe: Apartheid's Dilemma', in
      Martin and Johnson (eds), *Destructive Engagement: Southern
      Africa at War* (Harare, 1986), pp.43-72. See also H.H. Patel,
      'Zimbabwe', *Survival*, XXX (1988), pp.38-58. Despite their profile
      none of these writers was invited to the Zimbabwe Staff College
      to teach on security issues, although Patel did lecture on the non-
      aligned movement and international relations.

50   See R. Martin, 'Regional Security in Southern Africa: More
      Angolas, Mozambiques or Neutrals?', *Survival*, 29 (1987), pp.387-
      402.

51   All of these problems were identified by BMATT and pointed out
      to the Ministry of Defence and ZNA Headquarters.

52   Zimbabwe Staff College 3/1/1, 'The Development of Tactical
      Doctrine at the ZSC', (restricted), 27 June 1985.

53   BMATT were reluctant to teach Total Strategy on the basis that it
      was really a theory of international relations. But the British did
      assist in procuring reading resources. The works of such scholars
      as H. Giliomee, H. Adam, D. Moodie, L. Thompson, P. Frankel,
      K. Grundy, D. Geldenhuys and R. Jaster were amongst the works
      obtained by the ZNA.

54   See R. Weitzer, 'Responding to South African Hegemony: The
      Case of Zimbabwe', paper presented at the annual meeting of the
      American African Studies Association, New Orleans, 23-26
      November 1985, pp.2-7.

55   See for instance the Catholic Church's report, 'Reconciliation is
      still possible', Zimbabwe Catholic Bishop's Conference, Harare,
      19 March 1983.

56   According to Weitzer, 'In Search of Regime Security: Zimbabwe
      Since Independence', *Journal of Modern African Studies*, 22 (1984),
      pp.529-527.

57   A ZANU-ZAPU unity agreement was signed on 22 December
      1987. Under this accord ZAPU was absorbed into ZANU-PF.

58   The treaty was signed on 12 January 1981. Some ZNA officers
      compared the commitment to a 'mini-Vietnam', interviews with
      STF officers.

59   For a discussion see Evans 'The Security Threat', pp.227-231.

60   One of the major operational problems was the determination to
      direct the campaign from Harare as opposed to developing
      responsibility to a forward field headquarters. This resulted in
      severe inflexibility in the field deployment.

61   See Mugabe's remarks in *Herald*, 12 November 1986.

62 'Mozambique Confusion at home, silence abroad', *Africa Confidential* 32 (1991), pp.6-7.

63 For ZNA force levels see *The Military Balance 1990-1991* (London: International Institute for Strategic Studies, 1990), p.147. This indicates an even further rise to 51,600.

64 There is also a Police Internal Security Intelligence Service (PISI) alongside the CIO and the Special Branch.

65 This was the position up until the ZANU-ZAPU unity agreement. Since then, the Politburo has been expanded to include six former ZAPU members in a body of 24 persons. However, it is significant that the service commanders remain Shona and ex-ZANLA leaders.

66 I am indebted to ZNA officers, especially former black Rhodesian regulars, for an insight into this system and its mechanics. Several guerrilla veterans also provided information on the importance of regional affiliations.

67 The definition is drawn from S.P. Huntington, *The Soldier and the State: The Theory and Politics of Civil-Military Relations* (Cambridge, Mass., 1957), p.83.

68 See A.R. Luckham, 'A Comparative Typology of Civil-Military Relations', *Government and Opposition* 6 (1971), 5-35; E.A. Nordlinger, *Soldiers in Politics: Military Coups and Governments* (Englewood Cliffs, 1977), pp.15-19.

69 The current ZNA Commander, Lieutenant-General Solomon Tapfumaneyi Mujuru (formerly known by his Chimurenga *nom de guerre* of Rex Nhongo until 1986) is alleged to have extensive business interests and appeared before the 1989 Sandura Commission into official corruption. He appears to have survived the inquiry. Mujuru has commanded the ZNA since its inception.

70 Discussion with a British Chief Instructor at the Zimbabwe Staff College.

12

Reviewing the Origins of the Freedom Charter

Paul B. Rich

Introduction

The gathering of the Congress of the People (COP) on a stretch of
wasteland at Kliptown outside Johannesburg on the 25 and 26
June 1955 has traditionally been seen as a key turning point in
post-war South African politics. Some 2884 delegates debated
and passed the Freedom Charter under the watchful eyes of a
further 7000 spectators before lorry loads of police armed with
sten guns broke up the meeting on the afternoon of the 26th. The
evidence taken by this extensive police operation was used the
following year in the trial on charges of treason of 156 people.[1]

The holding of the Congress of the People indicated that a new
phase in oppositional politics was developing in South Africa. A
number of different political groupings were brought together in
an attempt to form a common front against the entrenchment of
apartheid under the Nationalist government of JG Strydom.
Albert Luthuli, who was then President of the ANC, considered
that the COP was 'perhaps. . . the first really representative
gathering in the Union's history'.[2] The drawing up of the
Freedom Charter gave a more populist tone to Congress politics
than previous strategies. Petitions, deputations and lobbying
through white 'natives representatives' had failed to stem the
tide of apartheid legislation. Those active in Congress politics

have seen the COP as a successful example of a 'peoples parliament' (though this was not the original objective), producing an anti-imperialist 'peoples document', attempting to lay down the guidelines for a future democratic South Africa, but not laying down a precise blue-print for a future society.[3]

The COP, indeed, developed a language of populist politics based on the concept of 'the people' which continues to have major political resonances in contemporary South African politics. This chapter has three objectives. First, it will examine the significance of this populist discourse and its linkage to a wider tradition of radical politics in Britain and the US. Second, the chapter will situate the Congress at Kliptown in the context of internal generational and ideological divisions within the ANC. It will argue that the strategy of calling such a Congress developed out of an attempt by moderates in the Congress leadership to contain the more militant demands of the radicals and anchor the ANC's policy in parliamentary politics rather than the revolutionary terms of national liberation. This attempted containment broke down, though, as the COP movement developed an increasingly radical momentum of its own. Finally, the chapter will assess the longer-term repercussions of the COP on South African politics and its relevance to contemporary political struggles.

The Notion of 'the People' in Politics:

The centrality of 'the people' in the deliberations of the COP was a new theme in South African politics in the mid-1950s, though it drew on a much longer radical tradition in Europe and America. Politics derived from the notion that governments are made and broken by 'the people' owe much to the breakdown of alternative fictions of governance. As Edmund Morgan has shown in studies of the English revolution of the seventeenth century and the American revolution of the eighteenth, popular sovereignty emerged when the fiction that government could be based upon the Divine Right of Kings broke down. The revolutionaries who embarked on a quest for political liberty from such restricted rule were forced themselves to invent a set of political fictions.

The reality behind these formulations was that the notion of popular sovereignty 'found expression most often in disputes among the few over the possession of the powers and privileges allegedly surrendered'.[4] As these disputes intensified, each side would refer to the 'people' in a seemingly never-ending series of contracts between governments and people which could be made and then unmade. This process ultimately ensured the long-term entry of 'the people' into the political system of Britain and the United States via a progressive extension of the franchise in the late nineteenth and early twentieth centuries.[5] For the majority in South Africa, a similar path into the political system was denied by the entrenchment of white settler power in the decades after Union in 1910. The political marginalization of black Africans under segregationist and apartheid legislation represented in one sense their subordination to a twentieth century form of political divine right built on the doctrine of white racial supremacy.

Meanwhile, black politics remained hidebound by poor organization and the diffusion of energies into the rival ideological groupings of the African National Congress (ANC) and the All African Convention (AAC). These divisions became compounded by generational rivalries by the end of World War Two as a younger group inside the ANC formed the Congress Youth League (CYL) and began pressing for more radical policies to mobilize mass support in opposition to the structures of 'natives representation' established in 1936. Initially, hopes focussed on a common platform emerging through an amalgamation of the ANC and AAC. Once this avenue was closed by the failure of unity talks in 1948 between leaders of the two organizations, the radicals concentrated on transforming the ANC from within in order to make it the focus for African nationalist revival.[6] From this point onwards there was a steady shift towards seeing black opposition to apartheid as a 'national liberation' struggle. African nationalist theory in South Africa, as elsewhere on the African continent, sought the mobilization of a collective popular will which was broadly part of a set of theories of 'revolutionary democracy'.[7] There was thus increasing pressure for the voice of 'the people' in South Africa to be heard in the form of a national convention.

Alongside these pressures within African nationalist politics, a number of white radicals who had been active in the South African Communist Party until its suppression in 1950 also campaigned for a more populist strategy. One of the most prominent strategic theorists of this group was the architect Lionel ('Rusty') Bernstein, who became one of the founding members of the Congress of Democrats in 1953. In an address at COD's first conference, Bernstein warned against trying to impose ideological blueprints upon the resistance movement to apartheid. This might have been possible 'in other times before the opposing forces have presented themselves so forcibly' but to do so now 'would be to isolate ourselves from the forces that are already in action for democratic advance and to attempt to superimpose our ideas, our visions, on what they have already tried and found to be unworkable. We have to work with what we have.'[8]

Thus, while COD did not appear initially to welcome the proposal for a Congress of the People, many of its activists saw it as an opportunity to forge over the following two years an alliance with the ANC national executive based in Johannesburg. It was probably encouraged in this by some of the black members of the old SACP such as Moses Kotane who championed a popular alliance against Nationalist rule embracing sections of the white working and middle class, who, he claimed, were disaffected by a United Party dominated by 'representatives of finance capitalism'.[9] The forging of this alliance would prove crucial to the political direction that the COP would take.

Generational and Ideological Divisions:

The Congress Youth League had initially been formed in 1943-44 by a younger group of radicals strongly influenced by the ideas of Anton Lembede. They became impatient with the prevaricating and authoritarian leadership of AB Xuma, the ANC president, and keen to steer the movement into an increasingly nationalist direction. At the ANC's annual conference in December 1949 the Youth League succeeded in removing in a constitutional coup Xuma as president and replacing him, first, by the wealthy medical doctor James Moroka and, after the Defiance Campaign, by Albert Luthuli (in December 1952). At the 1949 conference the Youth League also secured the passing of the *Programme of Action* which laid the foundations for a programme of militant action against government-inspired bodies such as the NRC along with the promotion of ideals of 'National Freedom' against prevailing white political doctrines of segregation, trusteeship and apartheid.[10]

The Youth League radicals injected a rhetoric of political militancy into the ANC which often had similar features to the ideology of Black Consciousness in its search for a subjective black liberation from colonialism.[11] This quest for political identity had a strongly Africanist flavour. The National President GM Pitje claimed in 1950 that the ANC had at last rediscovered its spiritual roots by assuming the 'revolutionary role of a liberatory movement'. It no longer simply demanded its share in the government of the country but government by the majority, the 'African people'.[12]

The Africanist dimension to Youth League ideology got rather watered down, though, over the following years, once a number of Youth Leaguers found themselves in positions of authority inside the ANC. Working alongside the radicals from COD, the Youth League leadership became attracted to a national liberation ideology that avoided simply *African national* liberation and emphasized instead a more general *popular* or *national* liberation from imperialism. Long-standing radicals such as JB Marks urged the CYL leadership to move out of its 'intellectual domain' and reach out to 'suffering African youth' at the local level.[13] Youth Leaguers such as the Secretary-General Walter Sisulu were also influenced by the more general international climate of rising colonial nationalism. Sisulu visited China in 1954 and was deeply impressed by the apparent success of the Communist government of Mao-tse-Tung in freeing such a large country from imperial influences.[14]

Many of the Youth Leaguers such as Sisulu, Oliver Tambo and Nelson Mandela were keen to move in the direction of a popular alliance with other organizations in the wake of the

Defiance Campaign. The National Action Committee that had been appointed to oversee the running of the Defiance Campaign reported in December 1953 a 'disquieting lull' in political activity since the previous year. It noted that there had been no major preparations to implement Nelson Mandela's suggested 'M-Plan' based upon street-based cells in order to resist penetration of the organization by police spies.[15] The Committee confessed to being isolated from the general activities of Congress and strongly favoured the proposal for a Congress of the People as a means of regaining the political initiative. There was the added consideration that the COP would also be a means of preventing the Congress leadership being diverted from the path of 'mass struggle' by proposals for 'disruptive talks' by the South African Institute of Race Relations and other white liberal organizations.[16]

The National Action Committee's support for the COP was also strengthened by a feeling among many Congress leaders, including Albert Luthuli, that the movement had to think through an alternative agenda to that of apartheid and not simply react to the initiatives of the Pretoria government.[17] The President of the Cape African Congress, Professor ZK Matthews, was particularly keen to spell out the principles of what he hoped would continue to be constitutional opposition to the government's policy. Matthews taught at the University of Fort Hare and was one of the leaders from the inter-war generation who had tried to work through state-created institutions as part of a strategy of progressively expanding African political rights.[18] Though critical of the miniscule powers of the NRC, Matthews did not want to see the institution abolished after it went into voluntary adjournment in protest at the government's handling of the 1946 African mine strike.[19] Throughout the late 1940s Matthews had remained implacably opposed to calls for an immediate boycott of the NRC and became somewhat of a *bete noire* in radical circles. The Communist paper *Inkululeko* castigated his opposition as 'not worthy of a leader of his stature'.[20]

Matthews was not a politician who bent easily to the pressure of popular opinion. He adopted a rather donnish approach by seeking to articulate what he felt from informed analysis was the chief political mood of the time. He had chaired the committee that drew up the 1943 ANC statement on the Atlantic Charter entitled *Africans Claims in South Africa*. This document looked back to the Woodrow Wilson's Fourteen Points, asserting the rights of nations to self-determination; it also caught some of the new mood engendered by World War II by combining this with the demand for the self-determination of subject peoples. In the case of those parts of Africa under white settler control, it demanded the international recognition of Africans' full citizenship rights as well as their 'direct participation in all the councils of the state'.[21]

Matthews viewed African claims for full citizenship rights as accruing from international standards of justice linked to Christian ethics.[22] He did not consider that it was necessarily the case, as the Youth Leaguers maintained, that the ANC was the spiritual embodiment of this demand for national liberation. At the time of deliberations within the ANC national executive committee on discussions regarding possible amalgamation with the All African Convention in 1948, Matthews refused to accept that the ANC leadership necessarily had to have a mandate to prosecute the talks. On the contrary, 'the absence of a mandate' was 'a mandate also'.[23] In an article in the journal *Foreign Affairs* a few years later he considered that the ANC had not 'captured the masses of the African people and its accomplishments do not altogether justify its claim to speak for them effectively'.[24]

Matthews felt by the early 1950s that successful resistance to apartheid depended upon the development of an alternative code of political ethics to those of the white state. The figure of Gandhi in India served as a reminder that there were limits to rational persuasion when dealing with imperial powers, which would not abandon their power without a bitter struggle.[25] The concept of the *assimilation* of Africans into a common society he considered politically difficult to realize in South Africa since it invoked 'conglomeration of inter-mixture and dull conformity'. Similarly, the notion of the *integration* of Africans into a common political system, then fashionable in liberal circles, did not offer much hope either since it implied a 'kind of passive becoming in which things happen to the individual instead of the individual consciously shaping or participating in shaping his own destiny'.[26] To Matthews it appeared essential to concentrate upon individual rather than group initiatives. It was important to remember that 'in every institution the unit of cooperation is not the group but the individual and the emphasis should be placed upon individual merit not upon group lack of it'.[27]

Nevertheless, Matthews became increasingly aware of the growing collective power of the Youth League among the ANC's younger membership. His refusal along with Moroka to resign from the NRC brought him under growing attack from 1950 onwards by the Youth League radicals. In December 1950 at a meeting of the ANC's national executive Moroka and Matthews found themselves isolated as they were called upon by Nelson Mandela to resign from the NRC, particularly after it emerged that the Secretary of Native Affairs, Dr WWM Eiselen, had himself requested them to do so.[28] During the following year there were demands from the Youth League in Johannesburg for both Matthews and Moroka to be expelled if they failed to resign.[29] Further pressures came from Z K Matthews' son, Joe, who had come under Youth League influences as a student at Fort Hare in the late 1940s and was a radical exponent of Pan Africanism. Joe Matthews was bitterly critical of attempts by the South African Institute of Race Relations (of which his father was a member of the National Executive Comittee until 1953) to try and mediate between the govenment and the ANC in the Defiance Campaign. He saw the Defiance Campaign producing a 'revolutionary situation' which was 'too large' for the SAIRR and which even armed force would be unlikely to crush.[30]

On his return in May 1953 from a year's sabbatical at the Union Theological Seminary in the United States, Z K Matthews realized that the Defiance Campaign had escalated internal divisions within the ANC rather than developing an impetus for revolution. The campaign's strategy had emerged for expedient reasons rather than from any deep commitment to Gandhian precepts of non-violence.[31] Its failure to shift government policy left the ANC without a clear sense of political direction and prone to political factionalism. Even Albert Luthuli did not appear to command the full support of his executive in Natal.[32]

Matthews' proposal for a COP at the Cape Congress in Craddock on 15 August was due to his anxiety that the banning orders imposed on so many leaders of the ANC in the wake of the Defiance Campaign could lead to a loss of control to more radical elements keen to precipitate an escalation of racial violence. He felt that the ANC leadership had generally acted as a 'restraining influence' throughout the Defiance Campaign. But the general state of race relations was 'explosive' and 'irresponsible action or utterances on either side of the colour line might easily touch off something worse than what is happening in other parts of the continent'.[33] He later recollected at the Treason Trial that he saw the Congress of the People as a representative gathering of different organizations in South Africa. This would in turn avoid the 'completely amorphous body' of the All African Convention founded in 1935 to oppose the Native Bills which consisted of 'lots of people representing nobody at all'.[34]

Matthews also hoped the COP would sharpen up the objectives of the ANC and lead to the outline for an alternative 'non racial' constitution in South Africa.[35] Within Congress circles, though, it was viewed more as a means of reviving the organization's rather poor political fortunes. At the ANC's annual conference in Queenstown in December 1953 a resolution was passed instructing the executive to make 'immediate preparations' for the organization of the COP, in conjunction with the executives of the SAIC, COD, SACPO and 'any other democratic organization', for the holding of a 'truly representative convention of the peoples of South Africa'.[36] Matthews' name continued to be seen as vital to the prosecution of this goal and, following a request from Albert Luthuli in a letter to Matthews of 9 February 1954, Matthews spelt out the purposes of the COP in a memorandum.

Matthews' memorandum indicated the degree to which his thinking had moved since *African Claims* a decade previously. Indeed, comparing the final memorandum with a surviving early draft, it is possible to see the drift of his thought as he identified the objectives of the COP on increasingly populist lines. The guiding principle of the early draft was that 'the essence of *good government* is that the policy and programme of government must be an expression of the will of the people'.[37] This was changed in the final version to the less Westminster-inspired notion that 'the essence of *democratic* government, as commonly understood, is that its policies and programmes *of action* must be an expression of the people' (emphases added). Similarly, the notion of history as a kind of biblical morality tale contained in an early draft's statement that 'the people must and will speak, and woe be unto my regime which tries to ignore the voice of the people' was abandoned in the final draft in favour of a more complex notion of historical destiny. This declared that 'The voice of the people cannot be stifled indefinitely. The people must and will speak in the end, however long they may have remained silent in the past. Human history shows that it is disastrous for the Voice of the People to go unheeded for too long'.[38] The evolution of the memorandum pointed to a shift away from the idea of trying to make the existing political system perform on 'good' lines to the notion that it had sooner or later to accord with the inherent tendencies of populist democracy. The memorandum provided a clearer ideological statement of this world view: not only was it the case that regimes the world over were ultimately made by 'the people' but they would sooner or later be broken by the same force if they refused to recognize this general law of history.

Organizing the Congress of the People:

Some of the leaders involved in the planning of the COP recognized at an early stage that there would be dangers involved if it was seen as an alternative 'government' or 'parliament'. A conference of executives of the organizations behind the COP (known as the 'sponsoring organizations') was held at Fraser in Natal on 25th March 1954. Here the COP was envisaged as being beholden to the sponsoring organizations. A Joint Planning Committee was established with not more than 5 members appointed by each organization, though the ANC was appointed to act as convenor of the Planning Committee. This Committee in turn submitted a draft plan to a further meeting of the executives of the sponsoring organizations at Evaton in the Transvaal on 9 May 1954 which established a 'National Action Council' to organize and run the campaign. There was a strong grouping from COD on the NAC consisting of Joe Slovo, Piet Beyleveld, Lionel Bernstein and Rica Hodgson. In addition PQ Vundla, Oliver Tambo, EP Moretsele and ET Tshunungwa were appointed from the ANC along with Ahmed Kathrada from the SAIC and two SACPO representatives.[39] In turn at a subsequent meeting at Fraser in Natal on 15 August 1954 a 'secretariat' of the National Action Council was established.[40]

The National Action Council (NAC) decided at a meeting at Stanger in Natal on 16 August 1954 to cast as wide a net as possible by inviting a large number of organizations to affiliate to the COP. It was hoped that 5000 volunteers would be initially recruited to launch the campaign, along with a series of provincial and regional committees, so that plans could be made on a local basis. These committees were charged with organizing the distribution of 10,000 posters and 250,000 stickers, establishing links with newspapers and printing their own fortnightly bulletins of activities.[41]

The organizers placed considerable emphasis upon the recruitment of volunteers and their planning was similar to the ANC's M-Plan. Ahmed Kathrada saw the volunteers as providing nothing less than the 'hard core of men in our army of liberation'.[42] Pete Beyleveld, one of the leading COD activists on the NAC, suggested that volunteers should start organizing in factories and work places as well as holding meetings covering a single street or neighbourhood block. Volunteers were encouraged to 'work like missionaries, without resting', for the aim should be that 'no citizen of South Africa' was 'left out of the discussions of the Freedom Charter'.[43] By November of 1954 Albert Luthuli increased the effort by calling for some 50,000 'freedom volunteers' to promote the aims of the COP. It was hoped this would lead to a considerable infusion of funds since each volunteer would be charged with collecting £1 a month from each individual branch or group that he or she organized.[44]

The COP was part of a wider effort to revive sagging membership levels in the ANC which dropped from a maximum of 100,000 in 1952 at the height of the Defiance Campaign to a mere 32,000 by 1955.[45] Over the following months, though, the COP had only a sporadic impact at the local level and remained continually dependent on Congress branches and visits by outside organizers.[46] Some discussions on the Freedom Charter were held in factories during lunch hours, although this did not always lead to formal demands being sent to the NAC in Johannesburg .[47] In some cases, the volunteers in the townships and locations had only a vague idea of their task. This led in the Transvaal to a series of fortnightly lectures being organized to explain what they should try and do.[48] There were frequent complaints by the organizers that funds and demands were not being passed upwards.

Problems in mobilizing mass support led the NAC Secretariat to try centralizing political decision making, despite ZK Matthews' original conception of the COP as being simply a campaign created by the respective sponsoring organizations.[49] The white activists from COD were particularly keen for the Secretariat to adopt this strategy since they envisaged the Congress of the People developing an organizational autonomy over and above the sponsoring organizations. They saw this as a means of fulfilling the COD goal, spelt out by its National Executive, of securing the 'maximum possible' participation by whites in the COP.[50]

The COD position was strengthened by the refusal of the Liberal Party National Executive Committee on 26 January 1955 to involve itself in the campaign through fear that it was being secretly dominated by former members of the South African Communist Party.[51] In various parts of the country, COD organizers found themselves in positions of considerable political influence due to the relative weaknesses of the other Congresses. In the Western Cape this came about through the absence of any strong local ANC tradition and COD proved to be one of the most important supporters of the COP effort.[52] In the Transvaal, on the other hand, COD's influence was helped by its relatively effective organization as well as the bannings imposed upon the ANC leadership. It easily proved itself to be the most important source of funds in the province despite its tiny membership, contributing some £38-16-5d out of total funds of £45-15-7d collected by the sponsoring organizations by February 1955 (The ANC contribution was nil).[53]

COD's efforts to improve the organizational efficiency of the COP, however, did little to speed up the rate of popular mobilization. The COP organization on occasions found itself by-passed as people in rural areas simply wrote out their own demands on scraps of paper rather than use the forms provided by the National Action Council in Johannesburg.[54]

Part of this organizational breakdown was due to harrassment by the government and the banning of a number of political leaders. There were also conflicting notions about what the COP was for. Not all those active in it shared ZK Matthews' view that the COP was simply a campaign of the respective organizations belonging to it. One speaker at a meeting in Cape Town, Perry Simon Manana, saw the COP as replacing parliament in its authority to 'write all the laws with which the people will be ruled in this country'.[55] In the Transvaal, furthermore, the Provincial Organizer reported that the COP was generally viewed at the branch level as a separate organization to that of the ANC.[56] Other organizers on the NAC, such as the leading COD activist Ben Turok, tried to appeal for working class involvement in the COP in the hope that this would lead to a wider popular following.[57]

The National Action Council, however, did not initially start out by trying to raise particular local issues but maintained more of an educational emphasis. Considerable importance was attached to a series of lecture notes which were distributed at intervals to regional organizers to be studied by the volunteers, trade unionists and general members of the Congresses. The rather slender response to this material from the regional committees indicated that the lectures were not particularly popular.[58] In the case of the Transvaal, it was reported that most of the members of branch committees did not even see the lectures.[59]

In the late stages of the campaign a different strategy began to be adopted of relaxing central control and moving to a looser interpretation of the NAC's original plan of campaign. The organizers in the Transvaal recognized that if popular interest was to be mobilized it needed to relate to particular issues. By early April, the Transvaal Committee of the COP suggested to regional committees that they encourage groups of 5, 10 or 20 people to get together to write their demands for the Freedom Charter on any piece of paper. This could be done at the same time as elections were held for delegates to the Congress itself. The election meetings were to be held as a 'gala festival' in order to attract maximum attention. It was also suggested that ANC members organize in their home areas when they returned for holidays and write to relatives publicizing the COP.[60] There was no long-term campaign to mobilize support from organized groups of workers. Only three unions agreed to support the COP campaign on a national level, the African Laundry and Dry Cleaning Workers Union, The Textile Workers Union and the Food and Canning Workers Union. There were also few attempts by the COP organizers to mobilize workers themselves. It was only in early May 1955, some seven weeks before the Kliptown meeting, that approaches began at last to be made to African mine workers on the Witwatersrand.[61]

The delegation of authority to the local level helped save the Congress of the People from near disaster, for it was becoming increasingly clear that the leadership of the ANC was embroiled in far too many other issues to allow it to be of much practical assistance. On February 9 the government began to implement its policy of removal of people from the Western Johannesburg suburbs of Sophiatown, Martindale and Newclare to land in Meadowlands thirteen miles outside the city. The ANC was rather caught unprepared and started organizing resistance, despite evidence that many families were in favour of the move.[62] The following month, the ANC executive also decided to boycott the schools established under the 1954 Bantu Education Act. The ANC's energies became increasingly diverted into efforts to co-ordinate a national campaign of boycott of the government schools despite a chronic lack of knowledge of activities being conducted by its various local branches.[63] At the national level the ANC leadership was hindered by a shortage of funds which left it by May of 1955 with no full-time secretary to run its Johannesburg head office.[64]

Drafting the Freedom Charter

As the COP campaign reached its final stages in May and June 1955, there was a worry among some ANC activists that it might be diverted from the original task of drafting the Freedom Charter. With Chief Luthuli confined under a banning order to the magisterial district of Stanger, there seemed to be a risk that the ANC leadership would be eclipsed by a more multi-racial political grouping centred upon Johannesburg which had learned to work together and was now anxious to form its own permanent organization.[65] Though this group had made considerable efforts to gather a national following, it did still appear highly urban in complexion with many rural areas poorly organized. Robert Resha, for example, only reached Umtata in the Transkei on a tour for the NAC on 21 June some four days before the start of the COP at Kliptown.[66]

A large majority of the delegates to the COP came from the urban areas. It was later estimated that only 300 delegates came from Natal, 250 from the Eastern and Western Cape and only 50 from the Orange Free State. The balance of some 2194 came from the Transvaal and the majority of these from Johannesburg.[67] The sparse numbers of those coming from outside the Transvaal was a result of poor local organization as well as the expense of travelling to the Witwatersrand.

The COP organizers intended that a wide range of political figures and organizations would make the gathering in Kliptown representative of the broad mass of people in South Africa. Several key individuals such as Albert Luthuli and Nelson Mandela could not attend or give speeches due to banning orders. ZK Matthews, on the other hand, declined to give the opening address on the grounds that he had prior commitments to Fort Hare.[68] The NAC turned to Trevor Huddleston, a priest from the Community of the Resurrection who had for a number of years worked in the slum of Sophiatown. Though he had not been involved politically in the COP up to this point, he was broadly sympathetic to its aims. His passionate opening of the Congress of the People at Kliptown struck its radical tone. This was partly induced by the reluctance of a number of bodies to be associated with it. The Liberal Party's refusal to attend cut it off from much of the mainstream white liberal establishment while churches such as the Catholic and Methodist Churches in South Africa also declined to be affiliated on the grounds of its political nature.[69]

The absence of these bodies weakened the political checks on the Secretariat of the NAC, which proceeded to draft the Freedom Charter in conjunction with a sub-committee appointed for this task. There is no indication that the demands sent to the NAC had a particularly clear ideological content. For the most part, they opposed apartheid legislation and demanded direct parliamentary representation by 'our own people'. The demands were couched in such general terms as 'more facilities for cultivation and grazing', 'equal education for all races', 'freedom of movement', 'houses for all' and 'votes for all'. These demands were woven into a document which gained a clearer ideological focus as it evolved from the NAC, but which was not even given to leading Congress leaders like Albert Luthuli or ZK Matthews for their critical comments. The first draft was only considered at a meeting of the NAC on 23 June, two days before the Kliptown Meeting. It was, in the words of the defence at the Treason Trial, 'the first time that anyone connected with the Congress of the People, other than the drafting sub committees, had seen any text of the Freedom Charter whatsoever'.[70]

The first draft makes strong statements about the need for close popular control over the organs of government. 'The bonds between the people, the organs of public opinion and their elected representatives', it declared, 'should be close, and consultation between the people and their representatives should prevail at all levels and at all times'.[71] This was changed in the final draft to a more centralist conception of South Africa as a 'democratic state, based on the will of all the people', with no specific provision for direct consultation. Likewise, the first draft spoke of an active 'state encouragement' for every 'national group' to 'use and develop its own folk culture and national customs'. If it had been retained it would have staked an early claim for a multi-cultural programme in South Africa. However, it was changed in the final draft to the notion of 'equal status in the bodies of the state, in the courts, and in the schools for all national groups and races'.

On economic issues the first draft considered that the wealth of South Africa derived from the labour of all its 'citizens'. The basic industries of the country were to be 'worked for the benefit of the people' with only the mines being specifically nationalized. By the final draft the language of citizenship had been replaced by a more populist demand that the 'national wealth' of South Africa should be 'restored to the people' with the banks and 'monopoly industry' being added to the mines for nationalization. The final draft only once referred to 'citizens', when it declared that 'teachers shall have the rights of other citizens', which appears to mean more or less the same thing as 'people'.

The first draft made a clearer commitment to the family as a distinct social unit in a future South African society. It considered that the family was 'the natural and fundamental unit of society' and was 'entitled to protection by society and the state'. By the final Charter the emphasis had shifted to the demand that 'laws which break up families shall be repealed'. The first draft also favoured schemes of agricultural modernization by linking demands for an 'equitable distribution of land' for the peasants with the adoption of 'advanced and mechanical ways of farming, by planned irrigation schemes and anti erosion work'. This was altered in the final Charter to the demand that the state 'shall help the peasants with implements, seed, tractors and dams to save the soil and assist the tillers'.

The final draft of the Freedom Charter marked an ideological shift towards a more populist language that asserted the collective will of 'the people' and put rather less emphasis than the first draft on other countervailing rights of groups such as families or bodies of citizens. Its focal point was the future state in South Africa as the embodiment of the people's collective will. 'South Africa', it declared, 'belongs to all who live in it, black and white, and ... no government can justly claim authority unless it is based on the will of the people'. It was far less concerned than the first draft with fulfiling goals of economic modernization than with achieving social and economic equity.

There was an also important shift in the tone of the two documents. The first draft simply made demands which 'should' occur while the final Charter confidently asserted that its demands 'shall' occur. The first draft showed traces of the presupposition that by reasonable persuasion and argument its just demands could be conceded by the existing state. This had effectively vanished by the final Charter which asserted its demands as non-negotiable processes which would reach fruition by the inherent logic of events. As Nelson Mandela was later to claim, the Charter was 'a revolutionary document precisely because the changes it envisages cannot be won without breaking up the economic and political set-up of present South Africa'.[72] Likewise, Walter Sisulu saw the Charter as a pivotal document in a national liberation struggle which was also socialist in content. It was nothing less than the 'basic law of the liberatory movement, a declaration of principles unifying all the people in our land, black and white, except for the small section of reactionaries who see in the Charter the end of their long-established domination and exploitation. The Charter is the picture of the future South Africa in which oppression and exploitation shall be no more'.[73] Other writers, such as 'Inkululeko' in the newspaper *New Age*, tried to play-down the Charter's socialist features and stressed instead its democratic demands. A complete change of 'state form'' was essential if these were to be realized and 'Inkululeko' attacked the 'illusion' of liberals in South Africa that a democracy could be achieved 'within the existing constitutional set-up'.[74]

The Freedom Charter was a radical populist document which accurately reflected the trends within the discourse of the COP over the preceding two years. For the organizers, the COP marked the 'spontaneous assertion of unity in thought, in action and in spirit for a better South Africa'.[75] The event was broadly welcomed in the Congresses. Albert Luthuli publicly declared that no greater democratic document had ever been drawn up in South African history, though he had some doubts over the Charter's nationalization proposals and also felt that many of its provisions such as for a 48 hour week would have been better left for 'the time when the Principles outlined in the Charter are being implemented'.[76]

The COP, however, did not produce the expected unity within the political opposition in South Africa. Over the next few years considerable opposition also emerged within the Africanist wing of the ANC to the multi-racial nature of the Freedom Charter's demands, eventually leading to the splitting of the movement in 1958-9 and the creation of the PAC. The Kliptown gathering had served to inject an intensely optimistic set of expectations among the Congress following which could not ultimately be fulfilled.

The Repercussions:

The COP was a considerable political triumph, given the increasing government harrassment of political leaders in the Congress Alliance. It also represented a radical political platform which many of the surviving leaders from the inter-war years found hard to accept. The reluctance to engage in mass political action was epitomized in ZK Matthews' failure even to attend the Kliptown Meeting on the grounds that he could not get a flight to Johannesburg.[77] The drift of the ANC's policies was not really to his liking. He tried to dissuade Oliver Tambo and the ANC's National Executive Committee from concentrating upon joint meetings with the executives of the other organizations of the Congress Alliance and to concentrate upon preparing for the ANC's own December conference.[78]

However, on 31 July 1955, the Joint Executives of the COP decided to meet Chief Luthuli at Stanger in Natal as the continuing National Consultative Committee (NCC).[79] Matthews felt isolated from the trend of political events and, given the need to attend to matters at Fort Hare, decided not to seek re-election at the end of 1955. He warned of 'swollen-headed' political leaders embarking on ambitious schemes with limited resources.[80] But he was reluctant to attend the ANC's annual conference in December 1955 to give the Presidential Address in Luthuli's absence caused by a banning order.[81] Matthews did address the conference and described the COP in laudatory Churchillian tones as 'the people's finest hour'.[82] Though he captured some of the prevailing mood it was his own political swan song. Increasingly, he distanced himself from the ANC and concentrated upon academic politics at Fort Hare.

The COP had given new life to pressures from the ANC's radical wing to relate the movement's strategy to particular political issues in which African people were engaged. Walter Sisulu charged that ANC leaders had not really understood the COP, preferring to see it as 'nothing more than just a big conference unconcerned with the positive struggles of the people'.[83] The COP itself tried to draw out the lesson that if 'just over 8000 volunteers were able to shake the country' then it should be possible to do far more in terms of issues like opposition to Bantu Education. 'The activities of a political movement are not alone significant because *all* the people participate in them', it declared. 'They are significant also because they are activities that represent the best ideas and feelings of the masses of the people even when they do not take active part in them' (emphasis added).[84]

This report helped persuade a meeting of the Joint National Executives of the Congress Alliance at Stanger at the end of July 1955 to press ahead with the creation of a more permanent body. Despite the small number of representatives at Kliptown, the COP was widely viewed as representing a far wider population. Norman Levy of COD put this at 350,000 while ZK Matthews suggested an even larger figure of half a million. The meeting refused to be daunted by the poor turn-out of some 5000 volunteers. Matthews pointed out that the term 'volunteer' had put many people off through its associations with the previous Defiance Campaign. Some leaders wanted to establish a 'standing' or 'coordinating committee' but Matthews proposed instead a 'consultative committee', which formally maintained his original principle that the COP was only a campaign of the 'sponsoring organizations' behind it. It was agreed that the committee would consist of two members from each of the sponsoring organizations.[85]

The NCC committed itself to a million signature campaign in support of the Freedom Charter which it hoped would be complete by June 26 the following year. It was not at first clear, though, how a campaign of these proportions was to be organized. From the start, provincial branches of the old COP structure appeared confused by the lack of clear guidelines from the centre.[86] The Million Signature Campaign also repeated many of the over-ambitious objectives of the Congress of the People. The Transvaal alone was set the task of gathering 450,000 signatures, and its organizers hoped in October 1955 that 100,000 of these could be gathered before the end of the year.[87] In the event it managed to collect 50,000 signatures by June of the following year and this was more than any other province. Though the NCC met some 22 times during the year and the Secretariat on a further twenty-eight occasions, the campaign was hampered by poor communications with the representative organizations and the failure of these organizations to nominate representatives to the Committee.[88]

The political strategy of mass political mobilization proved to be overly ambitious in the context of the South Africa in the 1950s. Those involved hoped to broaden the existing political base of the Congress Alliance forged in the passive resistance of the Defiance Campaign. In the process, it was hoped a mass movement could be forged which would lead to a development of 'non racial' political consciousness. With the establishment of SACTU in 1955, furthermore, this would put the black working class in a vanguard role of an essentially revolutionary struggle to overthrow the South African state.

In practice, the COP did encourage an increasingly 'multi-racial' or 'non racial' political climate in South African politics in the middle to late 1950s, though not necessarily one with a revolutionary edge. The campaign for mass mobilization divided informed African opinion and alienated many key figures of the older generation of political activists who had been involved in Congress politics since the middle 1930s. The ANC leadership appeared to have adopted an increasingly confrontational course with the government leaving no space for political moderates.[89] The remaining moderately-inclined leadership felt increasingly isolated after the arrest of suspects in the Treason Trial at the end of 1956 and tended to look for political influence through white liberal allies. ZK Matthews, along with his son Joe Matthews and Albert Luthuli, met Quintin Whyte from the South African Institute of Race Relations during the Treason Trial and stressed the necessity of cooperation with liberal bodies in order to fight the government's apartheid programme. Luthuli and ZK Matthews even denied that the ANC was a strongly nationalist body and said, Whyte noted, that 'if anyone got up and spoke in these terms at an ANC meeting, they would get short shift'.[90]

Despite these efforts to present the ANC as a body that was still anxious to negotiate with the South African state, it was clear that from a longer-term perspective the Congress of the People had been crucial in radicalizing the movement and squeezing out more liberally-inclined elements. If the older, moderating influences had been shaped in some degree by the model of black economic and political advance in United States, the model that gained increasing attraction in Congress circles by the middle to late 1950s was that of third world national liberation.[91] To this extent, the Freedom Charter was a landmark in the progressive inculcation of a radical political culture in the ANC that some observers, such as George Fredrickson, perceived as a continuing drag on the movement's capacity to enter into serious constitutional negotiations with the government of FW De Klerk.[92]

Conclusion

The thrust of the movement clearly underwent a fundamental shift in the course of the 1950s. It changed from seeking to pressurize the government via persuasive argument into a push for mass political mobilization. In the course of this transformation, the notion of the movement articulating the demands of the 'people' in South Africa became increasingly salient. In one sense it reflected an internal power struggle between the younger generation of Youth League-inspired militants and older figures such as ZK Matthews and Albert Luthuli. It also reflected a conflict of strategy over whether to build a mass movement based on tight control from the leadership of the Congress Alliance or whether to follow ZK Matthews' original design of building a looser movement representing different organizations without a strongly autonomous leadership. The latter course would probably have secured a wider set of political alliances, including very probably the Liberal Party, while the former course involved a rather tighter set of political relationships that many critics saw as securing considerable political influence for the white radicals in COD.[93]

The Freedom Charter, nevertheless, has survived as a key political document in contemporary South African politics. It is not the rigid ideological statement that it has been made out to be by both right and left. It was the product of a historical process. It provides the basis for the political platform of the ANC, despite the present movement's commitment to 'non racialism' and the avoidance of any legal recognition to ethnic group entities. To Cyril Ramaphosa, for instance, now Secretary-General of the ANC, the Freedom Charter 'is a simple, unpretentious statement of the aspirations and responses to the problems of apartheid'.[94] Ramaphosa has interpreted the Charter's provisions in an instrumental manner, emphasizing less its populist content than its potential as a set of principles for a socialist programme of state control of the economy and redistribution of wealth. Some critics have cautioned against such an approach, urging that the Charter tends to stress *goals* as opposed to *means* and it is still important to consider how wealth is going to be created.[95] Ramaphosa, however, employing a rather crude labour theory of value to predict future behaviour, has retorted that the removal of apartheid structures will release an enormous pent-up capacity in the South African economy. 'Workers are prepared to work even harder after the attainment of the Freedom Charter', he has claimed, 'in order to generate the necessary wealth that would give their children free and compulsory education'.[96] To this extent, the Freedom Charter still inspires its followers with a sense of political destiny as apartheid faces its demise.

Notes

1   The Congress Alliance consisted of the ANC, the South African Indian Congress (SAIC), the South African Coloured Peoples Organsiation (SACPO), the Congress of Democrats (COD) and the South Afrtican Congress of Trade Unions (SACTU). It was estimated that of the 2884 delegates, 360 were Indians, 317 Coloureds and 113 Europeans and the rest African; Treason Trial Papers, Church of the Province Archives, University of the Witwatersrand, AD 1812/Eg 3.2.4 undated mss.

2   Albert Luthuli, *Let My People Go*, (London: Collins, 1962), p.158.

3   Raymond Suttner and Jeremy Cronin, *30 Years of the Freedom Charter* (Johannesburg: Ravan Press, 1984), p.86.

4   Ibid, p.289.

5   Asa Briggs, 'The Language of "Mass" and "Masses" in Nineteenth Century England' in Asa Briggs (ed), *The Collected Works of Asa Briggs*, Vol. 1 (Sussex: Harvester Press, 1985), pp.35-54.

6   In May 1948 the ANC in the Transvaal rejected a proposal for the holding of a Transvaal-Orange Free State Peoples' Assembly for Voters for All unless the committee that proposed it resigned and surrendered its powers to an alternative committee consisting of the ANC (Transvaal), The Transvaal Indian Congress and the African Peoples' Organisation; *Bantu World*, 15 May 1948.

7   Thomas Hodgkin, 'A Note on the Language of African Nationalism' in Kenneth Kirkwood, ed., *African Affairs*, 1 (1961), p.40.

8   Carter Karis Collection (Hereafter, CKC), Reel #2D C2:30/2; L. Bernstein, 'The Road to Liberty', ms, n.d. (1953 COD Conference paper).

9   Moses Kotane, *South Africa's Way Forward* (Cape Town: New Age, 1954).

10   Anthony Sampson, *The Treason Cage* (London: Heinemann, 1958), p.79; Edward Feit, 'Generational Conflict and African Nationalism in South Africa: the African National Congress, 1949-1059', *International Journal of African Historical Studies*, 5 (1972), pp.181-202.

11   'Subjective Liberation — An Immediate Necessity', *Africa*, (1953).

12   *Inkundla ya Bantu* , 21 January 1950. Other Youth Leaguers such as M. B. Yengwa, who became Secretary to Albert Luthuli in 1952, claimed that the Youth League's nationalism was 'moderate', for it was recognized that there were 'other communities in South Africa who had made South Africa their home', *Ilanga lase Natal*, March 11 1950.

13   J. B. Marks, 'Address to the Conference of the African National Congress (Transvaal) in the Western Native Township, September 30-1 October 1951', unpub. mimeo, p. 5.

14   Treason Trial Records, AD1812 Ea 1.4.19 Notebook of Walter Sisulu, n.p., n.d., noting that Mao was 'guided by a clear scientific line in which he never inverted for a moment. This has been proved by history.'

15   CKC, reel #5B, Report of the National Action Committee, 5 December 1953. Fatima Meer in her biography of Nelson Mandela suggests, without any supporting evidence, that the M-Plan was implemented in 1953, *Higher Than Hope*

(Harmondsworth: Penguin, 1988), p.60. For details of the M- Plan see Edward Feit, Urban Revolt in South Africa: A Case Study', *Journal of Modern African Studies*, 8 (1970) 55-72.

16   National Action Committee report.

17   *Let My People Go*, p.149.

18   He felt that some aspects of the Smuts government's policies deserved African support and praised the 'truly herculean efforts' of the officials of the Native Affairs Department to 'grapple' with the 'problems' of African agricultural development despite severe shortages of funds. Z.K. Matthews, 'The Rehabilitation and Development of the Reserves', *South African Outlook*, 1 November 1945, p.170. For a more detailed study of some of Matthews's views see Cynthia Kros, 'Z.K. Matthews and Education', *Perspectives in Education*, 12 , (1990/91) 21-40.

19   Jan Hofmeyr to J.C. Smuts, 7 October 1946 in Jean Van der Poel, ed., *Selections from the Smuts Papers* (Cambridge University Press), p.95.

20   *Inkululeko*, 28 April 1948.

21   ANC, *Africans Claims in South Africa* (Johanesburg, 1943), p. 5.

22   Z.K. Matthews Papers, (microfilm, University of the Witwatersrand) B4.30, 'Racial Antagonism', n.d (1952-3). Racial antagonism was the supreme test of human relations; it brought out the main assumptions behind human actions. 'If faith without works is dead', Matthews concluded, 'works without the right faith can be positively pernicious'.

23   CKC, Microfilm Roll #3B 2 DA 21/2 30/1; Minutes of Executive Meeting (in James Calata's handwriting) 14 December 1948.

24   Z.K. Matthews, 'The African Response to Racial Laws', *Foreign Affairs*, 30 (October 1951) 101.

25   Z.K. Matthews Papers, B4.27 'Gandhi and South Africa', unpub. mss. of lecture delivered in the USA (1952-53).

26   Z.K. Matthews, 'An African Policy for South Africa', *Race Relations*, 16 (1949), p.80.

27   Ibid. In this consideration Matthews was probably stimulated by the figure of Reinhold Niebuhr who was Professor of Christian Social Ethics at the Union Theological Seminary when he went on sabbatical there in 1952-53.

28   CKC, Roll #2B 2.DA 14/2 30/13 Minutes of the National Executive (in James Calata's handwriting), 15 December 1950. The Youth League in the Transvaal had started criticizing

Moroka for refusing to resign from the NRC from as early as the previous June, see *African Lodestar*, 1, 2 June 1950.

29   Jordan Ngubane, 'African Traders and Apartheid', *The Forum*, 15 January 1951.

30   Z. K. Matthews Papers, Joe Matthews to Z. K.Matthews 5 August and 3 September 1952. Joe Matthews was at this time a radical Pan-Africanist seeking the creation of a 'purely African state' as the 'prelude to its inclusion in a United States of Africa', JG Matthews, "Africa for the Africans", *Inkundla ya Bantu* , 29 April 1950.

31   Leo Kuper, *Passive Resistance in South Africa*, (New Haven: Yale University Press, 1957), p.103.

32   The former Youth League activist Selby Ngcobo, for example, expressed doubts to Matthews as to whether Albert Luthuli really commanded the full support of his executive in Natal. 'The rising middle classes in Natal', he wrote, 'are too much dependent on the Europeans for positions in Joint Councils, for trading licences in locations and for other small material benefits. Selling a birthright for a mess of potage', Z. K. Matthews Papers, B2.94 Selby Ngcobo to Z. K. Matthews 21 October 1952. Ngcobo was probably referring to such conservative figures in Natal as A.W.G. Champion who had only been removed from the Presidency of the Natal Africa Congress by Albert Luthuli in December 1951.

33   Z. K. Matthews Papers, C2.296, Z. K. Matthews to Henry P. Van Dusen, 2 November 1953.

34   *Treason Trial Record*, p.17995.

35   CKC, Roll #5B 2:DC15:92/9 Statement from Z. K. Matthews' wife, 1955 or later.

36   'Resolutions, ANC Annual Conference, December 18-20, 1953', in Thomas Karis and Gwendolen M. Carter (eds), *From Protest to Challenge*, Vol. 3, Stanford, Hoover Institution Press, 1977, p.126.

37   CKC, Roll #5B 2:DC15:92/2 draft (in ZKM's handwriting) entitled "The Congress of the People". n.p, n.d.

38   Ibid.

39   Treason Trial Papers, AD1812, Eg1.2.3, Minutes of the National Action Council, COP, 5 August 1954.

40   CKC, Roll #5B 2:DC15:92/6 memo, 'The Congress of the People Campaign and the Freedom Charter', n.d submitted as part of the Treason Trial defence.

41   Treason Trial Papers, AD1812, Eg1.2.12 W. Sisulu to The

Secretary, the Joint Working Comittee encl 'Draft Plan of Campaign', 1 July 1954.

42   Ibid, AD1812/Eg.7.3 Meeting of the ANC, SACPO, TIC and SACOD in the Trades Hall, Johannesburg, 25 July 1954.

43   *Speaking Together*, No 2, End of August 1954.

44   *Forward to Freedom* , No 1, 27 November 1954.

45   Edward Feit, *African Opposition in South Africa: The Failure of Passive Resistance* (Stanford: Hoover Institute, 1967), p. 65.

46   Tom Lodge, *Black Politics in South Africa Since 1945*, (London and New York: Longman, 1983), p. 70.

47   Suttner and Cronin, p.36.

48   Treason Trial Papers, AD1812 Eg7 Minutes of the Provincial Action Council of the Congress of the People, 12 September 1954.

49   Ibid, AD1812 Ea1.9.1, African National Congress (Cape) Minutes of Executive Meeting, Cradock, 11 September 1954

50   Ibid, AD1812 Ef1.1 Statement by National Executive Committee, SACOD, n.d.

51   Lodge, p.72; Janet Robertson, *Liberalism in South Africa, 1948-63* (Oxford: Clarendon Press, 1971), p.161.

52   Congress of Democrats Papers, Church of the Province Archives, University of the Witwatersrand, AD2187 J(111) B. Gosschalk to Y. Barenblatt 21 June 1956.

53   Ibid, AD1812 Eg.7.4 Treasurer's Report, encl. in Minutes of a Meeting of the Transvaal Provincial Committee of the Congress of the People, Johannesburg, 22 February 1955.

54   Suttner and Cronin, p.50.

55   Treason Trial Papers, AD1812 Eg5.3 Meeting on Parade, Cape Town 13 February 1955.

56   Ibid, AD1812 Eg7.4.3.4 Freddy Morris, Report on the Congress of the People, n.d.

57   Ibid.

58   CKC, Roll #5B 2:DC 15/4 41/3, P. Beyeleveld (?) for NAC to the Sec, Cape Western Prov. Action Committee 29 March 1955; to Dr A.H. Sarder, Ladysmith, 29 March 1955; to T.E. Tshunungwa 20 April 1955. Treason Trial Papers, AD 1812 Eg6.4 NAC to the Sec, Food and Canning Workers Union 5 February 1955 reporting a lack of activity in the Transvaal. In the Western Cape, though, it was difficult to get a response to the NAC's lectures as the groups there were so decentralised, ibid, Eg1.2.1 J. Motloheloa, Cape Western Action Council to the Sec, NAC, 4 May 1955.

59   Treason Trial Papers, AD1812 Eg7.4 Minutes of the Meeting of the Transvaal Committee, COP, 24 May 1955.

60   CKC, Roll # 6B 2:DC 18:30 Sec, Transvaal Committee for the COP to the Sec., Johannesburg Regional Committee for the COP, 3 April 1955.

61   Ibid, #6B 2:DC 18:30, Minutes of a Meeting of the Johannesburg Regional COP, 7 May 1955.

62   Thomas Karis and Gwendolin M. Carter, 'Introduction' in Karis and Carter, *From Protest To Challenge* ,Vol.3,   pp.24-25; Feit, *African Opposition in South Africa*, pp.92-142.

63   Treason Trial Papers, AD1812 Ea1.9.4 O. Tambo circular to all Provincial Secretaries 19 April 1955; T.E. Tshunungwa to the Prov Sec, Transvaal, 22 April 1955.

64   Ibid, AD1812 Ea1.6.2 O. R. Tambo to W. Z. Conco 6 May 1955. It was estimated that the ANC would need at least £30 a month to maintain its head office, ibid, Ea1.6.2 R. Resha to W. Z. Conco, 17 February 1955.

65   Ibid, AD1812 Ea1.10.4 , M. B. Yengwa to W.Z. Conco, 17 June 1955.

66   Ibid, AD1812 Ea1.6.2, Secretariat to E. T. Tshunungwa, 1 June 1955.

67   Ibid, AD1812 Eg1.2.3, Report of the National Action Council of the C.O.P. to the Joint Executives of the ANC, SAIC, SACPO and the SACOD, n.d., p.3.

68   Ibid 2186 Eg1.2.1 R. Resha to Z.K. Matthews 30 May 1955; Z. K. Matthews to the Secretariat NAC, n.d.

69   CKC, Roll #5B, J. B. Webb to Secretariat, NAC, 9 October 1954; Chairman, Advisory Board of the South African Catholic Bishops Conference to the Secretariat, NAC, 20 October 1954.

70   CKC, Roll #5B 2:DC15:92/6 mss., 'The Congress of the People Campaign and the Freedom Charter'.

71   Treason Trial Papers, AD1812 Eg4.1 draft of the Freedom Charter n.d. (June 23 1955?).

72   Nelson Mandela, 'Freedom In Our Lifetime', *Liberation*, June 1956, rep. in Nelson Mandela, *The Struggle Is My Life* (London: IAAF, 1990), p.55.

73   CKC, Roll #5B 2:DC15:92/13, W. S. ms n.d.

74   'Inkululeko' (Ben Turok?), 'Does the Freedom Charter Mean Socialism?', *New Age* , November 17 1955.

75   CKC, Roll #5B 2:DC15:92/10, Report of the Congress of the

People.

76   Ibid ,2:DC 15:92/11 AJL, mss., 'The Congress of the People — A
        Milestone in the People's Struggle'; Treason Trial Papers,
        AD1812 Ea1.10.5, A. Luthuli unpub. mss., n.d.

77   Treason Trial Papers, AD1812 Ea1.9.4, Z.K. Matthews to O.R.
        Tambo 27 June 1955.

78   Ibid, AD1812 G6, Z.K. Matthews to O.R. Tambo, n.d.

79   Ibid, AD1812 Eo3.1.2, Minutes of the Joint Executive of the ANC,
        SAIC, SACOD, SACPO held on 31 July 1955 in Stanger Natal.

80   Ibid, Ea1.9.4.3, Z. K. Matthews to T. T. 6 February 1956.

81   Ibid, AD1812 Ea1.9.4, Z. K. Matthews to A. J. Luthuli, 9 December
        1955.

82   'Address by Professor Z.K. Matthews', in Karis and Carter, vol.3,
        pp. 218-9.

83   CKC, Roll #5B 2:DC15:92/13 W.S. ms., n.d.

84   Treason Trial Papers, AD1812 Eg4.4, 'Suggested Programme',
        n.d.

85   Ibid, AD1812 Ec.3.1.2, Minutes of a Meeting of the Joint
        Executives of the African National Congress, S.A. Indian
        Congress, S.A. Congress of Democrats and the S.A. Coloured
        Peoples Organisation held on the 31 July, 1955, in Stanger, Natal.

86   Ibid, EO 2.2, Secretary, Joint Congress Committee, Cape Town, to
        The Secretary J.C.C. 17 July 1955.

87   Ibid, E.P. Moretsele, circular letter, 24 October 1955.

88   CKC, Roll #5B 2:DC 15/5:62 Report of the Secretariat, N.C.C. n.d;
        Lodge, p.74

89   Leo Kuper Papers, Microfilm Reel 2, Box 2, Interview with Selby
        Ngcobo.

90   Quintin Whyte Papers, Church of the Province Archives,
        University of the Witwatersrand, AD1502 Bb3.8, Notes of
        Meeting with Chief Luthuli, Professor Z. K. Matthews, Mr Joe
        Matthews and Mr Ncwana, n.d.

91   A.P. Walshe, 'Black American Thought and African Political
        Attitudes in South Africa', *The Review of Politics*, 32, January 1970,
        pp.51-77.

92   George Fredrickson, 'African Americans and African Africans',
        New York Review of Books, 26 September 1991.

93   Interview with Peter Brown.

94   Cyril Ramaphosa, 'The Freedom Charter and the Economy:

Fundamental Workers Rights' in James Polley, ed., *The Freedom Charter and the Future* (Johannesburg: A D Donker, 1988), p.43.

95 Hermann Giliomee, 'The Freedom Charter and the Future' in ibid, p.19.

96 Ramaphosa, 'The Freedom Charter', p.45.

13

The ANC and Black Workers

Peter Limb

Introduction

Characterization of the ANC as petit-bourgeois is all too common in scholarly writing. This image deserves to be questioned. It cannot be denied that the ANC had elite or middle-class elements. However, almost from its inception it had an important worker constituency that grew with the passage of time. In 1918-20, and again in 1928-30, ANC leaders moved to the left and expressed solidarity with black worker struggles, and by the 1940s there was a slowly increasing worker membership of Congress. Even in the intervening periods, including a period of stagnation in the 1930s, there were considerable visible and invisible threads binding the ANC and working people. This chapter uses examples drawn from several periods and from the lives of notable individuals to show how African workers and the ANC related to each other. It also shows that black workers were frequently presented with a dilemma: the ANC seemed to offer some prospect of relief from race-defined oppression, but often appeared little able, or at times willing, to mobilize workers.

1912-40

The more overt concern for workers shown by ANC leaders of the 1940s had its roots in earlier times. The ANC in its first decade may have adopted resolutions in keeping with the aspirations of blacks in general, and even of African workers in particular, but it remained small, weak in resources, and without an effective nation-wide apparatus.[1] Hence many African workers probably simply did not know much, if anything, about Congress. This should be qualified by the fact that most urban Africans (except miners in compounds) lived in close proximity to each other, and that the identity of Congress, once established in a location, could easily spread, especially by oral means and by tapping inherited traditions. Govan Mbeki recalls that:

> When Inqindi [ANC] was formed, all strata of African society took part: the middle class led by the intellectuals, the peasantry represented by chiefs and their amaphakathi [councillors], and the working class consisting of the then urbanized Africans ... before 1920 ...the working class took an active part. The presence, of men like Letanka ... arrested in a workers' strike in 1917, in the executive ... cannot be ignored.

He recollects that in 1923 [at the age of 13] he attended South African Native National Congress meetings and concerts among peasants in the southern Transkei. While acknowledging that the leadership of Congress was provided by intellectuals, Mbeki maintains, 'it was a people's organization ... we must not allow weaknesses of organization to obscure this fact'. Congress itself was the product of diverse regional branches, some, such as the Transvaal Congress, more militant than others.

The ANC by 1928-30 was capable of attracting thousands of people to mass rallies, such as those in December 1929 organized by the Western Cape branch, or in Johannesburg in 1928 for ANC President Josiah Gumede on his return from the Soviet Union. Campaigns against passes continued. *Abanthu-Batho*, the Congress newspaper, continued to support workers rights and Garveyism until its demise in 1931. But from 1931-36, the nadir of the ANC, according to Peter Walshe, it turned away from mass actions, 'drawing its executives and the proportion of its members from the new "middle class"'. Although radicals were at this time frustrated at ANC moderation, going so far as declaring the body dead, [and there is plenty of evidence to sustain this view], they frequently acknowledged the strength of its heritage.[2]

John Gomas, a working tailor and SACP activist, saw the ANC and ICU as having been 'two mighty mass organizations of the non-European masses', that at their militant best awakened mass support, now lacking leaders with 'the experiences and tradition of struggle of the international working class', but capable of being re-built. Although hostile to reformism, Gomas acknowledged the ANC as a mass   organization, and clearly thought it had a future.[3] By its 1938 conference, the ANC was paying greater attention to black workers' demands. Dr. AB Xuma, ANC President-General 1940-48, had already taken an interest in social and working conditions in the 30's, contributing to commissions on health, wages and living conditions, giving detailed analyses of the role of cheap labour and discrimination against black workers, noting that 'because of low wages . . . the wife was sometimes driven to resort to illegitimate means of supplementing wages — such as illicit liquor traffic'.[4]

ANC members continued to keep alive those symbols of resistance capable of politically uniting blacks — land, historical traditions, the ANC image itself. Alfred Xuma told a Mendi Memorial meeting in Johannesburg in 1939 that the 1913 Land Act had left 'hundreds of thousands of Africans . . . homeless, landless, moneyless and hopeless'. Land was a major symbol, and it was closely linked to nationalism. But interest in labour issues was also noticeable amongst black political figures. To some it was obvious:

> To us Africans the chief 'colour problem' is the problem of discrimination. The spear-thrust of the whole campaign of discrimination is economic . . . The African is undernourished and diseased because he is ignorant ; he is ignorant because he has not the money to go to school . . . cannot bargain his labour in the open market.[5]

The evidence of JB Marks is paradoxical, for it both confirms and denies ANC effectiveness. Marks, the son of an African railway worker, led a strike as a student teacher, was banned from teaching in 1931 due to political activities, becoming a full-time union, SACP and ANC activist. He joined the ANC in 1928. He estimated, in a 1964 interview, that the ANC had reached its nadir in 1935, and that it was not until 1937 that there were definite attempts made to revive its remnants. Meetings were called up and down the country, with strong support shown for the ANC, even in small dorps and villages: 'The ANC had a very very wide influence, even at the time when it was dead, literally dead. It had a very strong ideological influence'. Touring the Orange Free State and Transvaal to give the message that Congress had 'come back', he noted there 'wasn't much difficulty' in getting this across, and little opposition from chiefs. It is possible some of this ANC 'tradition' included memories of the ICU or other groups. At this time in the provinces Congress tackled local grievances such as passes, land and permits, taking up court cases, yet there was no concrete policy and the 'ANC had very little to do with the trade union movement. Up to very late. I think it comes to the 40s where they convened a conference and conceded the plight of 300,000 African workers. At the time they were not dealing with trade unions.'[6] The Conference of African Leaders, which convened to revive the ANC in 1937 elected the communist JB Marks its secretary, and leftists such as Edwin Mofutsanyana and Gert Sibanda played an increasingly active role in regional ANC affairs. Hidden amongst the verbiage of the Annual Congress was a growing interest in the burgeoning urban worker constituency of Congress.

1940-46

Increasing urbanization, and industrialization, begun in the 30's with steel foundries and engineering plant, accelerated in World War II. This stimulated greater African proletarianization, rising inflation, and low wages, as well as harsh industrial and social legislation which precipitated large-scale African worker strike actions in the 40s. The ANC-worker relationship was here at its most problematic. Some workers clearly did not see the organization as relevant to work issues. Moreover, 'moderate' ANC leaders could be expected to be especially reticent about support of strikes during a World War. Some strikes were organized and led even without formal unions — such as the 1942 power workers' strike. Kin-ethnic based groups may have supplied the social 'cement' for these actions, as Dunbar Moodie and Baruch Hirson suggest, though industrial discipline, shared work experience and associated bonding of workers can also aid united action. Those (formally) 'unorganized' workers such as domestics and farm labourers, as well as the majority of workers who were simply not unionized, left few records and their attitudes to the ANC are only rarely glimpsed.

The 1940s were marked by widespread urban protests over issues such as housing and bus fares. Over 70,000 Africans took part in squatter movements which established shanty towns at Orlando in 1944, and at Albertsville in 1945. Large-scale bus boycotts took place, with some involvement by SACP and ANC figures, but often led by residents or other political identities. High labour turnover in factories and very low wages contributed to increased activity of criminal gangs, which, whilst often apolitical and difficult to organize, sometimes liaised with the ANC — political gang-leaders mobilized in Benoni for the Defiance Campaign in 1952.[7] Strikes and boycotts may have made some moderate African nationalists feel uncomfortable, but could still be of some use to the ANC cause if solidarity was expressed.

African Miners, their Union, the '46 Strike, and the ANC

The beginnings of the first real mass trade union for South Africa's black miners was a small event — so small that history records very little about it, save that the initiative came from a meeting of the Transvaal African National Congress Executive in 1941.[8]

ANC writers can, with some justification, claim that the organization was, together with the SACP, responsible for the creation of the African Mine Workers' Union (AMWU), whose founding conference in August 1941 was arranged with the aid of both the Transvaal ANC and the SACP. James Majoro (SACP), Gaur Radebe (ANC/SACP) and SP Matseke, Chairman of the Transvaal ANC were prominent. Edwin Mofutsanyana (ANC/SACP) stated that 'the mines are the starting point and backbone of the national movement'.[9] The Committee to Organize African Mineworkers, formed in 1941, which made representations to the government that led to the Lansdowne Commission on Native Mine Wages, regarded itself as representing the ANC, and conveyed to Prime Minister Smuts a resolution from the August mineworkers conference (called by the Transvaal ANC) protesting 'against the exclusion of African Mine Workers from the cost of living allowance' and low wages.[10]

Xuma, endeavouring to incorporate the views of African miners and mine clerks, addressed the 1943 Lansdowne Commission on behalf of the ANC, forthrightly stating that Congress experience that many commissions were simply a device to 'quiet public clamour for certain reforms', and that the terms of the inquiry served 'to protect, and to entrench the position of, the Gold Mining Industry and the European mine workers'. The latter 'in his relation to the African mine worker, is more a capitalist than a worker'. He presented detailed statistics on the labour force, causes of its poverty and social ills, argued that 'we ... do not believe that some must enjoy the cream [of the gold industry] while others get only skim milk', and then related these facts to the political exclusion of Africans. The ANC called for abolition of the compound system, increased wages, repeal of anti-labour laws, and recognition of the AMWU. 'Conditions of African mine workers can never be what they should be until they have a recognized and registered trade union and the Mines & Works Act, the Native Labour & Regulations Act and the Pass Laws have been repealed'. Xuma has been portrayed as the 'chief motivator' of ANC resurgence. He helped introduce a more centralized structure and concise constitution to ensure the ANC became more than an annual meeting. He presented evidence, or represented Africans, to numerous commissions, including the Lansdowne and Smit committees. During 1946-1947, Xuma rejected government offers of union recognition excluding miners and farm workers, as a deliberate denial of 'fundamental rights of workers, namely collective bargaining'.[11] What is important here is not that Xuma, by occupation a doctor, was not a worker, but that politically the ANC was allying itself with workers.

JB Marks had not been involved with the union at the start,

but became President after Radebe. The committee formed to establish the union was an 'absolutely independent [from the ANC] body' according to Marks. Although the ANC 'supported [AMWU work in 1944-5] . . . there was no direct liaison, except that anytime I wanted speakers to go to a meeting . . . they would have ANC speakers there'. Xuma also supported the AMWU: 'he did on more than one occasion come to address our conferences . . . I think it had the full support' of the ANC. On the other hand, Marks insists that the Council of Non-European Trade Unions, CNETU, had nothing to do with the ANC.[12] The ANC had co-operated with CNETU, the latter noted, 'but the lack of finance and sufficient staff . . . makes it impossible to cope'.[13]

There is some evidence of communication between Xuma and the AMWU. In 1942 secretary James Majoro wrote to Xuma issuing an appeal for aid, as the large number of complaints were handled in 'spare time, we have no paid official'. Xuma also corresponded with mine labourers and clerks, writing in June 1943 to Enoch Njozala requesting information on miner housing, compounds, 'sex perversions', family separation, wages and recruiting, for the ANC's Lansdowne submission.[14] The venerable doctor maintained a healthy interest in miners, even if he was not given to taking part in radical strikes. Addressing the Lansdowne Commission Xuma outlined the history of the ANC and stated that its aims included to 'protect and raise the status of the African people in all spheres'. Miners faced deleterious social and health effects of compound life, and 'starvation wages' tempted some to 'traffic with their bodies'.[15]

Organizers of the African trade unions expressed the wish not to appear to be in 'conflict in any way' or to usurp 'any of the functions' of the ANC in the movement for recognition of the unions, according to Michael Scott. Paying greater attention to miners was also perhaps stimulated by a growing intellectual interest in miners and their world by African literati. Dhlomo and B.W. Vilikazi (died 1947) had begun to write of the mines in the 30s; Peter Abrahams' *Mine Boy* (1946) was a pioneering literary analysis of black miners' lives.[16]

Escalating prices, wages more or less static since 1900, food shortages, and frustration sparked a major mine strike of between 70-100,000 Rand mine workers in August 1946. Moodie suggests that *izibonda* (room leaders in the mine compounds) were responsible for much of the coordination of compound actions, especially on the East Rand.[17] One miner, Palama Lelosa, recounts his experience of how employer attitudes, the return of white miners from the war and the consequent demotion of blacks influenced his decision to join the strike:

> What I expected was that something would be done with it, to show that I had proved to be a faithful servant during the time of the difficulties [war]. But this wasn't done. Instead I was demoted on my job without any increment. I felt that now if people should suffer even when they had done their best under conditions that were trying, that because I am black I must be neglected. That is why I joined the 1946 strike.[18]

What was the attitude of the miners to class and national struggles? Walter Sisulu states that in his opinion he and other miners in the 30's did not know about the ANC. It is likely that many shared this ignorance. Here is a prime case of ANC leaders being portrayed as 'petit-bourgeois'. Xuma is accused by Hirson of lack of enthusiasm for the 1946 strike and of failing to attend mass meetings. Xuma, who had the year before addressed union conferences, did try and meet with Marks, only to find him arrested. But the ANC was not simply Xuma, and other members besides Marks were involved in the strike. The National Executive Committee met during the strike, with Xuma in the chair, in a a gathering which included trade unionists Dan Tloome, Gana Makabeni and Gosani. The call of the AMWU for all Africans to assist was noted, Xuma stating 'Congress was a national movement fighting side by side with African trade unions for the status of all Africans'. Another meeting on 26 August, after the strike, agreed to give the union financial aid.[19] Moodie suggests that the union delayed the strike for one week to mobilize supporters in the SACP and ANC to print and distribute leaflets, and Meli notes that 'a crucial role was played by CP and ANC members . . . who went out night after night to distribute union leaflets [and] . . . because of this work, the strike kept spreading'. On the other hand, inside the mines, Moodie has shown that, at least on the East Rand, it was the *isibonda* that mobilized miners. The ANC annual conference in December

1946 passed an unopposed motion by Cele 'for the fallen men in the African Mine Strike', and another for the 'fallen women of Springs'.

The fact that ANC and unions were 'organizationally distinct, each with separate membership, leadership and interests', should not be seen as unusual. They had different raisons d'être. If the ANC had been more closely involved it could have been accused of domination. What is important is that cooperation between the two groups did increase, that worker membership of the ANC increased, and that the strike accelerated these processes. Marks, asked about the level of ANC support for the union, stated:

> No, there was no support. Just because of not having been oriented towards the trade [union] movement . . . I didn't keep them well informed. There was not a regular report as to what developments were taking place in the trade union field . . . they also had to rely just on the atmosphere that was created.

Yet once the strike was on, the SACP 'were on the spot and so with the members of the ANC it was all hands on deck . . . they were all there'. Marks seems to be saying that the ANC was not involved in union affairs, but expressed solidarity in struggle. Characterization of the ANC as simply 'middle class' must come to terms with these facts,

A Worker-ANC Dialogue? Some Case Studies

The ANC's 1945 African Claims was drawn up by a committee of twenty-eight, including Xuma, Rev. James Calata, businessman Baloyi, journalist Richard Godlo, and the radicals Kotane, Mbeki, Mofutsanyana and Makabeni. It spoke of the right of self-determination of Africans in the face of 'the peculiar circumstances of a politically-entrenched European minority ruling a majority non-European population'. It also called for better labour, welfare and housing conditions, for peace, a Bill of Rights, a common voters roll, full female ANC membership, equal pay, a minimum wage, and union recognition. Xuma's preface referred to the ANC as 'the mass liberation movement'.[20] The ANC by now was 'profoundly influenced by their economic environment and responded to the widespread frustrations [and recognized] African emancipation involved more than the organization of the 'middle class'. . . Vigorous trade unions were recognized as an essential means to a just wage structure and a vital support for the national movement'.[21] ANC strategy now largely coincided with CPSA and union policies, facilitating ANC-worker unity. Workers active in the ANC, SACP or unions now had no major ideological obstacles to united action, although anti-communism influenced the ANCYL until the late 40s. Already by 1945 the ANC had declared that it was:

> Looked upon . . . by the broad masses of the African people as a National Liberation Movement . . . It is high time it is realized that our struggle . . . is two fold, not only are we nationally oppressed but we are also economically oppressed . . . It is, therefore, of prime importance that the African National Congress should take up the dual oppression as a whole, marching side by side with the African Trade Unions . . . The Africans and their Trade Unions have no semblance of democratic rights . . . That being the case we are inclined to think that the most important field is the 'INDUSTRIAL ARENA' wherein African Trade Unions have been, and are waging a fairly promising fight [but] fight as an isolated group. It is, therefore, incumbent upon the [ANC] to co-operate with the Trade Unions and fight the issue as a whole . . . to foster a spirit of national consciousness ; and to propagate the necessity of all Africans in industry to join Trade Unions and the National movement. Congress and the Trade Unions must march together. They are merely different aspects of one and the same movement and objective. All Trade Unionists must become members of Congress so that we can have a Labour Government in the African National Congress. [emphases added].[22]

This is a remarkable document in several respects. It was issued in an official National ANC bulletin in 1945, four years before the 1949 program, and one year before the miners' strike. It specifically identified unions as the most important field of work. It was possibly written by Dan Tloome; it had earlier appeared as a memorandum to Xuma under his name, although it may have been a joint work. However, it is inconceivable that Xuma did not know or approve its contents. Here is clear evidence that important ANC leaders identified closely with the workers.

HIE Dhlomo noted that 'of recent years the political struggle

has been given a new impetus by organized African labour ...
today the African is turning to the weapon of economics... for to
him it is a question of survival'. The way in which black workers
and unions approached ANC leaders also shows the close
interrelationship felt by both sides. CR Masekela, Secretary of the
Bantu Trained Nurses Association wrote to ZK Matthews of the
ANC and Natives Representative Council member, about
discrimination against black nurses. Martin Ncayo of Craddock,
employed by the Railways, wrote that:

> We blacks, work 10 hours a day while Europeans... take turns in
> resting at our expense... We have no holidays ... if you feel unwell
> and stay away from work, you are immediately dismissed... We
> have no houses in which to live... We live in tin shanties... We
> don't know what pay we can get per hour. We can not ask any
> questions for fear of being dismissed.[23]

Had he first contacted the union, or was that considered
dangerous? Why then write to an ANC/NRC leader unless
workers felt the ANC in some way represented their interests?

Albert Luthuli had worked as a teacher, and in 1950 drew
attention to legislative barriers to African workers 'limited by
state legislation and general attitudes of racial prejudice to the
category of unskilled worker', disadvantaged from the start by
poor nutrition and low wages which barely covered family
expenditure. This sort of awareness of industrial issues by
nationalist leaders of the ANC has been given too little attention.
The 1949 ANC Program of Action referred explicitly to the need
for 'consolidation of the industrial organization of the workers
for the improvement of their standard of living'.[24]

In 1952 the Defiance Campaign was launched and the ANC
was again moving amongst workers, but this time on a much
larger scale. The mass approach resulted in a swelling of
Congress ranks, from an estimated 7,000 to 100,000, particularly
in the Eastern Cape where membership was put at 60,000. Port
Elizabeth Africans called for a general strike, and at the regional
conference of the ANC at New Brighton in 1952, with delegates
representing 30,682 members, condemned the City Council for
suppressing African unions and the ANC. Walter Sisulu
addressed Port Elizabeth ANC supporters in 1954, stressing the

pivotal role of black workers:

> There is no need for me to tell you about the disabilities of the
> African people. You know that thousands are arrested every week
> under the notorious pass laws . . . living below the bread level
> because of low wages . . . We say to the Minister that the lovely
> homes, the schools . . . of the European children . . . are almost
> entirely due to the sweat and toil of the African worker.

Born in 1912, in a poor rural family, Sisulu stands apart from
many of the inner core of ANC leaders. He had neither higher
education nor professional credentials. He left school at age 15 to
work in the mines, cutting rock below ground, and in kitchens
and bakeries, before being sacked for leading a bakery strike. At
28 he joined the ANC, apparently after hearing AB Xuma speak.
He became prominent in the Youth League, and in 1949 was
elected as ANC Secretary-General. He recalls the ICU and
Garveyist Wellington movements, strong in the Eastern Cape, as
at 'the first time that political ideas began to work in my mind...
during the Wellington period linked with . . . Garvey'. Personal
resentment against the pass laws strengthened his radical
nationalist beliefs: 'I think the thing which pushed me, more than
anything else, is the question of the pass laws — that irritated me
right from the beginning'. However, when a gold miner on the
Rand, he and other miners generally did not know about the
ANC, indicating its remoteness, or inaccessibility, to the world of
miners. Yet lack of education was not an obstacle to class or
national consciousness:

> When I was fired from my job as a baker's 'boy', it was not
> necessary for me to read a book to understand that what I was
> experiencing was national oppression. When I was assaulted on
> the job, I did not need a degree to know that this was gross injustice
> . . . we did not accept the history that was taught to us. I remember
> in standard one being taught that Shaka was a murderer. But this
> was not what we understood from the lesson. Our understanding
> was that he united the Zulu people.[25]

A few months later, along with other ANC leaders, he was
banned. 'Despite all this', he wrote, [the] 'movement is growing
in strength, gaining new adherents and reaching new levels of
effectiveness'. Nelson Mandela asserted trade union and worker

rights, noting 'ties between the working people and the Congress have been greatly strengthened', urging members 'if you are not allowed to have your meetings publicly, then you must hold them over your machines in the factory, on the trains and buses'.[26] There is thus evidence of growing worker-ANC dialogue.

Some African wage earners were motivated to join the ANC by their work experiences.[27] Alfred Nzo qualified as a health inspector in 1951, the same year that he joined the ANC. 'As a health inspector I was brought face to face with the conditions under which the African people lived, and having known that there was an organization which concerned itself with their suffering, I became a member'. Mary Ranta had been a herd-girl, then a 'tea lady' at the Pretoria mint, and a typist for the African Iron and Steel Workers Union in 1946, becoming a union organizer in 1949. The previous year she had joined the ANC, apparently after watching a huge Congress demonstration. This may have led her to become an active unionist. A common slogan of the period, popularized by Luthuli, but preceding him, was for every unionist to join the ANC, and vice versa.

Wulf Sachs' psycho-portraits of John Chavafambira, an African *nyanga* (doctor) who turned to political activism after experiencing deep alienation, and Tshakada, a well-educated clerk, describing himself as a 'New African', show how office workers and others were swept up in the mass movement. Politicized by the 1945 Johannesburg bus boycott Chavafambira 'was no more merely a *nyanga* . . . [he] had become an effective propagandist . . . addressed small groups', and joined the protests of Mpanza, whilst Tshakada attended SACP and ANC meetings.

In some cases unionism can clearly be identified as a reason for people to affiliate themselves to the ANC. Eric Mtshali became a factory worker in the Lion matches factory in Durban and was active in campaigns on behalf of the Freedom Charter. Mtshali was a dock worker in Durban from the early fifties, at age 18, joining the dockers' union after encouragement by the radical Wilson Cele. He recalls that 'on the docks there were Indian workers, but it was mainly African unions on the docks at the time. But in Durban there is . . . a big group of the Indian working class. I must say in the 50's the Indian working class was very active and revolutionary'.

He did not immediately join a union on the docks, and adds that it was not strikes that determined his early political consciousness but the personal role of Cele. 'When I joined the unions it was through this comrade and he was the one who shaped my political thinking . . . he was my political mentor'. When first introduced

> to ANC politics, it did not appeal to me, because it was speaking of freedom which was a little bit far from my problems as a worker . . . a little bit abstract . . . as a trade unionist I thought my problems were going to be solved immediately because it means going to the boss, asking for higher wages, better conditions of work . . . But with the encouragement and education that I got from this comrade . . . and of course with other later, it became clear to me that trade unionism was not a solution to the problems of South Africa. It was at that time that I decided to join the ANC. It was 1953, I think, or 1954.

He joined the Clermont branch, 'a very big one and . . . mainly working class . . .it was not very difficult to organize the ANC in Clermont because the same people . . . we were organizing to join the ANC were the same workers [who] were in the unions'. Luthuli was also an important influence. Though he

> was a Christian . . . he had extraordinary qualities of combining Christians and Communists, workers and other sections of the population. I remember his call . . . that every ANC member must be a trade unionist, and every trade unionist must be a member of the ANC, and he went on to say SACTU is the spear and ANC is the shield. And that call . . . did not only help to build the ANC, but SACTU as well. It also cemented the relationship between ANC and SACTU to an extent that you can hardly find a person, even those days, who would say I'm a member of the ANC, a worker but not a trade unionist, or that I'm a trade unionist but I'm not in the ANC'.

Mark Shope, born in 1919, a herd-boy in Letaba village near Tzaneen in the northern Transvaal, son of a rail worker, supported his family from the age of seven until all the family cattle died during the depression. He recalls 'we used to make our living by going along picking bones along the river . . . and then you get a packet of mealie meal'. He 'had no chance of going to school' and began working as a farm labourer, earned 3/6 a month, picking oranges and watering oranges trees, then as a kitchen worker. He took part in his first strike at the age of sixteen, and worked in the gold mines from 1935-39, experiencing the 'ruthless regimented' compounds and indunas,with no complaints avenue. Shope then worked in the railways, and for the Johannesburg City Council in 1940. In 1941 he was employed as a messenger in the Director General of War Supply. After the war he was a laundry worker, becoming an organizer for the Laundry Workers Union, then union chairman in 1952, the same year that he was inspired by the Defiance Campaign to join the ANC, later becoming General Secretary of SACTU. This was the same period, and appears to be the same sort of inspiration that influenced Mabooe, as noted above. Shope was in a mine strike in 1935 'but it didn't mean anything to me'. By the time of a laundry strike in May 1946, and the miners' strike of August, 'for the first time I became aware of what was happening ... beginning to understand ... what life is all about' and he recalls attending the miners' strike meeting. His awakening was probably related to the radical political traditions of the laundry union, but he states that it was 'only after the Nationalist Party came to power that most people began to realize that now we are faced with a real enemy and we must fight'.

This suggests that strikes, per se, do not necessarily precipitate a change in political consciousness, but that it is the interaction of political forces with economic struggles that are more likely to induce changed thinking. Although more advanced, more politically conscious sections of the labour movement may have been aware of the gambits of Smuts and the creation of false consciousness about union recognition amongst Africans, it took a major political shock to rouse large numbers. Although Shope's evidence may well be coloured by a desire to justify the Congress Alliance, his recollection is that:

> From the trade union point of view, the African trade unions, since their very inception in 1919 . . . have never found themselves separated from the main political, or immediate, goal, that is of joining hands with the ANC. It is true that at certain stages, the ICU

was so popular among the people that it nearly overclouded [the ANC], but as time went on there was this question of looking at the struggle of South Africa not only from the trade union point of view but also from the national liberation struggle . . . the African trade unions in South Africa had always found themselves on the progressive side of the trade union movement . . . In the 1940s CNETU . . . always fought not only just for higher wages, better working conditions . . . it fought also for the freedom of our people, that is, it was in line with the national liberation movement, the African National Congress . . . We believe that the working class has got a role to play in politics and . . . that in any struggle, or in any revolution, the outcome . . . in history has always depended on what role the working class is playing. Whether it plays a passive role . . . or it plays a real political role . . . After all, what is politics if its not food that you have to eat, if its not the roof under which you have to sleep, the clothes you've got, the education of the children. These affect the workers daily.

After finishing only primary school, John Nkadimeng, born in Sekhukhuneland in 1925, was a domestic worker in Germiston. Becoming a factory worker in Johannesburg he lived in a hostel and recalls where he read Roux's *Time Longer than Rope* (1948) . He took a job in a tobacco factory where he experienced harsh conditions and strikes, joining the Tobacco Workers' Union in 1950, and, following another strike for wages, the ANC : 'I was shop steward. We were vomitted by our factory'. Others were re-employed but he and the union secretary were arrested, and then sacked in 1952. He became a CNETU organizer, then first National Organizer, and General Secretary of SACTU.

Stephen Dlamini, born in 1913, was at first a teacher, but as a result of discrimination left his teaching job and also stopped going to church. 'When I left my schooling, I became a teacher, and then because of the exploitation of teachers and so on and so forth, then I decided to go and work in a garage in Durban'. In the 1930s he was selling petrol in the Transvaal and Free State. Later he became a factory worker in the textile industry, helping create the African Textile Workers' Union, of which he was eventually chairman. He was also active in the Municipal and Milling Workers' Union. In 1954 he was elected to the ANC Natal executive in 1954:

In fact I created the union and got the comrades in the industry together . . . a hard job, getting together, to fight the employers for higher wages... We used to also hive [out] newspapers, party newspapers... I became a member of the CP in Durban in 1935 ... I stayed in the textile industry until I got to Robben Island, for 29 or 28 years.

He is clearcut on the relationship between workers and the ANC, in fact the workers were 100% behind the ANC, behind the Defiance Campaign, behind the Revolution, because they were conscious of the fact that there could be no freedom unless you get rid of the bourgeoisie in South Africa'.

Ben Baartman joined the ANC the year after the 1946 mine strike, at the age of 23, while working in Worcester. He suggests there was flexibility in the ANC, that 'if you couldn't pay [dues], you still got the [ANC] membership card'. He later became a textile worker and joined the Textile Workers' Industrial Union, which worked closely with the ANC. 'The ANC and TWIU didn't have separate ways of working. You would find that the leaders in the trade union were also leaders in the ANC... In Worcester you could not separate a trade unionist and an ANC member'.

Another poorly educated worker was former herd-boy, Greenwood Ngotyana, born in 1922, who did not pass standard 6 until aged 20. He later worked as a rail labourer in Cape Town, and organized for the Non-European Railway and Harbour Workers' Union. In 1951 he was assistant secretary of the Western Cape ANC, as well as being secretary of the Cape Western Advisory Boards and Vigilance Associations.

The list can be expanded with case after case. Alpheus Maliba, the son of a peasant, was born in 1901 in the northern Transvaal, became a factory worker in Johannesburg in 1935 but maintained close links with the rural areas. He founded the Zoutpansberg Cultural Association and the rural sister-organization, Zoutpansberg Balemi Association. Joining the SACP in 1936 after contact with the party night school, he edited Mbofolowo, the Venda language section of *Inkululeko*.. He was also a leader of the ANC. Pious Mei, born in 1912, joined the ANC in 1936, went on to become a leader of the African Textile Workers's Union and of the Natal ANC in the 1950s. Peter Nthite, born 1929, son of a labourer, worked as a driver after leaving school, joining the ANC in the 1952 Defiance Campaign.

Conclusion

From its inception, the development of the ANC has been entwined with the aspirations of the black workers of South Africa. Characterizations of the ANC leadership as petit-bourgeois do not tell the whole story. Without the support of workers the ANC could not have become a mass movement. Its aspirations to dominate the political landscape of 'the new South Africa' likewise depend on its continued ability to attract support from workers.

Notes

1   The ANC was then the South African Native National Congress (SANNC).

2   See *Cape Times,* 17 December 1929; P. Walshe, *The Rise of African Nationalism in South Africa : the African National Congress 1912-1952* (London : Hurst, 1971), p. 243 ; P. ka I. Seme, The African National Congress: Is it Dead? (s.n.:n.d. [ca.1933]) in Carter Karis Collection (henceforth CKC), reel 14A, pp.1-4, & his 'Support Congress Clubs and Ensure Employment', Umteteli wa Bantu 10 November 1934, in which he supports Congress Clubs to 'encourage all Native business enterprises ... [and] help the Native shopkeeper, the hawker and the pedlars ... The chiefs will be able to get their motor cars more cheaply ... we should always remember that it is the duty of the Congress to satisfy the Minister of Native Affairs of our good intentions'. Little wonder that radicals such as Gilbert Coka gave the ANC a wide berth at this time ; J. G. Coka, 'Congress Wash-Out', Umsebenzi 25 Aug. 1934, counted 12 participants at one ANC conference session ; Umsebenzi 25 April 1930 ; Abantu-Batho 30 April 1931.

3   Walshe, pp. 256-263. See J. Gomas, *100 Years of 'Emancipation of Slaves': Smash the Chains of Slavery! (a Call to National & Social Emancipation)* (Cape Town : CPSA , 1934), pp.5, 9, 15-16; D. Musson, *Johnny Gomas: Voice of the Working Class* (Cape Town : Buchu, 1989) pp. 88-94 ; R. Alexander, 'Johnny Gomas as I Knew Him', *South African Labour Bulletin,* 15 (1991), pp.80-83; J. Gomas, "Now How is this 'Civilised Labour Policy' to be Fought", *Umsebenzi* , 16 February 1935.

4   A.B. Xuma, 'Bridging the Gap Between White & Black in South
         Africa', paper presented to Conference of European & Bantu
         Christian Student Associations, Fort Hare, 27 June-3 July 1930
         (Lovedale : Lovedale Press, n.d.): 'when one complains ... Native
         wages in the mines are low ... one is, at once, told that the Native
         miner receives more wages in kind ... However when the Native
         worker becomes a phthisis victim, the wages in kind are never
         included in ... compensation'; Evidence to Native Economic
         Commission, 22 May 1931, Xuma, Evidence Given Before the
         Kaffir Beer Commission, September 1941 (S.l: n.d.), p.6 ; Xuma
         Papers (henceforth XP) reel 2 ; Africans were 'working for the
         same wage in cash or in kind as was paid my father some fifty
         years ago', p.2. Xuma experienced the rigours of manual work
         when a student in the U.S.; J. Burger, [Leo Marquard], *The Black
         Man's Burden* (London : Gollancz, 1943), p.210.

5   Umlindi we Nyanga 15 March 1939 ; speech of a 'Bantu delegate
         to a Conference held at Adams College in Natal' cited in C.F.
         Miles-Cadman, *Socialism for South Africa* (Johannesburg: SA
         Labour Party, [1941]), p.97.

6   Interview by Sheridan Johns, April 1964, in CKC reel 2:XM42:94.

7   T. Moll,'Did the Apartheid Economy "Fail"', *Journal of Southern
         African Studies*, 17 (1991), pp.271-291; CPSA, 'House for All'
         (n.d.); CPSA, 'The People Overflow' (CPSA, n.d.), pp.7-8 ; By
         1947/8 Africans in manufacturing comprised 308,080, compared
         to 210,355 whites and 74, 795 'Coloureds'. Nationwide they
         comprised 47% of the total manufacturing, 88% of the mining
         and 92% of the farming work force. Over all, urban Africans
         were about 23.1% of the national African population in 1946, up
         from 12.5% in 1921: see Report of the Industrial Legislation
         Commission of Enquiry (U.G. 62-51) (Botha Commission), pp. 7-
         11, 18; *Union of South Africa. Population Census, 7 May 1946*, v. 1 p.
         39. S.B. Ngcobo, 'The Response of Africans to Industrial
         Employment'. *Race Relations Journal*, 21 (1954), pp.10-17 noted
         an increase of urban African women from 147,000 in 1921 to 357,
         000 in 1936, and 642,000 in 1946. B. Hirson, *Yours for the Union*
         (London: Zed, 1989), chapter 12 ; P. Bonner 'The Politics of Black
         Squatter Movements on the Rand, 1944-1952', *Radical History
         Review*, no.46/7 (1990), pp.89-116 Features of the Grievances
         Regarding the Passenger Transport Operating between
         Alexandra Township & the City of Johannesburg: Specially
         Presenting the Women's Case [s.n., n.d.], in XP reel 10, also noted
         in Hirson, pp.138-41 ; A.B. Xuma, Memorandum of Evidence on
         Behalf of the Residents of Alexandra Township 27 September9
         43, XP, reel 10.

8   'Toussaint', [pseud.], *A Distant Clap of Thunder* (London:

Inkululeko, 1986), p.1.

9   F. Meli, *South Africa Belongs to Us: a History of the ANC* (London: Currey, 1988), pp.103-4: 'the ANC played a crucial role in establishing the union, with the active participation of a number of communists'.

10   M. Scott, *A Time to Speak* (London: Faber, 1958), p.115 ; Transvaal African Congress, Circular letter of Gaur Radebe, Secretary for Mines, 9 June 1941, re 'African Mine Workers' in CKC reel 3B 2:DA21:41/1; letter of Committee to Organize African Mineworkers to Smuts, 12 Sept. 1941, signed by Radebe and A. Msitshana, annexure B to AMWU Evidence. XP reel 4; C.R. Diamond, 'African Labour Problems on the South African Gold Mines with Special Reference to the Strike of 1946', M.A. thesis, University of Cape Town 1969, p.114.

11   A.B. Xuma, ANC, Evidence Given Before the Native Mine Wages Commission ... July 13 1943 ... on Behalf of the ANC, pp. 9-17, XP reel 4 ; 'The interests of the ANC and the SACP in the mine workers were not entirely new although the vigour ... unionization was ... pursued was unprecedented' ... the Transvaal ANC was 'less inclined towards parliamentary politics, partly because blacks never had the vote in the Transvaal and partly because the gold mines were such an overwhelming reality for most blacks'; W. James, 'From Segregation to Apartheid: Miners and Peasants in the Making of a Racial Order, South Africa 1930-1952', Ph.D, University of Wisconsin, 1982, pp.64, 94-98; J.P. Hendricks, 'From Moderation to Militancy: a Study of African Leadership & Political Reactions in South Africa, 1936-1960', Ph.D., University of Michigan, 1983, pp. 3, 8-9; Xuma, Evidence to the Interdepartmental Committee of Enquiry Concerning Economic, Health & Social Conditions of Africans in Urban Areas, 11 Oct. 1941, XP reel 6.

12   Notes of interview by S. Johns, April 1964, pp. 12-13, in CKC reel 2:XM42:94. In an earlier interview with the late Gwendolen Carter, Marks stated that the union reached a maximum of 20,000 members, enroling members by the lights of police cars. A.K. Brooks, 'From Class Struggle to National Liberation: the Communist Party of South Africa, 1940 to 1950', M.A. thesis, Sussex University, 1967, p.71 suggests the ANC was incapable of launching the AMWU alone.

13   ANC (Transvaal). Report of the Provincial Secretary to the Annual Provincial Conference, Sept. 29 - Oct. 1 1945, p. 2, in CKC reel 3B, 2:DA21:30/3.

14   Letters: Majoro to Xuma, 30 May 1942, XP reel 3 ; Xuma to Njozala, 30 June 1943 ; reply by Njozala 4 July 1943, XP reel 4,

who estimated a miner could only save £18 a year on their current wage of 2/- per shift.

15   A.B. Xuma, Evidence to the Natives Mine Wages Commission, in XP, reel 5. Xuma sent a form letter to African contacts regarding mine conditions. One reply was from induna Daniel Denalane of the Robinson Deep Mine, who on the question of sexuality claimed 'every Shangaan youngster leaving his father's home to work on the Mine is destined to be a 'wife' ... Faction fights have been known to be caused by this filthy thing'; letter to Xuma, 25 June 1943, in XP reel 5.

16   See letter Michael Scott to Xuma, 3 September 1943, XP reel 3; E. Gunner,'Literature and Apartheid', in J. Lonsdale (ed.), *South Africa in Question?* (London : Currey, 1988), pp.217-233, pp. 221-7.

17   T. Dunbar Moodie, "The Moral Economy of the Black Miners' Strike of 1946," *Journal of Southern African Studies*, 13 (1986), pp.1-18, 33.

18   Interview, Apartheid, producer Brian Lapping (Granada TV, 1986), with permission (transcripts ICS archives).

19   *Strike Bulletin of the AMWU* , 4 (15 August 1946), pp.1-2; *Cape Times* 16 August 1946; Hirson, pp.178-9: Xuma 'was not a keen supporter of trade unions and wanted funds for the ANC from the Bantu Welfare Trust, which had connections with the Chamber of Mines' (p.170) ; ANC. National Executive Working Committee Minutes, 13 August 1946, in S.M. Molema Papers, ICS (M842); Moodie, p.31.

20   ANC. African Claims [1945], pp. i-ii, 5-6, 9, 15-16. The ANC produced 10,000 copies of African Claims, costing £160.15/- ; invoice 2 September 1944, Xuma Papers, reel 8.

21   Walshe, pp.275-77, 294, 307, 320.

22   'The ANC & the African Trade Unions', *ANC Bulletin*, [1945], XP reel 10 ; Hirson, pp. 116,121. See also, D. Tloome, The African National Congress & African Trade Unions [n.d.] handwritten memorandum to [A.B. Xuma] President- General ANC, in XP, reel 8.

23   H.I.E. Dhlomo, 'The African Artist & Society', *Ilanga lase Natal* 5 March 1949, in N.W. Visser (ed.), 'H.I.E. Dhlomo: Literary Theory & Criticism', in *English in Africa*, 4 (1977), pp.71-72;; letters to Z. K. Matthews 14 April 1944, 30 December 1942, in Z.K. Matthews Papers ICS Archives (M932) B.1.1.

24   A.J. Luthuli, 'The Policy of the State in the Union of South Africa Hinders the African from Making His Fullest Possible Contribution to the Development of the Country', Mss. of address to Pietermaritzburg City Parliamentary Debating

Society, 25 September 1950, pp.7-8, in *Luthuli Papers* ; statement by G. Mzamane, D. W. Bopape, Bloemfontein, 17 December 1949 in H. Joseph, *If This Be Treason* (London: Deutsch, 1963), pp.185-7.

25   Walshe, pp. 402-3 ; *Advance,* 6 November 1952 ; Speech Delivered by W.M. Sisulu, Secretary-General of ANC, [Port Elizabeth], 28 March 1954, in CKC, reel 14A; *Walter Max Ulyate Sisulu* (London: SATIS, 1982), pp. 6-8 ; N. Gordimer, 'Walter Sisulu' [a biographical essay] in CKC, reel 14A. He 'did not go beyond standard two', W. Sisulu, *The Road to Liberation* (30th University of Cape Town T.B. Davie Memorial Lecture, 1990), p.3 ; 'Walter Sisulu : a Leader Rooted in Challenging Racism', *New Nation*, 27 October 1989; comment to the author, Perth, 23 August 1991.

26   Statement of W.M. Sisulu, 20 August 1954, in CKC, reel 14A. In the fifties, as Tom Lodge notes, there was little history writing by the ANC; 'Charters from the Past: the ANC & its Historiographical Traditions', *Radical History Review* 46/7 (1990). But there was J. A. Calata's, 'A Short History of the ANC' (1957), mimeo, [in ICS Archive, *Horvitch Papers* E/5]. This was more a set of notes for Congress members than history, but exhibited two interesting points : that historical tradition was alive in the ANC, and that the move to defiance was seen as having little alternative ; N. Mandela, 'No Easy Walk to Freedom' [not the book, n.d., ca. 1953], pp. 5-6 mimeo, in CKC, reel 2: XM33:84/2.

27   The remaining case studies in this chapter are taken from: *Counter-Attack,* 5 August 1959; J. Hadebe, 'Mary Ranta', *Fighting Talk* , March, 1957; W. Sachs, *Black Anger* (New York: Grove Press, 1947), pp. 316-22 (Tshakada: 'we are organised workers ... we want to create leaders, organise masses, establish contact' *ibid.,* pp.136-37, 164, 303) ; T. Karis and G. Carter, *From Protest to Challenge:* v. 4, *Political Profiles 1882-1964* (Stanford : Stanford University Press, 1972), pp. 70,87, 113, 121, 159; CKC, reel 14A; interviews of author with Mark Shope, Eric Mtshali, and John Nkadimeng, Lusaka, May 1989 ; M. Shope, 'Black Gold', *Sechaba*, v.8, no.6 1974, pp.8-11, p.10; M. Shope, 'SACTU's Role in the Developing Struggle', *Sechaba*. 2, no.8 (1968), pp.3-6, p.6 ; 'John (Kgwana) Nkadimeng', 'Treason Trial Bulletin Biography' no.6 [n.d. c1956?], in CKC, reel 13A 2:XN39:91/2; Walshe, p.257; interview, Steve Dlamini, Lusaka, May 1989 ; B. Baartman, *The Autobiography of a South African Textile Worker* (London : SACTU, 1988), pp. 11-12, 19 ; 'Alpheus Maliba', *Umsebenzi* (n.s.) 4, no. 2 (1988), p.8 ; H.J. & R. Simons, *Class & Colour in South Africa 1850-1950* (London: IDAF, 1969), p.538; CKC, reel 13A 2:XN21:96/1.

14

Unions, Direct Action and Transition in South Africa

Glenn Adler, Judy Maller, and Eddie Webster

Introduction

F van Zyl Slabbert, a leading theoretician of the transition process in South Africa recently proposed that 'the nature, extent and outcome of transition (away from racial domination) in South Africa is determined primarily by the internal dynamics of our situation and not by external pressures'.[1] He distinguishes between planned and unplanned pressures, identifying dramatic black population growth, the accelerated flow of black people to the cities, the growth of a disaffected youth in the cities, and the demands of the economy for a more rational utilization of resources, as the major causes of unplanned internal change.

However, when van Zyl Slabbert turns to identify the 'planned' causes of transition, he becomes curiously opaque. While acknowledging that 'the struggle' against white domination had 'the most profound impact on the current transition', he makes no references to the character or composition of the extra-parliamentary opposition. Instead he points to the extent to which President FW De Klerk's speech on 2nd February, 1990 (where he began the process of political transition by unbanning the African National Congress [ANC], the Pan-Africanist Congress [PAC] and the South African

Communist Party [SACP]) 'caught the opponents of the regime by surprise'. 'They were', he says, 'simply not prepared for the speed of De Klerk's shift to transition politics . . . . Until 2 February the conventional paradigm of change prevalent, in at least the ANC, was one of revolutionary transition and seizure of power over decades, not one of negotiated transition over months.'

This chapter focuses on a neglected factor — and actor — in the process of transition away from white minority domination — the labour movement. The labour movement in South Africa played an important part in precipitating and is playing an equally crucial role in securing the transition to a democratic order. The centrality of the labour movement in the South African case thus has important implications for comparative discussions of transitions to democracy.[2]

In a comparative study of Southern Europe and Latin America, Valenzuela argues that the labour movement occupies a special place among the forces of civil society during the transition from authoritarianism.[3] He gives several reasons for this: the organized network of the labour movement gives it greater capacity for effective and extensive mobilization at critical moments than other social groups, its mass base normally has specific common interests and a politically tinged collective identity rooted in a lived history, and, most important, the labour movement can disrupt the economy. Labour's demands, says Valenzuela, cannot be lightly ignored.

However, for labour to achieve its specific objectives and an overall transition to democracy, the labour movement needs to be able to mobilize in certain circumstances and restrain its membership on other occasions. For this mobilization-restraint sequence to happen a number of conditions are necessary. First, it requires a strong labour movement; second, a movement which is relatively united; third, a close alliance between the labour movement and political movements; finally, and most important, the labour movement needs to have a close working relationship with the transition elites during the transition process, but should not be in government itself. 'This should insure', says Valenzuela, 'that the labour movement's narrow goals will not be completely neglected in the course of re-democratization, while the fact that the transition's leading elites are not directly identified with labour should facilitate the creation of industrial relations and other labour related institutions that business will accept.'

All of the conditions identified by Valenzuela are present in the process of transition currently underway in South Africa. The labour movement in South Africa is both strong and united. 45% of the work force, or approximately 3 million workers covered by the Labour Relations Act are now organized into unions.[4] Although there are five different union federations, the largest, the Congress of South African Trade Unions (COSATU) with one and quarter million members, has more members than the others combined.[5] COSATU consists of 14 nation-wide industrial unions with extensive and strong shop floor structures, giving them power from the factory floor to the national level.[6] These unions have extensive constitutional requirements entrenching worker control over the union's office-bearers, and have strong traditions of accountability of leadership to rank-and-file members. During the last four years there have been important moves towards greater unity between COSATU and the next-largest federation, the National Council of Trade Unions [NACTU]. Finally, through the last decade a close working alliance emerged between COSATU and, first, internal organizations in the political traditions of the ANC, and later the ANC itself. These developments were consolidated after 1990 in the form of a tripartite alliance between COSATU, the ANC, and the SACP.[7]

With regard to the fourth condition — the relationship with the transition elites during the transition process, indications are that the labour movement is increasingly likely to want to maintain its distance from any government that emerges during the transition process. Jayendra Naidoo, COSATU negotiations coordinator argues that the nature of the tripartite alliance will change once the ANC is in government as a result of its cross-class electoral base. An ANC government, Naidoo writes, 'will have a broader responsibility and constituency beyond the working class — including people who are our so-called class enemies'.[8] As Valenzuela argues, 'Not forming direct part of the government should spare the labour-linked political leadership from becoming identified with possibly unpopular economic measures, allowing the labour movement leadership as a whole to focus more on rebuilding and extending labour's political and union organizations'.[9]

The combination of these factors can lead to a situation where labour's goals and the process of transition to democracy are complementary rather than antagonistic.   The labour movement has the power to shape policy in the interests of workers, and the capacity to restrain its members when its actions are likely to antagonize established interests. But this restraint depends on the possibility that labour can achieve its specific objectives within the transition process; if this occurs, Valenzuela argues, the labour movement will accord legitimacy to the transition process itself, which will be a strong foundation for the ensuing democratic regime.

We argue two points about the process of transition. First, we maintain that it was the increasingly mass character of internal resistance to white domination that was decisive in challenging the legitimacy of the regime. The labour movement was a crucial actor at the centre of this challenge, employing a strategy of non-violent direct action, especially in the form of the political strike, or as it is referred to in South Africa, the 'stayaway'.[10]

South Africa's overt racial oppression and political authoritarianism has ensured that the concerns of organized workers are not limited to collective bargaining issues, but extend to broader social and political issues involving equality and democracy. The labour movement has therefore been characterized as 'social movement unionism', because it attempts 'to link production to wider political issues'.[11] Social movement unionism combines organization around factory-floor issues with an engagement in community and state policy. As Ronaldo Munck has argued, social movement unionism involves 'trade unions who turn to political answers for their members' problems'.[12] They therefore engage in alliances with political organizations, coordinating action and advancing their common interests.   Finally, they reach out to a broader constituency beyond their own members.

The notion of social movement unionism engages with the

classical debates on the role of trade unions in capitalist society and social transition. It contests what Hyman has labelled the 'pessimistic tradition', descended from Lenin and also Michels, which holds that unions play a limited if not conservative role due to their foundation in capitalist relations of production and their subsequent bureaucratization.[13] Instead, social movement unions by virtue of their overt political intervention and alliances can play a key role in political and economic change.

Our second point about the labour movement's role in the process of transition is that the use of the stayaway tactic changed in the late eighties, marking a significant shift in union strategy from *demonstrative opposition* to *conditional participation* with employers and state structures such as the National Manpower Commission (NMC). The NMC is a state body with power to investigate labour affairs and advise the Minister of Manpower on labour legislation. Until very recently, it was made up entirely of business representatives, white state functionaries, and representatives from the white trade unions. Although officially open to the unions with large black memberships which emerged in the 1970s, these unions systematically boycotted the NMC, along with all other state structures in light of their racist and undemocratic nature. Their non-participation was part of a broader rejection of state structures by the anti-apartheid movement, a policy known as militant abstentionism.[14]

By treating state structures such as the NMC as negotiating forums, and backing-up its bargaining position with mass action such as stayaways, the labour movement has developed practices of *radical reform* rather than adhering to a Leninist notion of *revolutionary rupture*. Thus the campaign of mass action between 1988 and 1989 against the amendments to the Labour Relations Act ushered in a new era characterized by the politics of reconstruction.[15] In the process, the labour movement has logically extended a strategy of negotiation backed up with industrial action first developed on the shop floor to contest managerial authority. More recently this strategy has been employed to influence state policy. 'It's another stage of advance in the negotiating process', according to COSATU Negotiations Coordinator Naidoo, 'that we've been participating in for the last

20 years, moving it logically onto a higher level because we are unable to solve certain things unless we bring the government in'.[16]

The chapter is concerned with exploring the relationship between the labour movement, direct action and the process of transition. First we trace the emergence and development of the stayaway as a tactic of resistance to apartheid, and show how the effectiveness of the tactic was closely linked to the growth of the labour movement in the eighties and its evolving relationship with community organizations. Next we trace the shift in the use of the stayaway tactic in the late eighties, when it was used as part of the anti-Labour Relations Act campaign, which resulted in an historic accord between labour, employers, and the state over the restructuring of labour relations. The third section analyses the November 1991 stayaway which formed part of a campaign against the unilateral imposition by the government of Value Added Tax (VAT). These two campaigns propelled the emergence of a National Economic Negotiating Forum (NENF) between labour, employers and the state to negotiate macroeconomic policy.

The chapter concludes by raising the question as to the impact on the labour movement of its involvement in corporate-like state and employers structures. Will participation demobilize the movement, leading to a decline in its mass character as it is distanced from its base? Or, will participation help to ensure that the goals of the labour movement are achieved and that there is a successful transition to a new democratic order in South Africa?

It is of course true that certain forms of participation could lead to the first result. However we conclude that there are reasons to be optimistic that the second course will be more likely in South Africa. We identify four factors in the labour movement which will facilitate both a successful transition to democracy, and a transition which favours labour's interests. These are 1) the continuing power and unity of the labour movement; 2) its traditions and practices of democracy; 3) its character as social movement unionism which actively represents working class interests in the political arena; and 4) its independence from, yet good working relationship with the opposition political groups who are likely to form the next government.

The Emergence of the Stayaway Tactic in South Africa

The stayaway emerged as a specific tactic of black resistance to apartheid when, in December 1949, the ANC adopted the Program of Action aimed at non-collaboration, a disobedience campaign and a general withdrawal of labour.[17] The stayaway was first used as a tactic on 1 May 1950 as a protest to mark the general dissatisfaction of the African people with their position in the country. A further seven stayaways were called by the Congress Alliance over the next decade with varying degrees of success.

Activists soon realized that the question of organization was the key to a campaign's success. As the Congress newspaper *New Age* concluded after the failure of the 1958 stayaway 'it is significant that the stoppage was most complete wherever organization was best . . . . The only answer is to build the strength of the people on sure foundations, to organize the workers, to give them machinery in which they have confidence.'[18]

Table 14.1
Black Stayaways in South Africa Since World War II

Date	Proposed duration	Area	Objective	Organizer	Success rate
1 May 1950	1 day	Witwatersrand	General political protest: Communism Act	CP , ANC & Indian Congress	Partial success
26 June 1950	1 day	National	Racial Discrimination Communism Act	ANC & Indian Congress	Partial success
7 May 1951	1 day	Western Cape	Against removal of 'Coloured' vote	Franchise Action Council	Partial success
26 June 1957	1 day	National	£ a day	Congress Alliance	Success
14-16 April 1958	3 days	National	Protest General Elections	Congress Alliance	Failure
21 March 1960	Indefinite	National	Pass Laws	PAC	Partial success

Date	Proposed duration	Area	Objective	Organizer	Success rate
28 March 1960	1 day	National	Day of Mourning	Congress Alliance	Success
29-31 May 1961	3 days	National	National Convention	National Action Council	Partial success
4-6 August 1976	3 days	Johannesburg	Bantu Education & detained students	Soweto SRC	Success
23-25 August 1976	3 days	Johannesburg	" "	" "	Success
13-15 Sept. 1976	3 days	PWV	" "	" "	Success
16-17 Sept. 1976	2 days	W. Cape	" "	?	Success
1-5 Nov. 1976	5 days	PWV	" "	SSRC	Failure
16-17 June 1977	2 days	PWV	Commemorate 1976 Soweto Rising	" "	Failure

This change in emphasis led to the establishment of factory committees which were to combine both industrial and political functions. Congress argued the need to combine both functions, because wage issues were very often unrealisable in straight trade union terms. Workers would be prosecuted if they made demands that led to strike action; the only way to take up wage issues was in the context of a climate which would force the government and employers to give concessions.[19]

The last stayaway of the 'decade of defiance' was in May 1961 when the Congress Alliance called for three days of protest action against the declaration of a Republic and demanded a genuine national convention. Although the stayaway was only partially successful nation-wide, a high degree of success was recorded in certain industries. A survey carried out by SACTU at the time concluded that workers who are organized into trade unions are more responsive to a political call than unorganized workers. 'Their trade union activity has given them heightened political consciousness and they also respond more readily when the appeal is made on a factory as opposed to a residential basis, as they feel that there is less chance of dismissal if the whole factory is involved.'[20]

1961 marks the end of the decade of non-violent extra-parliamentary political activity. The partial success of the stayaway in April and the tightening up of state repression, led to a change in strategy. Congress leaders began to ask whether it was appropriate to continue to follow a non-violent strategy when dealing with a government that was now determined to crush such actions as stayaways. In June the ANC decided to launch a sabotage campaign, aimed at government property and mounted by the newly-formed secret ANC armed wing *Umkhonto we Sizwe* in December 1961.

In the wake of this decision to embark on armed struggle, anti-apartheid activists abandoned a fifty-year tradition of exclusively non-violent methods of struggle. Thereafter, despite the ANC's expressed commitment to continuing the 'political struggle' — mass mobilization — the organization devoted its energies increasingly to the sabotage campaign inaugurated in 1961 and to the training of guerrillas in preparation for armed struggle. A gradual withdrawal of resources within the

Congress Alliance from a program of non-violent direction action followed.[21]

In addition to the rechannelling of cadres, intellectuals and material energies toward guerrilla warfare, the ANC's decision had a widespread and profound ideological effect on political activists. Similar shifts toward armed struggle took place in smaller organizations, including the PAC and sections of the Liberal Party known as the African Resistance Movement (ARM). The perception of non-violent sanctions as an ineffective form of struggle was underscored by Nelson Mandela's statement at the Rivonia trial, that in the aftermath of the Sharpeville massacre in March, 1960, the leadership had decided that the 'time had come to fight'. The fact that the campaigns of the fifties and early sixties had produced no political and social change was taken as evidence that non-violent direct action had tried and had failed. It was a conclusion that entailed limited evaluation of ANC strategy, tactics and organizational capacities, and instead was broadly translated as a rejection of non-violent methods of struggle in existing conditions in South Africa. The ideologically negative connotation that non-violent sanctions acquired, together with massive state repression, produced a long hiatus in popular struggle until the seventies.

Important structural changes took place in the economy in the sixties which laid the grounds for the emergence of new black trade unions. The South African economy expanded rapidly, economic growth, bringing important changes in the relations of production in industry. The growing concentration and centralization of capital led to the growth in the absolute size of workplaces and a tremendous advance in their technological sophistication. Most manufacturing industries experienced increasing demand for semiskilled and skilled labour, which could not be met either by local white or immigrant workers. The changes allowed for large numbers of black workers to fill the void.

These structural changes in the economy created an important base on which black workers could build industrial unions. The unofficial erosion of job reservation was accompanied by growing awareness and confidence by black workers in their economic power. With recognition of this emerging terrain for direct action came renewed efforts to revitalize and develop black trade unions. Gradually a few surviving black trade unions as well as newly-formed ones began testing their strength, suffering numerous defeats, but also gaining important victories.[22]

These fledgling unions made important strategic innovations which profoundly affected trade union development as well as the course of political struggle in South Africa. Their adoption of a *strategic* use of power introduced a new way of operating. Where possible, these unions sank deep roots on the shop floor, transformed as it was by the dramatic economic changes of the 1960s and 1970s. On the shop floor, unions could develop a strong factory-based leadership, less prominent than head-office activists, and closely tied to their members. With the strong backing of their workers, factory leaders had the power to push for concessions from management, which not only created space for further advances, but also won concrete improvements in workers' conditions, thereby reassuring them of the efficacy of direct action. There were two important components to the union's approach to the strategic use of power: 1) democratic processes to win voluntary consent from members for action and for restraint when necessary; and 2) tactical flexibility which included a capacity to distinguish principles from tactics, and to choose those tactics most likely to succeed, including negotiation and compromise. These strategies, in the new economic conditions of the 1970s, facilitated the growth of the trade union movement, ultimately resulting in the government's legal recognition of black trade unions in 1979 — a decades-long demand on the part of black workers.

In its emphasis on gradualism, flexibility, and compromise with employers and the state the strategy stood in marked contrast to the armed struggle being waged by the ANC, which aimed at the state's overthrow. Furthermore, in place of a vanguard movement to smash the state, the unions sought to build a broad movement based on strong factory structures, held together through practices of democratic accountability. This is not to suggest that non-violent struggle was adopted by the labour movement as a principle; rather, in the context of the security clampdown of the 1960s and 1970s it was an appropriate strategy for internal opposition. It was for this reason that when the newly formed Soweto Students' Representative Council (SSRC) called a series of stayaways from August 1976 to June 1977 (Table 14.1), the new trade unions, with the exception of one Black Consciousness-aligned union, remained aloof fearing that their modest organizational gains would be destroyed by the power of the apartheid state.[23] While large numbers of workers participated in the stayaways, it was certainly not with the support from their trade union leadership.

Stayaways only re-emerged as a tactic with the return of mass mobilization in the early 1980s, but this time the labour movement was centrally involved. In November 1984 the unions were thrust into a leading role in the Transvaal stayaway on 4th and 5th November, in which up to 800 000 workers stayed away from work and 400 000 students boycotted classes.[24] It was the beginning of united mass action between organized labour, student, and community organizations, with unions taking a central role. (Table 14.2) For the trade unions it marked a decisive break with its previous strategy of remaining aloof from township struggles.

Table 14.2
Black Worker Stayaways, 1984–86

Area	Demands	Organization	Employer Response	Date	% Effective	Days
Sharpeville	Rent	Civic Assoc. & shop stewards		3 September 1984	60%	1
Soweto	Solidarity on rents; police	RMC		17 September 1984	35–65%	1
Springs	Student demands	Parent Student Committee		22 Oct 1984	80%	1
PWV Area	Student demands repression cost of living & rents	Unions students community	No work no pay except SASOL who dismissed all 6000	5-6 November 1984	80% in union factories approx. 800 000	2
Port Elizabeth	Retrenchments & prices	PEBCO & PEYCO	No work no pay	18 March 1985	35–90%	1
Uitenhage	Solidarity for victims of repression	UYCO	No work no pay	21-22 March 1985	16–98%	2
East Rand	Solidarity over death in detention	CWIU & FOSATU	Dependant on form of action	14 May 1985	Partial; up to 100 000 involved	1

Area	Demands	Organization	Employer Response	Date	% Effective	Days
Pieter-maritzburg	Support of striking workers	MAWU	No work no pay	18 July 1985	100%	1
Cape Town	State of Emergency	Unclear	No work no pay	10-12 August 1985	37% on 11/9/85; overall unsuccessful	1
Nationwide	Day of prayer	Bishop Tutu		9 Oct.ober 1985	unsuccessful	1
PWV Area	Release of detained union leader	MAWU	No work no pay	5 March 1986	58%	1
Port Elizabeth/ Uitenhage	Commorate Sharpeville & Langa	UDF & COSATU	No work no pay also authorized leave	21 March 1986	82-99%	1
Port Alfred	Conviction of a rapist	Port Alfred Womens' Organizat'n		5 May 1986	100%	5
Nationwide	Recognize May Day as holiday	COSATU & NECC	No work no pay	1 May 1986	15-99%	1
Nationwide	Commeorate Soweto rising & protest State of Emergency	COSATU UDF NECC CUSA & National Foundation	No work no pay	16 June 1986	39-90%	1

The sheer scale of the stayaway must be understood in terms of the build-up of conflict and struggle in three key spheres in the Transvaal: the townships, schools and factories. The occupation of the townships by the army was the catalyst that was to lead to the stayaway. The Congress of South African Students, the largest student organization in the townships until its banning in 1985, whose demands had not been met, wanted to widen its short-term goals. As a result, it called for the support of the UDF organizations and the trade unions. Responding to this call, parent-student committees were formed in a number of townships. The beginning of a working relationship between community-student organizations and trade unions was formed in the Transvaal between August and November 1984.

The stayaway was most effective where trade union and community-student organizations coincided, Furthermore, 70% of the sample of unionized plants had a stayaway rate of over 80%. Unlike in the past, where extended stayaways faded after the first day, in November 1984 there was no weakening of the stayaway on day two, as had been anticipated by some observers. There was also no significant difference between the participation of migrant workers and township dwellers. In contrast with 1976, when migrants were mobilized against student protesters, many of these hostel dwellers, particularly on the East Rand, were now unionized.[25]

The November 1984 stayaway came at the start of a period of unprecedented mass mobilization, marked by a closer working relationship between the early shop-floor based unions and those unions organized under the umbrella of the United Democratic Front. The unity culminated in the formation of COSATU in December 1985. Over the next year COSATU and the UDF launched a number of extremely successful stayaways, including two country-wide actions on May Day and 16 June (the tenth anniversary of the 1976 Soweto uprising). (Table 14.2) These actions were generally demonstrations of power — pure protests — and were not tied to any on-going negotiation or to the achievement of specific goals.

The state responded by declaring a series of states of emergencies beginning in 1985. Over 143 trade unionists were detained between 1985 and 1989, and in December 1986, the first direct attacks on trade unionists began. Three NUMSA shop stewards were killed in Howick, Natal, for belonging to a COSATU union and participating in a strike. Since then there have been approximately sixty-five cases of attacks upon the premises of trade unions and individual trade unionists who have associated with COSATU. There have been very few prosecutions and even fewer convictions.[26]

Despite — and to some extent because of — the emergency, strike activity reached an historic peak in 1986 and 1987.[27] The state responded with increased repression. In April police shot at striking railway workers during a protest march in Johannesburg. The South African Broadcasting Corporation mounted a vicious propaganda campaign against COSATU, presenting its Head Office as a 'house of torture'. On the 5th and 6th May, 1987 COSATU held a successful nation-wide stayaway against the white general election; early the following morning COSATU house was destroyed by a bomb.[28] Later in the year, 340 000 miners went out on a three week strike over wages. The strike was characterized by a management offensive to try and break the power of the National Union of Mineworkers which had been built up over the previous three years.

The attacks on the unions were part of a broader shift in employer and state attitudes towards the labour movement; both felt that the unions had made unacceptably deep in-roads into management power and that it was time to roll back labour's gains. In September 1987 after extensive consultations with employers, the government tabled new legislation in the form of the Labour Relations Amendment Bill which sought to reverse the decade-long trend liberalizing the industrial relations system.[29] The response of the labour movement to this offensive and its impact on the strategy of the movement — and its use of the stayaway tactic — shall be explored next.

Shifting Strategy: the Emergence of Radical Reform

The labour movement was intent on opposing the new Labour Relations Amendments which they saw as a 'clear attack on COSATU' by mounting a campaign of resistance. During the first half of 1988, letters, stickers, pamphlets, public demonstrations, protest meetings and weekly shopfloor protests were organized by shop stewards intent on stopping the bill. Demonstrations were in contravention of the security laws, and some were forcibly broken up by the police. Members from COSATU and a smaller federation, NACTU took to the trains and buses to publicize the dangers of the bill. COSATU also found other avenues of public pressure: representations were made to parliament listing their objections to the bill and recommending changes, but none of their major proposals were accepted. International publicity was sought to increase pressure on the government to abandon the bill.[30]

Mounting popular opposition to the labour bill took place in the context of the bannings of 17 organizations in February 1988, including the United Democratic Front, and a prohibition on COSATU's engagement in politics. The state's repressive response gave impetus to COSATU's decision to call for a three day stayaway on 6, 7 and 8 June to protest both the labour bill and the bannings and restrictions imposed by the state. Lengthy stayaways had not previously been successful because the depth of organization required to sustain workers' adherence to the call had not been present. There was widespread scepticism that COSATU could meet the challenge it had set itself. However, NACTU agreed to back the call and the message was spread from workplace to workplace.

On 2 June the South African Employers' Consultative Committee on Labour Affairs (SACCOLA), which represents all the major employers' associations, initiated its first meeting with COSATU to discuss the planned stayaway. SACCOLA called on COSATU to abandon the stayaway and pursue other avenues of protest. COSATU refused and the meeting ended in public acrimony. But it was to be the first of many meetings in which COSATU, NACTU and SACCOLA would negotiate the terms of future labour legislation. COSATU went ahead with the stayaway, combining mass action with protracted negotiations with SACCOLA to amend the legislation.

The 1988 Stayaway

The first-ever successful three day national stayaway demonstrated the mass base that the labour movement had developed.[31]　Workers in the manufacturing sector in the industrial heartland of the Pretoria-Witwatersrand-Vereeniging (PWV) area displayed overwhelming support. Despite a drop in the percentage of workers observing the stayaway over the three day period, 70% of manufacturing workers remained at home for the entire time. The commercial sector was unable to sustain its high response rate of the first day and the transport sector improved its response somewhat over the course of the three days. In the public sector, the numbers of workers who observed the stayaway varied enormously, and declined over the three days.

Table 14.3
African Workers Staying Away (PWV)

Sector	Day 1	Day 2	Day 3
Manufacturing	81%	78%	72%
Commercial	67%	52%	48%
Transport	11%	28%	28%
Public (Range)	0-62%	0-50%	0-30%

The Natal region showed strong and sustained support for the stayaway, despite the public opposition from Inkatha and Chief Buthelezi:

Table 14.4
African and Indian Workers Staying Away (Natal)

Sector	Day 1	Day 2	Day 3
Clothing/Textile	93%	89%	86%
Metal/Motor	84%	84%	84%
Chemical	82%	82%	82%
Retail	68%	77%	75%
Food	65%	66%	65%

Sector	Day 1	Day 2	Day 3
Transport	57%	57%	56%
Footware	51%	48%	47%
Paper	43%	29%	24%
TOTAL	80%	78%	72%

Table 14.5 provides an overview of the stayaway rates across all sectors in the Eastern Cape. The manufacturing sector — dominated by the heavily unionized automobile and components sector — saw a higher response than that of commerce and retail.

Table 14.5
Black workers staying away (Eastern Cape) *

Town	Day 1	Day 2	Day 3
Port Elizabeth	61%	57%	55%
Uitenhage	89%	89%	89

* (Eastern Cape results were not tabulated by sector)

In the Western Cape the response to the stayaway was negligible. Historically, participation in the region has been highly erratic. The factories tend to be smaller than those in the other urban areas with a predominance of clothing factories traditionally organized by conservative unions. The racially divided nature of the regional workforce of Africans and Coloureds has also had an impact on low levels of participation in stayaways.[32] The stayaway was successful in only a small number of companies, notably in the construction and food industries.

The stayaway was also weakly supported on the mines. According to the optimistic figures of the NUM, only 6% of all African workers employed in the mining industry stayed away. The low response rate could be attributed to the fact that the union had not yet recovered from the long and debilitating miners strike of 1987, as well as to the isolation of the

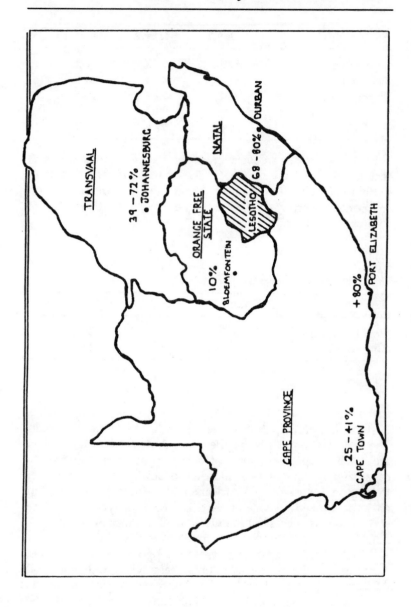

mineworkers from the broader community due to the compound system and the stringency of mine security.

COSATU cautiously estimated that altogether 3 million workers participated in the stayaway on its first day. The magnitude of the stayaway shows the labour movement's ability to mobilize its own mass base, as well as a capacity to mobilize workers far beyond the membership of the two union federations.

One of the results of the stayaway was that SACCOLA quickly asked COSATU to reopen talks on the Labour Relations Amendment Bill and the talks took place the very next day. Unlike previous meetings, however, this time union and SACCOLA negotiators were joined by the Director General of Manpower in the first tripartite meeting of its kind on labour affairs. The participants agreed to delay promulgation of the bill until September to 'allow a process of negotiation to take place that would impact on the bill'.[33] The true significance of the stayaway was therefore to link the mass demonstration of workers' power with negotiations over legislation with the state and employers. In doing so COSATU had forged a new, more strategic approach to resistance.

Early on NACTU and COSATU agreed to collaborate in their negotiations with SACCOLA and the Department of Manpower. SACCOLA and the two union federations agreed upon a set of 'offensive clauses' to be left out of the bill, and to subject the clauses to further negotiations. Nonetheless, the Government ignored these agreements, and went ahead and gazetted the Act in full on 1 September. Negotiations were abandoned and the new Labour Relations Amendment Act (LRAA) was enforced. The turn of events forced COSATU to re-evaluate its approach: it did not abandon the linkage of negotiations to mass action, but instead realized that this coupling should in fact be more direct by ensuring representivity and rank and file involvement in the negotiation process. They also realized it would take far more mobilization and pressure before labour's interests would be taken into account by the state.

The LRAA changed the balance of power in the industrial court and its provisions reversed major gains made previously by the trade unions, particularly with regard to strike legality and recognition of minority unions. While the labour movement was not yet on the receiving end of the full force of this new law, COSATU continued its resistance and efforts to change it.

COSATU and NACTU convened a Workers' Summit in March 1989 to discuss amongst other items, their action against the Act.[34] The summit resolved to campaign actively around six demands: the right to strike and picket, no dismissals without proper hearings, no retrenchments without negotiations and fair selection procedures, recognition of majority unionism, and the right to secondary industrial action. These demands went to the heart of the LRAA.

At COSATU's third national congress in July 1989 delegates agreed to ballot members as to whether COSATU should take further 'sustained' action to back up their six demands. The congress decided to stage the resistance in September, when whites-only general elections were scheduled, so as to voice COSATU's protest of the racist political system. 'The two issues are related', said COSATU General Secretary, Jay Naidoo, 'It is after all, this racist parliament that passed the LRA, and it is precisely because the vast majority of workers have no say in this parliament that an Act like this can be passed'.[35]

The COSATU congress resolution was carried through to the second Workers' Summit, this time attended by NACTU in its official capacity, along with other unaffiliated unions. The summit was subject to intense police harassment; the police imposed restrictions, surrounded the summit venue, and videotaped the entire proceedings. Nonetheless, a plan of action concerning the LRA campaign was devised and adopted, calling for brief stoppages or demonstrations in all factories on 1 September, a two day stayaway on 5 and 6 September, followed by a month-long consumer boycott of white-owned shops starting on 13 September. Finally, workers would invoke an indefinite overtime ban, although this decision would be reviewed on a monthly basis.

NACTU issued a slightly different programme calling on its members to stayaway on the 6th (election day) and the 12th of September (the anniversary of Steve Biko's death in detention). The different calls created some confusion as to when the stayaways would take place. Despite these differences, the summit resolved to continue meeting with SACCOLA and other employer bodies to strengthen the link between negotiations and mass action.

The September 1989 Stayaway

LMG monitoring of manufacturing and commercial concerns recorded that in the PWV area only 39% of black workers stayed away on the 5th September, while the following day, 72% observed the stayaway call.[36] (see map below) The higher response on the second day was attributed to a number of factors: the second day coincided with election day and so the political aspect of the stayaway was clearer and elicited a wider response. Furthermore, there was no confusion about the call to stay away on the second day, unlike the first, as NACTU unions also participated on the second day.   Finally, buses were unavailable on the second day as the local bus company recalled its vehicles from the African townships for fear of retaliation (although trains and private taxis continued to operate). The greater Durban district, Natal's foremost industrial area, reported a 68% stayaway on the first day and a 80% stayaway on the second. Significantly, a large number of Indian workers participated in the stayaway on both days, in contrast to previous experience.   The Eastern Cape matched its past experience and recorded the highest stayaway rate in the country. More than 80% of black workers stayed away on both days, although coloured participation in the Port Elizabeth area fell off slightly on the second day.   In the Western Cape approximately 25% of workers stayed away on 5th September and there was a large increase in participation on the second day, when 41% of black workers did not report to work. Though the response in Cape Town was lower than in other urban areas, it was considerably higher than the area recorded in the June 1988 stayaway.[37]

The stayaway tactic had now become part of a wider programme of sustained protest rather than a one-off demonstration of collective power. Unlike previous stayaways, the aim of both the 1988 and the 1989 actions was not simply demonstrative, but was primarily designed to facilitate changes to the Labour Relations

Amendment Act, through the judicious use of popular protest to increase the labour movement's leverage in negotiations with employers and the state.

The success of the stayaway strengthened labour's hand in negotiations with SACCOLA, though not immediately. Shortly after the stayaway SACCOLA announced that it was suspending talks with the unions, although around the same time the NMC invited proposals for an investigation into the LRA. Following newly-installed President De Klerk's liberalization of restrictions on public gatherings, COSATU organized marches against the LRA. Talks with SACCOLA were reconstituted and the employers agreed to make concessions. The September mass actions ensured that employers and the state would continue to negotiate the terms of the law, as union members would not let the issue die. The talks led to an accord between COSATU, NACTU, and SACCOLA [CNS Accord] in May 1990 to redraft the LRA, leaving out the offensive clauses, and endorsing basic labour rights for all workers, including those previously excluded from the LRA in the agricultural, domestic and public service sector, as well as workers in homelands. Unlike 1988, when the Government ignored agreements between the labour movement and SACCOLA, in 1990 the Minister of Manpower published the accord in the Government Gazette almost immediately. Between those dates, De Klerk assumed power and introduced his package of reforms which began the process of normalizing politics. De Klerk's government was certainly more receptive to negotiated solutions, and these changes gave further impetus to labour's strategy of radical reform. But it is worth noting that labour's adoption of the radical reform strategy preceded by more than a year the change in government.

A large number of employer objections prompted the Cabinet to call for further consultations, and the amendments to the Act were postponed again. COSATU and NACTU members immediately called demonstrations across the country, and even occupied the Department of Manpower offices in Johannesburg. The protests led to an historic meeting between President De Klerk and COSATU, NACTU and SACCOLA leaders on 26 June which set up a joint working party to resolve the impasse.

While the working party continued its deliberations, COSATU backed up its negotiating position with a call for further protest action in early October and announced plans for another national stayaway. However, there was no need for this threat to be carried out: the pressure led to settlement and the 'Laboria Minute' was completed. The agreement extended basic collective bargaining rights to all workers and instructed the NMC to draft a new bill, while the unions agreed to participate in a restructured NMC. The minute also scheduled the tabling of the CNS accord before parliament in February 1991, and resolved that future labour law would be subject to consultation with both SACCOLA and the unions. The COSATU Central Executive Committee's position was 'to make the NMC a fully representative body of the major unions and employer organizations. This restructured NMC would then be a negotiating forum and not merely an advisory body.'[38]

The unions were extending the logic of their radical reform strategy by agreeing to participate in the NMC while continuing to engage in mass action. For COSATU, participation in such state structures did not mean abandoning its mass base nor its strategic use of power. On the contrary, the radical reform strategy could *only* be effective for as long as it was linked to mass action. Negotiation in state structures was not an alternative, but an extension of labour's long-established strategy.

In February 1991 the Labour Relations Act was finally amended along the lines of the Laboria Minute. The new Act was hailed as the first piece of post-apartheid legislation, and consolidated a democratic industrial relations system accepted by labour, employers, and the state. The timing of these reforms was crucial for the entire transition process: the labour movement entered the transition phase not as a wounded giant hobbled by authoritarian laws, but as a movement with unprecedented freedom of action, and flushed with the success of the anti-LRA campaign. The anti-LRA campaign marked the victory of the labour movement's struggle against those forces attempting to turn back the clock, demonstrating that real gains could be made through the strategy of radical reform.

Extending the Strategy of Radical Reform to the Political Arena

The unbanning of political organizations in 1990 and the growing movement towards a negotiated transition to democracy fundamentally changed the political terrain in South Africa. In the context of transition, the government was no longer able to restructure economic and political life unilaterally. The political changes — and the seemingly unresolvable and long-standing economic crisis — opened up the possibility of the democratic movement influencing the direction of the economy.

COSATU's ability to mobilize its mass base was demonstrated once again in the November 1991 stayaway, called to protest against the implementation of VAT. What distinguished the November stayaway is that the labour movement was now mobilizing to protest against a state policy not directly related to the workplace, but against a general economic policy which affected everyone. In doing so, they were making an unprecedented frontal political challenge to the state's core prerogative: its power to determine fiscal policy. The labour movement was asserting its right as a representative of the aspirations of workers to participate in macroeconomic change.

COSATU's third National Congress in July 1991 decided to embark on another stayaway and other forms of mass action if VAT was implemented by the government without further consultation. Although at the eleventh hour the Minister of Finance hurriedly exempted a number of subsistence foodstuffs from VAT, the government implemented the tax in spite of the objections from the labour movement and major political organizations. COSATU, NACTU, the ANC and other political groupings went ahead with the stayaway.

There were three significant features of the stayaway: first it was the largest ever recorded, involving an estimated 3.8 million workers on the first day and 3.4 million on the second. It also saw the highest stayaway rate by coloured workers and it elicited the most antagonistic response from employers yet seen.[39] The results showed broad support from black workers in all sectors except mining and agriculture.

Table 14.6
Sectoral Breakdown of 1991 Stayaway

Economic Sector	Day 1	Day 2
Finance/Insurance	94%	91%
Manufacturing	81%	60%
Construction	73%	73%
Retail/Wholesale	71%	68%
Transport	59%	56%
Personal Services	46%	44%

While the finance and insurance sector in particular saw a high response, the manufacturing sector was strongly affected mainly due to its high levels of unionization. The mining sector once again showed a low rate of participation, but was a flashpoint of violence.[40] The stayaway was widespread across regions:

Table 14.7
Regional Breakdown of the 1991 Stayaway

Region	Day 1	Day 2
PWV	81%	68%
OFS Metropolitan	80%	73%
Western Cape	78%	76%
PE/Uitenhage	98%	98%
East London	67%	67%
Durban Metropolitan	84%	82%
Rest of Natal	73%	72%

Large proportions of the Indian workforce in Natal and coloured workers in the Western Cape responded to the stayaway call. Unionization was a key factor in determining the extent of the stayaway. The majority of companies surveyed employing more than 50 black workers were unionized, and it was in these companies where the stayaway was most successful. Companies employing more than 50 black workers showed higher stayaway rates, particularly on the first day of the stayaway for the very large companies.

Table 14.8
Stayaway Rate by Number of African Employees

Number of African employees	% STAYAWAY	
	Day 1	Day 2
1 - 50	57%	54%
51 - 100	63%	64%
101 +	74%	64%

Management responses were also monitored. On the whole, management adopted the traditional approach of 'no work, no pay'. At those companies affected by the stayaway, the following occurred:

Table 14.9
Management Response to the 1991 Stayaway

Management Response	Percentage of Managements[*]
Paid workers	32%
No work, no pay, no penalty	53%
Applied penalties	14%
Intend to dismiss workers	6%

[*] (Percentages do not total 100% as some companies opted for more than one response, penalizing some of their workers, while dismissing others)

The percentage of companies which intended to dismiss workers was the highest ever recorded. They were located mainly in the unionized manufacturing and construction industries. A relatively common penalty imposed by companies was the withdrawal of end-of-year bonuses from workers who stayed away. Many of the management respondents were very hostile to the stayaway and did not recognize the legitimacy of trade union involvement in issues outside of the shopfloor. A surprisingly high percentage of companies agreed to pay workers who participated in the stayaway because employers believed they were not individually to blame for the downtime.

These employers attributed their employees absence to 'intimidation' and threats of violence.

The implications of the VAT stayaway were far-reaching. Firstly, the labour movement established itself as a key actor in negotiations over the transition to democracy due to its unique capacity to mobilize a large mass base. Second, labour reasserted its strategy of mass action to back up its negotiating position, and confirmed the wisdom of extending the strategy to the political sphere. Since the release of Nelson Mandela and the start of the process of political negotiations, this strategy had been downplayed and negotiations had taken place exclusively between leaders of the various parties and organizations. The VAT stayaway ensured that negotiating positions were supported with pressure from mass mobilization.

Two broad demands emerged from the stayaway. The first and most obvious was political: 'no taxation without representation'. On this demand the labour movement succeeded in altering the VAT policy, but did not achieve its goal of stopping its implementation. The many concessions offered by the Minister resulted from the labour movement's threats of mass action, however. In March, when the zero-rating on basic foodstuffs was set to expire, the labour movement threatened another round of mass action, and further concessions were granted by the Minister.

But through the fight over VAT, it became clear to the labour movement that merely delaying VAT would not achieve their overall goals of participation in economic decision making. Furthermore, their frustrations with the NMC led to COSATU withdrawing from the body, complaining that the government was dragging its heels on the restructuring of the forum and on extending labour legislation to workers not previously covered. These experiences motivated the labour movement to seek a new general forum where economic policy could be negotiated, and intensified the importance of their second demand: for a macroeconomic negotiating forum where economic policy could be discussed in a more coordinated, global manner. Piecemeal interventions, such as tinkering with the terms of VAT were no basis for addressing macroeconomic policy issues. 'Our country', said Jay Naidoo, General Secretary of COSATU, 'faces major economic problems which cannot be solved unilaterally by a minority government on a piecemeal basis . . . . We believe a macroeconomic negotiating forum comprising employers, the major political parties, unions and the state should be established as a matter of urgency to negotiate socio-economic issues. We cannot wait for political democracy before addressing the need for socio-economic development.'[41] The anti-VAT campaign brought home the necessity for the negotiating process to deal with both economic and political issues simultaneously.

Not only did labour claim the right to participate in the process of restructuring the economy through the proposed Economic Forum, but it also demanded membership rights at the Conference for a Democratic South Africa (Codesa).[42] Although the demand was not met, COSATU leadership participates through a working group consisting of its allies, the ANC and South African Communist Party [SACP], who sit in Codesa; furthermore, four COSATU representatives sit in the SACP delegation to Codesa.[43]

The VAT stayaway consolidated the broad coalition in opposition to the government. The event not only strengthened the alliance within the labour movement between COSATU and NACTU, it also, for the first time, widened labour's support base to include white collar unions, the small business sector, coloured and Indian workers on a mass scale, and even professional groups such as doctors who closed their surgeries for two days. Labour demonstrated a capacity to reach beyond the ANC's traditional constituency and to provide leadership in this broad coalition.[44]

Labour's initiation of and participation in the National Economic Negotiating Forum was based on its concern with the growth of the economy in the long term. The labour movement has moved beyond short term collective bargaining issues to a concern with the long term viability of the economy. COSATU and some of its affiliate unions have embarked on a number of research initiatives to explore the possibilities of restructuring work and the economy and producing viable industrial strategies.[45]

Union initiatives culminated in meetings with a number of employer organizations during early 1992 to establish a National

Economic Negotiating Forum. In May 1992, labour, together with business representatives, met the newly appointed Minister of Finance and the three parties agreed to meet informally to discuss economic issues. COSATU backed down on its previous insistence that a formal structure should be established to develop economic policy and appears to have accepted the Minister's argument that this should wait until an interim government is established through Codesa. However, the labour movement's position at the centre of new economic policy formulation is the result of its strategic approach to negotiation and its ability to mobilize a large base of support.

Conclusion

The new strategy employed by the labour movement since the 1988 stayaway indicates a significant shift in its politics and those of the anti-apartheid movement in general, from a historical policy of abstention from participation in policy formulation, to one of active engagement.[46] The labour movement is clearly willing to participate in state structures, as long as participation is premised on an independent and mass base. The stayaways have demonstrated the labour movement's ability to mobilize in a disciplined manner beyond its own membership and this suggests that labour will have a substantial impact on the process of transition.

The strategy has generated widespread debate inside the labour movement between those who argue that the trade unions will be incorporated into state structures and will lose both their mass base and militancy, and those who argue participation is a tactical necessity which will enable the labour movement to influence the transition process as a whole.[47] We argue that while there are always dangers in participation, there is little new in the strategy: it extends an approach forged in labour's struggles with employers in the 1970s and 1980s, and later applied to struggles with the state over the LRA from 1987. Risks of cooptation and demobilization were present in each of these earlier phases and the labour movement survived; the knowledge, practices, and self-confidence gained in those experiences are not likely to disappear quickly, and serve as some insurance against an incorporationist result.

The labour movement is hardly the poor relation of the transition. First, in Valenzuela's terms, it is powerful and united: it is arguably the largest, best organized, and most strategically placed actor in South African society, with proven capacity to mobilize — and as conditions demand, to restrain — its membership. Indeed, it is perhaps more developed and powerful than any labour movement in countries undergoing fundamental political transitions.[48]

Second, it has developed traditions and practices of democracy, which have been reliable means to mobilize mass support. Third, its social movement character has seen its growing political engagement and influence as the only member of the tripartite alliance with a proven mass base. Fourth, the labour movement has thus far maintained relative independence of decision making. In combination, these factors have elevated labour's status within the alliance.

Unlike the examples cited by Valenzuela, where the labour movement's role in transition was relatively limited, our research points towards a more dramatic role for the South African labour movement in the transition to a new democratic order. The labour movement was the initiator of the anti-VAT campaign, and extended the negotiation process to include the restructuring of the economy. At the time of writing, the labour movement has encouraged the ANC to adopt the strategy of radical reform in its dealings with the government at Codesa. The tripartite alliance has established a 'Commission on Negotiations' to plan a campaign of mass action to strengthen their position at Codesa.[49] The overwhelming success of the ANC mass action in August 1992 owed a great deal to the experience of previous stayaways.

Rather than being 'caught by surprise' by the events of February 1990, the labour movement pointed in the direction of an alternative strategy of transition, one in which the subject group is able to challenge the dominant group through the mobilization of an independent power base. This had led to a change in the balance of power in the workplace that has not led to the revolutionary seizure of power, but to compromise and radical reform. Indeed the shift in the strategy of the labour movement in the late eighties foreshadowed and laid the foundations for the negotiated restructuring of South Africa's economic and political institutions in the early nineties.

Through this process of radical reform new institutions emerged which enjoyed a high degree of legitimacy. The recognition agreement between a union and an employer — the embryo of a social accord — is one example. The non-violent mediation of conflict is another. The most significant achievement of the labour movement is the set of procedures which ensures the democratic representation of the interests of ordinary workers. Through the strategic use of collective power it created democratic practices and procedures that provide South Africa with a model for a negotiated transition to a new democratic order.

The transition in South Africa cannot be understood without focusing on the neglected actor — the labour movement. Its strategy of radical reform in pursuit of workers' interests stands in contrast to an elite-centered strategy of negotiation — the favoured path of the government, and until recently, the practice of the ANC, as well. The characteristics of the labour movement: its strength, unity, independence, and mass base give it a potential to influence both the form and content of political and economic change in South Africa.

Notes

1   Frederick van Zyl Slabbert, 'The basis and challenges of transition in South Africa: A Review and a Preview', in Robin Lee and Lawrence Schlemmer, eds., *Transition to Democracy: Policy Perspectives 1991* (Cape Town: Oxford University Press, 1991).

2   See Guillermo O'Donnell, Philippe C. Schmitter, and Laurence Whitehead, eds., *Transitions from Authoritarian Rule: Prospects for Democracy* (Baltimore: Johns Hopkins University Press, 1986); Margaret E. Keck, 'The New Unionism in the Brazilian Transition', in Alfred Stepan, ed., *Democratizing Brazil: Problems of Transition and Consolidation* (New York: Oxford University Press, 1989); and Leigh A. Payne, 'Working Class Strategies in the Transition to Democracy in Brazil', *Comparative Politics*, 23, (January 1991).

3   J. Samuel Valenzuela, 'Labor Movements in Transitions to Democracy', *Comparative Politics*, (July 1989).

4   Andrew Levy and Associates, *Annual Report on Labour Relations in South Africa, 1991-1992*, (Rivonia, 1992).

5   Eddie Webster, Evidence to International Labour Organisation Fact Finding and Conciliation Commission Concerning Freedom of Association, February 1992.

6   Eddie Webster, 'Taking Labour Seriously: Sociology and Labour in South Africa', *South African Sociological Review*, 4 (October 1991). See also Sipho Pityana and Mark Orkin, eds., *From the Factory Floor: a Survey of COSATU Shop Stewards*, (Johannesburg: Ravan Press, 1992).

7   Rob Lambert and Eddie Webster, 'The Reemergence of Political Unionism in Contemporary South Africa', in William Cobbett and Robin Cohen, eds. *Popular Struggles in South Africa* (London: Africa World Press, 1988).

8   Jayendra Naidoo, 'Thumping the Table', *South African Labour Bulletin*, 16 (May/June 1992).

9   Valenzuela, 'Labor Movements in Transitions to Democracy', p.464.

10   The stayaway has emerged as a tactic used by political organisations and trade unions which entails a specific form of withdrawal of labour: workers stay at home in support of a variety of demands, political or economic. The stayaway emerged in the context of legislation which prevents gatherings for political purposes, pickets, or other public demonstrations.

11   Rob Lambert and Eddie Webster, 'The Re-emergence of Political Unionism', p.21.

12   Ronaldo Munck, *Third World Workers and the New International Labour Studies* (London: Zed Press, 1987), p.233.

13   Richard Hyman, *Marxism and the Sociology of Trade Unionism* (London: Pluto Press, 1971).

14   Karl von Holdt, 'Towards Transforming South African Industry: a Reconstruction Accord between Unions and the ANC?' *South African Labour Bulletin*, 15, (March 1991).

15   See Geoff Schreiner, 'Fossils from the Past: Resurrecting and Restructuring the National Manpower Commission', *South African Labour Bulletin*, 16 (July/August 1991).

16   Naidoo, p.18.

17   Eddie Webster, 'Stayaways and the Black Working Class: Evaluating a Strategy', *Labour, Capital, and Society* 14 (April 1981).

18   As quoted in Rob Lambert, 'Black worker consciousness and resistance in South Africa, 1950-1961', M.A. thesis, University of Warwick, 1978, p.20.

19   Ibid, p.30.

20   Lambert, ibid, pp.145-148.

21   Tom Lodge, *Black Politics in South Africa Since 1945* (Johannesburg: Ravan Press, 1983), pp.236-239.

22   Steven Friedman, *Building Tomorrow Today* (Johannesburg: Ravan Press, 1986).

23   Webster, 'Stayaways and the Black Working Class', p.26-36.

24   Data on this and subsequent stayaways was produced by the Labour Monitoring Group (LMG), a group of academics (including the authors) at the Universities of the Witwatersrand, Natal, Cape Town, Rhodes, and Port Elizabeth. The data was gathered through telephone surveys of employers nation-wide.

25   Labour Monitoring Group, 'The November Stayaway', *South African Labour Bulletin*, 10 (May 1985).

26   Labour Monitoring Group, 'Detention Reports', (unpublished), 1986-1987.

27   Andrew Levy and Associates, *Annual Report on Labour Relations in South Africa, 1991-1992*, (Rivonia, South Africa, 1992).

28   Alan Fine and Eddie Webster, 'Transcending traditions: Trade Unions and Political Unity', in Glenn Moss and Ingrid Obery, eds., *South African Review 5* (Johannesburg: Ravan Press, 1989.

29   Jeremy Baskin, *Striking Back: A History of COSATU* (Johannesburg: Ravan Press, 1991).

30   Baskin, *Striking Back*, pp.265-266.

31   Statistics on the 1988 stayaway drawn from Labour Monitoring Group, 'Stayaway survey, June 6-8', *South African Labour Bulletin*, 13, (September 1988).

32   Hilary Joffee, 'Stayaways in Cape Town, 1986', Paper presented to the Association for Sociology in Southern Africa Conference, Durban, July 1986.

33   Baskin, *Striking Back*, p.290.

34   NACTU withdrew at the last minute from the summit, although a number of its affiliates did attend in an unofficial capacity.

35   Baskin, *Striking Back*, p.386.

36   Statistics on the 1989 stayaway are drawn from Labour Monitoring Group, 'Stayaway: 5th & 6th September 1989', *South*

African Labour Bulletin, 14 (October 1989).

37 The overtime ban did not elicit the same degree of support. The consumer boycott reflected variation in regional effectiveness. Labour Monitoring Group, 'Overtime Ban Survey', *South African Labour Bulletin,* 14 (November 1989).

38 *Flame* (Newspaper of the Chemical Workers' Industrial Union), No. 31, September 1991.

39 Labour Monitoring Group, 'Survey of the November 4th and 5th Stayaway', *South African Labour Bulletin,* 16 (January 1992).

40 At President Steyn mine in the Orange Free State more than 60 miners were killed and hundreds injured as tensions reached breaking point after management threatened dismissal, and due to the high level of layoffs in the industry. This was however the only incidence of violence during the course of the stayaway.

41 *Finance Week,* 7 November 1991.

42 Codesa, set up in December 1991, includes most of the major political groupings in South Africa, and its aim is to lay the ground rules for an interim government and a forum to draw up a new constitution.

43 'National Economic Forum: Parallel to Codesa?' Interview with Sam Shilowa, Assistant General Secretary, COSATU, South African Labour Bulletin, V. 16, No. 3 (January 1992).

44 Duncan Innes, 'Cosatu bid to shake off "Junior" Role', *Sunday Star,* 3 November 1991.

45 Avril Joffee and Dave Lewis, 'A Strategy for South African Manufacturing, *South African Labour Bulletin,* 16 (March/April 1992).

46 Karl von Holdt, 'Towards Transforming South African Industry: a Reconstruction Accord between Unions and the ANC?' *South African Labour Bulletin,* 15 (March 1991).

47 See the special issue of the *South African Labour Bulletin,* 'COSATU: Gaining Influence, Losing Power?' 16 (May/June 1992); Glenda Daniels, 'Will labour Agree to a Social Contract?' *Work in Progress,* 23 April 1992.

48 If we take membership figures as an incomplete (but the only available) index of union strength, then South Africa's degree of unionisation is higher than any other examples given in Valenzuela's case studies. See Valenzuela, 'Labor Movements in Transitions to Democracy', p. 453. For details on degrees of unionisation, see Table 1.1 and 1.2 of International Labour Organisation, *World Labour Report 2* (Geneva: ILO, 1985).

49   'ANC Paves Way for Mass Action', *Sunday Star*, 31 May 1992;
       'What COSATU demands', *Sunday Times*, 31 May 1992.